HANNA AND BARBERA
CONVERSATIONS

TELEVISION CONVERSATIONS SERIES
DAVID LAVERY, GENERAL EDITOR

HANNA AND BARBERA
CONVERSATIONS

Edited by Kevin Sandler and Tyler Solon Williams

UNIVERSITY PRESS OF MISSISSIPPI / JACKSON

The University Press of Mississippi is the scholarly publishing agency of the Mississippi Institutions of Higher Learning: Alcorn State University, Delta State University, Jackson State University, Mississippi State University, Mississippi University for Women, Mississippi Valley State University, University of Mississippi, and University of Southern Mississippi.

www.upress.state.ms.us

The University Press of Mississippi is a member of the Association of University Presses.

Copyright © 2024 by University Press of Mississippi
All rights reserved

∞

Library of Congress Cataloging-in-Publication Data

Names: Sandler, Kevin S., 1969– editor. | Williams, Tyler Solon, editor.
Title: Hanna and Barbera : conversations / Kevin Sandler, Tyler Solon Williams.
Other titles: Television conversations series.
Description: Jackson : University Press of Mississippi, 2024. | Series: Television conversations series | Includes bibliographical references and index.
Identifiers: LCCN 2023048941 (print) | LCCN 2023048942 (ebook) | ISBN 9781496850430 (hardback) | ISBN 9781496850447 (trade paperback) | ISBN 9781496850454 (epub) | ISBN 9781496850461 (epub) | ISBN 9781496850478 (pdf) | ISBN 9781496850485 (pdf)
Subjects: LCSH: Hanna, William, 1910–2001—Interviews. | Barbera, Joseph—Interviews. | Hanna-Barbera Productions—History. | Animators—United States—Interviews. | Television producers and directors—United States—Interviews. | Animated television programs—United States.
Classification: LCC NC1766.U52 H35 2024 (print) | LCC NC1766.U52 (ebook) | DDC 741.5/80922—dc23/eng/20240103
LC record available at https://lccn.loc.gov/2023048941
LC ebook record available at https://lccn.loc.gov/2023048942

British Library Cataloging-in-Publication Data available

CONTENTS

Introduction   ix

Chronology   xxiii

Hanna and Barbera: After Fifty Years, Opposites Still Attract   3
MORRIE GELMAN / 1989

Cartoon Creator Joseph Barbera Takes Tom and Jerry to Movies   10
TOM PROVENZANO / 1993

Hanna and Barbera at MGM   15
MICHAEL BARRIER / 1999

Roundtable Discussion with Mike Lah   25
DARRELL VAN CITTERS / 1977

Interview with Ray Patterson   28
MICHAEL MALLORY / 1998

Oscar Goes to Author of Cartoon   33
FRED QUIMBY / 1944

They Paint a Million Cats   34
BARRETT KIESLING / 1956

The Influence of *Crusader Rabbit* on *Ruff and Reddy*   37
KARL COHEN / 1989

Ed Benedict   41
AMID AMIDI / 2002

Daws Butler: The Master's Voice   45
BRIAN LOWRY / 1987

Don Messick: Vocal Hero 50
BRIAN LOWRY / 1986

Cartoonists Turn to TV for Work 55
CHARLES WITBECK / 1959

Lance Nolley 57
DON PERI / 2011

A Few Words from Jerry Eisenberg 59
YOWP / 2011

TV Hit from a Cartoon Factory 70
THOMAS E. STIMSON JR. / 1960

Close-Up on Huck and Yogi: Hanna and Barbera with Antoinette Bower 75
ANTOINETTE BOWER / 1961

TV without Terror 84
JANE KESNER ARDMORE / 1962

Doug Wildey on *Jonny Quest* 88
DAVID W. OLBRICH / 1986

Hanna-Barbera and Taft Broadcasting 97
LAWRENCE H. ROGERS II / 2000

It'll Cost $40 to $50 a Day to Enjoy Area's New Park 108
GEORGE PALMER / 1969

The Improbable World of Hanna-Barbera 112
BILL HANNA AND JOE BARBERA / 1967

The Purveyor of Saturday's Fare 116
JOHN STANLEY / 1968

Hanna-Barbera Presents Saturday Morning and Comedy 119
HANNA-BARBERA / 1969

The Men behind Dastardly and Muttley 121
JOHN CULHANE / 1969

Iwao Takamoto   133
AMID AMIDI / 1999

Joe Ruby and Ken Spears on *Scooby-Doo, Where Are You!*   137
STU SHOSTAK / 2012

Roundtable Discussion with Mike Maltese   141
DARRELL VAN CITTERS / 1977

Hanna-Barbera Australia   146
DAN TORRE AND LIENORS TORRE / 2018

Darrell McNeil on *Super Friends*   161
MARC TYLER NOBLEMAN / 2011

Hanna-Barbera School to Keep an Art Alive   166
LEE MARGULIES / 1977

My Adventure in the Hanna-Barbera Animation Training Program   169
TOM MINTON / 2024

Tom Sito on Hanna-Barbera   178
KEVIN SANDLER AND TYLER SOLON WILLIAMS / 2021

Margaret Loesch and Joe Barbera   184
SONNY FOX / 1979

Squire Rushnell at ABC   194
KEVIN SANDLER / 2021

Hanna-Barbera: The Cartoonists Who Own Saturday Morning   200
JOHN MARIANI / 1979

The Smurfs   207
GERARD BALDWIN / 2015

Hanna-Barbera: Will *Heidi's Song* Be Its *Snow White*?   217
JOHN CANEMAKER / 1981

Yabba Dabba Crew: Working with Hoyt Curtin at Hanna-Barbera   225
JEFF BOND / 2001

Fred Seibert at Cartoon Network   232
JESSE KOWALSKI / 2017

Brian Levant on *The Flintstones* Movie   238
KEVIN SANDLER / 2021

Joseph Barbera: An Animated Life   243
SCOTT SHAW! / 2007

Suggested Resources   245

Index   249

INTRODUCTION

> We have the largest animation studios in the world. It's a little sad. Other cartoon studios, in their anxiety to grow, love to run us down, to call us a factory, or a sweatshop. But when Bill and I started, in 1957, our industry was finished. Disney wasn't making any shorts. We had been together at M.G.M. for 18 years, making Tom and Jerry, when they closed their doors. The "factory" reputation came about because we employed different methods of production. We never belittle our competitors, but a competitor who makes only five cartoons a year and calls us a factory is forgetting how many people we give work to.
> —JOE BARBERA TO THE *NEW YORK TIMES*, NOVEMBER 23, 1969[1]

These were Joe Barbera's reflections on the state of the animation industry in 1969, for a profile piece on the company he and Bill Hanna cofounded in 1957: Hanna-Barbera Productions. The year represented the near-midpoint of Hanna and Barbera's storied fifty-year partnership, beginning with their 1940 Tom and Jerry theatrical short *Puss Gets the Boot*, through their success on television with primetime's *The Flintstones* and Saturday morning's *Scooby-Doo, Where Are You!*, and ending with their 1990 theatrical animated feature, *Jetsons: The Movie*. Arguably, Bill Hanna and Joe Barbera were the most prolific animation producers of the twentieth century. They directed 114 Tom and Jerry cartoons at MGM and, while presidents of Hanna-Barbera Productions, produced over 200 animated and live-action television series and specials. They directly employed about 600 employees in 1969, increasing to as many as 800 by the late 1970s, making this the largest animation studio in the world; Hanna-Barbera outflanked its once-competitor Walt Disney in output and, for many years, influence in the industry.

Admittedly, Bill and Joe's legacy is and should be open for debate. On one hand, they standardized an assembly-line mode of cartoon production for television at odds with the established artisanal norms of theatrical animated shorts production in the Hollywood studio system; on the other hand, essentially every other television cartoon studio followed a similar model, both out of necessity and choice. Hanna and Barbera called this "planned animation";

nearly everyone else called it "limited animation," particularly those who still practiced full animation, which by comparison became dramatically more expensive and time-consuming. Chuck Jones, the renowned Warner Bros. Looney Tunes director, who actually went on to make thirty-four semilimited theatrical Tom and Jerry cartoons for MGM in the mid-1960s, denigrated the television cartoons of Hanna-Barbera and other studios; in 1969, he told Michael Barrier and Bill Spicer of *Funnyworld* that these were nothing more than "illustrated radio," aesthetically bankrupt in their "eternal flatness and repetition."[2] In *Film Comment* in 1975, Leonard Maltin called stripped-down limited animation television cartoons like those from Hanna-Barbera "consciously bad: assembly-line shorts grudgingly executed by cartoon veterans who hate what they're doing."[3] Despite these criticisms, both Maltin and Barrier acknowledge in their oral histories of studio era animation—*Of Mice and Magic* (1987) and *Hollywood Cartoons* (1999), respectively—that television's economic and temporal demands were what drove animation studios like Hanna-Barbera toward quantity and predictability.[4]

Documenting Bill Hanna and Joe Barbera's career for the University Press of Mississippi's Television Conversations Series, with its focus on interviews with celebrated filmmakers and television creators, is similarly complicated. While the pieces published in this volume cumulatively address the elements that most define Hanna and Barbera (the directing team behind MGM's Tom and Jerry series from 1940 to 1957) and Hanna-Barbera (the animation studio Bill and Joe ran from 1957 to 1989), slightly less than half feature conversations with the two men. There are reasons for this. For the majority of their time at MGM, despite not being involved in the creative process, animation studio head Fred Quimby largely asserted authorship over Bill and Joe's cartoons, speaking on their behalf to the press and accepting their Academy Awards on stage at the Oscars. When Quimby retired in 1955, Bill and Joe became co-heads of the studio and asserted their proper credit over Tom and Jerry—for two brief years, before MGM shuttered the cartoon division. Hanna and Barbera would found Hanna-Barbera in 1957, and after *The Huckleberry Hound Show* became a breakout success the next year, they granted interviews to journalists to talk about their life stories, craft, and studio. Hanna-Barbera's reputation began to wane as the 1960s progressed, however, and fewer interviews took place. Between 1961 and 1965, each of the studio's primetime follow-ups to *The Flintstones* failed to last beyond one season. Saturday morning would change their fortunes. While their new action-adventure cartoons proved exceedingly popular with children, Hanna and Barbera faced great public criticism over depictions of violence. The 1969 publication in the *New York Times* of the deeply probing piece cited in our epigraph may have caused Bill and Joe to subsequently shirk attention from the press, to avoid criticism of their studio. Thereafter, they largely shut out the contentious discussions about Hanna-Barbera's own Saturday morning cartoons that were happening widely elsewhere, making only periodic exceptions to discuss their amusement parks and feature films. For the remaining twenty years of their careers, Bill and Joe rarely gave interviews. Ultimately, in the twilight of their lives in the mid-1990s, they each told their life story in a widely distributed autobiography.

Consequently, interviews with Hanna and/or Barbera are few and far between; more frequent are profile pieces of the Hanna-Barbera studio that quote Bill and Joe. As the more charismatic, talkative, and outgoing of the two, Joe is the subject of most interviews. His voice dominates the studio's history in print, skewing coverage toward his domain: the front end of television production (development, sales, writing, casting, and voice recording). Bill was humble and reserved, but a tireless, hands-on manager. Typically, by comparison, his responsibility for handling the grueling back end of production is overshadowed (planning the actual animation, inking and painting, checking, and photography). In fact, we found only one solo interview with Bill that was published during his long career, and it is already available in another collection.[5] When Hanna and Barbera did go on the record in interviews, they were often less than forthcoming about their work. They tended to echo familiar talking points, like about their brave founding of the studio in a time of industrial uncertainty, the hard-won early success of *The Flintstones*, and their struggles to make "nonviolent" cartoons in the 1970s. Joe would often resort to praise rather than introspection, making his public comments feel more like public relations than journalism. Importantly, such interviews and profiles rarely even acknowledged the army of producers, writers, animators, inkers, painters, and other artists who did the day-to-day work of outputting nearly ten thousand feet of finished animation each month at Hanna-Barbera's peak in the late 1970s. Since the mid-1960s, the studio's increasing volume of work caused Bill and Joe to step back into more supervisory roles. Joe acknowledged this fact in 1964; when asked if he still drew, Joe responded with amusement: "Well, only to the extent that I'll show an artist what I might have in mind, rather than try to tell him . . . but otherwise it's up to the unit to do its own work."[6]

Rather than republish a series of pieces that repeat Bill and Joe's well-worn stories, serve as self-promotion for Hanna-Barbera, privilege the front end of production, or elide the contributions of their countless employees, *Hanna and Barbera: Conversations* opens up discussion about the men and their studio. Interviews and profile pieces here indeed contain conversations *with* Hanna and Barbera, on their intertwined careers at MGM and their own studio; others involve conversations *about* Hanna and Barbera, by individuals who worked alongside them. These pieces include previously published articles, profiles, recollections, and corporate statements, as well as unpublished and newly conducted interviews. We have edited some pieces for length, focus, interest, and accuracy. We order the pieces in this volume approximately chronologically, not by the original publication date, but according to the years addressed. In this manner, Hanna and Barbera's careers, their modes of producing film and television cartoons, and their lasting impact on the animated art form can be more fully and accurately represented.

Two retrospectives celebrating the longstanding partnership between Bill Hanna and Joe Barbera open this volume, introducing the familiar memories they would share throughout their half-century-long careers. These late accounts mirror what Bill and Joe said in what is likely the earliest print piece about the pair, a brief 1940 Associated Press profile not included here, published just months after the successful release of *Puss Gets the Boot*. Joe is described as "both artist and story constructor," and Bill as someone who "doesn't draw much, but [has] done about everything else in film cartoonery"; they "complemented each other so well that the boss, Fred Quimby, put them in the same cubby-hole office."[7] Nearly fifty years later, in *Variety* in 1989, Bill echoed the same sentiment on beginning of their collaboration: "[Joe] did the drawings and I did the animation direction . . . and we've been together ever since."

Bill and Joe frequently told the story that they originated their limited animation technique for television in making preproduction "pose reels" for their Tom and Jerry cartoons. Bill would time and expose the 1,200 or so rough pencil sketches Joe made of key poses and extreme shots, before getting into the labor- and time-intensive stage of inbetweening and ink-and-paint. The early Associated Press piece describes this process as a "new technique and their own idea"; later, Joe told *Variety* that this preliminary test film would provide a blueprint for the finished film. "We were able to get an idea of what this cartoon would look like with this simulation. We got more laughs on that penciled drawing reel than anything that had ever been made there."[8]

Joe shared the same tale in *Drama-Logue* in 1993 to promote the release of *Tom and Jerry: The Movie*, the other introductory career overview featured here. Like many interviews about Hanna-Barbera before it, Hanna is absent. Joe recounts enduring stories about their film and television careers: most people believing that their cat and mouse was a "stupid, unoriginal idea" for a cartoon; MGM unexpectedly closing the animation studio in 1957; he and Bill facing down the apparent impossibility of making five-minute television cartoons for $3,000, after averaging $45–60,000 for seven-minute theatrical Tom and Jerry shorts; and the studio's milestone of making *The Flintstones*, the first half-hour primetime animated sitcom. These anecdotes speak to Joe and Bill's time-honored approach of putting likeable, charismatic characters into entertaining scenarios. "The idea is to make them funny," Joe told the Associated Press in 1940. "The purpose of the cartoon is to make people laugh. That's all we're trying to do."[9] In 1993, Joe saw his cat-and-mouse cartoon series come full circle in 1992 with *Tom and Jerry: The Movie*, although just as a "creative consultant" to Warner Bros., rather than the creative force he was behind the original theatrical series. Joe's surprising enthusiasm for his cat and mouse now talking (and singing!) may be one of his public relations tactics.

Subsequently, we return to the beginning of Bill and Joe's careers together in the Los Angeles area. They emerged as a production duo at MGM in 1939 while working under production supervisors Hugh Harman and Rudy Ising. Michael Barrier's account of their time at the studio until 1957 in *Hollywood Cartoons* is based upon interviews with Hanna and other animators. Barrier interprets Hanna and Barbera's contrasting personalities and work histories as defining the look and feel of the Tom and Jerry cartoons. Their "aesthetic incompatibility . . . entailed clothing a Terrytoons sensibility in a Harman-Ising shell," which he sees as hardening over the years into a glossy but increasingly monotonous formula of feverish pacing, sentimentality, and brutality. Despite his misgivings, Barrier's account of Hanna and Barbera's unit sheds light on their production methods, detailed further by animators Mike Lah and Ray Patterson. Director Tex Avery joined MGM in 1941, and his wild style shaped Bill and Joe's own approach to writing and directing. Producer Fred Quimby's hands-off management ensured their general creative independence. By the late 1940s, Bill and Joe's crew operated as a "cohesive infantry squad" with a "high level of expertise," as Barrier puts it; Joe remembered this time with his artists as "a state of splendid creative isolation."[10]

While Tom and Jerry may have lacked the variety and depth of the animated shorts coming from Avery's MGM unit and those from UPA, Warner Bros., and Disney, popular audiences and the industry at the time embraced Bill and Joe's cat-and-mouse cartoons with enthusiasm. After early, unremarkable attempts with other characters, Quimby had Bill and Joe make nearly all Tom and Jerrys during their tenure at MGM, because, said Barrier, Bill and Joe's series "was proving to be too popular . . . to waste them on anything else." Tom and Jerry eventually won seven Academy Awards out of thirteen nominations; Quimby celebrates the first award, for *The Yankee Doodle Mouse*, in his syndicated piece included here. After Quimby's retirement in 1955, Hanna and Barbera received another Oscar nomination for a non–Tom and Jerry cartoon, *Good Will to Men* (1955), an update of Hugh Harman's *Peace on Earth* (1939), about a postapocalyptic world populated only by animals. Barrett Kiesling, previously the publicity director at MGM, captures Bill and Joe's brief tenure as studio heads in a 1956 portrait of their production process for *Films and Filming*. Six months later in May 1957, after a disastrous year at the box office, MGM infamously shut down their cartoon studio; instead of making new cartoons, the studio began simply reissuing earlier Tom and Jerrys.

Like many other Hollywood animators in the 1950s, Hanna and Barbera were thrown into unemployment. In their mid-forties, they were not about to retire. With theatrical animation studios closing across Hollywood, attempting to make cartoons for television seemed like their only real option. To do this, Bill and Joe formed a new television cartoon studio, H-B Enterprises, soon renamed Hanna-Barbera Productions. To carve out a niche in the new medium, the two producers had to abandon longstanding organizational and aesthetic principles of full animation they cultivated so deeply during the studio era. "Gone forever were the deep pockets and lenient deadlines that allocated dollars and indulgent production schedules to us with such golden profusion," Bill says in his autobiography. "In their place appeared initial shoestring budgets of daunting severity and that implacable television specter known as the air date."[11] To make their early television cartoons, Hanna and Barbera pieced together their planned animation process, a newly limited but versatile mode of cel animation that restricted character movement, relied on simpler character design and minimal background design, and emphasized voice acting and sound effects; with techniques like these, they found ways to work within television's temporal and financial constraints.

Along with Bill and Joe, several MGM and Hanna-Barbera artists present during this transition share their thoughts here on the limited animation cel techniques and production processes that defined the early years of the new studio. Bill and his brother-in-law Mike Lah refined the MGM demo reel process at Shield Productions, a short-lived studio documented by Karl Cohen. This then became the basis for planning character movement at Hanna-Barbera: Characters' distinctive neck accoutrements seamlessly enabled the head and arms to be animated separately from the body, as Ray Patterson and character designer Ed Benedict recall; meanwhile, Brian Lowry documents in two profiles that voice artists Daws Butler and Don Messick became the "two-man stock company" whose wide vocabulary of distinctive voices and sounds conveyed vibrant character in the absence of much movement. At this time, Bill and Joe began to sell journalists on the superiority of planned animation for television over more fully animated theatrical shorts. "[O]ur [TV] cartoons are better than our fancy Tom and Jerry movies," Bill claimed to syndicated columnist Charles Witbeck in 1959. "We use close-ups, our shows are easy to watch, and we let the viewer use a little imagination." Bill and Joe's ballyhoo was self-serving and survivalist, a response to common complaints about the aesthetic sacrifices they made in their television work. Despite the limitations of the home medium, layout artist Lance Nolley, one among many Disney-trained artists hired by Hanna-Barbera in the early 1960s, believed Bill and Joe "tr[ied] for perfection, as close as they can." Nolley probably spoke for many in saying that "Hanna and Barbera are the two men who kept us all in the cartoon business by cutting down costs."

The 1960s saw Hanna-Barbera refine the basic blueprint of its planned animation model for half-hour television cartoons, either as three individual, seven-minute segments for syndication like *The Yogi Bear Show* or a single three-act episode for primetime like *The Flintstones*. Developing relatable characters and composing witty stories became the focus at Hanna-Barbera; the studio's characters at the time, according to Hanna, "could generally carry the show based upon the charm of their cuteness, wit, and humor, with minimal suggestive movement."[12] Layout artist and character designer Jerry Eisenberg, who worked full-time at Hanna-Barbera from 1961 to 1977, chronicles much of the history of the studio during these years in his interview with blogger Yowp. Eisenberg speaks to Hanna-Barbera's planned animation process by describing roles he assumed over the years, as story director, animation director, and production manager. A 1960 *Popular Mechanics* piece documents the cost-saving animation techniques in use on *Huckleberry Hound*: the reduction of speech to nine standard mouth positions, the general minimization of in-between drawings, and the photographing of each cel twice. A 1961 profile on the Canadian Broadcasting Corporation's news series *Close-Up* has Joe presenting a *Top Cat* storyboard to journalist Antoinette Bower, much like he would do for prospective sponsors. When Bower asks about a "code of ethics" for their characters, Joe explains: "We never have a real bad villain. This is taboo. They frown or they pout but they never have teeth, are never vicious. . . . And I think this is the key to everything we do." *Parents Magazine & Better Homemaking* was glad that Hanna-Barbera left behind the "sadistic action" of their Tom and Jerry cinema shorts. In 1962, the publication approvingly described how this emphasis on character-based humor "prove[d] that youngsters can be entertained without violence, mayhem or villains."

However, the studio's reliance on broad comedy, in each succeeding year of the early 1960s, was producing diminishing returns. While *The Flintstones* remained successful for years, the studio's next two primetime sitcoms, *Top Cat* and *The Jetsons*, were cancelled after one season. Syndicated packages *The Hanna-Barbera New Cartoon Series* and *The Magilla Gorilla Show* failed to produce breakthrough stars. Playing defense, Hanna-Barbera took the huge risk of fundamentally reconceiving their house style for 1964's *Jonny Quest*, their ambitious action-adventure series inspired by the radio drama *Jack Armstrong, the All-American Boy*. This science fiction cartoon featured tales of a team of unlikely but intrepid male heroes, who battled demented scientists, invisible monsters, and oversized carnivorous lizards, dramatized through a realistic illustrated aesthetic. For the first time, Joe largely ceded the central creative role. Comic book artist Doug Wildey took on this responsibility, recounting to *Amazing Heroes* the difficulty Hanna-Barbera's animators had drawing convincingly in this realist mode, network objections to the use of Kolkota orphan Hadji, and his own perception that the comedic dog Bandit compromised the show's integrity. While *Quest* remains a memorable high-water mark for the studio, high production costs doomed it to a one-season run.

Despite the disappointments of this period, Hanna-Barbera was becoming the world's largest cartoon factory. In 1963, Bill and Joe moved most of their 250 employees into a newly built, three-story, forty-thousand-square-foot headquarters in Studio City, a space-age building reminiscent of *The Jetsons*. By this time they were pursuing a vast cross-media portfolio, including their first theatrical feature, 1964's *Hey There, It's Yogi Bear!*; a theatrical short series, Loopy de Loop; comic strips and comic books; commercials and industrial films; a music division, Hanna-Barbera Records; and licenses for over 500 manufacturers to make some 2,500 branded products.[13] By 1965, the studio had produced thirteen network and syndicated series. Sensing opportunity, given the scale of their operation, Bill and Joe began to explore the prospect of selling Hanna-Barbera; they finalized a sale in December 1966 to the Taft Broadcasting Group, a Cincinnati-based owner of television and radio stations. While Bill characterized the transition to Taft as a "relatively rippleless switch,"[14] the studio became increasingly oriented around commercial profitability; the conglomerate's chief operating officer and president, Lawrence H. Rogers II, provides a frayed account of the acquisition and its aftermath. Bill and Joe would continue to run the studio, but Taft required a major retooling of their business operations, which Rogers reports lost money during their first years of ownership. This included the creation of worldwide distribution and character merchandising sales departments, and expansion into amusement parks. In 1969, Rogers, Hanna, and Barbera explained to the *Cincinnati Enquirer* that they would establish the first park, Kings Island, near Cincinnati, Ohio; it would open there three years later, as planned, in 1972.

Taft now owned the company that would emerge as the largest supplier of Saturday morning cartoons to the three US broadcast networks for the next two decades. For the 1967–68 season alone, Hanna-Barbera supplied programming for ten of the eighteen 9 a.m.–12 noon timeslots. Their six new series contained "29 new cartoon stars and costars. . . . creations for the ever-never land of the home screen," Joe and Bill pronounced in the first edition of their studio's in-house newsletter, *The Hanna-Barbera Exposure Sheet*. Elided here is the violent nature of *Space Ghost* and *The Herculoids*, action-adventure fantasies of terror and peril ordered by the networks to capitalize on the space, spy, and superhero crazes. Public outrage over the effects such violent television shows allegedly had on children increased significantly after March 1968, following continuous television coverage of the Vietnam War, student protests, the assassinations of Martin Luther King Jr. and Robert F. Kennedy Jr., and the riots and panic that ensued after their deaths. Responding to the controversy over violence in his cartoons that April, Joe told the *San Francisco Examiner* that "I can't really defend it," but assured readers that "superheroes are a fad on the way out," to be replaced by "a Mary Poppins kind of whimsy, fantasy, magic." Indeed, the violence that permeated these action-adventure cartoons would soon be exiled from the Saturday morning lineup for nearly a decade.

The studio's press kit promoting the upcoming 1969–70 season, "Hanna-Barbera Presents Saturday Morning and Comedy," announces the studio's shift away from action-adventure to "fun-violence." This was the period when John Culhane was granted unusually generous access to the studio for his profile in the *New York Times*. While visiting, he elicited candid reflections about the increasingly vexing artistic constraints of Saturday morning programming—not only from Bill, Joe, and their employees at the studio, but also from network executives, children's television advocates, and competing television animation producers. Culhane essentially concludes his lengthy discussion of Hanna-Barbera with a heavy sigh: "Saturday morning TV is an American tragedy. . . . We are wasting the fleeting time of childhood and men's talents[.]" Nevertheless, Iwao Takamoto, head of design and layout at the studio during this time, later proudly told *Animation Blast* about his artistic process in shaping the overall design aesthetic of the studio's popular series *The Perils of Penelope Pitstop*. Writers Joe Ruby and Ken Spears share with Stu Shostak the creative freedom Joe granted them in developing their comedy-mystery, *Scooby-Doo, Where Are You!* Longtime animation writer Mike Maltese, a creative force behind the studio's early cartoons, offers a contrasting perspective in a roundtable discussion at the California Institute of the Arts, lamenting that, by the 1970s, "you have to fight the network boys, who tell you how to write cartoons."

Saturday morning proved immensely profitable for the three broadcast networks and its animation suppliers, particularly Hanna-Barbera, throughout the 1970s. However, the studio's creative standards seemed to further erode each season, as they continued trotting out an endless reintroduction of familiar characters, animated versions of primetime series and music groups, and uninspired variations on previously successful formulas. A number of pieces shed light on the myriad industrial, institutional, and cultural forces affecting the quality and quantity of Hanna-Barbera's work in the 1970s. Dan Torre and Lienors Torre's oral history, "Hanna-Barbera Australia," provides a case study of one factor shaping US children's animation in the 1970s: "runaway production." They chart the history of Hanna-Barbera's first outsourcing venture, in Sydney, Australia, from 1971 to 1988. Met with great resistance by American animators, the Sydney studio enabled Hanna-Barbera to lower labor costs by shifting some production overseas. Hanna-Barbera's offshore studio provided higher wages and better working conditions than other Australian studios, but it also caused friction in the Australian animation industry, because it largely supported Hanna-Barbera's US efforts rather than pursuing local productions. For one of these Australian productions, *Super Friends*, Darrell McNeil worked as layout/assistant animator for Hanna-Barbera in Los Angeles. The first Black artist on the studio's teams, he tells the *Noblemania* blog about the creation of original DC characters for the show, efforts to appease network executives with nonviolent storylines, and Hanna-Barbera using in-town, nonunion subcontractors to finish productions on time.

Hanna-Barbera had another labor problem in the 1970s: their older animators from the 1930s and 1940s, experienced artists they still relied on, were retiring and dying. To train new people into the practices of planned animation, the studio started an in-house animation training program, covered in a 1977 *Los Angeles Times* profile. Tom Minton, in an original contribution written for this volume, looks back at his time learning official and unofficial lessons in animation production at this "tuition-free night school." After a time, Hanna-Barbera placed Minton into their overflow unit, only to terminate him and others soon after, he suspects, when the studio jointly opened Cuckoo's Nest, also known as Wang Film Productions, in Taiwan as an outsourcing studio. Tom Sito, who would serve as president of industrial union The Animation Guild (IATSE Local 839) from 1992–2001 but in 1977 was also a young animator at Hanna-Barbera, recalls his own on-the-ground experience: staring down unrelenting production slates, miniscule budgets, tight airdates, and the unwelcome competition of cheap overseas labor. The increasing amounts of work being performed overseas led to a strike by television animators in 1979; Hanna-Barbera was caught off-guard, and the workers won antirunaway production rules. When similar tensions boiled over in 1982, however, the studio was prepared, and held out. After ten weeks, Hanna-Barbera defeated the union, and then sent virtually all labor-intensive animation production work overseas, to a growing array of outsourcing studios.

Much of the power in the 1970s, though, still lay with the three broadcast networks, a near triopoly that largely determined the cost, schedule, and content of Saturday morning cartoons. NBC children's programming executive Margaret Loesch joined Joe in 1978 for an interview about the network-supplier relationship, providing a nuts-and-bolts account of a single Hanna-Barbera series, *Godzilla*. ABC network executive Squire Rushnell later recalled his unorthodox creative process with Joe in developing Scrappy-Doo and the Pound Puppies: "I didn't want Hanna-Barbera to create a series that was going to be a hit for the other networks . . . I wanted them to create hits for ABC." Both network executives were struggling to respond to pressure exerted by media reform groups, particularly Peggy Charren's Action for Children's Television. *Saturday Review* in 1979 presented a typical finger-pointing match over the state of Saturday morning animation: Charren accuses Joe of "racial stereotyping" in *Jabberjaw*; Joe blames the networks for "kill[ing] all the creativity" in cartoons; Rushnell faults his own network's standards and practices department for "sanitizing" them. Author John Mariani ultimately finds Bill and Joe responsible for the studio's tepid offerings: "[T]he men who own Saturday morning have become too successful at what they once loved best... and now there's little heart left in them or the characters they create."

While Hanna-Barbera probably reached its peak production volume in the late 1970s, the studio's power and influence began to fade in the 1980s, in the face of the Federal Communication Commission's deregulation of the television industry under President Ronald Reagan. New animation studios, often partnering with toy and greeting card companies, entered a marketplace greatly expanded by after-school broadcast syndication and its lucrative licensing and merchandising opportunities. A commune of imaginary blue forest sprites was brought to the studio by NBC head Fred Silverman around 1980; beginning in 1965, as a network executive at CBS and ABC, Silverman occasionally wielded more creative direction over the studio's concepts than Bill or Joe. Loesch, now a development and programming executive at Hanna-Barbera, placed line producer Gerard Baldwin in charge of *The Smurfs*. In an excerpt from his autobiography published here, Baldwin recounts shepherding the labyrinthine production onto television: it quickly expanded from thirty minutes to a ninety-minute block and ran for nine seasons, essentially bankrolling Hanna-Barbera through the end of the 1980s.

Joe didn't understand the Smurfs at all, said Baldwin; his great hope at the time was *Heidi's Song*, a fantasy musical theatrical feature lushly rendered in full animation at Hanna-Barbera by some of the last surviving studio-era cinema animators. Joe told *Millimeter* in 1981 that the film would be proof that he and Bill could make a Disney-quality animated feature when provided the time and money denied to them for their television work. However, Joe ruefully recalled what happened when *Heidi's Song* was released in 1982: "The picture was dumped on the theaters and just sat there."[15] Meanwhile, the thriving *Smurfs* was serving as Hanna-Barbera musical director Hoyt Curtin's final flourish. Hired by Bill in the 1950s to provide the continuity music that thematically unified many of the studio's most famous cartoons, Curtin now ushered classical music into television cartoons for possibly the first time. As he gradually retired, Curtin trained multiple young score composers throughout the 1980s; they later recalled his formative influence on their careers in *Film Score Monthly*.

A lack of non-*Smurfs* hits, old age, and regime change at Taft successor Great American Broadcasting led to Bill and Joe's ouster as presidents of Hanna-Barbera in 1989; David Kirschner, the thirty-four-year-old producer of *An American Tail*, succeeded them, lasting a mere three years. When Ted Turner bought Hanna-Barbera in 1992 for its vast cartoon library, Kirschner was replaced by Fred Seibert, a former creative director at MTV and brand consultant at Nickelodeon, and tasked him with setting up a new, all-cartoon cable channel, Cartoon Network. At a 2017 exhibition on Hanna-Barbera at the Norman Rockwell Museum, Seibert recounted his challenges in remaking the studio. He felt that Bill and Joe "had lost the mojo, in terms of what to do for the contemporary market," and that their lingering influence, despite no longer running Hanna-Barbera, was impeding the studio's creativity. Ironically inspired by the hands-off approach Fred Quimby took with the production of Bill and Joe's theatrical shorts at MGM, Seibert reinvented the Hanna-Barbera studio by soliciting and financing original animated shorts from artists near and far. *What a Cartoon!* was the result, an anthology series debuting in 1995 that aired a total of forty-eight seven-minute films, yielding Cartoon Network's first six original half-hour "Cartoon Cartoons," including the series *Dexter's Laboratory* and *The Powerpuff Girls*. In what would be their final work as animators, Bill and Joe each wrote and directed two shorts for *What a Cartoon!*, although independently of one another. While Bill and Joe served on Cartoon Network's advisory board, their once commanding production authority was granted to younger artists. Hanna and Barbera largely became symbolic figureheads of the company they founded for the remainder of their lives.

Although they were not creatively involved, the project from this time that aligned most directly with Bill and Joe's legacy was *The Flintstones* movie, a 1994 live-action adaptation produced by Steven Spielberg's Amblin Entertainment. "My job was to walk the tightrope between animation and reality," director Brian Levant states in an original interview here. He recalls the "100,000 square feet of soundstages that were devoted to literally creating Bedrock out of foam. Bill and Joe had brief cameo roles in the film. When they saw the film for the first time, both "jumped out of their seats, [with] tears in their eyes." The success of *The Flintstones* was likely a redemption for the two men of their five decades of hard work spent shaping and reshaping the animated art form.

Bill and Joe continued to come into the office most every day throughout the 1990s, and into their last years. Joe wrote and published his autobiography in 1994, *My Life in 'toons: From Flatbush to Bedrock in Under a Century*. Barbera shares many historical details related to their collaboration, but also frequently spins his memories for credibility and humor. Bill, also generally without work for one of the first times in his life, coauthored his own autobiography in 1996, *A Cast of Friends*. Hanna's account is more firmly grounded in the production techniques and historical vicissitudes of his and Joe's collaboration. Joe gave several late interviews, although attempts to get Bill on the record in his later years were pockmarked by gaps, tragically revealing the noticeable progression of his Alzheimer's. Bill died at age ninety in March 2001. Joe survived a handful of years more, seeing the formal closure of Hanna-Barbera in 2001, as it was absorbed into Warner Bros. Animation; he died at ninety-five in December 2006, to widespread tributes. Studio artist Scott Shaw! closes this volume with a brief remembrance of Joe, and a remark that applies equally to Bill: "[W]e lost the last old-time animation studio boss who actually knew how a cartoon was made."

Many people have helped us with this book over two and a half years. We send our thanks to the authors, interviewees, and rights holders who have made this collection possible. The project would have been quite different had Patrick Sullivan not connected the two of us in the first place. Yowp has been a guide since the beginning, through his stuff about early Hanna-Barbera cartoons. The last surviving early Hanna-Barbera artists have provided invaluable assistance: Tony Benedict, Iraj Paran, Jerry Eisenberg, Willie Ito, and Bob Singer. Several animation figures have been resources at key moments: Jerry Beck, Tom Minton, Linda Simensky, Tom Sito, and Darrell Van Citters. We acknowledge Ana Martinez at the Hollywood Chamber of Commerce, Martin Gostanian and Maria Pagano at the Paley Center for Media, and Linda Steele at the Canadian Broadcasting Corporation for their assistance. We personally wish to thank Dennis Bingham, Lev Cantoral, Adam Dix, Tamara Falicov, Maureen Furniss, Timothy Havens, Timothy Jones, Jim Korkis, Jesse Kowalski, and Michael Mallory. Several organizations and people have contributed financially, supporting our ability to pay permission fees for these pieces: the Society for Animation Studies, Dan Torre and Lienors Torre, J. Scott Williams, Arizona State University's Department of English, and the University of Virginia's Department of Media Studies. Our editor at the University Press of Mississippi, Emily Bandy, embraced this book from the beginning and fielded questions large and small through the project's tenure. Lastly, completing this project would have been more difficult had our families not lovingly listened to us go on and on and on about Hanna-Barbera.

The work of Bill Hanna and Joe Barbera and their Hanna-Barbera studio has been routinely downplayed and even completely omitted from all manner of books and publications. Yet it is undeniable that the pair has indelibly shaped the aesthetics and economics of television animation. There is much more to write about these under-discussed figures, despite our attempts to cover their whole careers. Numerous prominent examples of the studio's range of productions deserve more attention than we provide. These include: primetime animation series *The Flintstones* and *The Jetsons*, syndicated animation series like *The Huckleberry Hound Show* and *Wait Till Your Father Gets Home*, the animated theatrical film *Charlotte's Web*, live-action and animated television films like *Jack and the Beanstalk* and *The Gathering*, Hanna-Barbera Records, direct-to-video release *The Greatest Adventure: Stories from the Bible*, and Hanna-Barbera's myriad commercials, title sequences, and industrial, recruitment, and educational films. Our hope in publishing this volume and making these texts available is to aid in restoring Hanna and Barbera, and Hanna-Barbera, to the historical record.

KS
TSW

Notes

1. John Culhane, "The Men Behind Dastardly and Muttley," *New York Times Magazine*, November 23, 1969, 110.
2. Quoted in Michael Barrier and Bill Spicer, "An Interview with Chuck Jones," *Funnyworld* 13 (1971). Reprinted in Maureen Furniss, ed., *Chuck Jones: Conversations* (Jackson: University Press of Mississippi, 2005), 38, 43.
3. Leonard Maltin, "TV Animation: The Decline and Pratfall of a Popular Art," *Film Comment* 11, no. 1 (January–February 1975): 77.
4. Leonard Maltin, *Of Mice and Magic: A History of American Animated Cartoons* (New York: Plume, 1987; first edition, New York: McGraw-Hill, 1980); Michael Barrier, *Hollywood Cartoons: American Animation in Its Golden Age* (New York: Oxford University Press, 1999). Nevertheless, Maltin would conduct a kindhearted three-and-a-half-hour interview with Joe Barbera in 1997 for the Academy of Television Arts & Sciences Archive of American Television series.
5. Eugene Slafer, "A Conversation with Bill Hanna," in *The American Animated Cartoon: A Critical Anthology*, edited by Danny Peary and Gerald Peary (Theme Park Press, 2017), 287–92. This book was first published in 1980 by E. P. Dutton.
6. Quoted in Ruth E. Thompson, "Hanna Barbera Increased Staff 100 Times in Seven Years," *Times Argus* (Barre, VT), October 24, 1964, 7.
7. Hubbard Keavy, "New Animated Cartoon Process Proves Entertaining in Hollywood," *The Sun* (Baltimore), May 5, 1940, sec. 1, 6. Syndicated by the Associated Press.
8. Keavy.
9. Keavy.
10. Joseph Barbera, *My Life in 'toons: From Flatbush to Bedrock in Under a Century* (Atlanta: Turner Publishing, 1994), 85.
11. Bill Hanna with Tom Ito, *A Cast of Friends* (Dallas: Taylor Publishing Company, 1996), 136.
12. Hanna, 144.
13. Buz McCarthy, "Hanna-Barbera Plans New Show," *Syracuse Post-Standard*, June 21, 1964.
14. Hanna, 147.
15. Barbera, 230.

CHRONOLOGY

1910   William Denby Hanna is born into an Irish American family on July 14 in Melrose, New Mexico Territory, USA, a frontier town of fewer than one thousand people.

1911   Joseph Barbera is born into an Italian family on March 24 in a tenement apartment in Little Italy, Manhattan, New York City, New York, USA. He would largely grow up in bustling Flatbush, Brooklyn.

1917   Hanna's family settles in the Los Angeles neighborhood of San Pedro, California. Previously, his father's engineering work moved the family to remote areas of Oregon and Utah.

1922   Hanna becomes a Boy Scout, an avocation he continues until late in life. In 1985, at age seventy-five, Hanna will receive the Distinguished Eagle Scout Award, which he reports to be his proudest life achievement.

1929   Barbera begins submitting and publishing single-panel cartoons as J. Roland Barbera in magazines including *Redbook* and *Collier's*.

1930   Hanna joins the Harman-Ising animation studio, working from cel washer up to leading the ink and paint department. Hanna works with Hugh Harman and Rudolf Ising for about ten years, and is influenced by their sentimental, Disney-style approach to animation.

1932   Barbera joins Van Beuren Studios as an animator and storyboard artist. The studio, formerly led by Paul Terry until 1929, maintains Terry's wild, slapstick New York City cartoon style, which shapes Joe Barbera's personal cartooning style. In 1936, after Van Beuren closes, Barbera works at Terrytoons for one year.

1935   Barbera marries Dorothy Earl, his high school sweetheart. They are married for twenty-eight years (until 1963) and have four children (Neal, Lynn, Jayne, and a short-lived baby boy).

1936   Hanna directs his first cartoon, *To Spring*, together with animator Paul Fennell, for Harman and Ising's Happy Harmonies series, for MGM. Hanna marries Violet Wogatzke. They are married sixty-five years, and have two children (David and Bonnie).

1937   Barbera joins the newly formed MGM cartoon studio, after driving across the country from New York to Los Angeles.

1939   After working around each other for two years, Bill Hanna and Joe Barbera begin collaborating on their first original project, a cat-and-mouse cartoon. Barbera draws the characters and story frames; Hanna directs the cartoon by timing Barbera's layout drawings with bar sheets.

1940   *Puss Gets the Boot*, Hanna and Barbera's first collaboration, is released in February. It is nominated for the Academy Award for Best Short Subject: Cartoons.

1941   *The Midnight Snack*, the first official Tom and Jerry cartoon, is released in July. With this cartoon, Hanna and Barbera begin leading their own animation unit at MGM. Tex Avery assumes control of MGM's second animation unit in 1942, influencing the evolution of Hanna and Barbera's series. The pair would predominantly produce and direct cartoons for MGM's Tom and Jerry series for eighteen years.

1943   *The Yankee Doodle Mouse* wins the Academy Award for Best Short Subject: Cartoons. The Tom and Jerry series—including *Puss Gets the Boot*—would be nominated a total of thirteen times, winning for six additional cartoons: *Mouse Trouble* (1944), *Quiet Please!* (1945), *The Cat Concerto* (1947), *The Little Orphan* (1949), *The Two Mouseketeers* (1952), and *Johann Mouse* (1953).

1945   MGM releases the theatrical feature film *Anchors Aweigh*, directed by George Sidney, showcasing Jerry Mouse in a rotoscoped dance sequence alongside a live-action Gene Kelly. As animated characters, Tom and Jerry will also appear with Esther Williams in *Dangerous When Wet* (1953), and again with Kelly in *Invitation to the Dance* (1956).

1951   Hanna and Barbera moonlight after hours to produce the first opening-title sequence for the television sitcom *I Love Lucy*. The original stick-figure credits will remain in place for the full eight-year production run of the series. Beginning in 1959 for syndication, the credit sequence will be replaced by the now-recognized satin heart. In 1964, Bill and Joe would also create the credits for the television series *Bewitched*.

1952   Barbera writes a stage play, *The Maid and the Martian*, which debuts in Los Angeles. Barbera's script would partially inspire the 1964 film *The Pajama Party*.

1955   Hanna and Barbera assume responsibility for MGM's animation division, after studio head Fred Quimby retires and Tex Avery departs to direct animated television commercials. They remake the 1939 Hugh Harman film *Peace on Earth* as *Good Will to Men* (1955).

1956   While at MGM, Hanna cofounds Shield Productions, a short-lived animation studio, without Joe Barbera. Partnering with brother-in-law and fellow animator Mike Lah, Hanna attempts to create a color version of the first television cartoon, *Crusader Rabbit*. Ultimately, the series is revived by Shull Bonsall's studio TV Spots without them.

1957 MGM closes its cartoon studio on May 15, forcing Hanna and Barbera, and the rest of the studio's staff, into unemployment. On July 7, Bill Hanna and Joe Barbera open a new animation studio, H-B Enterprises, with several MGM colleagues, to make cartoons specifically for television. George Sidney and Columbia Pictures president Harry Cohn provide financial backing, and Columbia's Screen Gems television division distributes their product. Their first office is at Kling Studios, 1416 N. La Brea Avenue, formerly Charlie Chaplin's studio. Bill and Joe would take turns as president and vice-president of the company for the next thirty years. Hanna-Barbera's first television cartoon program, *The Ruff and Reddy Show*, debuts December 14 on NBC's Saturday morning schedule. Two four-minute *Ruff and Reddy* cartoons starring a chummy cat and dog bookend a children's program starring live-action host Jimmy Blaine that also features older Columbia theatrical cartoons.

1958 *The Huckleberry Hound Show* begins syndicated broadcast on September 29, on local stations between 5:00 and 8:00 p.m., and lasts three seasons. The series, starring a blue anthropomorphic coonhound with a North Carolina Southern drawl, also introduces future star Yogi Bear, and becomes the young studio's breakout hit. Hanna and Barbera begin expanding their studio by hiring experienced Hollywood artists and creatives from across the animation and live-action industries. The studio would assume its now-familiar name the next year: Hanna-Barbera Productions.

1960 Hanna-Barbera receives an Emmy Award for Outstanding Achievement in the Field of Children's Programming for *The Huckleberry Hound Show*, the first Emmy awarded to an animated television cartoon. *The Flintstones* premieres in primetime on September 30 at 8:30 p.m. on ABC. The prehistoric sitcom lasts six seasons, becoming a lasting signature for the studio.

1961 *Top Cat* begins airing on September 27 in primetime on ABC. The cartoon about city alley cats lasts only one season in the United States, but becomes widely popular in Latin America and the United Kingdom. *The Yogi Bear Show* also debuts in syndication, giving the rascally bear his own program.

1962 *The Jetsons* premieres on September 23 in primetime on ABC. The science fiction sitcom, while initially only lasting one season, would become perennially popular in syndication, leading the studio to later produce new episodes from 1985 to 1987.

1963 Hanna-Barbera, previously dispersed across different buildings, move the growing company into a large new studio building at 3400 Cahuenga Boulevard in Studio City. As the studio's number of cartoon series in simultaneous production begins growing around this time, Bill Hanna

1964   *Jonny Quest* debuts September 18 in primetime on ABC. A popular success that foreshadows future action-adventure cartoons on Saturday morning, the series lasts only one season due to high production costs. Other than Hanna-Barbera's *Where's Huddles?* (1970), it is the last network primetime television cartoon until Fox's *The Simpsons* in 1989. The musical comedy *Hey There, It's Yogi Bear!*, Hanna-Barbera's first animated feature film, is released by Columbia Pictures. The studio's second feature, the spy-themed *The Man Called Flintstone*, will be released in 1966.

1965   Hanna-Barbera Records is founded to release recordings of original pop music and Hanna-Barbera–themed records. It would close just two years later.

1966   Hanna-Barbera Productions is acquired by the Taft Broadcasting Company on December 28 for $12 million. Hanna and Barbera remain presidents of the studio. Hanna-Barbera produces its first major Saturday morning hit, *Space Ghost and Dino Boy*. Barbera marries Sheila Holden, a cashier and bookkeeper.

1967   The studio produces the live-action/animated fairy tale telefilm *Jack and the Beanstalk* for NBC, earning an Emmy for Outstanding Children's Program.

1968   The comedy cartoon *Wacky Races* debuts on CBS, spawning two spin-offs the following year, *The Perils of Penelope Pitstop* and *Dastardly and Muttley in Their Flying Machines*.

1969   *Scooby-Doo, Where Are You!* premieres September 13 on CBS. The mystery-comedy would be continually renewed in differing iterations across numerous media formats for decades, becoming Hanna-Barbera's most popular creation.

1970   The studio has a modest success with its Saturday morning series *Josie and the Pussycats*, the first US television cartoon to feature an African American woman.

1972   Hanna-Barbera opens its first overseas animation studio, in Sydney, Australia, known as Hanna-Barbera Australia, to share growing production responsibilities. H-B would coorganize further international subcontracting with studios in South Korea, Mexico, Argentina, Spain, and Poland, and cofound Cuckoo's Nest in Taiwan in 1978 and Fil-Cartoons in the Philippines in 1987. Taft Broadcasting opens Kings Island, an amusement park modeled after Disneyland, on April 29 outside Cincinnati, Ohio. Subsequent H-B-themed parks opened by Taft would include Kings Dominion in 1975 (near Richmond, Virginia) and Hanna-Barbera Land in 1984 (outside Houston, Texas).

1973 *Charlotte's Web*, Hanna-Barbera's iconic and ultimately most successful animated feature film, is released by Paramount Pictures. "Last of the Curlews," an hour-long *ABC Afterschool Special* telefilm, wins an Emmy in 1972 for Outstanding Achievement in Children's Programming: Informational/Factual.

1976 Hanna and Barbera are jointly awarded a star on the Hollywood Walk of Fame (as "Hanna-Barbera"), on the 6700 block of Hollywood Boulevard, for their television work.

1977 The studio begins its animation training program to train young artists to replace retiring elder studio animators. H-B's live-action adult drama *The Gathering* airs on ABC, winning the Emmy for Outstanding Special—Drama or Comedy.

1979 Television animators walk out of Hanna-Barbera and other studios on August 13, as part of a successful eleven-day industry-wide strike, winning protections against international outsourcing. A subsequent ten-week strike in 1982 would fail, leading to most animation and ink-and-paint work being sent overseas.

1981 *The Smurfs* debuts on NBC's Saturday morning schedule on September 12. The fairy-tale comedy, based on the long-running Belgian comic begun by Peyo in 1958, is an immediate hit with audiences, expanding into a ninety-minute block and running for nine seasons. The series and its primetime specials will be regularly nominated for Emmy Awards throughout the 1980s.

1982 *Heidi's Song*, an ambitious, Disney-style fantasy musical produced by Hanna-Barbera and distributed by Paramount Pictures, is released, to disappointing box office results.

1988 *The Smurfs* episode "The Lure of the Orb" wins a Humanitas Prize. *The Flintstone Kids* also wins, for its 1989 episode "Rocky's Rocky Road."

1988 Hanna and Barbera receive the Governors Award from the Academy of Television Arts & Sciences for their lifetime's work.

1989 David Kirschner, the producer of the *American Tail* and *Child's Play* film franchises, succeeds Bill and Joe as president of Hanna-Barbera.

1990 *Jetsons: The Movie* is released by Universal Pictures. It is the last project Bill Hanna and Joe Barbera are creatively involved in jointly producing and directing.

1991 The Hanna-Barbera studio and library are sold by Taft successor company Great American Broadcasting to Ted Turner's Turner Broadcasting System on October 29 for an estimated $320 million.

1992 Former MTV creative director Fred Seibert is appointed president of Hanna-Barbera in June to oversee the studio's reorganization as a subsidiary of Turner Broadcasting. Cartoon Network is launched as a cable network on October 1 by Turner Broadcasting System. Classic

Hanna-Barbera cartoons form much of the network's early programming, along with programs packaging together classic cartoon film shorts, including Looney Tunes and Merrie Melodies, Popeye, and MGM series. Bill Hanna and Joe Barbera become symbolic figureheads, creatively advising artists at the studio and serving on the new network's advisory board. Numerous shows featuring Bill and Joe's characters will be reimagined at Cartoon Network in the 1990s, the earliest within three years: *Space Ghost Coast to Coast* and *The Real Adventures of Jonny Quest*.

1993 Hanna and Barbera are inducted into the Academy of Television Arts & Sciences' Hall of Fame. In 2005, the two are immortalized together with classic characters in a bronze wall sculpture portrait on the Academy's Hall of Fame Plaza.

1994 Barbera publishes his autobiography, *My Life in 'toons: From Flatbush to Bedrock in Under a Century*. The live-action film *The Flintstones*, produced by Hanna-Barbera and Steven Spielberg's Amblin Entertainment, is released by Universal Pictures. Bill and Joe both appear in brief cameo roles in the film, as well as its sequel, *The Flintstones in Viva Rock Vegas*, released in 2000.

1995 The Museum of Television & Radio in New York, which would become the Paley Center for Media, organizes an exhibit, screening series, and catalog book titled *The World of Hanna-Barbera*.

1996 Hanna publishes his autobiography, *A Cast of Friends*, coauthored with Tom Ito.

2001 Bill Hanna passes away at home on March 22. Hanna-Barbera is absorbed into Warner Bros. Animation, formally closing the studio. It is renamed Cartoon Network Studios.

2006 Joe Barbera passes away at home on December 18.

2016 The Norman Rockwell Museum presents Hanna-Barbera art, organizes talks, and conducts interviews with surviving studio creatives for the exhibit and book "Hanna-Barbera: The Architects of Saturday Morning."

2021 Cartoon Network Studios Europe is rebranded as Hanna-Barbera Studios Europe.

HANNA AND BARBERA
CONVERSATIONS

Hanna and Barbera: After Fifty Years, Opposites Still Attract

MORRIE GELMAN / 1989

From *Variety*, July 12, 1989, 57, 68, 70. © 1989 Variety Media, LLC. All rights reserved. Used by permission.

February 5 was a night to remember. The B'nai B'rith Lodge in Beverly Hills honored William Hanna and Joseph Barbera as Men of the Year at its annual dinner.

The five hundred men, women and children at the black-tie event held at the Beverly Hilton Hotel celebrated the fiftieth anniversary of the Hanna-Barbera partnership. Costumed actors representing H-B's most memorable creations danced to music from some of the team's almost three hundred series and specials. Numerous small fry, including the kids of Pia Zadora and husband Meshulam Riklis, joined them on the dance floor.

The pair were lauded for "a half-century of the art of animation to thrill and delight and make lives bright for children worldwide" by the dinner's chairman, Leonard E. Wasserstein.

MCA Inc. president Sid Sheinberg, honorary chairman of the event, said Hanna and Barbera had "entered the realm of the immortals." He praised the would-be engineer (Hanna) and the onetime bank clerk (Barbera) for bringing wit and intelligence to cartoons instead of "mindless violence."

There was good reason for celebration. According to the US Census Bureau's Office of Marriage and Family, only 26 percent of the men and women married in 1930 were still together fifty years later. For business partners to still be together after fifty years is even more remarkable.

CHOICE VOICES

What hath this fifty-year partnership wrought? After twenty years of doing Tom and Jerry theatrical cartoons at MGM and starting their own banner with a single order for a six-minute short in 1957, Hanna-Barbera has become one of the world's largest producers of animated entertainment. It has been a spawning ground for some of the best voice talents in the world, and a wellspring of all sorts of related merchandise forever identified with kids, laughter, and good times.

Turner Network Television will commemorate this half-century of achievement with *A Yabba Dabba Celebration: 50 Years of Hanna-Barbera*, a two-hour special premiering July 17. Spec will combo live action with classic cartoon footage, plus new animation featuring some of the team's best-known characters.

The Hanna-Barbera story is quintessential "only in America" material.

Bill Hanna, seventy-seven, as different from seventy-eight-year-old Joe Barbera as an English muffin from a pizza pie, didn't figure to enter the realm of showbusiness immortals. [Editors' note: Bill was actually seventy-nine.] Born in New Mexico, almost a continent away from Barbera's native Brooklyn, he found himself working on construction of the Pantages Theatre in Hollywood during the Depression. He fell off the scaffolding and wound up in the hospital—and, indirectly, in showbiz.

Seeking less-strenuous employment, Hanna signed on with Pacific Title & Art, where he learned how to ink cells. He worked with pioneer cartoonists Rudolph Ising and Hugh Harman.

"I learned the business from Harman and Ising," Hanna recalls. "By the time I was twenty-one, I was writing music and doing animation direction."

Hanna then went to MGM, writing and directing cartoons. There, in 1937, he met Joe Barbera, a fledgling animator.

As a child in Brooklyn, Barbera remembers his mother being infatuated with show business. She would pick up Joe and his brother at school and go to see Jack Benny or another top-flight vaudeville act. Showbiz soon seeped into young Joe's blood.

"You don't know enthusiasm until you see Joe try to sell you something," Sid Sheinberg observes about Barbera, the natural performer. He's still one of the best pitchmen in Hollywood, a place that has seen more pitches than Yankee Stadium.

Contrast this with Hanna quietly learning his craft at the feet of the masters.

The duo's opposing personalities mesh very well, perhaps one of the reasons for their longtime success. Barbera is the showman, the front man, Mr. Outside. Hanna is the nose-to-the-grindstone inside man, turning the ideas into reality.

A prime example of Joe Barbera's colorful demeanor is his description of his former boss Paul Terry, creator of Terrytoons and one of the pioneers in the animation business. "He always had a cigar in his mouth," Barbera remembers. "He even had a dent in his lip where the cigar fitted, and he talked like Sydney Greenstreet."

Barbera was recruited for MGM by Ted Sears, who acted as a go-between for an exec named Fred Kelly. "They asked Sears to locate some talent for MGM, which was about to start its own cartoon studio," Barbera recalls. The salary was $87.50 a week.

WHAT'S THE STORY?

Barbera is fond of anecdotes—how situations worked out fortuitously because of some chance circumstance. Ask Bill Hanna a question, and the reply is self-effacing and unembellished.

This is the laconic way Hanna describes his five-decade partnership with Barbera: "We teamed together; we wrote. He did the drawings and I did the animation direction, as I had been doing with Harman and Ising, and we've been together ever since."

Hanna is not comfortable speaking about himself or his accomplishments. He's much more at ease buried in his work or talking to longtime associates.

Hanna and Barbera's first collaboration was *Puss Gets the Boot*. It was nominated for an Academy Award.

The new team came up with a technique called "limited animation," which was later to serve them well in television. Barbera would not do storyboards, but instead gave his initial drawings to Hanna for timing and photography right off the paper sheets. They simulated an entire cartoon with about 1,200 drawings instead of the 26,000 needed for full cel animation.

"We were able to get an idea of what this cartoon would look like with this simulation," Barbera explains. Colleagues at the studio were called in to view the limited animation. "We got more laughs on that penciled drawing reel than anything that had ever been made there," he remembers.

Fred Quimby, the animation unit boss, told Hanna and Barbera to complete their project. So was born the team.

Barbera would illustrate the story, and Hanna would time and expose it. The same holds true even today. Barbera still works on the story end, and Hanna is still getting the stuff through production.

Puss Gets the Boot was really Tom and Jerry but not under that name. In Barbera's evaluation, "It was a hysterically funny picture."

Puss was successful and the duo made a second cartoon, [the first] "Tom and Jerry."

Originally, H-B were going to call the characters Jinx and Jasper. "We were trying to be different," Barbera points out. "But you find out that the simplest approaches are often the best."

FACE TO FACE

Hanna/Barbera became a separate unit at MGM. Bill and Joe sat at facing desks, and worked that way for twenty years.

Did they argue? Barbera has a running gag to answer that question. "We did fight," he says. "The very first week we had a real knock-down, drag-out fight. And we haven't spoken to each other since. That's the secret."

Typically answering the question more seriously, Hanna recalls an argument very early in his association with Barbera, long before there was a Hanna-Barbera company.

"We have never had a fight or a violent argument," says Hanna. "I respect him, and he shares that same respect and consideration for me."

It has been a friendly relationship but not a particularly close one. Hanna and Barbera don't mix socially. Barbera is much more into the Hollywood scene, palling around with film and TV honchos. Hanna's buddies are high school chums, people he has worked with for thirty to forty years.

Barbera is the company president and spokesman, and Hanna is glad for it.

"I really think Joe does what he does better than I would do it," Hanna says. "While he may not always speak for both of us, it doesn't take anything away from me. I know what I do and he knows what I do, and he would have kicked me out a long time ago if he didn't respect me."

Hanna's title is senior VP. In the early years, both developed the material together, but Barbera drifted into sales and marketing and Hanna into production. Joe hired the writers, and Bill hired the animators. Hanna also sets up foreign distribution and production facilities.

The only time it bothers him to be in a secondary position, Hanna confesses, is when Barbera gets all of the credit "for some of the things I do." It's not, Hanna adds quickly, that Barbera seeks or even accepts such credit; it sometimes comes out that way in the retelling of their joint enterprises.

Barbera remembers Hanna, ever the dedicated worker, speaking on the phone with his eyes closed and head back, totally concentrated.

"It was funny," Barbera reminisces. "You'd walk in and open his desk drawers, go through his pockets, take his wallet, stack the stuff up and leave it there. Then he'd open his eyes and wonder who was in his office."

Hanna and Barbera turned over fifty minutes of animation a year at MGM: seven to eight pictures of six to seven minutes each. Their first budget was about $32,000, Barbera recalls. This grew to maybe $65,000 per cartoon at the peak.

To keep the original Tom and Jerry within budget, the pair kept scaling back the cartoon's length until they got a five-minute product.

OUT BUT NOT DOWN

By 1957, Hanna and Barbera were not only scaled back, they were out. MGM closed its animation department. "The studio told us to finish what we were doing and then let everybody go," Barbera remembers.

Sticking together as a team, Hanna and Barbera tried to break into television. They didn't own the rights to Tom and Jerry, nor did they have much money.

At MGM, Barbera confirms, "We signed contracts and MGM owned everything we did. They owned all of the Tom and Jerry material; we were just salaried people under contract."

Ironically, more than thirty years after leaving Tom and Jerry behind at MGM, the cartoon series is still paying dividends to Hanna-Barbera. Following the showings of *A Yabba Dabba Celebration*, TNT will offer a special Tom and Jerry feature, *Dangerous When Wet*, in which Esther Williams stars as a fitness buff who takes a dip with the cat and mouse team.

The Turner organization, which acquired the MGM library from Kirk Kerkorian in 1986, now controls the rights to Tom and Jerry. H-B will be making a series for TNT called *Tom & Jerry Kids*.

Barbera says that after MGM, he and Hanna had "a two-bit deal" at Screen Gems, the TV arm of Columbia Pictures. Screen Gems made a deal with the duo for five five-minute cartoons, paying an average of $3,000 each, for a cat and dog story, *Ruff and Reddy*.

H-B used the limited animation technique they had developed for the Tom and Jerry series. Between Barbera's drawings and Hanna's timing, the team was able to do TV cartoons for $3,000 or less.

George Sidney, a producer-director who worked with Bill and Joe on *Anchors Aweigh*, during which live action was comboed with animation, was an original investor in Hanna-Barbera Prods. The company found office space in the former Chaplin Studios in Hollywood.

Sidney has claimed he founded Hanna-Barbera Prods., financed the organization 100 percent, was the largest single stockholder and was president for the first five years, the period of the firm's greatest growth.

Per Barbera, Sidney should get credit for helping start Hanna-Barbera and "that's it. He's a nice man, goodbye."

From *Ruff and Reddy*, Hanna-Barbera went on to their first major success, *The Huckleberry Hound Show*, which featured Yogi Bear. The series started in 1958, and H-B won an Emmy for it in 1960.

The hits kept rolling from there, including their first primetime network series, *The Flintstones* for ABC, *Yogi Bear* as a spinoff of *Huckleberry Hound*, *Quick Draw McGraw*, *Top Cat*, and *The Jetsons*.

Barbera's pitch for *The Flintstones* established his reputation for doing dynamite presentations. He'd tack two half-hour stories on all four walls and narrate them, doing all the voices and sound effects.

"It was like doing a play or a comedy act," Barbera says. Each presentation would take an hour and a half, and he would sometimes do five a day.

Barbera remembers pitching to Jim Aubrey, then prexy of CBS-TV, in "a rotten, dark room" where he couldn't see anything. Aubrey passed on *The Flintstones*, saying, per Barbera, he didn't want to take a gamble on that kind of show.

Barbera finally sold the show to ABC in about fifteen minutes.

He remembers the license fee as $50,000 a week, with H-B bringing in the half-hour for about $30,000. H-B segued from *The Flintstones* to other primetime series. *Top Cat* sold to ABC on the strength of one drawing, according to Barbera, followed by *The Jetsons* and the action-adventure *Jonny Quest*.

He also remembers selling *The New Adventures of Huck Finn* to NBC programming chief Mort Werner as a primetime series. Barbera and agent Ted Ashley went in to see Werner and sold the series in two minutes."

Taft Broadcasting bought Hanna-Barbera for $12 million in December 1966 and paid off George Sidney with $2 million, says Barbera.

The sale was the first big money Hanna and Barbera ever realized. "We were never big movie moguls with a lot of money," Hanna emphasizes. "We were salaried people just like any of the animators we worked with." He claims that some of those animators "made a lot more than we did."

Barbera claims he and Hanna gave the company away. "You could look back now and say, 'Well, it's worth $300 million today,'" he explains.

Previously, Screen Gems had been Hanna-Barbera's selling agency. "They represented us, taking a 60 percent chunk out of each deal," Barbera says.

"After MGM closed us down, we made Screen Gems something like $24 million in five years. They were getting a big piece. They were getting the sixty and we were getting the forty."

He says Taft was "a terrific outfit"; Great American Communications acquired Taft's assets in 1987.

Under the new arrangement, Hanna-Barbera has been restructured almost from scratch. While not abandoning animation, H-B is now diversifying into many other areas.

Asked if H-B has become MCA-Universal's hired gun in its well-publicized disputes with Disney, Barbera says, "It's a natural step if someone wants to have well-known cartoon characters in their park (Universal's theme park in Orlando, Florida)."

"They really do a job," Barbera says about the Disney organization. "They really know how to do it over there, and it behooves us to learn from them."

There are no thoughts of either he or Hanna retiring. Hanna says his wife often tells him, "You'll probably die doing what you're doing."

Barbera claims he wanted to retire four years ago, but then adds that this isn't the kind of job you retire from. It's not exactly all carefree "because I have a problem every damn day," but he draws, writes, tells jokes, and "has a lot of fun."

Ask about their favorite H-B characters, and Hanna will cast his vote for The Flintstones; Barbera likes Yogi Bear.

Hanna likes Fred, Wilma, and crew because "there are so many human frailties in some of the characters." He also likes the husband-wife relationship.

Barbera likes Yogi because he's a nonconformist, "freewheeling and always fighting the establishment."

Cartoon Creator Joseph Barbera Takes Tom and Jerry to Movies

TOM PROVENZANO / 1993

From *Drama-Logue*, July 29–August 4, 1993, 28. Copyright © *Backstage*. Reprinted with permission.

In the midst of redesigning the large Hanna-Barbera studio compound, suites of offices look like they have been through a war. But at the far end of the dust, plaster, and twisted metal is an oasis of order. Through the threshold we find ourselves in an enclave of dark wood and memories. From the richly furnished room it might be the office of any successful Hollywood executive, but the distinctive trappings make it unmistakably the working habitat of one of the seminal animators of the film industry, Joseph Barbera.

His office looks more like a toy shop than a workspace. Hundreds of stuffed Hanna-Barbera cartoon characters, pictures, and cels cover the furniture, line the walls, and flood the floor. Each item details a specific memory in the long productive life of Barbera, a sentimental and very happy man.

For some forty years he and his partner, William Hanna, have dominated television cartoons. From the early days of Huckleberry Hound and Fred Flintstone to the modern mania for "kiddie" versions of popular cartoon shows like *The Flintstone Kids* or *Tom & Jerry Kids*, no one has put out as much successful product as Hanna-Barbera.

Now with feature films looking to television and cartoons for inspiration, Joseph Barbera has a new career as a creative consultant to major studios creating full-length versions of his comic creations. First out is *Tom and Jerry: The Movie*, a funny and touching story of hopelessness and pulling together. The filmmakers knew they needed more than just the comic violence of the six-minute Tom and Jerry shorts, so they turned to Barbera, the storyman, to come up with a well-crafted plot. In this film, Tom and Jerry find their home destroyed. In order to survive, this constantly feuding pair must rely on one another. In a highly amusing moment, about twenty minutes into the film, they discover they can both talk—they are surprised at one another since they have not shared a word in their fifty-[plus]-year partnership.

Tom and Jerry is far more than just one of Hanna-Barbera's most successful creations. The cartoon is the engine that created animation's most prolific team. Joseph Barbera was brought out to MGM from New York in the mid-1930s. The studio was dissatisfied with its animation company and wanted to create its own division to make cartoon shorts. Among the local talent in the new division was William Hanna. He and Barbera hit it off quite well, though the new animation department didn't seem to be paying off.

"The whole thing wasn't working. I suggested to Bill, 'Why don't we do a cartoon ourselves?' The question is what kind of characters do you use? People seem to think it is just a breeze to take a purple spotted pig and a tall yellow giraffe and make them characters. It doesn't work. So I leaned towards the most unoriginal idea in the world, a cat and a mouse. Very basic because I knew wherever you went, no matter where you ran it—in Somalia or Beirut—you see a cat and a mouse and you know what's going to happen. A chase. The question is: How do you do it? They had been doing cat and mouse cartoons all over the place. There was Felix the Cat, Krazy Kat. A whole bunch of cats. Then Mighty Mouse. So when we started, Oh hoo! Such dialogue about what a stupid, unoriginal idea—an old idea. How many can you do? One, two? All this conversation about these two idiots trying to do a new series."

Meanwhile, the brass had decided that the next cartoons should be based on the famous comic strip *The Katzenjammer Kids*. "A German family speaking in German dialect at the time we were at war with Germany. These mucky-mucks in the research department said this is the one. It was out every Sunday in the comic sheets. It is popular. Surefire! It was the worst idea in the world."

The studio soon saw that the idea was headed for disaster, as was the entire department. Barbera was sent to work with Friz Freleng, who would later make his name with Warner Bros.' brilliant Bugs Bunny cartoons. "I was the story man. Although I was an animator when I came out, I segued into storyboards. I liked to do the story. Our greatest accomplishment was throwing pushpins at our shoes. Go right through the leather. A big sport in the cartoon industry. I became the best in the studio."

While Barbera was throwing pushpins at shoes, the studio came up with the idea of bringing in famous, high-class cartoonists to head the department. That idea soon went bust, but Barbera and Hanna had returned to their simple idea of the cat and mouse cartoon. "I would lay the whole thing out while I was writing the story. Then I'd turn it over to Bill who would concentrate on getting it out to the animators. We shot all these drawings I did and previewed them before we even started the cartoon. They got the best reaction."

So they made the cartoon [*Puss Gets the Boot*] and it was a success. "However, in their infinite wisdom, the head honcho from MGM said, 'We don't want to do any more cat and mouse cartoons. Don't want to put all our eggs in one basket.'" Fortunately, intervention came from a distributor in Texas who demanded more of the "cat and mouse cartoons." Barbera and Hanna went back to work, though the rest of the department still felt it was a hackneyed concept. "Once we began, the hue and cry went up again, 'Oh God! What a stupid idea.' We had to have a name for the characters. Once again, a very unoriginal name, Tom and Jerry, a Christmas drink!"

The first film they did with the official name won an Oscar—the first of seven. [Editors' note: Actually, the first Oscar went to *The Yankee Doodle Mouse* in 1943.] Still the studio resisted doing more. And they resisted for twenty years. Then the downward spiral hit MGM. In the middle of one of the busiest schedules ever, the phone rang and they were ordered to shut down the studios. The animators had no idea that MGM was in terrible financial straits. But they did find out why their successful branch was cut loose. "The head honcho was looking through the books. He said, 'What the hell is this? You reissue the Tom and Jerry cartoons you did four years ago and you do as well as a new cartoon. What do we need new cartoons for?' You can't believe this kind of thinking."

So Barbera was out of work. "Here we are in our early forties, making fair money but figuring this is it. I'd reached the peak of my career. What do I do now? Do I go open a hamburger stand, try to sell insurance? What the heck do you do? Successful, working here for twenty years; suddenly you are cut off."

At the time, television was beginning to emerge as a force. "Television was a dirty word at MGM. If you mentioned television it was ruthless, they wanted you out of there." Nevertheless, Barbera and Hanna saw the possibilities of television. They wrote a six-page memo to the company detailing the way to make money from television, but they received no reply.

They peddled their wares all over town and were rejected by everyone. Finally they landed a slim deal at Columbia's Screen Gems, the television division. Money was so tight they were forced to recreate animation art. "To give an example of how tough things were, we were averaging $45–60,000 for a five-minute Tom and Jerry cartoon. They offered us $3,000 for a five-minute cartoon for television. You say, 'How do you do this?' You use all the knowledge you gathered over twenty years. Basically, you limit the number of drawings. A five-minute Tom and Jerry cartoon was about 23–28,000 drawings; for television we did about 1,800–2,300 drawings. It's a matter of exposure and camera work, tricks you use to make it work."

The success on television was dramatic. Soon they had three half-hour anthology shows, *Huckleberry Hound*, *Quick Draw McGraw*, and *Yogi Bear*, all through deals with Kellogg's. Then a strange new idea came along: . . . a prime-time cartoon. "It had never been done before. We tried working with a whole bunch of characters—a pilgrim family, a Roman family, a hillbilly family—[and] went on and on until we hit the caveman family. The minute we put them in skins and bare feet and went into what I call the window dressing (Stoneway piano, Ann Margrock, Stony Curtis, Polarock camera), it hit. All these things worked. It held the adults, but we never lost the kids."

It was through the success of *The Flintstones* that Barbera gained a real insight into merchandising tie-ins. "I remember sitting in this chair getting a call from New York about us planning for them to have a baby. No one had had a baby in cartoons. He asked, 'What is it?' 'It's a boy, a chip off the old block, Fred Jr.' 'Too bad. We had the Ideal Toy people, and if it is a girl we could really clean up.' I said, 'It *is* a girl.' Just that quickly. Pebbles, another little chip off the block. . . . Boy dolls weren't selling."

Hanna-Barbera has continued to dominate television and Barbera keeps on top of those projects. But now he is fascinated with the new feature projects. [Hanna and Barbera are] not coproducing. Barbera chose to take the title "creative consultant" to the producing studios.

He is thrilled with the reaction to *Tom and Jerry: The Movie*. The idea came when he was trying to find out who controlled the short films he had spent twenty years creating. He learned Ted Turner owned them, and he went to see that company. Through conversations, the concept of a feature was developed and Barbera mapped out the story.

Barbera knows the characters are popular here in America, but he was thrown by the reaction in Europe. "I just came back from Germany and Paris. In Berlin, not only was the house totally sold out, there were four thousand people milling around outside who couldn't get in. When I walked down the aisle, the whole theater got up for a standing ovation. In Paris, the same reaction. The big surprise is that Droopy makes a ten-second cameo appearance, a yell goes out taking the roof off. Droopy! At the Paris opening, all in French, here comes Droopy again and another scream goes up! So now I am doing a new Droopy series: *Droopy, Master Detective*."

The *Flintstones* movie came about in much the same way. Barbera went to see Universal Studios about adding his cute and cuddly characters to the scary shark and gorilla on the theme park tours. Soon conversation led to Barbera's idea, which included a *Flintstones* movie. Suddenly they made a deal and Universal and Spielberg were on board with the idea. "The beauty of Amblin being involved is they have money. I went to the set where they have duplicated the town of Bedrock. They created twenty-two vehicles. I drove around in Barney's sports car. Unbelievable. The interest is amazing. Catch the trailer with [John] Goodman in the theater—the reaction is astonishing."

Barbera's love for his work shows through his kindness and his utter delight. "My pleasure is seeing something started thirty years [ago] booming. Something we started fifty-six years ago is [now] a full-fledged feature. It is really a thrill."

Hanna and Barbera at MGM

MICHAEL BARRIER / 1999

Excerpts from "MGM, 1939–1952," from *Hollywood Cartoons: American Animation in Its Golden Age* (New York: Oxford University Press, 1999), 403–10, 419–21, 422–24. Copyright © Oxford University Press, Inc. Reproduced with permission of the licensor through PLSclear.

When Bill Hanna and Joe Barbera began making cartoons together, it was at Fred Quimby's instigation. Hanna said that Quimby asked him and Barbera "to develop a cartoon" because Hugh Harman and Rudy Ising "were not able, physically, to turn out as many cartoons per year as MGM wanted."[1] It was probably Friz Freleng's departure from the MGM studio in April 1939 that triggered Quimby's interest in finding someone to make more cartoons. Hanna was the obvious candidate. From the time he was directing Captain and the Kids cartoons in 1937 and 1938, his diplomatic skills apparently served him just as well in his dealings with Quimby as they did while he was handing out work to his animators. In contrast to many of his colleagues—Barbera among them—Hanna had no criticism of Quimby: "My feeling with him was that he wanted us to make good cartoons.... We'd give him a paragraph [summarizing an idea for a cartoon], and he'd say fine, go ahead. He never turned down an idea."

Barbera, who was Hanna's almost exact contemporary (he was born in 1911, Hanna in 1910), had become a gag and story-sketch man for Freleng soon after he began working at MGM. Hanna had first known him as an animator, though ("I can remember handing out Katzenjammer animation to Joe"), and he saw in Barbera's draftsmanship a way to plug a gap in his own skills: "I had always been shy that talent that I felt I needed." Both Hanna and Barbera were members of Rudy Ising's unit, and Ising worked with them on the story for *Puss Gets the Boot*, which pitted a large gray cat against a small brown mouse, after they began writing it on May 8, 1939.[2] Ising acknowledged that his role was minor. "Joe did most of the story sketches," he said, and Hanna "most of the direction."[3]

Even before Hanna and Barbera finished their first cartoon together, Quimby decided to put them at the head of their own unit.[4] Ising said that he got "fed up" with Hanna and Barbera "because of the conniving they were doing with Quimby.... I finally said, 'Go ahead and give them their own unit if you want to,' or something like that."[5] MGM announced the unit's creation in the trade press in September 1939.[6] Although Hanna and Barbera took *Puss Gets the Boot* with them to their new unit, it still bore Ising's name as producer when it was released in February 1940; in keeping with MGM's practice at the time, his was the only screen credit for an individual.

Puss resembles Ising's own cartoons in the way the characters look: Bob Allen, who designed Ising's characters, drew a model sheet for the cat and the mouse that is dated August 8, 1939, or about three months after story work began. *Puss Gets the Boot* also mimics Ising's cartoons in its rather labored pace. A subtle difference surfaces, though, when the mouse slugs the cat in the eye. Ising muffled such gags when he used them at all, but Hanna and Barbera show no comparable diffidence—the mouse quite literally does not pull his punch. The cartoon's Ising-like pace does not soften the gag's impact; if anything, it makes the gag more graphic by permitting a clear view of fist hitting cornea.

Quimby thus had good reason to believe Hanna and Barbera could bring to the screen cartoons more aggressively comic than those Ising was willing to make. They started *Swing Social*, their second cartoon together, while they were still in Ising's unit; then, on their own, they made two cartoons, *Gallopin' Gals* and *The Goose Goes South*, that were essentially blackout-gag cartoons like those that Tex Avery had been making at Schlesinger's and that every other studio had been copying. These were cartoons of the kind that Quimby had sought in vain from Rudy Ising; from the start, Hanna and Barbera were giving the boss what he wanted.

It was with their fifth cartoon, *The Midnight Snack*, that Hanna and Barbera returned to the cat and mouse that had starred in *Puss Gets the Boot*. They started writing *Midnight Snack* on April 18, 1940,[7] almost exactly two months after the release of *Puss Gets the Boot*—long enough for favorable exhibitor reaction to get back to the cartoon studio.[8] A black maid in *Puss Gets the Boot* addresses the cat as Jasper, and he kept that name during early work on *Midnight Snack*, but by the time the cartoon was released in July 1941, the cat and mouse had become Tom and Jerry—a familiar coupling of names for cartoon characters since Barbera's former employer Van Beuren had used it for two human characters ten years earlier.

The two new codirectors hewed to the pattern they had established in making *Puss Gets the Boot*. Hanna said: "I would do all the timing on the bar sheets, and [Barbera] would do the sketches. We worked full size, and we didn't do storyboards.... I used to take those character layout sketches and time them, and then we shot them," as "pose reels," that is, each sketch was photographed under the animation camera for however long Hanna prescribed. The resulting reel, in its total effect, gave a rough idea of what the finished film would be like. In addition, Hanna said, he, and not Barbera, "always handed the animation out to the animators."[9]

Hanna thus directed much as Ising did, not by drawing but through the writing and control of the timing. Barbera played a role roughly comparable to Bob Allen's, telling the story not through a storyboard—although Ising's writers turned out lots of sketches, he rarely if ever put up a complete storyboard of the Disney kind—but through character layout drawings that doubled as story sketches. Hanna also inherited the use of pose reels from Ising, who made such reels from Allen's layout drawings. In the eyes of some members of the Hanna and Barbera unit, though, Barbera contributed much more than Hanna did.

Gus Arriola began working for Hanna and Barbera as a gag man around the time they were making *The Midnight Snack*. Not only did Barbera draw the character layouts, but he also came up with "about 75 percent of the gags," Arriola said. "He would inspire the rest of us to come up with material, because he was so fast."[10] Jack Zander, as an animator in the new unit, also noticed that Barbera drew very rapidly. More explicitly than Arriola, Zander described Barbera as the superior codirector: "The pictures were all Joe's, and the only thing that Bill did was write out the sheets. . . . Mostly we directed those pictures ourselves because all you needed were some good layouts, which Joe Barbera would provide. . . . We'd time it the way we felt like it."[11]

Barbera had the legs of his desk extended so he could work standing up, Arriola said, "and I remember seeing long layout sheets hanging over the end of it because he would be laying out the whole background." There were limits even to Barbera's energy, though: after a few more pictures, Harvey Eisenberg began drawing finished layouts, for both characters and backgrounds, from Barbera's rough sketches. From then on, Hanna said, "we both spent most of our time on stories."[12]

It was in the writing of the cartoons that the two directors might have been expected to clash because they came out of such contrasting environments—Hanna from Harman-Ising, Barbera from Van Beuren and Terrytoons—and their taste in animated comedy varied accordingly. Hanna, said Michael Lah (who animated on *Puss Gets the Boot*), "loved cutesie stuff. . . . Joe was the other way, wild as hell."[13] Similarities to Ising's cartoons lingered in the early Tom and Jerry cartoons, especially in their deliberate timing, which was clearly attributable to Hanna. The Ising influence—and behind it the Disney influence—could also be felt in more constructive ways. *The Night Before Christmas*, released in December 1941, hinges on the successful characterization of the two antagonists. That characterization (which arises through Tom's response when Jerry kisses him under the mistletoe) is adequate to the purpose: it makes plausible Tom's change of heart near the end of the cartoon, and Jerry's consequent saving of Tom from getting his paw caught in a mousetrap. Cat and mouse are more like rival siblings than hunter and prey.

A Terrytoons flavor is, however, just as strong in *Officer Pooch*, released in September 1941. In this cartoon without Tom and Jerry, the title character is a canine policeman whose low-slung design and rubbery animation evoke the characters in mid-thirties Terry cartoons. As if it were a Terrytoon, *Officer Pooch* boils with activity, but there's no thought visible behind it; watching such a cartoon is like watching a plant grow in time-lapse photography. The Tom and Jerry cartoons themselves were rooted in a conception they shared with a great many Terrytoons: Barbera wrote many years later about how hackneyed cat-and-mouse conflict was in the eyes of his MGM colleagues at the time he and Hanna started making *Puss Gets the Boot*,[14] but such conflict was, in fact, far more common in the Terry cartoons than in any other studio's.

After *Officer Pooch*, Hanna and Barbera made almost nothing but Tom and Jerry cartoons. Even though Quimby had apparently planned for them, like Harman and Ising, to make cartoons with a variety of characters, the Tom and Jerry series was proving to be too popular—or was judged as potentially too popular in a theatrical environment newly filled with aggressive, energetic characters like Woody Woodpecker—to waste them on anything else.[15] Any reconciliation of Hanna's and Barbera's different styles of cartoon making would have to take place within the confines of that series.

Closing the gap was, in part, simply a matter of picking up the pace. Tom and Jerry themselves, as relatively simple and inherently active characters, all but dictated faster timing. By 1942, in releases like *Dog Trouble*, Hanna's timing was becoming sharper than in the earlier entries; he was starting to break free from the music-based timing that he inherited from Ising. There are in *Dog Trouble* some animated equivalents of turning on a dime (as Tom flees from a bulldog), even though much of the timing is still dull and regular.

Increasingly, though, Hanna and Barbera dealt with their aesthetic incompatibility simply by ignoring it. A cartoon like *Fine Feathered Friend*, released in October 1942, was the result. Scott Bradley's music often sounds like the slightly sentimental score for a Harman or Ising cartoon, a hen looks like a Bob Allen design, and so on, but some of the gags are far more brutal than anything in an Ising cartoon (or, for that matter, in the earlier Hanna and Barbera cartoons). Twice, Jerry almost cuts Tom's head off with hedge clippers. In *Sufferin' Cats*, released in January 1943, there is prolonged business at a chopping block, first with Jerry, who is on the verge of being cut in two, and then with Tom, when a devil urges him to bring his axe down on another cat's skull. (This is one of the rare cartoons in which Tom pursues Jerry as a potential meal.)

The accommodation that Hanna and Barbera reached in cartoons like *Sufferin' Cats* entailed clothing a Terrytoons sensibility in a Harman-Ising shell. The drawing style and the animation—literal at its core, for all that it had speeded up—encouraged accepting the cartoon's world as a sort of reality. Translated into such a visual language, Barbera's broad and careless gags often suggested that the characters were suffering severe and extremely painful injuries.

That was the significance of the clippers and the axe. By 1937, when a memorandum titled "Tips to Remember When Submitting Gags" circulated in the Disney studio, many people in animation had recognized that preserving the body's integrity was critical to the success of animated comedy involving characters like those in the Disney and Harman-Ising cartoons. As the memo said, "When a sharp, pointed weapon is used as a prop, it should never pierce any living character."[16] In the early forties, all the Hollywood cartoon studios were exploiting their characters' resilience (itself the fruit of a decade's experience with stretch and squash) by using those characters in gags more violent than the gags of a few years before. But sharp objects threaten to violate a cartoon character's body in a way that a blunt object does not: resilience is no real protection against a spear or an axe, as it is against a club.

Strictures like those in the Disney memo never had any force at a studio like Terrytoons; any shift toward aesthetic coherence tended to take place not out of conviction but out of a dim awareness that better-received cartoons were doing things differently. Hanna, by giving Barbera's gags respectable dress, alleviated any pressure for change that might have originated in such unfavorable comparisons, so that the Tom and Jerry cartoons of the middle forties actually manifested the Terrytoons sensibility more powerfully than did the contemporaneous Terrytoons themselves.

The MGM studio, as a physical facility, was the class of the industry, next to Disney; for Richard Bickenbach, who had been an animator for Friz Freleng at Schlesinger's, going back to MGM (where he first worked soon after the studio opened) "was like going from the slums to the elite."[17] The MGM directors also had more time to do their work; they made as few as four or five cartoons a year, half as many as the directors at some rival studios. The MGM cartoons were more finished looking than the norm for the period, just as the parent studio's features were, and that superficial gloss further obscured the Tom and Jerry cartoons' base origins.

Having no real center, the Tom and Jerry cartoons changed over time, but they did not evolve in the way that Disney's did. Even Tom's design differed markedly from film to film, as if Harvey Eisenberg never got a firm grip on the character. On into the middle forties, the Hanna and Barbera cartoons swayed back and forth between brutality and sentimentality, sometimes within the same film. The first half of *Baby Puss*, released in October 1943, is almost like an Ising cartoon—full of cute stuff, with no really violent gags. But its tone changes sharply as soon as three other cats appear and begin manhandling Tom. From that point on, even the sound effects contribute to the violence: when Jerry applies a nutcracker to Tom's tail, the resulting crunch is all too realistic.

In *Tee for Two*, released in July 1945, there is in one striking gag the suggestion that even Barbera's brutal comedy could have been reshaped into something more satisfying. Tom, fleeing from hornets, takes refuge in a pond, breathing through a reed—but the hornets pour down through the reed and, by implication, into Tom's mouth. "Then," as Mark Kausler has described it, "after we have waited *just* long enough, *all* the water . . . *flies* up in the air, and there is the most terrifying drawing ([by the animator] Ken Muse) of Tom being stung in his wide open mouth and throat by the angry bees, accompanied by the most anguished scream ever put on film."[18] As dreadful as that scene may sound, the sheer scale of Tom's reaction—so big it's preposterous—cancels out his pain.

By then, though, what had begun in the early Tom and Jerry cartoons as an accidental mating of incompatible elements was hardening into a formula, one in which the intention to inflict pain, and the suffering of pain, were everywhere present. Not only did Tom show no interest in eating Jerry, but the characters' sibling-like rivalry in the early cartoons gave way to an unshaded thirst for damaging each other.

The Tom and Jerry cartoons were by the middle forties starting to pick up Academy Awards almost as regularly as Disney had in the previous decade. Hanna and Barbera's strong position with Quimby, and MGM's strong position in the industry, probably accounted for most of the five Oscars that the Tom and Jerry cartoons won during the forties. (Only one of Avery's MGM cartoons, *Blitz Wolf*, from 1942, was even nominated over that period; a Tom and Jerry cartoon was at least nominated every year from 1943 on [through 1950].) Quimby seems not to have cut as much slack for Avery as he cut for his favored directors. Quimby "had no sense of humor," Avery said. "He was a dog, he was rough."[19] Then again, Avery tested Quimby's patience in a way that Hanna and Barbera never thought of. . . .

What gave Hanna and Barbera such authority in the MGM cartoon studio was not simply success in the theaters and at the Academy Awards, or their being on good terms with Fred Quimby. By the middle forties, the Tom and Jerry cartoons exuded the powerful self-confidence that a successful formula bestows. For one thing, the cartoons *looked* slick. By the time of *Solid Serenade*, released in August 1946, the inconsistencies in Tom's appearance from cartoon to cartoon had been almost entirely smoothed away; he was sleeker, his body not so bulky as before, and his design less cluttered by hair and by superfluities like dots on his muzzle (although those still turned up in some scenes, no doubt thanks to animators who were used to drawing Tom that way). Jerry underwent fewer changes, probably because his design was more economical to begin with; he mainly became cuter.

Dick Bickenbach began drawing layouts for Hanna and Barbera in 1946. Like Harvey Eisenberg before him, Bickenbach redrew Barbera's sketches as character layouts and sometimes, as he explained, added drawings: "Whenever I had a chance, like if somebody turned, I'd throw in about three drawings for a turn." Bickenbach's drawings were polished and very much on model, and such detailed guidance contributed mightily to the cartoons' glossy surface, but his drawings, unlike those of Tex Avery's layout artists in the early forties, did not bend the cartoons in a direction that was recognizably the layout artist's rather than the director's. "It was tied down very tight for poses—what they wanted to see," Bickenbach said. "If [Barbera] wanted a certain look on Tom or Jerry, he would have it down there, and I had to get that in this pose, in the size that they wanted."[20] When Hanna handed out sections of a film to the animators, Ed Barge said, he gave them not just the exposure sheets and Bickenbach's layout drawings, but also Barbera's story sketches.[21] Barbera "really was my boss," Bickenbach said. "He was the one I had to please."

Hanna and Barbera worked together on the stories, seated at desks facing each other, with what sounds like the comfortable familiarity of an old married couple. Bickenbach, who worked in the next room, observed them as they assembled stories: "They talked it over all day long, between the two of them. . . . 'Well, the little guy does this, and he goes here, and he does this'—that's the way their story came out. It wasn't written, to begin with. They had a basic plot, maybe . . . and they'd work at it as they went along."

As in the early days of their collaboration, Barbera probably came up with most of the gags, but during the handouts to the animators, Hanna was clearly in charge. Said Irv Spence: "When I would pick up . . . Bill would have all of the timing on the exposure sheets, for every little thing, every little accent, every little bit of action. . . . Bill acted out *everything*."[22] It was Hanna, Ed Barge said, who "was just a genius at picking out a few frames here and adding a few there to make something stand out a little better" when he reviewed an animator's pencil tests on a Moviola. Hanna and Barbera both looked at pencil animation in the early years, Barge said, but later Hanna alone looked at the pencil tests, while "Joe stuck strictly to boarding," that is, to drawing the sketches that Bickenbach transformed into layouts. It was, however, Barbera to whom the animators went if they wanted to make a significant change in a Bickenbach pose: "Joe was the drawing man."[23]

The sense always in the Tom and Jerrys released in the late forties and early fifties is that directors, animators, and layout artists are pursuing their objective as relentlessly as a cohesive infantry squad. A high level of expertise manifests itself literally down to the frame, as in the razor-sharp timing in *Kitty Foiled*, released in May 1948: at one point, Jerry, disguised preposterously as a tiny, lethargic Indian, turns around very slowly to look back toward Tom, and then breaks into a high-velocity run with Tom right behind him. In contrast to typical practice, Jerry begins running instantly; there's none of what animators call "slowing in," no building up of speed, and the comic contrast between Jerry's very slow walk and very fast run is all the more striking as a result.

By the late forties, too, Scott Bradley's music was very much of a piece with what was happening on the screen. Bradley had been the composer for Harman-Ising in the thirties, and in the early years of the Tom and Jerry series his scores didn't always fit: his score for *The Million Dollar Cat*, released in May 1944, sounds like ordinary dance band music, related only tenuously to the cartoon action. But as Hanna and Barbera perfected their formula, so did Bradley: in *Puttin' on the Dog*, released in October 1944, a cartoon filled with furious activity, his music stokes the feverish atmosphere as much as mirrors it. He was cultivating a musical equivalent for the screen violence, and within a few years he had achieved it. . . .

In their music, as in every other way, the Tom and Jerry cartoons were the fruits of painstaking calculation and highly developed skills. But the cartoons' very polish—because it made so clear that nothing got into them by accident—emphasized the contradictions that had been integral to the Tom and Jerry series from the beginning. Hanna and Barbera never addressed the aesthetic issues that the violence in their cartoons constantly raised; there's no reason to believe that they ever recognized that such issues existed. The collaborative effort that went into making the Tom and Jerry cartoons was so thoroughly harmonious that it foreclosed anyone's raising such fundamental questions.

As if to compensate for their consistently high level of violence, the Tom and Jerry cartoons in the late forties began to offer ever larger helpings of sentimentality. It consumed whole cartoons, like *Heavenly Puss*, released in July 1949. There is remarkably little comedy in that cartoon, which has Tom seeking a seat on the "Heavenly Express," a train headed for Paradise, after he has been crushed by a piano; at one point, some kittens come sloshing up to the reservation desk in a water-logged sack. *Heavenly Puss* confesses its fraudulence when the cartoon's feline equivalent of Saint Peter reveals that Tom's mortal sin is "persecuting an innocent little mouse"—a sin that is convenient rather than credible, since every cat would be guilty of it.

In other cartoons, sentimentality manifested itself in the formulaic adorability of characters like Nibbles, the baby mouse who is the title character in *The Little Orphan*, released in April 1949. Cute kittens that could have come straight from Bob Allen's model sheets for Rudy Ising turned up with increasing frequency in the Tom and Jerry cartoons of the late forties and early fifties. In some cases, such characters *did* come from old model sheets: a model sheet for the goldfish in *Jerry and the Goldfish*, released in March 1951, is exactly the same as the model sheet for Ising's *Little Goldfish* of a dozen years earlier.

As sentimentality grew in importance, those rare moments when the violent gags had any real emotional content—some point other than pain—all but disappeared. In the 1946 cartoon *Solid Serenade*, Jerry hits Tom with a cream pie that has a comically superfluous iron in it. Although Tom's face is flattened momentarily, he looks not injured but disturbed—his song has been interrupted, as if by a heckler, and *that* is what bothers him. Nuances of that kind gave way in the late forties and early fifties to generalized, repetitious facial expressions; Tom and Jerry (and the supporting characters, too) all scowled exactly the same way—brows knitted, lower lip stuck out—and they scowled a large part of the time.

The Tom and Jerry formula, like any successful formula, could not be sustained indefinitely, and cracks were starting to show by the early fifties. A cartoon like *Cat Napping*, released in December 1951, suffers not just from gags that are often unpleasant, but from gags that are just too silly: it defies belief, on the terms already set by the cartoon itself, that Jerry could kick a frog so precisely that it would land in Tom's drinking glass and that Tom would not notice that he was sucking the frog through his straw and into his mouth.

In addition to such failings, the Tom and Jerry cartoons of the early fifties were very noisy. The same loud sound effects—glass breaking, explosions, crashes—turned up, over and over again. That was, however, just what the stories called for. The monotony was built in. It was no wonder that even Hanna and Barbera were finally getting tired of it.

Notes

1. William Hanna, interview with author Michael Barrier, November 2, 1976.

2. A very brief synopsis for *Puss Gets the Boot* (then called "The Mouse and Cat Story"), probably prepared for submission to Quimby early in the writing for the film, shows a start date for story work of May 8, 1939 (a Monday). USC/MGM: MGM Collection, USC Cinema-Television Library, University of Southern California.

3. Rudolf Ising, interview with author, June 2, 1971.

4. Bob Allen and Jim Pabian both spoke of Ising's having turned over the story for *Puss Gets the Boot* to Hanna and Barbera in something close to finished form. "He had just written the first story of Tom and Jerry," Pabian said. "Rudy's story department had written it. To get them out of his hair, Rudy gave them this; it was intact, all it needed was timing, and Bill . . . had already learned how to do that." James Pabian, interview with Milton Gray, April 6, 1977. Allen said, similarly, that "I designed the first model sheet for Rudy's unit and the storyboard and models were handed over to Bill and Joe incomplete—Bill and Joe finished the picture." Allen to author, December 29, 1989. Both men could only have had in mind the transfer of the story to the new Hanna and Barbera unit since there's no question but that Hanna and Barbera did most of the writing while they were still in Ising's unit; they were, in other words, "Rudy's story department," at least as far as *Puss Gets the Boot* was concerned.

5. Rudolf Ising, joint interview with Hugh Harman with author, October 29, 1976.

6. *Motion Picture Herald*, September 23, 1939.

7. That is the date shown for the start of story work on a one-page synopsis like the one for *Puss Gets the Boot*. The synopsis itself is dated October 9, 1940. USC/MGM.

8. According to both Hanna and Barbera, one letter from a major exhibitor was the stimulus for the second cat-and-mouse cartoon. Bill Hanna, *A Cast of Friends* (Dallas: Taylor, 1996), 43; Joe Barbera, *My Life in 'toons* (Atlanta: Turner, 1994), 76.

9. Hanna interview.

10. Gus Arriola, interview with Milton Gray, January 31, 1977.

11. Jack Zander, interview with author, March 24, 1982.

12. Hanna interview.

13. Michael Lah, interview with Milton Gray, January 4, 1977.

14. Barbera, *My Life in 'toons*, 73.

15. Barbera, *My Life in 'toons*, 75. Barbera's book is typical of such Hollywood autobiographies in that it includes anecdotes that are difficult to credit in their literal form—he has Quimby wanting Hanna and Barbera to drop Tom and Jerry entirely, after *Puss Gets the Boot* had been well received in the theaters—but that clearly have some basis in fact. For an MGM director to concentrate so heavily on one series was a sharp break with precedent (the failed Captain and the Kids series apart).

16. "Tips to Remember When Submitting Gags," February 12, 1937. Walt Disney Archives, Burbank, California.

17. Richard Bickenbach, interview with Gray, February 25, 1977.

18. Mark Kausler, "Tom and Jerry," *Film Comment*, January–February 1975, 74–75.

19. Tex Avery, interview with Gray, February 18, 1977.

20. Bickenbach interview.

21. Ed Barge, interview with Gray, November 26, 1976.

22. Irv Spence, interview with Gray, November 29, 1976.

23. Barge interview.

Roundtable Discussion with Mike Lah

DARRELL VAN CITTERS / 1977

Edited from the transcript of an event organized by Darrell Van Citters at the California Institute of the Arts, March 28, 1977. Printed with permission.

Mike Lah: I started at Disney in 1934, and I saw the old *The Tortoise and the Hare* thing going on. I got to the assistant stage at Disney, then went to Harman-Ising for about a year, and to MGM [in 1937]; I was there for fifteen to sixteen years. I helped develop all the Tom and Jerrys and [Barney] Bears and all, and Tex Avery's cartoons. When I left there, I went into the freelance field in 1954 and 1960. . . .

In the meantime, the Hanna-Barbera thing was developing on the outside. George Sidney, [Harry] Cohn, Bill Hanna, and Joe Barbera got together and formed this company. I was supposed to be part of it but never quite came up with . . . [I helped them develop the really limited animation technique, a process which we had actually done prior to the animation stage at MGM.] We got a story, and we'd make a pose reel, and shoot it in pencil test form. We'd look at it and it would be funny as hell. Then we handed out the animation, and it would come back and, because of all our training in animation, making things move slow and anticipate and overlap and come back and all that, then we found out that the pacing was so fast and so funny in pose reel that after it came back from animation, it lost a certain amount of snap and guts in it. We always said for twenty, thirty years, "One of these days we will be making a cartoon just moving the heads and mouths, and just animate it very funny like Charlie Chaplin, and you have a funny picture." So that's what happened after MGM closed up. The guys got together and presented this [process to Screen Gems]. . . .

Nancy Beiman: A question on the set-up at MGM: When you were there, did you alternate between the Hanna/Barbera and Avery units?

Lah: When I first went there [in 1938], I [was] in Rudy Ising's unit. We worked on the Barney Bears and the Silly Symphony–type things that he was doing. Joe [Barbera] came from New York. He was an animator. He was animating for Hugh Harman. He was really a storyman; he loved stories. And Hanna was doing some timing and directing before Rudy came. . . . MGM started with Friz Freleng from Warner Bros., and Bob Allen from Harman-Ising, and Bill Hanna. Those were the directors that they started on cartoons. Actually, that's [when] they started undermining us . . . but most of the guys remained at Harman-Ising, including Rudy and Hugh. And they couldn't get any of us—we were going to stay there until the end and all that stuff. Finally, MGM moved in. They got Rudy, they got Hugh Harman, and Friz left, and everybody else [including Bill Hanna] was relegated back into their positions. They literally picked up the Harman-Ising unit and moved it to MGM.

[Editors' note: To clarify, in August 1937, MGM decided to found an in-house cartoon studio, headed by Fred Quimby, rather than continue to rely on outside contractor Harman-Ising Productions for their animated shorts. MGM poached Freleng from Warner Bros. and many Harman-Ising animators to make their own first series, The Captain and the Kids; however, the cartoons were unpopular. To save his studio, in October 1938, Quimby hired Harman and Ising to each oversee their own separate animation unit at MGM, joining many of their former employees.]

Now, it was me stuck with a lot of New York animators [in Rudy Ising's unit, along with Bill and Joe]. . . . They, Bill and Joe, [started] the story for the first Tom and Jerry. It wasn't Tom and Jerry then. [It was] *Puss Gets the Boot*. And what [Quimby] did, he credited Rudy Ising as the producer. But Bill and Joe actually did it. They directed it; they did the layouts and a few of us animated on it. . . . Rudy took the credit as producer. But the outcome . . . was that [*Puss*] was so successful that when they got the returns out of it, Quimby decided they were going to put names on it, and of course, "Tom and Jerry" came out of it. Everybody was [asked], for fifty dollars, to come up with a name, and Jack Carr came up with the name "Tom and Jerry." . . . [Soon,] there were three units: Hanna and Barbera's unit, Rudy Ising's unit, and Hugh Harman's unit.

Ultimately, Hugh was out of there, Rudy was still there, and I was working between [the units]. I jumped from Rudy's unit to Bill and Joe's unit and back and forth as an animator, as a posing artist. We found that posing was the way to go. That put everything in control of the director—the timing, the animation. They sort of developed that.

Then Tex [Avery] came into the picture and took that third unit, Hugh Harman's old unit. Then they started moving guys around again: who is going to have what and all that. Quimby took me out of Bill and Joe's unit and put me in Tex's unit. I became Tex's man, as far as posing was concerned. We posed our reels with him.

He was a funny guy. [Tex] brought this fast timing [from Warner Bros. to] MGM. It was so fun—his pictures began just overwhelming everybody. And of course we enjoyed being competitive. [The other directors] decided they were going to learn from Tex Avery and speed up their cartoons. So they sped up their cartoons. And Tex would say, "That's pretty damn good. I can go faster." The timing was so fast that you didn't have any time to put in in-betweens. You'd lose the meaning of the poses, you know? When we finished it off and Quimby looked at the thing, he got up and said, "I've got to tell you something. I must be Mr. Average Punk. I don't understand a thing I'm seeing."

And yet, when we [had seen] the pose reel, he laughed. See, that was a signal right there to all of us guys that there's a lot of creativity that came out of an accident. The pose reels—the pose reels were funny. When they came back [from animation], they were mushy. A lot of the stuff that was funny was because of the way it was timed: not just the speed, but comparative timing between pieces of action. We made them with acting and pantomime. Like Charlie Chaplin. That's pantomiming, and that came out of these pose reels. But when the pose reels were animated, the poses needed in-betweens [and] that just wrecked it. It's not to say that it was wrong. It was wrong for that particular gag or that particular action, because there are other actions that need a lot of in-betweens. . . .

[Tex] had a funny sense of humor, just really quick. He was a great innovator—he changed a lot of things. Bill and Joe also got the same criticism from Quimby: "You guys have got to quit making them so fast. You're making them for yourself and the people over here [in the studio]. You're not making them for the public. Nobody can understand what goes on. They miss the gags." And he was right. He was sharp enough to recognize that. You know, you can get involved in what you're doing on the desk there and just listen to the critiques around you, and all of them are in the same boat as you are. You're not out there in the public going to the theater and looking at them and watching them, and seeing a reaction. Some of those things would just go right over people's heads. They wouldn't even get it. We laughed our heads off in the theater at the studio. Those were great developing days. . . .

Bill and Joe did some very, very wonderful things with Tom and Jerry, the kind of things that Tex wouldn't even touch. They had certain things that happened in their pictures that Tex just couldn't feel and wouldn't even attempt to feel. He wasn't a guy who felt that you could get warmth or get teary-eyed in animation. Animation was a cartoon and it had to be slapstick and funny. That was it. On the other hand, some of that wiped off in the Tom and Jerrys by Bill and Joe, but they also had a little bit of the other thing in their pictures that Tex never had in his. Not that I think it's good or bad, it's just that they're different personalities. And each has his own way.

Interview with Ray Patterson

MICHAEL MALLORY / 1998

Edited from the transcript of an unpublished interview. Conducted at the Smoke House restaurant, Burbank, CA, January 20, 1998. Printed with permission.

Michael Mallory: When did you start at MGM?

Ray Patterson: I started in '41. I was there and then spent a year in England and came back, and I was [at MGM] until '53, I think. . . .

Mallory: You went straight to the TV studio.

Patterson: We had our own studio, Grantray-Lawrence, for fourteen years [1954–68]. We did a lot of commercials and won a lot of awards. We did the first fifteen half-hour *Spider-Man* [episodes] for ABC [in 1967]. Ever see it?

Mallory: The recent ones?

Patterson: These were from 1967, '68. [But] I closed the studio [around that time] and went with Bill and Joe . . . animating. I animated a lot on the features they did. *Charlotte's Web*: I did most of the rat on it, working at home.

Mallory: They seem to use a lot of people at home.

Patterson: [At Grantray-Lawrence, we also] did an awful lot of subcontracting. As a matter of fact, we did one of the first *Jetsons* for [Hanna]—the whole picture. . . .

Mallory: You and Irv Spence are sometimes referred to as the artists who really crafted Tom and Jerry's personalities.

Patterson: Bill [Hanna]'s always said that, yeah, kind of brought their personality into it. I used to animate a lot of the bulldog, I loved to animate him, because he was . . . the dialogue, I just loved to get him. The voices are so important to animation. . . .

Mallory: Did Irv specialize on Jerry?

Patterson: Tom or Jerry. He could jump back and forth. I used to animate on Jerry and Tom, and the bulldog. So did Irv.

Mallory: Would you analyze characters or just draw?

Patterson: Just went and drew. The thing was, Joe was the artist on the thing and his little sketches had the moods, exactly what expression Jerry should have or Tom should have—mad or happy or whatever—and then Bick Bickenbach [was] the guy who'd draw those up for layouts for us. . . . And then Bill's timing . . . They were a team that worked like this.

Mallory: Bill's timing is pretty incredible.

Patterson: I know, that's where I learned it. . . .

Mallory: Tom and Jerry are among the fastest cartoons around. That seems to be an MGM trait.

Patterson: With Bill and Joe, they had a little story running through, and they never lost that. That was always through the whole thing. Some of these others, they'd time it fast and you'd hardly know what's going on. . . .

Animation isn't really how good you can draw. It's being able to visualize and put down on paper what you visualized. I'd get that model sheet for Tom and Jerry, or the elephant in *Dumbo* [while at Disney], . . . but if you asked me to sit down and draw you an elephant, I couldn't do [it]. Now, Irv could sit down and draw you a cartoon elephant. I couldn't do it. I guess I was able to visualize a feeling: if Tom is really mad, he's mad. I could get that on the paper. . . .

Mallory: How long would it take to do a classic Tom and Jerry?

Patterson: About nine weeks.

Mallory: That was the animation?

Patterson: That was the whole thing: about nine weeks, ten weeks. [Editors' note: Surely, it look longer.] I'm trying to think how many . . . I think we did nine a year. . . .

Mallory: Were you involved in the MGM commercials?

Patterson: I know I animated on the opening [credits for *I Love Lucy*]—the little stick figures.

Mallory: You did that one?

Patterson: Yeah, we had to hide it when Quimby came by, because they didn't want him to know [*laughs*]. They were doing it on the QT. . . .

Mallory: Did he come by very often?

Patterson: He didn't know what was going on. He'd come down the hall, you'd hear his [heavy] footsteps, and "Here comes Fred!" . . . He was a hard-headed businessman, but he stayed out of Bill and Joe's hair. . . . He was smart enough to let the guys alone. . . .

Mallory: Did you have contact with Scott Bradley?

Patterson: He worked down the hall from me. He was very gifted, he could get the pencil test and run down and [write] everything right to the pencil test. What Bill and Joe did, they'd shoot layout drawings—before we even got a picture. They'd run it for us, and we could get kind of an overview feeling of where the whole thing was going, before we'd even start to animate. Which is very good for practical purposes, and that would help Bill with his timing and everything. Then Scott would take the pencil test and write music to it. . . .

Mallory: So there would be three stages: a pose reel, a pencil test, and a final?
Patterson: Yeah.
Mallory: I heard somewhere that the pose reels were where Joe got the idea for limited animation for TV. Do you know anything about that?
Patterson: [No.] When we started, everything used to go on ones, no matter what. . . . *Dumbo* was the first picture where they did everything on twos, except where you have to have fast action. [Disney] saved all that money in in-betweening—a guy sitting there making his other drawings—it saved an awful lot of money. With Bill and Joe, it was the same thing at Hanna-Barbera. [But] in Tom and Jerry in the old days, most of the stuff was on ones.
Mallory: But the audience probably doesn't know.
Patterson: You can't tell the difference. . . .
Mallory: Tom and Jerry is a lead-in to the later TV work, since both rely so much on pose and attitude.
Patterson: Yeah, attitude and poses meant so much. You've got to have the right poses. . . .
Mallory: You said that you left MGM in 1953. . . . Were you ever at [Hanna-Barbera's original location], the Chaplin Studios?
Patterson: My studio [Grantray-Lawrence] was down at 716 La Brea, below Chaplin Studios.
Mallory: What was the size of the staff when they first went into TV?
Patterson: Up there in the Charlie Chaplin Studios, there wasn't too many. . . .
Mallory: People said [that] when MGM closed down and TV was starting, there was a lot of unemployment.
Patterson: That's right. There were periods in there where they'd have lay-offs all over the place. It wasn't steady work like on Tom and Jerry, where you'd have a year's work and two weeks vacation. . . .
Mallory: How did the Tom and Jerry animators feel about limited animation?
Patterson: It was a completely different medium. But working with Bill and Joe, we were all friends—we kidded around and played jokes on each other. I was animating on a feature, [the] "Dance of the Hours" [sequence] in *Fantasia*, and we did three feet a week. With [the] Tom and Jerrys, it was eighteen feet a week when I started, and it went up to twenty-five feet a week. [Interviewer's note: Per Bill, a foot in full animation can sometimes contain sixty drawings.] Ken Muse was really a footage man. He'd turn in forty feet, then turn in his twenty-five feet a week and bank it.

When I went to England [to work for David Hand at Gaumont Animation] we were doing eighteen feet and when I came back, they were doing twenty-five feet a week. I had a letter from Quimby. I had my job back, and I said, "How 'bout a raise? The other guys are getting it." He was a tough old businessman. Finally, I got it. He had us all in the office one day, the four of us sitting there, and he said, "I need more footage, fellas." We said, "No, it will hurt the quality, Mr. Quimby." Finally, he said, "Can't you fellas get me one more frame?"

But going to [limited] animation wasn't too hard, because they just kind of count the drawings: We're going to have so many drawings in this. And it got so where you would animate something fully every drawing [Editors' note: We think he means an action], and you'd hold it, and animate an arm or a mouth. A good animator could make it almost look like full animation, but it wasn't. The price was way under what they'd been getting [at MGM].

Mallory: Would arms be done on a separate cel?

Patterson: Separate cel. And like, mouths would turn here [gestures], and sometimes you'd have the head go up and down and the body held. . . . I guess Bill's the one that really started that whole thing because you had to have a system like that. It had to be done fast. . . .

Mallory: Did you have contact with the story guys, like Mike Maltese or Warren Foster?

Patterson: They were real talented, and they were a real big help to Bill and Joe when they started. That was before I started, while I still had my studio. . . . You're only as good as your story. If you don't have a story, great animation is not going to go. If you have a good story and bad animation, the story's [still] there. It'll work. Of course, if you have both, it works out better. . . .

Mallory: Bill and Joe were always credited as producers and directors [on H-B's television cartoons]. But you always see Nick Nichols credited as animation director. What would [Bill] do as opposed to what Nick did?

Patterson: Nick Nichols—I finally took over and did the same thing—we'd take the storyboards and time them for the animators. . . . [Nick would] get the board all finished, but then you have to bring in certain footage. One year Bill said that we were losing about $250,000, $300,000 by overanimating—you had to throw it away. It had to come down right to the exact frame. So we used to try and get it down to maybe ten or fifteen feet over footage—otherwise you're throwing money away. That's what Nick did.

Mallory: He controlled the footage?

Patterson: And handed it out to the animators.

Mallory: Would Bill set the timing and do exposure sheets?

Patterson: No, that was up to Nick. . . . Bill used to do all [the timing] himself, but then Nick came in. But Bill [still did] some of it . . . [H]e had a boat, the *Gallatea*, and Bill would sit there with Carl Urbano and myself. We'd time shows, and then we'd fish, and then we'd have cocktail parties with other boats around there at five o'clock. But we'd turn out 2,000 to 3,000 feet a week on the boat. One year, we had so many . . . I had about seven guys that I'd hand out the boards to, [to] time on the boards. Like I said, we'd do [the timing] all on board. George Gordon was one, Rudy Zamora, Don Lusk . . . I still see Don Lusk. He animated on *Snow White* but he didn't get any credit because they didn't [put] it in the picture. . . .

All I can think of is how nice it was to work with the guys. We'd just have more fun—the gags and stuff. It wasn't like working for a boss. I worked mostly with Bill. But Joe, we used to have a lot of fun and martinis together. . . .

Mallory: What era was that?

Patterson: Oh 1989, or '90, in there. [Editors' note: We think he means 1979 or 1980.] There were so many shows going. We produced an average of 7,000–8,000 feet a week. One year Bill said, "Good God—do you know we did 10,000 feet last week?" That is over feature picture-length. We couldn't believe it.

Mallory: Has that been duplicated since?

Patterson: I doubt it. I don't think anybody turned out the amount of work that Bill and Joe did.

Oscar Goes to Author of Cartoon

FRED QUIMBY / 1944

From *Big Spring* [Texas] *Daily Herald*, June 2, 1944, 3. Syndicated by the Associated Press.

Like Jennifer Jones and Paul Lukas, there were two other Hollywood stars who won an Academy Award this year. But little was said about them. Withal, each mail brings requests for their photos. They're known from Teheran to Terre Haute—from Paraguay to Podunk.

Success is theirs yet these stars work for nothing. They are never given a vacation—they never complain. Actually, they don't even know the meaning of the word "temperament." Neither are they ever bedecked in sable or ermine, nor do they attend the swank night clubs, albeit they were born in a bottle!

Yes, they emerged from an ink bottle, February 10, 1940. Though christened "Tom Cat" and "Jerry Mouse," they are more familiarly known to millions of fans as just "Tom and Jerry." Their introduction to the world was in the cartoon *Puss Gets the Boot*. Men, women, and children laughed as the brash, bullying Tom tortured the meek mite, Jerry, through the early stages of the film, but the rascally rodent managed to master the situation before the end.

Were they gifted with vision, Tom and Jerry would see their prototypes in the men who direct them—Bill Hanna and Joe Barbera. As is customary in cartoon production, humans first enact the roles of their pen-and-ink creations, thus aiding the animators who draw the animal characters. Hanna is the smirky, blustering Tom Cat. He stands before a mirror and mugs to his heart's content. Barbera is the Jerry Mouse. With exaggerated facial contortions, he is submissive to Tom's harangues—while the story is in preparation.

In reality, neither Hanna nor Barbera is an exhibitionist. Rather would you regard them as the type to inherit the earth, were you to meet them socially. The boys joined my cartoon staff in 1937 as story and layout men. Their ability was soon discernible and promotion to the directorial ranks followed.

We were all very proud of Tom and Jerry for the award—the first ever won in Academy competition with Walt Disney. Could they have made an acceptance speech, I'm sure they would have said, with typical Hanna-Barbera modesty, "Thanks, folks. It's a great honor. I guess we were just lucky."

They Paint a Million Cats

BARRETT KIESLING / 1956

From *Films and Filming*, November 1956, 10–11.

It takes eighteen months to make a seven-minute animation cartoon. This is 50 percent longer than the time required to prepare, photograph, and complete an average ninety-minute "live action" film. Photography, alone, of a live action feature, averaging eight weeks, takes only one-tenth of the time required to bring forth a cartoon.

These comparisons were developed during a discussion with William Hanna and Joseph Barbera, producers of MGM cartoons. Winning eight Academy Oscars since 1940 gives the MGM studios a valid claim to the title of being the industry's most consistent source of successful animated cartoons. Seven of the MGM Oscars have gone to Tom and Jerry cartoons. No other cartoon character, or pair of characters, has won more than a single statuette.

"At our peak production of twenty cartoons annually," says William Hanna, "we will produce more than 1,500,000 separate drawings in twelve months."

The frequently quoted figure that it takes 25,000 drawings to make one film cartoon, say Hanna and Barbera, is misleading and inaccurate. Actually 58,835 drawings of many types are made to create a single seven-minute Tom and Jerry. This is 5,000 more than the average for other cartoon producers.

"The extra 5,000," says Barbera, who moved to film cartoons from drawing cartoons for *Collier's* magazine, "comes because we are the only producers to make every cartoon *twice*."

In working out a new cartoon story, the partners (together for eighteen years) pass across twin desks about 1,000 rough sketches. These are made rapidly on small three-inch or four-inch note pads, identical with the type found on executive desks in any business.

A character layout man then expands this picture story to 4,000 pencilled sketches on eight-inch by ten-inch paper. While details are missing, every major sequence is roughly worked out. These 4,000 pencil sketches are then photographed. The "pencil reel," as Hanna and Barbera call it, is a simple way to detect action flaws before actual animation starts.

The pencil reel approved, the story is handed to a team of twelve men: four animators, four assistant animators, four "inbetweeners."

FINDING RECRUITS

These men are all fine artists. Every cartoon producer recruits new talent for cartoon production from leading art schools. Cartoon artists are encouraged to paint and draw outside, and their work regularly appears in leading art exhibits.

The most experienced artists are called animators. They set the keynote for the action and facial expressions of a cartoon by doing every fourth sketch, numbers 1, 5, 9, and so on. The assistant animators "follow the leader" with sketches 3, 7, 11, 12 and so on. The "in-betweeners," clever young artists just beginning in the business, do one-half of the total sketches, numbers 2, 4, 6, 8, 10, and so on.

Completing its 25,000 sketches, the animating team hands them to the "inkers" and "painters." Inkers trace the sketches on 25,000 pieces of transparent celluloid. Before the painters take over to color the cells, 1,160 color samples have been made, using most of the 400 tints and hues in the cartoon paint stock to insure that each action sequence has the proper colors to accentuate character, build a mood, create a laugh.

When the cels are painted, and before the cartoon has been photographed, thirty to forty backgrounds have been prepared. These paintings, 8 by 12 inches for normal size cartoons, 6½ by 15 inches for Cinemascope, correspond to the timber and plaster sets of "live" films.

The mountain of 58,835 sketches required before a cartoon can be photographed is now complete.

To guarantee authenticity, research is just as thorough as for a feature picture. Over a hundred hours of study into the period when Johann Strauss wrote his great waltzes in gay Vienna preceded the making of Academy Oscar winner *Johann Mouse.*

While the animators made their thousands of sketches, William Hanna prepared a "detail sheet." It's a sixty-page book of rules. In it each of the 25,000 drawings has a space as each drawing is one frame of the finished picture. Words spoken by the voices of the cartoon characters are written in, frame by frame. (The "voices" are those of radio, television, and film personalities.)

Music also goes on the detail sheet, note by note, frame by frame. This insures that cartoon dancers, for example, are always "on the beat." Dancing has been well done in *Down Beat Bear* and *Muscle Beach Tom,* to name only a few.

The MGM cartoon studio has also worked closely with MGM feature picture producers in inserting into features novelty sequences where human actors dance with cartoon characters. *Anchors Aweigh* pioneered this field. In it Tom and Jerry danced with Gene Kelly. More recently, the "Sinbad the Sailor" sequence of the studio's all-dancing *Invitation to the Dance* presents Kelly dancing with the amorous Dragon and other specially created cartoon characters. Eighteen months of laborious detail is over.

Cartoon and feature film photography are very different. Instead of straight ahead, the cartoon camera shoots downward to a camera table. On this the cinematographer places the painted background for the sequence. Over the background he puts the transparent "cel" with the action of the first frame of that sequence.

CAMERA WORK

He presses a pedal to photograph each frame. The camera mechanism then moves the unexposed film ahead another frame, and a second shot is made. When the cinematographer has pressed the pedal approximately 25,000 times, the picture in its entirety is on color film. It then goes to the Technicolor laboratories for processing.

Unlike feature production, where in some cases only one or two things can be done at a time (sound recording and photography can be done on one stage for only one feature picture at a time), cartoon production can be carried on for as many as twenty pictures simultaneously.

Earlier this year, as a new Tom and Jerry was being planned, the cartoon cinematographer was photographing *The Flying Sorceress*, *Busy Buddies*, and *Muscle Beach Tom*.

Across their twin desks, Hanna and Barbera were tossing the first rough 3-inch-by-4-inch sketches of three cartoons, which will not be ready until mid-1957. Their tentative titles are *What Is a Pup?*, *Grandpa Tom*, *Pets in the Park*.

"Turning out a million and a half drawings a year," say the partners, "we are not surprised it takes a year and a half to do one cartoon. We are amazed that we can do it in that short a time."

The Influence of *Crusader Rabbit* on *Ruff and Reddy*

KARL COHEN / 1989

Edited from *Animatrix* 5, 1989, 39–42. Copyright © UCLA Animation Workshop. Printed with permission of the author and Chuck Sheetz.

New material has been discovered that suggests Bill Hanna had more than a passing interest in *Crusader Rabbit*, and that several members of Hanna-Barbera's first production staff had worked briefly on a version of *Crusader Rabbit* that never aired. In a conversation about the demise of the Ward-Anderson production of *Crusader*, Lucille Bliss mentioned that in 1957, Bill Hanna hired her and Daws Butler to do the soundtracks for eleven color *Crusader Rabbit* shows. She recalled that Hanna had formed a partnership with several people that did not include Joe Barbera, and that they were in production on their *Crusader* show before Hanna and Barbera started to develop *Ruff and Reddy*.

Bill Hanna has a different version of the events. He recalls that he was interested in obtaining the rights to *Crusader* and flew to New York to meet with Jay Ward about obtaining the property. He also met Alex Anderson in San Francisco. . . . Hanna said that after the meetings took place, he and Joe Barbera decided to set up production on their own. He went right into the development of *Ruff and Reddy*. He did not recall doing any soundtracks with Bliss and Butler.

Hanna didn't feel *Crusader* influenced him in script design or animation techniques. He said his knowledge of limited animation came from pose reels used in checking animation at MGM. They were used to check timing before final animation was done. His first use of "limited animation" came in 1938, when he and Joe Barbera made a reel to show Fred Quimby what a Tom and Jerry cartoon would look like. [Editors' note: We believe this was in 1939.] None of the pose reels were shown to the public.

Alex Anderson remembers being excited about meeting Hanna, a celebrated animation director. He says that they would not have talked about the business end of the company because that was Jay Ward's responsibility. He assumes they talked about his ideas, about what works well in limited animation, and about production techniques, including the importance of building a library of stock reaction shots, walk cycles, and other standard images. He was unaware of what happened to Hanna's project after their meeting and was surprised to hear [Hanna] had recorded tracks with [Bliss and] Daws Butler.

Jay Ward confirmed having discussions with Hanna about the sale of *Crusader*. He writes that Hanna never owned the rights to the show but they "did work on some ideas. Very preliminary work." He doubts that the sound recording session Bliss remembers could have been for anyone else. Ward suggested contacting Mike Lah.

Mike Lah is head of Quartet Films, Inc. in Studio City, California, and is a former MGM animation director. He recalls that after MGM terminated their animation department (spring 1957), Shield Productions, Inc. was formed to produce *Crusader Rabbit* cartoons in color. The four partners in Shield were Bill Hanna, Mike Lah, Don Driscoll, and Don McNamara. Most of the staff members were former MGM employees.

The company was in production for about three months when they heard [that] the rights to *Crusader Rabbit* were being litigated. They found out that Shull Bonsall of TV Spots had obtained the rights to the property. Jay Ward assured the Shield people that he owned the rights to the show, and that they could continue working on the project. They did not have any written contract with Ward protecting them from Bonsall's claim, so after consulting with their attorney, they decided to end production.

Bonsall's claim was based on distribution rights Fairbanks Productions sold in a package deal when they ended syndication operations in 1951.[1] Ward and Anderson's company owned the copyright,[2] but Bonsall had Fairbanks's rights and was making it impossible for Ward and Shield to continue. Anderson says they couldn't afford the legal battle necessary to defend their rights, so they settled by selling them to Bonsall.

Lah says that at the time work stopped about six shows were in production. They offered to sell Bonsall their work, but he refused their price and didn't counter with another.

Lah said that their limited animation style was based on the pose reels done at MGM to check timing, proper attitudes, and acting. He described them as pantomime poses, in pencil, without animation. Tex Avery and other directors also made them from time to time at MGM. "In taking on *Crusader Rabbit*, a better product was inevitable by applying our experiences with these pose reels."

During this period of demise, Bill Hanna and Joe Barbera joined forces with George Sidney of Columbia's Screen Gems to form a separate company. The new company became Hanna-Barbera and several staff members from Shield Productions, Inc. joined the new firm (but not Lah, Driscoll, or McNamara).

The new company, located on La Brea in Chaplin's old studio, made two half-hour shows on speculation, and presented them to the Leo Burnett Company, Kellogg's ad agency. The rest is history.

When *Ruff and Reddy* went into production there was a growing trend to produce half-hour shows named after animated characters.³ These shows kept costs down by either including theatrical cartoons or a great deal of live material. *Ruff and Reddy* consisted of new animation made for the show, a live emcee, and classic Columbia cartoons. . . . *Ruff and Reddy* premiered on TV December 14, 1957. . . .

When Hanna and Barbera opened their now-famous studio, Hanna told Lucille Bliss he would like to use her as the voice of Ruff the cat. Bliss says Hanna discussed giving her a four- or five-year exclusive contract.

At the time Hanna was considering Bliss for the voice of Ruff, Bonsall was getting ready to go into production on his new *Crusader Rabbit* shows.⁴ Bonsall wanted Bliss to do the voice of Crusader for considerably less than union scale. She refused. He eventually cut a new soundtrack using GeGe Pearson, a regular on the Red Skelton radio show, who tried to copy Bliss's style. To save money he also used bits and pieces of old soundtracks, according to Bliss.

Although Bliss never worked for him, Bonsall made it known in the animation world that he had the rights to *Crusader* and that Bliss went along with the show. No such contract ever existed, but the rumor was so effective that for a three-month period it was impossible for Bliss to find voice-over work in Los Angeles' animation industry. During this period, Hanna-Barbera chose someone else to do the voice of Ruff.⁵ [Editors' note: This person was Don Messick.]

The characters of Ruff and Reddy have a lot more in common with Rags and Crusader than they do with Hanna and Barbera's Tom and Jerry. Unlike Tom and Jerry and other cartoon stars of the 1950s, they were not adversaries, but were an unlikely pair of friends. Ruff is a cute cat and Reddy a large dog. Crusader is a lovable rabbit and Rags a tiger. All walked upright and talked. The new team battled evil just as Ward and Anderson's stars crusaded against the unjust. Both Ruff and Crusader are strong, aggressive personalities in shy, diminutive bodies, while Rags and Reddy are not too smart and play the part of the "patsy," with large, strong bodies. *Ruff and Reddy* had the three elements Alex Anderson thought were essential to make *Crusader* successful: cute things for kids under the age of ten, adventure for the older kids, and adult humor. Both shows were serialized adventures to unusual places. Finally, if Bliss was being considered for Ruff, it suggests there might be similarities in the characters of Ruff and Crusader. Daws Butler did the voices of both Shield's Rags and [Hanna-Barbera's] Reddy.

Considering the facts, it appears *Ruff and Reddy* evolved out of *Crusader Rabbit* and that the similarities are not totally coincidental. Hanna and Lah say [the original] *Crusader* was the successful show that proved TV animation was possible. They both studied it enough to know how they wanted to improve upon Anderson's approach to limited animation by adding ideas gleaned from doing pose reels at MGM. Also, Hanna had met Anderson and had probably discussed production concepts with him in San Francisco. *Ruff and Reddy* is by no means a copy of the earlier show, but a descendant of it. The importance then of *Crusader* was its success. It proved animation could be done for TV within the budget limitations of the medium if it was well written.[6]

Alex Anderson looks back on his pioneering work and wishes they had better budgets to work with. He writes, "The thing that always bothered me about limited animation was not so much the limitations on story action, but rather the restrictions on character reaction. 'Stunned' reactions to off-stage crashes were all very well, but, oh, how I longed for a full-blown Tex Avery–type response to many a situation."

When it was mentioned that other shows were descendants of *Crusader*, and that he should be recognized as the "father" of limited animation on TV, Anderson replied, "Me?? The father of limited animation?? What about Sir Leslie Lovelock, the inventor of the chastity belt? If this is a paternity suit, I demand a blood test!"

Notes

1. It appears that Fairbanks sold the package of TV shows to someone else, and that Bonsall obtained the rights to *Crusader* at a later date. . . .

2. On April 20, 1949, "The Comic Strips of Television" (*Crusader Rabbit*, "Hamhock Jones," and "Dudley Do-Right of the Mounties") was registered for copyright as an unpublished work. It was intended as a daily feature for TV. . . .

3. Shorter programs were available including the original five-minute *Crusader Rabbit* and the fifteen-minute *NBC Comics*, retitled as *Tele-Comics*.

4. Bonsall's production may have the dubious distinction of being the first children's TV show to be animated abroad. Bliss says it was animated in Mexico.

5. Bliss finally received a call from Bonsall telling her he had hired GeGe Pearson to "understudy" her voice, and that she was now free to "do as you damn well please." When she complained he had injured her career, he said, "You only have a phone call to prove it," and hung up. This episode resulted in her organizing a Screen Actors Guild chapter in San Francisco so that other actors who were young and vulnerable wouldn't be exploited. She was the chapter's first vice-president, and later served three terms as president. She was also San Francisco's representative to SAG's national board. . . .

6. George W. Woolery, *Children's Television: The First Thirty-Five Years, 1946–1981—Part 1: Animated Cartoon Series*, Metuchen, NJ: Scarecrow Press, 1983, 244–45, also notes similarities between the two shows. Fred Patten, "2½ Carrots Tall, TV's First Animated Cartoon Star," *Comics Scene* 6, November 1982, 54, has a brief mention of Shield working on *Crusader*.

Ed Benedict

AMID AMIDI / 2002

Edited from *Animation Blast* 8, 2002, 33–37. Reprinted with permission. Amid Amidi is the author of numerous books about animation, and the publisher and editor-in-chief of *Cartoon Brew*.

Amid Amidi: You were talking earlier about a meeting that took place at MGM? [Benedict had been working as a layout artist and character designer for Tex Avery at MGM since 1950.]

Ed Benedict: There was a notice put downstairs on the bulletin board at MGM about a meeting for every employee of Metro-Goldwyn-Mayer. Everybody—that's from the top executive to the maintenance guy—stars, everybody. We were to meet at this open place on the main lot at a certain time. They had a big platform built and the big wheels were all up there. Nicholas Schenck came from New York and Dore Schary was there.

And what this meeting amounted to was to ease our pain, and let us know that there was nothing to worry about with the growth of television. I remember them saying, "We've got our ears to the ground."

Amidi: The executives were probably more afraid of TV than the average employee?

Benedict: Oh, sure. They were upfront by presuming that there were a lot of people afraid for their jobs. These guys were looking ahead as best as they could, to protect themselves and prevent employees from leaving and going into another business. They did the right thing and they did it in a profound way.

Amidi: Around this time, you were already designing TV commercials for Bill and Joe's unit at MGM . . .

Benedict: Well, I'm still working in my room where I had been with Tex [Avery]. Before Bill and Joe cleared out of MGM [in mid-1957], Bill came to my room and he told me to do a model of a dog and cat. I don't remember whether he said it was for television, or whether he said to do it in a TV style—or something.

I did a couple of things that weren't quite in the area of style that he was thinking of. I finally did a dog and a cat in a frozen state. I had no idea what it was for and I didn't give a damn. All I know is I'm being paid. Not for the models, but I'm being paid weekly for sitting there. Anyway, this turned out to become *The Ruff and Reddy Show*.

Amidi: What happened after MGM closed down?

Benedict: After it completely closed down, I'm busy working from home on story sketches, layouts, and models for H-B and Tex Avery commercials. And let's keep it that way because now I was working half the time and making twice the money.

Amidi: So you continued working for Tex, too?

Benedict: Oh gosh, yeah. I did a hell of a lot of commercials for him at Cascade [Studios]. A few of the early "Raids" [ads]. I was busy as hell with Tex. I would take my work to him at his office on Santa Monica Blvd in West LA. . . .

Amidi: Now, in your work at Hanna-Barbera, you ended up designing many of their most famous characters.

Benedict: That's what happened.

Amidi: You never realized that you were creating these iconic figures of pop culture?

Benedict: Of course not, no.

Amidi: For example, let's take Yogi Bear. When you were asked to design Yogi, would the assignment have been to just design a bear, or with a character description? Like, it's a smart bear who likes to steal pies. . . .

Benedict: Joe [Barbera] would just tell me what he wanted. He'd make the voices, you know. He'd thought the thing up first and then he'd call me and tell me about it. I guess he described what the bear would be doing, what his character was. Very brief. But he wouldn't tell me the look, like whether it should be tall or squatty.

So, I'd just do bears until I got a few of them that I thought might fill the bill for the guy, and I'd take them up to him. Joe rarely made alterations, he usually picked them as they were.

Amidi: Did you like the finished H-B cartoons?

Benedict: No, no, no. I think the way the guys drew them stunk. I don't think they had any respect or regard, or gave a damn, what their things looked like. They paid little attention to the models, and in most cases the layouts I did of the characters.

Amidi: Did you enjoy the creative challenges of designing these characters?

Benedict: No, not particularly.

Amidi: But when your character showed up on the screen . . .

Benedict: When I saw them on the screen, it made me want to throw up.

Amidi: Every one of them?

Benedict: Most of them. The drawings were so god damn stinking and poorly drawn that it embarrassed me.

Amidi: Well, they had small budgets, too.

Benedict: I don't care about the budget. I don't care if they didn't have ten cents to make ten feet of film. The drawings were lousy. They didn't follow the goddamn model. They were too damn lazy or incompetent, or whatever it was—I don't know. There was no quality control at all.

I realize this stuff didn't have the luxury of time that the MGM pictures had. It's obvious in the "hold the body, just move the arms" animation style. But it shouldn't influence the drawing.

Amidi: Did the animators at MGM follow your models more closely?

Benedict: The models at MGM were followed much better than the ones for H-B. The ones for the TV cartoons were just awful.

Amidi: But still Yogi Bear looks like you designed him.

Benedict: So does Huckleberry Hound. It looks like my model—but it isn't. You must learn to look closer. They're horrible. Ugly and horrid. Like, on Huckleberry's nose. I had it rounded, but they put a sharp point on the end. You could stab yourself with the point on the end of his nose. I also had Huckleberry Hound with the hat a little above his head. On Yogi Bear, I've got one eye that goes over the lid of the cap, but they put it underneath the brim.

Amidi: But that would have been difficult to keep consistent in animation.

Benedict: No, it wouldn't. Not if you were earning your money.

Amidi: All those bowties and neck pieces that the characters wear, was that done purely to separate levels, or were there aesthetic considerations behind that?

Benedict: That was all mine. I just got into that and it seemed to work. I wanted to dress the characters up a bit and decorate them. They created color accents that would attract the eye beyond the bareness of the character's bodies. Take a nude dame standing up. She looks pretty blank, but if you put a thin black stripe around her neck, or some black gloves and a black stocking, it's a little bit of designing, a little black and white.

Amidi: Did you ever have ideas better than Joe's for a cartoon?

Benedict: No. I never thought of H-B stuff story-wise. I wasn't in the mindset. I never had any feeling about wanting to do it. . . .

Amidi: Your most famous works are the distinctive designs you created for the early H-B cartoons. How do you feel about your legacy being so closely associated with those cartoons?

Benedict: I don't think a thing about it. I'm conscious of it, and I'm aware of it. I can understand when people talk about the entertaining value of the things that I created. But, did I create them, or did I just design them? Or, did Joe create them, and I drew them? I drew his creations. What happened? I don't know.

There's a lot of people who create a lot of things that are great, but they're in a folder or drawer somewhere. And in this case, these may have gone into a file, too. The only thing is that Hanna-Barbera took and sold the thing. It's because of them that it is well known. And to some extent, in an extremely minute, microscopic way, my name might be known. But mostly to those in the business. And I think nothing of it, sincerely and truthfully. . . .

Daws Butler: The Master's Voice

BRIAN LOWRY / 1987

Edited from *Starlog*, March 1987, 58–60. Reprinted with permission of Kerry O'Quinn.

Unlike most actors, Daws Butler never yearned for the bright lights and the applause, the recognition that goes with having your name (and face) in lights.

Even if he had, it would have been difficult at best. A pleasant, likable man, Butler is all of 5' 2" and would have needed the old stand-on-a-box Alan Ladd trick to look down on a leading lady.

Nevertheless, Daws Butler *is* an actor, and one who takes great pride in his craft. It's a neglected art, he says. And who's to doubt him, for within this man lives Yogi Bear, Snagglepuss, Quick Draw McGraw, Baba Louie, Wally Gator, Augie Doggie, Dixie, and nine-year-old Elroy Jetson.

But that's only his Hanna-Barbera repertoire. Throw in Smedley the dog, Cap'n Crunch, and a horde of characters from *Fractured Fairy Tales*, countless commercials and incidental voices, and Butler becomes a one-man population explosion.

This smallish man . . . has a big mouth; however, to hear Butler tell it, it's equally important to have a big heart.

His vocal talent, he suggests, "is like a computer: you have your hardware and your software. You have the machine to do it and then you need the stuff inside to put into it.

"The hardware is your lips, your tongue, your chest—all the ways you get the voice projected. The software is in your head, and that's where your material comes from. That's what makes it work."

Work is something Butler does little of, these days. "I'm not concerned with other work," he admits. "I do the things I'm committed to, like *Yogi's Treasure Hunt* and Cap'n Crunch.

"It took many years to get to the point where I didn't have to worry about making a living and had a chance to pull back and relax. I don't need to work, financially, and my ego doesn't demand it."

He spends much of his spare time teaching acting workshops, writing short skits, and tutoring young actors in both physical acting and voicing. During the last decade, more than three hundred actors have passed through the workshops.

NIGHT CLUB COMIC

Butler received his own training in night clubs, working as an impersonator with two other performers after he graduated high school. Growing up just outside Chicago, he developed his talent by delighting friends with impersonations of teachers.

It was his on-the-job training in clubs, Butler says, that both honed his voicing and helped determine his career's course. Doing impersonations, three shows a night at times, "was like doing voice exercises—and I didn't even know it."

That experience also dampened any burning desire he might have had to be an on-camera star. "Playing the clubs as a youth, I was constantly in front of audiences, so I got it out of my system.

"What I ended up doing, the voicing, is all I ever wanted to do. I never really hungered to be on camera or be recognized in public. I don't see the point in it. That's flattery.

"The amazing thing is once in a while, somebody recognizes something in the timbre of my voice and says, 'Are you Daws Butler?' That's nice, that they like my work, but I really like being withdrawn and anonymous."

Butler's gift as a mimic served him well, since Joe Barbera wanted the Hanna-Barbera cartoons' lead characters to be patterned after recognizable voices. Consequently, there's Yogi, a fur-laden Art Carney; Snagglepuss, a ringer for Bert Lahr's Cowardly Lion; and Wally Gator, a quavery-throated reptile inspired by comic Ed Wynn.

On each, Butler made minor changes—exaggerating the distinguishing facets of the voice. "Yogi is a lot of chest and ebullience," he says. "It's really not as much an impersonation as a kick-off from an idea. The original is the springboard."

As a writer, Butler spent five years doing *Time for Beany* with Stan Freberg, and the two later produced "St. George and the Dragonet," a Jack Webb spoof that became, in the 1950s, the first comedy [single] to sell more than a million copies.

Armed with that background, and a fierce love for his characters, Butler frequently tinkered with the H-B writers' work. "I would do what we call interpolating. To me, all my characters are real—they have blood and bone and flesh.

"I would change a line occasionally, and I was good enough, apparently, that the writers wouldn't get mad. When I listen to old shows now, I can say, 'Oh, that's an ad lib.'

"I do it when it's permissible. I always wanted to say it the way the character would. Snagglepuss once had a line where he said, 'I don't agree with ya.' I changed it to, 'I beg to differ . . . I'm a differ-begger.'

"That's just a cuter way of saying it. I wasn't always going for laughs, but it had to be individual, to fit the character."

Don Messick, a self-proclaimed "second banana" to Butler, spent years doing the Boo Boo to Butler's Yogi, the Pixie to Butler's Dixie, etc. The two are still close, and Butler believes their friendship showed in their collaboration.

"It was almost like jazz," Butler suggests. "I would do something as Yogi, then Don would throw in a Boo Boo line saying the ranger wouldn't like it, and that would make Yogi even more adamant.

"It was the type of performing I really love, and we could work remarkably fast. Don and I would do four four-minute cartoons in about two hours."

Butler misses that situation, when he and Messick were doing dozens of voices and literally served as Hanna-Barbera's two-man stock company. By contrast, voicing today's cartoons is as uninspired as the limited animation. "Today, you have maybe eight people in a room, sitting around in front of microphones, each doing one or two voices. You don't have the rapport that developed between Don and me," he observes. . . .

Breaking into the business wasn't quite as simple. First, Butler dropped his first name, Charles, to go by Dawson, his middle name. People started calling him Daws, and it stuck. . . .

RADIO PERSONALITY

After leaving the army, Butler was an unemployed impersonator seeking a place to mouth off. He put together a demo tape, going from one ad agency to another trying to get commercial work.

"You would get a call, and no matter how small the part was, that would be a credit. That credit would help you get more credits," he explains.

He couldn't afford to be particular, either. One radio part called for a Hispanic voice. A native Midwesterner new to California, Butler had never heard one.

Before the show, he went to LA's barrio and spent the entire day listening to voices, hoping to master the dialect. "I was doing it pretty well, and then I had to say my name, 'Pedro,'" he relates. "I said, 'I'm *Pee*-dro.' It blew the whole thing."

Through his radio work, Butler met Freberg, a gifted comic who made his mark doing both commercials and albums. The pair churned out a number of comedy singles, locking themselves in a room for a day and usually coming out with two three-and-a-half-minute sides of material.

Eventually, however, the team drifted apart. "It's good it worked out the way it did," says Butler. "It was like a short and happy marriage. Our personalities were such that if we had stuck with it, I think Stan would have smothered me. There were other things I wanted to do."

On his own, Butler began doing voice work for the legendary Tex Avery at MGM, performing characters like [a Southern wolf], a forerunner to Butler's Huckleberry Hound. "Tex was the greatest talent I ever worked with," Butler comments. "He loved those laconic, laid-back characters."

Huckleberry Hound was a classic example, an understated mutt who made Gary Cooper seem talkative. Lapsing into the voice, Butler drawls, "Huck is kind of laid back. Normally, he's just walkin' along—then he'll turn his head an' say somethin' to ya. He don't move too much."

The character was so subtle that Butler found it difficult to change the pace. "The hardest thing was giving him a laugh. I just couldn't imagine him laughing for some reason. I finally gave him a snicker that followed the line: 'I'ma gonna sneak up on him from behind that tree. *Hee hee hee.*'"

Butler and Messick left MGM when Hanna-Barbera formed, becoming the resident voice-masters for the fledgling concern, as well as close friends. According to Messick, few voice-men have possessed Butler's range, from the high-pitched Chilly Willy for Walter Lantz to Wally Gator—a voice Butler describes as "sloppy, like eating a sandwich through a picket fence."

Still, Butler acknowledges there's one name that will always be synonymous with the craft: Mel Blanc. "*Everybody* knows who Mel Blanc is," he says. "People find out who I am and they say, 'Wow, did you ever work with Mel Blanc?' I say, 'Yeah, for about twenty years.'

"Mel does things that I couldn't possibly do, and I'm sure I do things he couldn't do. At Warner Bros., whenever they would have a character like a father or a kid, I would do it, because it just isn't Mel's bag."

Another kid is one of Butler's favorite characters, Elroy Jetson. That revelation, however, tends to disappoint *Jetsons* fans. "Everybody always assumed Elroy was really a kid," he says. "For me, it's like self-hypnosis. You must convince yourself you're nine years old again; let it go through your whole body."

Elroy had the benefit of a supportive space family, and, more importantly, some gifted writing. And that's what's sorely lacking in modern cartoons, Butler charges.

"The writing has gotten to a kind of pedestrian level," he observes. "I don't blame the writers. I blame the networks, the people who have the final voice."

As an example, Baba Louie has been excluded from *Yogi's Treasure Hunt*, he says, because execs fear the ethnic voice will lead to parental complaints. "That's ridiculous," Butler says. "He was always inoffensive, always much smarter than Quick Draw.

"They simply beat the scripts to death. They write and then they rewrite it, and then the director gets his hands in it."

Rather than lament limited animation's advent, Butler sees it as a challenge. If the characters don't move much, the voices have to be that much better—more emotive and more distinctive—to capture the viewer's imagination.

And that, after all, is the trick: for a 5' 2" man to make you believe he's an eight-foot bear or horse or a nine-year-old boy. "Sensitivity is at the bottom of the whole thing," he says, "and caring about what you do."

While the cartoons continue to play, there's a constant reminder of how much and how often that sensitivity came into play. Whenever you turn on the TV set and see a talking bear, there's a good chance the Butler did it.

Don Messick: Vocal Hero

BRIAN LOWRY / 1986

From *Starlog*, October 1986, 16–18. Reprinted with permission of Kerry O'Quinn.

Just because you haven't *heard of* Don Messick, doesn't mean that you haven't *heard* him. Indeed, it's hard to imagine a child growing up over the last twenty-five years who hasn't encountered his voice in one form or another, a voice which has been a significant presence in show business since just after World War II.

While Messick hasn't led a dog's life, he has on many occasions, worn a dog's voice—as well as the accents of rabbits, mice, and bears. Along with longtime friend Daws Butler, Messick formed half of one of the most prolific voicing teams in cartoon history, as the original voice men of Hanna-Barbera Productions.

A self-proclaimed "second banana" to Butler, Messick has sat in the star's chair as Scooby-Doo and Papa Smurf, as well as performing Boo Boo and Ranger Smith to Butler's Yogi Bear, Pixie to Butler's Dixie, Ruff to Butler's Reddy, Ricochet Rabbit, Professor Gizmo, Muttley, Mumbly, Atom Ant, Precious Pupp, So-So, and the future's favorite pet, Astro of *The Jetsons*. Throw in Dr. Benton Quest from the classic adventure series *Jonny Quest* and Snagglepuss's nemesis Major Minor and you've accounted for only part of Messick's repertoire of personalities.

Now sixty-one years old, Messick remains a highly sought-after voice, commuting from his home near Santa Barbara four or five days a week to create one character or another. In person, his genial, resonant baritone sounds nothing like the high-pitched pleas of Pixie or the gruff sagacity of Papa Smurf. That, of course, is his stock-in-trade.

"My approach is similar to Mel Blanc's," Messick says. "I've heard him say he always went for originality. All of his best-loved, best-known characters have been originals, not built on any particular impersonations. I've done the same."

An introverted child, Messick began to exploit his nimble voice at age thirteen with a ventriloquist act. Growing up listening to Edgar Bergen on the radio, he broke into radio himself at a local station in Maryland while still in high school.

"That got me into doing many different voices—never impersonations, but different character voices," he recalls. "I developed my own little radio skit when I was about fifteen."

Messick fell in love with performing and joined an acting class after graduating from high school. World War II sidetracked his thespian aspirations, but instead of returning home when he got out of the service in 1946, Messick, only nineteen, went directly to Hollywood, entering a radio workshop for returning GIs.

VOCAL HEROES

It was at about that time that Messick met Butler, as each made inroads into radio and a new, rapidly growing medium: television. Soon thereafter, the pair's long affiliation with Hanna-Barbera began.

"Prior to that, I had been doing live puppet shows on television," Messick relates. "The budgets for these local shows got to be unhandy, and at that time, the motion picture studios were making their backlog of theatrical cartoons available for television, which was much cheaper for the local stations than the production costs of these live shows.

"As that began to take hold, TV started using up that product enormously—as you know, it has a fantastic appetite.

"Meanwhile, Bill Hanna and Joe Barbera were the animation heads at MGM cartoons, and MGM was planning to phase out their cartoon department because they couldn't see the practicality, financially, of making cartoons for TV. Well, Bill and Joe had an idea to trim the costs and streamline the operation, so they started their own company.

"When I met them, they asked me what I thought Tom and Jerry would sound like *if* they had voices—of course, they never did—and I thought they were planning to take off on a new tack with Tom and Jerry. What they *were* planning was a series called *Ruff and Reddy*, which they would produce on their own, and that's how Daws and I became the original voice men for Hanna-Barbera."

Voices figured prominently in the new company's plans, with Butler and Messick schizophrenically hopping from personality to personality, trying to impart each one with a distinctive and recognizable style.

"I love doing that," Messick says. "Having started as a ventriloquist, I had developed this quick change, back-and-forth patter and a split personality. Often, our director would say, 'Don, you've overlapped yourself.'"

Character voices helped determine the look and movement of each talking rat, cat, or dog, with the producers working closely with the voice men on the kind of sound they wanted. In an effort to reach a larger following, Butler's familiar inflections usually dominated the duo.

"Daws, more than I, has the ability to base his characters on recognizable personalities, which is usually what Hanna-Barbera would want for a lead character—something that the viewer was already familiar with," Messick explains, offering Yogi Bear's similarity to Ed Norton and Snagglepuss's vocal resemblance to the Cowardly Lion as examples.

"As a result, I usually wound up as second banana," Messick adds. "My Boo Boo to Daws' Yogi, for example, was a perfect foil. He became like a sounding board—or a conscience—to Yogi.

"It wasn't really based on anything else. Joe Barbera wanted him to talk as if he had a cold all the time," he says, demonstrating a slightly more nasal Boo Boo, "but I thought that would have been kind of tiring on the ear over the long haul.

"Gradually, as so often happens, you start out doing a character pretty much the way you're told to do it, and as you get more familiar with the story's development and the writers get more familiar with the way the actor performs, it loosens up quite a bit—developing its own little quirks and characteristics. And that's always good—it brings the character *alive*."

Perhaps Messick's most famous character, Scooby-Doo, is an oddity in the sense that he doesn't "talk" the way most cartoon creatures do. "Both Scooby and Astro have these gravelly, what I call 'dog-produced voices,' but they're different," he maintains. "Astro, going back twenty-two years, has a voice in the midrange, whereas Scooby's voice comes from a little deeper down." Messick makes the familiar, guttural Scooby sound.

"Joe Barbera envisioned both Astro and then later Scooby as not being too articulate. It wasn't really my decision to make.

"All of Hanna-Barbera's characters have really been based on human-like characteristics rather than animal characteristics. Scooby-Doo was one of those rare instances when I tried to produce a sound that was akin to what an animal would talk like *if* it could talk."

Messick's personal affinity for dogs helped him produce voices for Precious Pupp, Muttley, and Mumbly, all of whom shared what he refers to as a "generic, mumbling voice."

Admitting to a special place in his heart for Scooby-Doo—whom he has spoken for (literally) over the past seventeen years—Messick has kept things in the family by also voicing Scooby's nephew Scrappy.

"He has had a pretty good education compared to his uncle Scooby," Messick muses wryly. "I mean, Scrappy can talk understandably. You would never know they were from the same family."

"They wanted a feisty little guy—a real spitfire who's afraid of nothing—and yet he has blinders on when it comes to his uncle Scooby, whom he hero worships, so he can't see Scooby's basic cowardice.

"The funny thing is, I didn't always do Scrappy's voice. They auditioned other people after deciding my Scrappy was too babyish, and ABC relooped it at considerable expense. Then, they decided they didn't care for the new voice, that it sounded like a Jerry Lewis, nasty little kid. They wanted more warmth.

"Eventually, I auditioned for it again, and the second season, I was back on Scrappy, doing the same voice I had done originally."

In addition to voicing most of the members of the Hanna-Barbera kennel, Messick has survived to the current era of children's animation—most notably, the robotic trend.

"There is an audience for the Star Wars syndrome of cartoons, I guess," he says.

"The toy companies are thrusting them upon us; they create the characters and then build a show around them."

Aside from the stiff, lifeless animation, some have suggested that amateurish voices further detract from modern cartoons. "I know," Messick groans. "I've been involved in some of those recording sessions. They're depending heavily on electronic distortions to give it the disembodied, robot-like characteristic vocally. Those things aren't really fun to do."

SMURFS UP

But fun is alive and well on Saturday mornings, according to Messick, in the form of *The Smurfs*. "It has a quality that was present in many of our earlier cartoons going back to Hanna-Barbera Productions—the fun, the warmth, and the comedy, which many of the adventure things *don't* have.

"I find *Smurfs* genuinely funny. It's well-written, and it usually has a moral without berating the issue."

Papa Smurf, one of Messick's favorite characters, is another original—"not based on anything," he says, "except my idea of what the character ought to be." Nevertheless, Messick's initial vocalization did undergo some changes.

"My concept was more of a pixie-ish kind of a guy," he admits. "After two episodes were recorded, we decided to change it a bit. So many of the characters had these whimsical, fey little voices, and Papa Smurf had to be the strength that would hold them all together. He should be more mature because the rest of them are all scatterbrains."

Speaking in his gruff Papa Smurf voice, Messick adds, "So now, Papa Smurf is much more in charge, in control of things—sort of a Santa Claus, all year round."

Messick's other famous papa appeared on *Jonny Quest*, a short-lived (but still popular) Hanna-Barbera adventure series that premiered in 1964. Messick played Dr. Benton Quest in twenty of the show's twenty-six episodes.

"*Jonny Quest* was a forerunner; it was ahead of its time," Messick suggests. "It was a good series and very well done, but it cost Hanna-Barbera a *fortune* to produce. I think it cost them about eight times as much to do a half-hour *Jonny Quest* as it did to do *The Flintstones*."

Dr. Quest presented a challenge, since Messick was supposed to keep the voice deep and urgent at the same time. "We were all shouting most of the time, and when you shout, you lose any distinctive qualities that your voice might have," he explains. "They kept saying, 'Keep it low, keep it down.' But you can't do that and shout, because you lose that mellifluous or resonant quality. It was a constant conflict to keep it different."

As extensive as Messick's vocal range is, past experience dictates that he take care of its delicate mechanisms. In his earlier days with Hanna-Barbera, he once lost his voice for two weeks by overspeaking his bounds.

According to Messick, only about fifty people actually make a living solely off of their voice, though opportunities have expanded recently. "They're doing more original animation for syndication rather than reruns, so voicers and animators are getting year-round work," he says. "It used to be rather seasonal, more or less April to September when they were preparing the fall lineup."

In addition to continuing stints on *Scooby-Doo* and *Smurfs*, Messick is currently working on *The Transformers* and *The Jetsons*. He also does many voice-over spots for TV and radio.

Ironically, Messick has very little understanding of why or how his craft works. "I never really analyzed how I do what I do," Don Messick says with a shrug. "It just happens automatically."

Cartoonists Turn to TV for Work

CHARLES WITBECK / 1959

From *Hutchinson [Kansas] News*, January 8, 1959, 22. Syndicated by King Features. Reprinted with permission.

A year and a half ago MGM's creators of the Tom and Jerry cartoons, William Hanna and Joseph Barbera, decided to do new cartoons for TV.

"MGM closed their cartoon shop, Disney stopped making animated shorts, and there we were—out of a job," said Joe Barbera, recalling the black day. "So we thought about TV. Where else could we go? We figured it was possible kids might get tired of old guys in clown outfits being real friendly, and then turning on old, old cartoons."

HIGH COSTS

The reason for the movie animated cartoon demise was high costs and low rentals. Also, it takes a cartoon about two years to get back its initial costs. The giant octopus confronting the two unemployed geniuses was how to make cartoons quickly—Hanna and Barbera only did eight Tom and Jerrys a year for MGM—and cheaply for the TV mill.

Old hands in the industry, tiny as it is, scoffed at Hanna and Barbera for thinking of the idea. One pro offered to lay a thousand to one against its success. H and B are considered two of the sharpest men in the business, but the idea still seemed too drastic to most.

"The costs came from all the drawings—the hand work," said Barbera, generalizing somewhat. "We figured we could cut down on the animation by planning. We call our TV cartoons 'planned animation.'"

"For instance, you want to show Huckleberry Hound about to go out on a chase, and you have him going into a closet, putting on an overcoat, walking out. You can get the same effect by cutting from Huckleberry outside the closet talking to another character to Huckleberry in the closet with his coat on. Time-consuming drawing is cut in two."

CUT ANIMATION

The two men cut the animation down to the point where they felt it wouldn't be missed and where a reasonable TV budget might be reached.

Then they talked MGM movie director George Sidney into helping out with backing, and hustled over to Screen Gems, Columbia Pictures' TV subsidiary, with budget and drawings. After five minutes of talking, Barbera had an offer.

It has been a year and three months, or 170 cartoon shows, since Hanna and Barbera's first effort appeared on TV. They now have two series running, *Ruff and Reddy* and *Huckleberry Hound*, during the dinner hour in 180 cities. Their technicians are currently dubbing the shows in Spanish and French for foreign markets.

"I think we've proved our point," says Barbera. "It's possible to make cartoons for profit on TV. No one else is doing it yet, but they will."

Of course, the two men have only been working practically seven days a week to turn out the huge quantity, using a staff of about twenty, and farming out animation segments. Both still appear in good health. Barbera even sports a tan, probably from his drawing-board lamp.

BETTER PRODUCT

"I think our cartoons are better than our fancy Tom and Jerry movies," says Hanna, who claims he isn't punch-drunk or prejudiced. "We use close-ups, our shows are easier to watch, and we let the viewer use a little imagination."

"We are coming up off the floor," Barbera chimed in. "We are even getting calls from ad agencies and cartoonists. UPA (maker of Mr. Magoo) has looked at our work and thinks we're on the right track."

Following Hanna and Barbera may save UPA, which had a charming series on TV for a few months, but its costs were so high as to make future programming impossible.

It's an encouraging Hollywood story. Not only because of the kids who get to look at new material, but it's the first note of hope for the dying cartoon industry. Others like UPA may take the hint—and the animators, artists, and story men who are now doing other things may have a chance to go back to the drawing board again.

Lance Nolley

DON PERI / 2011

Edited from *Working with Disney: Interviews with Animators, Producers, and Artists*, edited by Don Peri (Jackson: University Press of Mississippi, 2011), 75–76. Interview conducted August 11, 1978, by Don Peri. Copyright © University Press of Mississippi. Reprinted with permission.

Lance Nolley: I worked with [Disney] up to I think about 1960 and went over to Hanna-Barbera on *The Flintstones*. I stayed there about ten years, and then I retired. I'd had enough. But you know, I went back there last December [1977] and worked for six months at Hanna-Barbera. They don't do *The Flintstones* there anymore. It was all sent overseas to Australia. [Editors' note: Likely, he worked on *The New Fred and Barney Show*.] I worked on those, what we'd call adventure pictures, like *Godzilla, Captain Caveman and the Teen Angels, Scooby-Doo*. I worked on those sorts of things. And finally I'll tell you, that's such doggone hard work. It was really hard and tedious. It took a lot of concentration. I just had to give it up and go back to playing golf.

Don Peri: When you went from Disney to Hanna-Barbera, was that quite a contrast?

LN: Yes, it was. Every studio works a little differently, but basically, it all has to go through the same—more or less—process of story to layout to animation. I worked in layout with a chap named Richard Bickenbach. That's quite a name, but he was a fine man and a great artist. He's retired now. So I had good training. If you can draw, basically you can handle it.

DP: But as far as say the attitude towards the films, or degree of perfectionism, was there a big difference between Disney and Hanna-Barbera?

LN: Yes, some, but Joe Barbera was a perfectionist. You had to please Joe in your layout. Bill Hanna handled all of the animation. He was the director of the animation, the whole bit, and Joe handled story and layout. But if we had a particular question in layout concerning the design, say of a prehistoric automobile, we'd go to Joe, and he'd work very closely with us. He was a very fine designer himself, and he had a great story mind. No question about it.

DP: The reason I ask about Hanna-Barbera is that they are often regarded as somewhat of a factory-type operation, or at least not of the same quality as Disney. I was wondering if you found it to be that way.

LN: No. They try for perfection, as close as they can, but they have a tremendous program, a tremendous program. It is an insatiable appetite, this animation at H and B. You simply can't fill it up. There is always a demand for more artists, and frankly, all of the key artists, key animators at Hanna-Barbera, were Disney-trained men. All of them. There's Volus Jones, Bill Keil, and a number of other fellows who were Disney-trained and they grew up in that thing. So actually, pressure will bother anybody, but it will bother a Disney man less, because he's been through it all those years. It was a transition, I'll tell you.

DP: It wasn't necessarily going from good to bad or anything like that?

LN: No, no. Because, you see, actually Hanna and Barbera are the two men who kept us all in the cartoon business by cutting down costs. Now on *Sleeping Beauty*, there is some animation in that picture that costs as high as two hundred dollars a foot, and that's prohibitive with the average studio. Walt Disney, the Disney people, always had enough money that they could experiment and get perfection. No other studio had that kind of money, that they could spend months or years perfecting a character or perfecting a story.

DP: I guess Hanna-Barbera was under more pressure with television schedules—

LN: Yes. After the animation and the in-betweens are done, then it reverts back to the same system as any other studio—Disney and all the rest of them—of ink and paint, background painting. Background painters at Hanna-Barbera develop their own style, and of course, on *The Flintstones* it was a prehistoric approach. Actually, it was fun to work on. It was a lot of fun to draw that stuff.

A Few Words from Jerry Eisenberg

YOWP / 2011

Edited from the blog *Yowp: Stuff About Early Hanna-Barbera Cartoons*, March 11–17, 2011. Reprinted with permission of Jim Bennie and Jerry Eisenberg.

Yowp: How was it that you ended up at the Hanna-Barbera studio?

Jerry Eisenberg: I went [to MGM in 1956] from art school. I was only in art school for about a year and a half, and I had to go to work. My father—who was a cartoonist [Harvey Eisenberg]—he and Joe Barbera both lived in Brooklyn. They met each other at one of the [early animation] studios, became friends, and used to go to work together.

I needed to get a job. So my father called Joe over at the MGM cartoon studio in Culver City, and arranged for an appointment for me. I went with my portfolio and Joe hired me as an apprentice in-betweener in the animation department. So that's how I started. . . .

Yowp: At MGM, how many drawings would an in-betweener be responsible for?

Eisenberg: Well, it depends on the length of the scene. Let's say a scene is comprised of about fifty drawings. The animator will do the key drawings which would probably amount to maybe ten, eleven, twelve drawings. The assistant animator would then clean those up and then add more drawings. And the in-betweener does roughly half the drawings. So I would do twenty-five.

Yowp: I gather you were working with both units, Mike Lah's and Hanna and Barbera's.

Eisenberg: Yeah. At MGM, Bill and Joe would have their unit. I think at that point, they became producers; they were running the [animation] studio. There was Mike Lah's unit. Tex Avery . . . had already left before I worked there. In fact, he had his own little commercial studio. I did some freelance work for him, some in-betweening.

Seven months later, MGM decided to close the cartoon division. So I was out of work for about four months and then I got a job as an in-betweener at the Warner Bros. cartoon studio. . . .

Since I'd already had my seven months' experience with Joe Barbera [at MGM], I remember Joe called me when I was at Warner Bros. and he offered me a job to start in layout—that's what my father was, a layout man. That always interested me: layout, design. But my father said, "Why don't you stay at Warners a little bit longer and learn a little bit about animation?" So I took his advice, and I'm glad I did.

I finally left Warners [in August 1961] because I wasn't getting enough animation. . . . I just had an itch to get into the design and layout. Actually, I worked one week of my vacation [at Hanna-Barbera], and I loved it. So when I came back to work, I gave my notice and went to Hanna-Barbera.

Yowp: Was Joe Barbera the one who hired you to do layout at Hanna-Barbera?

Eisenberg: Right. [T]he layout department was Joe's department. Joe and Bill divided the duties. Joe was handling the creative end of things and Hanna was running the studio. The layout department was Joe's, because six months out of the year, several of us would do development work with him. And then, once the shows were sold, we'd work six months on production. Bill would run camera, and ink and paint, and animation. But Joe reserved the layout department [for himself], which was good, because we didn't have to deal with Hanna.

Yowp: Was Hanna-Barbera paying scale at that time?

Eisenberg: Well, whatever the union scale was—I guess so. There were probably some people making premium. I think when I started there, I was at assistant animation scale . . . then I remember after about four months, Joe Barbera called me in and said, "We're raising you to such-and-such." I guess in the contract it called for every so many months in layout, and you get a raise. Then you become a journeyman.

Yowp: How long did it take to lay out the shorts?

Eisenberg: Most of them were like, five, six, seven minutes, maybe. Probably seven, because you'd do three in a half hour, and you have to allow about nine or ten minutes for commercials. I used to lay them out in a week or less. I remember Hanna started an incentive thing. He wanted to get work done quicker, so he said, "Look, if you guys can lay it out in less than five days, you get extra money. So I used to average four days and get an extra day's pay. Instead of five days, I get six days. That was nice; the money came in handy. Willie Ito was [also] pretty fast.

Yowp: Art Lozzi was saying [that] he, Monte [Fernando Montealegre], and Bob Gentle, who were all painting backgrounds, had different styles. Can you look at a layout and figure that it's one guy's style over another?

Eisenberg: Oh, yes. I could tell the difference [between] my style and Iwao [Takamoto], Willie, [Dick] Bickenbach, Walt Clinton. And there was a funny guy from Texas, Lance Nolley. He'd come over from Disney. I think there was a big layoff at Disney, so Joe and Bill got the benefit of getting a lot of good people from there.

Yowp: Did the layout guys choose the color schemes for the cartoons?

Eisenberg: Sometimes. I remember being involved when I was supervising layouts for some of the shows later on: I'd work with the ink and paint people, selecting colors.

Yowp: I take it you'd get a [story]board from, say, Warren [Foster] or Alex . . .

Eisenberg: Oh, Alex Lovy. His stuff was terrific. We loved laying out off of his boards.

Yowp: How much of what they put on the board did you hew to when you started doing the layouts?

Eisenberg: Well, if it was Alex's board, his posing was terrific, you know. But he didn't really draw on model. Sometimes we liked his drawing better than the official model. Like, take Wally Gator, the alligator character [from *The Hanna-Barbera New Cartoon Series*]. Alex used to draw Wally—his was so funny-looking, we preferred it to the original model. But we had to do it like the model.

Yowp: So, when you arrived, was there a head of layout?

Eisenberg: Well, Bick [Dick Bickenbach] sort of was the head of layout, but it really wasn't formalized that much. We used to take our layouts for him to check. Even Joe Barbera liked to look over our layouts once in a while; we'd take them up to his office. I learned a lot from Joe. And Bick. Joe kept doing that up until, let's see . . . in '63 their building was built, up from where we were on Cahuenga. We moved in there, and Joe was still looking at our layouts maybe for a couple of years or so. Then he got too darned busy.

Yowp: How much direction did the layout guys give to the background people in putting together stuff?

Eisenberg: We would design the background and they would pretty much follow them. Sometimes they would add stuff. I remember on *The Jetsons*, Monte and the guys were doing a beautiful job on some of our backgrounds, 'cause I remember Iwao and I would go and look at the finished backgrounds. I saved some, thank goodness—they're just beautifully painted. But once in a while, they'd put in like a potted plant. My criticism was that sometimes it could be a little too strong and distract from, let's say, the characters. I always tried to be careful when I staged a scene that the background wasn't overly busy behind the character, or something wasn't going to distract from the character. So once in a while, we'd have to ask them to modify stuff like that, or tone it down.

Yowp: I imagine laying out a half-hour show like a *Jetsons* is somewhat different than a short. What kind of process was involved?

Eisenberg: Well, as far as the layout process, we had teams. Myself, Iwao Takamoto, and Jack Huber were a layout team. There were usually three acts to a half-hour show like that. We'd each do an act. We'd do the characters and the backgrounds and the props and everything. Then, of course, it would go to the animation director, who would do the exposure sheets and time it out. Then it would go to animation and background.

Yowp: Can you clarify some of the titles for me? You'd see Alex or Paul Sommer get a "story director" credit, and Nick Nichols would get an "animation director" credit. What's the difference between the two?

Eisenberg: Nick, you might say, was the animation timer. He would do the exposure sheets—time everything out. And he was so good and so fast at that. He was amazing. He could do so much work. He came over from Disney; he was an animation director on a lot of their shorts. But he was very fast, and he really developed in a different way on the television stuff. Of course, the story director was doing the storyboards. I don't know why they used those terms.

Yowp: They [the titles] changed somewhere during the middle of one of the seasons [1959–60]. Originally, Dan Gordon got a credit to do story sketches and then suddenly Alex got a credit as a story director.

Eisenberg: I think the "story director" title made more sense to me when they started doing storyboards from a script, rather than a writer's storyboard. Once things started getting so busy, especially with *The Flintstones*, Joe was hiring writers who had written on *The Honeymooners*. They didn't know how to draw, so we'd just get scripts. The storyboard guy would be more of a story director when you're doing a board off of a script.

Yowp: How long would it take to lay out one sequence from *The Jetsons* or *The Flintstones*?

Eisenberg: One week per act, I guess. Hanna was never that generous with the time. Later on, it was a little more generous, after he and Joe sold the studio. Joe always regretted that [decision].

I could tell you what became *The Flintstones*. Joe was trying to sell an animated *Honeymooners* show. I was working at Warner Bros. at that time. I remember that my father would once in a while help Joe with stuff, even though he was doing comic books at that time. He came to take me to lunch one day; he said, "I had lunch with Joe this week and I think I gave him a pretty good idea for nothing." I remember the exact words—I didn't question him that much about it, and my father never said a lot. One day when I was at Marvel [in the early 1980s], Alan Dinehart, who had been at Hanna-Barbera in those early years, was doing voice directing on a couple of my shows at Marvel, and he said, "Hey, I was there that day!" So he came in my room and filled me in on a lot of detail. My father came in to meet Joe, and he and Alan were showing him *The Honeymooners* stuff, and Joe said, "You know, nobody's interested." All three networks weren't that interested. So my father looked at it and said, "Well, why don't you put some skins on 'em, put them in the Stone Age, give them a pet dinosaur," and on and on.

I call that the "seed concept" idea because my father had already been thinking [about] prehistoric stuff. A year or two before that, he had created an idea for a prehistoric family for a TV cartoon. But the people he was supposed to go into business with changed their mind at the last minute about him being a partner with them. So he tore up the contract, which he wasn't going to sign, and he kept his artwork. And I remember seeing it. It was a prehistoric family with a pet dinosaur, a little kid and, I think, a teenage girl. It wasn't two families like *The Flintstones*—it was just like *The Honeymooners*.

Oh, I didn't even mention [Screen Gems sales executive] John Mitchell. When my father came back from lunch, he borrowed some pencil and paper and he made a drawing. He took it in to Alan and said "This is what they could look like." I've never seen that drawing. I'd love to see what that drawing looked like. So Alan took it over to Joe Barbera's office and Joe—he wasn't sure if he liked it. But I remember that over the years, Joe used to do that a lot with people, whether it was with me or somebody else. He'd like to come back the next day or so and act like it was his idea. So Alan said, "I took the drawing down the hall to John Mitchell's office, and John loved it." Then John said "Excuse me—" He took the drawing and went to Joe's office, closed the door, came out ten minutes later, came back to Alan, and said, "This is what we're going to develop." So John Mitchell made the decision on that. . . .

Yowp: You say that when the studio started, Lew [Marshall] and some others were promised a piece of the action?

Eisenberg: Well, I was talking to Lew one day—this was years ago. He told me when [Bill and Joe] were at the Chaplin Studio—that's where Hanna-Barbera started, there on La Brea—Charlie Chaplin had built a studio once, they were leasing part of it, and they were also renting space several blocks down for the ink and paint department. Lew said, "Hanna came into my room one day, he took the waste basket, turned it upside down, and sat down." I guess they didn't have any guest chairs. "And he said, 'Hey, Lew, listen. If you and the other guys (meaning Bick, Monte, and whoever the core group was that started out with them) . . . stick with us and we make a success and stay in business, well, we'd like you guys to share in a couple of points.'" It was nice of [Hanna] to say that, but he didn't keep his word. I don't like that; he didn't have to say that. I just figure "shame on him." Because, you know, [when Hanna] died . . . I'm sure he had more than a few hundred million dollars in his estate. What if he had a few million less? Big deal. Those things bother me, you know. If I give my word to someone, I keep it. I didn't like that about Hanna. I don't know why the guys didn't get together and call him on that back then.

Yowp: I guess probably because they didn't have anything in writing.

Eisenberg: Yeah, but they could have almost threatened a walkout. Hollywood has always done business with a handshake, so it was on that level. Like my father—he wasn't businesslike when he gave Joe that idea that became *The Flintstones*. I mean, if he had been more business-minded and really smart, since Alan [Dinehart] was there as a witness, he could have said, "You know, Joe, I've got an idea that might help you, but what's in it for me? I'd like to get a finder's fee or maybe something." Because Joe never mentioned it to me when he was alive. It was his ego, I guess. I said to Alan, "You know, he should have sent my father a check, maybe $25,000 after they sold the show." And Alan said, "Bullshit! He should have sent him $250,000." It's a shame, you know. That disappointed me about Joe. But I still liked him. I guess I always preferred him to Hanna. . . .

Yowp: You worked on *Jonny Quest*.

Eisenberg: Yeah, I remember Iwao and I helping to develop it with other people. We also laid out some of the episodes. Iwao and myself did the character layouts and the rough backgrounds, and we had a guy named Lew Ott who cleaned up the backgrounds. He was a very good artist. He did beautiful background work.

Yowp: How different is it to lay out an action-adventure cartoon like that as opposed to a comedy like *The Flintstones*?

Eisenberg: I don't know. It probably took a little longer with the realistic characters. We were pretty much used to doing the silly characters. That's always been my favorite, but I like doing the adventure stuff once in a while. It's a nice change.

Yowp: Was there a fair amount of interaction with Doug Wildey on layouts?

Eisenberg: I don't remember too much. I remember Doug, meeting him when he first came to the studio. It [the concept work on *Jonny Quest*] started at the old building. Joe called me up to his room and introduced me to Wildey. I really didn't know who he was at that time. Evidently, he's the guy who pretty much created the *Jonny Quest* idea. We were doing something about *Jack Armstrong, the All-American Boy*. I wish I would have asked more questions to find out how *Jack Armstrong* became *Jonny Quest*. Doug was a volatile guy. I remember starting to walk out of our cubicle one day. He came walking down the hall like he could kill somebody, he was so mad. I don't know what it was. He was probably coming from Barbera's office. It might have had something to do with credits. Maybe he felt he wasn't getting enough credit or money or whatever. I never questioned anybody about that.

Yowp: At that point, you were in the new building. How many guys would be working in layout? Were you in your own room or were the layout guys all together?

Eisenberg: Iwao and I shared a cubicle, sometimes with a third person. Like on *Jonny Quest*, Lew was in there with us. Other times it was just the two of us. Later on, Iwao ended up being the supervisor of the layout department, and we moved down towards the end of the hallway, and we each had our own cubicle.

Yowp: How did that go over, having Iwao take over? Because there were layout guys who had been there a lot longer, someone like Bick.

Eisenberg: I don't think Bick was interested in doing that much supervision, basically, because he was older. Bick was sort of like the layout supervisor when I started there. Iwao and I actually started there the same week [in 1961], full-time, though I had freelanced for Hanna-Barbera for a couple of years with Ken Harris; we would make commercials for them.

I think Bick just didn't have the energy anymore. By the time Iwao got into supervising, I would say it was maybe 1965 or something. We were doing quite a bit more work then than we were in 1961.

Yowp: You were mentioning that you spent six months in layout and six months in development. When did that happen?

Eisenberg: I know when I first started there, Joe wanted to do something with the Marx Brothers, and he asked me if I would do a presentation storyboard, which I worked on. But I don't remember working for six months in '61. Maybe it was in '63, '64, when we started doing more work. More development and selling more stuff.

Yowp: So which were the cartoons that you developed?

Eisenberg: A lot of the stuff, of course, didn't sell. But some of the things we helped develop sold, like *Jonny Quest*, *Squiddly Diddly*, *Secret Squirrel*. There were a few characters I created when I was there. I once brought some drawings to Joe with a hippopotamus, put a pith helmet on him, and a safari coat. He liked it, so he said, "Let's develop it." We got some writers involved. That's what became *Peter Potamus*. I don't know who came up with the name, but there used to be a disc jockey on the radio called Peter Potter in those days. It's like with Yogi Bear, it was like Yogi Berra, the baseball player.

Yowp: Were there other things in development where you thought, "It was a great idea. Gee, I wish they had bought it"?

Eisenberg: I remember one time Iwao and I were developing a thing based on that movie *Cat Ballou*. We were really enjoying it and having a lot of fun with it, but it didn't get sold. Joe had a cute elephant character called Fumbo Jumbo, but he never could sell that.

Joe did sell something that I had a lot of fun designing, with wacky airplanes. I think it was called "Stop the Pigeon" [the working title for *Dastardly and Muttley in Their Flying Machines*]. It had Dick Dastardly from *Wacky Races* in it. I designed about seven of those cars. I really like designing cars, things that would be animatable, almost. In fact, the next year Joe said, "Let's do 'Wacky Submarines.'" . . . I really enjoyed that. But it didn't sell.

Yowp: So, on *Wacky Races*, did you design the characters, in addition to the cars?

Eisenberg: Yes. I think we had about ten. . . . I remember when I did the Bouldermobile, I did one caveman. Then Joe came back—either him or the writers—and they said, "Let's do two cavemen." So we did two cavemen. . . .

Yowp: Did things change at the company a lot from a creative standpoint when Bill and Joe sold to Taft?

Eisenberg: Well, no, things stayed on for quite a few years after that. The sale was in '66. I remember that's when we met the Taft people. They came out and had kind of like a party out in the parking lot. And everybody got to meet them. The sale was supposed to happen in 1965. But there was an article in the trade paper [saying that] the widow of Harry Cohn, who was the head of Columbia Studios, had private stock in Hanna-Barbera. I think Harry owned a certain amount of stock and, of course, Bill and Joe, and their silent partner was that film director.

Yowp: George Sidney.

Eisenberg: What I read was that Bill Hanna, at some point, had bought the shares that Mrs. Cohn had, the widow of Harry Cohn. And [Hanna], or his people, represented to her that "This is what the stock is worth." But then, when the sale was announced in '66, from what I read, they were selling the studio for $25,000,000. Evidently, Mrs. Cohn's attorneys figured out that Bill Hanna really lowballed her, so they filed suit on her behalf, and that held up the sale for about a year, 'til that was settled.

Yowp: You said Joe would pitch to the networks, and they'd say, "No, we're not really looking for that." How much influence did the networks have toward the end of the 1960s in what you developed?

Eisenberg: When Fred Silverman first came on the scene—I first met him in 1965—he would be very involved. He had a lot of input. He was very creative himself. He was responsible for a lot of the *Scooby-Doo* thing [starting in late 1968]. He's the one who came up with the name. And he decided to make the dog and Shaggy the stars.

It was great to work with him. You know, of all the network executives, even when he became president of NBC [in 1978], he would still read Saturday morning scripts. We always felt that he had a respect for the cartoonists. He liked cartoonists and cartoons, and he was a fan. I kind of miss working with him.

Yowp: The original *Scooby* concept, before Fred modified it somewhat—who put that together?

Eisenberg: I wasn't involved in the early meeting. I remember helping to develop the show with some of the other guys. Well, Joe Ruby and Ken Spears had a lot to do with the initial creative development, and Barbera, and Silverman. Iwao, of course, designed Scooby-Doo. And he helped design some of the other characters. I think I helped on Shaggy. I don't remember doing anything on the dog. . . . I didn't work on production once it got sold because I was busy supervising some other shows.

Yowp: So you were supervising layout?

Eisenberg: Yeah, I would have maybe two different series, sometimes three, and keep track of everything. I was doing some layout work myself, but mostly supervising. Iwao was doing some of that. I don't know who else. We had a lot of shows.

Yowp: Was Joe difficult to work for?

Eisenberg: No, not Joe. Hanna was a bit difficult. At first, I would negotiate with Hanna, like if I wanted a raise. That wasn't very good, so I was . . . glad when I didn't have to deal with him anymore, when Joe really made layout . . . his department.

Yowp: I gather Schipek handled the production end of things, as opposed to the business end.

Eisenberg: That's right. Bill Schipek became the production manager [in 1969] after Howard Hanson left. Howard wasn't treated that well, and he worked with Bill and Joe at MGM.

Yowp: So what exactly did those guys do?

Eisenberg: Production managers? They would keep track of where everyone was. They'd have to deal with the animators, the layout men, or the department heads. They would be responsible for making up a production schedule, so to speak, and giving everybody the dates when stuff is due. And also coordinating with the camera department and ink and paint. Any kind of production, they would be manager-ing.

Yowp: Would they decide which animators would work on a series or a cartoon?

Eisenberg: No. That went through Nick Nichols. Later on, Nick had some of the animators helping him with the supervision. Like Ray Patterson, and maybe Jerry Hathcock, who came over from Disney. It's like in layout: they formalized the department and asked Iwao if he'd be the supervisor. But then there were, you might say, sub-supervisors. I was supervising a couple of shows or so in layout. Because [when] the studio really started growing big, you just can't have one person . . . managing [all of production]. Nichols came over from Disney. When I started full-time, I think Nick was already there.

Yowp: Were there a lot of guys, like [probably writer Karl] Kohler or [animation director] Manny Perez, that Hanna-Barbera brought in just to freelance?

Eisenberg: Probably. Gosh, I remember by [1973], when we were doing *Super Friends*, the studio got so busy. Boy, Joe sold a lot of shows. The previous year, we were averaging 1,200 feet of animation per week. All of a sudden, it went to 5,000 or so. That's what caused Bill Hanna to have to go out of the country looking for help. There weren't enough people here. That's when he started with Japan and, of course, went to Korea and the Philippines, and places like that, Australia. [Later, in 1988,] Disney bought [Hanna-Barbera Australia].

My complaint was, years later, by the 1980s and '90s, there was too much management and middle management. Hanna-Barbera used to run a very tight ship. You didn't have a ton of vice-presidents. But, by then, you'd have people under them. And everybody had to have an assistant. I felt there should have been "runaway management" sometimes, not so much runaway production.

Hanna ran a tight ship, because he was kind of a tightwad. He probably didn't want to spend the extra money. You know, a lot of us used to do stuff ourselves that maybe today they use a secretary or another assistant to do. A lot of featherbedding went on.

Yowp: You left Hanna-Barbera when?

Eisenberg: I left the first time in 1975. I was doing some freelance work, helping to develop a feature project [*Metamorphoses*] for a Japanese company [Sanrio]. I even took a leave of absence for six months to go to Tokyo for some final development.

Yowp: What was Joe's reaction to you giving your notice?

Eisenberg: He was always pretty cool about things. Who knows what he was saying privately. I was there for two years on that feature. During the second year, I was [also back in LA] helping Ruby and Spears. They were working in-house at ABC, which was near us in Hollywood. We were down on Sunset and Vine, and ABC was just down the street on Vine. Ruby and Spears would come over and ask me if I could do some freelance work for them, developing some stuff. The network was doing their own in-house development. Silverman was in charge in those days, and if he'd like something, he'd go to the studios and have them develop it further. . . . What was your question?

Yowp: What Joe's reaction was to your resignation.

Eisenberg: Oh, here's what I was getting at. A couple of times, I'd meet with Joe [Ruby] and Ken [Spears] for lunch, and they'd have one of the fellows from the network, Peter Roth, a really nice young guy. We were meeting at the Villa Capri in Hollywood—and that was one of Joe [Barbera]'s favorite places. When we got up to leave, I heard my name—and it was Joe [Barbera] calling. So I went over and spoke to him. He asked, "How's things going?" And I said "Well, things are winding down at Sanrio, and they want me to stay on for a year and do a comic strip for them. I'm not sure if I'm interested in that."

And Joe said, "Well, why don't you come and meet with me—I'd like to get you back at Hanna-Barbera." So, I ended up going back to Hanna-Barbera, and he treated me so well. It's interesting . . . In those days, you used to hear that after people would leave, they'd be treated better when they came back. That was my experience. He let me do what I wanted to do, and there was no haggling about how much money I wanted. I felt bad when Ruby and Spears approached me about three, four months later, and said, "We have an opportunity to open our own studio, and we'd like you to be our producer and art director." I was very interested, [and] I said, "I wish you guys were doing this about a year or so from now, because Joe just brought me back." I really had mixed emotions, but [I did go to Ruby-Spears Productions, and] it offered me more new experiences. I got to be a producer. And I was offered participation, besides net profits. I mean royalties on stuff I would design.

TV Hit from a Cartoon Factory

THOMAS E. STIMSON JR. / 1960

From *Popular Mechanics*, September 1960, 120–26. Copyright © 1960 Hearst Magazine Media, Inc. Reprinted with permission.

A group of little characters, whose real selves are scarcely more imposing than the place mats on your table, each week manages to capture the attention of some thirty-three million US television viewers.

And, remarkable as is the widespread appeal of the animated cartoon featuring Huckleberry Hound (the program is among television's top ten), even more remarkable is the fact that new cartoons appear each week. By ordinary standards, Huck should be just too expensive to produce.

In the past, a six-minute cartoon for theater showing cost $40,000 or more—enough, anyway, to keep an audience in popcorn indefinitely. On this basis, a half-hour television show—less time for commercials—would cost close to $200,000. Advertisers do not readily part with that kind of money on a weekly basis.

So when Bill Hanna and Joe Barbera, two of Hollywood's top cartoon producers, decided three years ago to break into television, they had some sharp-pencil-and-adding-machine-type figuring to do. Twenty years of producing MGM's Tom and Jerry cartoons had given them plenty of experience in animation techniques.

They invented shortcuts, new ways of achieving effects and new methods of treating action. They called the results "planned animation." Planned animation is much less expensive than the typical cartoons of only a few years back—and they've made the films even more entertaining.

Basically, they use the same animation process by which cartoons have always been made.

"First of all, we have to come up with a new story idea," Bill Hanna explains. "Joe Barbera and I contribute some ideas, the writers and other people on the staff contribute others. Next, we reduce the story to pictures by drawing a series of rough sketches that outline the action of the plot. These pictures are called the story board, since they originated on the drawing board. A story board for a six-minute cartoon may contain 140 drawings and as many as 600 for a half-hour show."

Once the story is approved, a layout story board is put together—this time with all the technical directions for the different departments written on each drawing.

Surprisingly, the voices of Huckleberry Hound and friends—plus all sound effects—are recorded before any of the actual animation begins. In the recording studio, the commentator speaks his lines, and the characters deliver their dialogue, while still in a disembodied state. Daws Butler, an experienced voice man with a repertoire of more than twenty-five voices and accents, handles many of the parts.

"These recordings are turned over to sound-track editors who listen to them and mark each syllable of speech on what are called animation sheets," Hanna continues. "These sheets will guide the animator so he can allow the proper number of frames for mouth action.

"The animators then make the actual drawings. Each bit of motion calls for several sequence drawings, possibly as many as six drawings to show a character taking a step. The drawings then go to the inking department where a girl lays a transparent sheet of acetate (known as a 'cel' because celluloid sheets were used in the old days) over the drawing and traces in the outlines with a broad pen. From here the cels go to the painting department where they are filled in with color, using quick-drying vinyl house paints. The cels are all painted in color because of the possibility of color television reruns in the future."

Actually, Huck and his friends exist in a rather fragmented way (for which there is probably some psychiatric or medical term). The inkers and painters make very few complete drawings. Huck's body may be painted on one cel, his head on a second, his legs and feet on a third. Stacked in register atop one another, the cels produce the full figure. This technique allows Huck to talk or walk merely by going through a sequence of heads or legs, and continuing to use the cels that make up the rest of the body.

Backgrounds are drawn on sheets of heavy paper and form the base under the stack of cels. If a character is to move to the left or right during a scene, a long background is used that shows a series of clouds or trees. The action then is created by moving the background one notch at a time in the proper direction. The animated character merely moves his legs and remains in the center of the scene.

The aim of all this work, of course, is to get the action on film. So each set of cels is photographed with a sequence motion picture camera that exposes one frame of film at a time. The cameraman places the background drawing on the flat easel under the camera, matches up the various cels on top of it (so that legs, arms, bodies, and other miscellany fit together), presses a button to make the exposure, and then consults his direction sheet to learn which cels should be replaced for the next exposure. Run at standard speed in a movie projector, the series of still drawings becomes a motion picture.

Animation is no pastime for a man who likes to let somebody else handle the details. It's tedious and time-consuming work. At the rate of twenty-four frames per second, a six-minute cartoon requires 8,640 exposures. That's probably more shutter snapping than you'll do in a lifetime with your Baby Brownie . . . and you might miss the whole 8,640-exposure sequence if you leave your TV set to put the cat out. That same six-minute cartoon may also require as many as 14,000 cels. A half-hour TV show consumes more than 43,000 exposures in all.

Until TV cartooning came along, a cartoon often was more expensive to create than a live action movie of the same length. A single six-minute short took all of six weeks to produce. . . . Today, with about the same size crew, Hanna and Barbera are producing as many as six shorts a week in the Hanna-Barbera Productions studio.

"One thing we do is take advantage of the small size of the home television screen," Joe Barbera says. "The small screen calls for close-ups instead of theater-wide scenes with babbling brooks and falling leaves in the background. We even like close-ups of a character's head instead of showing his full body, just to avoid the necessity of making more drawings.

"We've reduced the animation of speech to nine standard mouth positions, and a character has a full vocabulary with these nine expressions. More than that, you'll notice that we often finish a speech with a still picture of the character who is listening. Nothing is lost by this, and we can use the same drawing of the listener for many, many frames.

"Another thing, all the characters move either to the left or right, rarely away from you or toward you. This eliminates the need for tricky three-dimensional effects that require numerous separate drawings."

Other savings were achieved by eliminating entire departments, such as the test camera department formerly used to photograph each drawing before inking and painting. Too, the music sheet department in which cartoons were once timed to music is no longer used.

The biggest saving of all was obtained by eliminating the work of the "in-betweener." Previously, a chief animator would make most of the important drawings, and his assistant would fill in with some of the others. Additional sequence drawings, to be placed between the others, would be drawn by the in-betweener, actually a second assistant animator. His drawings accounted for half the cels.

By eliminating the in-between drawings, the number of cels is reduced by half. To make up for this, each cel is shot twice by the camera, on two frames of film. Thus, each drawing is seen for $1/12$ of a second when the film is projected instead of $1/24$ of a second. Action is speeded up, yet not to the point where it is jerky or displeasing. The cartoon effect is enhanced.

All this tells the story of how cartoons can be produced cheaply enough for television, but it doesn't explain the universal appeal of the Hanna and Barbera animations. College professors as well as schoolchildren, engineers, and kindergarten tots all delight in *Huckleberry Hound*.

"Part of the reason is that we have returned to the basic idea of a cartoon," Joe Barbera says. "In the old days of theater cartooning the animators tried to imitate people and animals as closely as possible in actions and voice. The cartoon effect was lost and results were not always funny.

"Today we exaggerate a character's appearance and actions on purpose. We hunt for plausible story situations, and we use satire and absurdity and slapstick. In a sense it's a return to the old Punch and Judy shows. We use simple drawings without too much detail. The result is fairly good comedy, good cartooning.

"The fact is that we used to make good cartoons in the old days and then throw them away. As soon as we had a story, we'd make a 'rough' preview reel to see how the story looked. The action was fast, everything was exaggerated, and the effects were pretty hilarious. After looking over this rough, we'd go ahead and produce the slower-paced animation. Today's cartoons to a great extent are the roughs of the past."

The results have scored with viewers and with the industry. Not only is *The Huckleberry Hound Show* distributed via 192 outlets in the US and Canada, it has gone worldwide as well. Much of Europe, most of Latin America, and Japan and other parts of Asia watch the *Huck* show every week. As if this weren't enough to keep the producers' cup running over, they were given the Emmy Award for the best program in the children's field at the twelfth annual TV award ceremony in June.

Cartooning is so popular, in fact, that about a year ago Hanna and Barbera introduced *Quick Draw McGraw*, a separate TV show that satirizes the gunmen of the old Wild West. And more recently a third show known as *The Ruff and Reddy Show* was put on the air, telling the story of a cat and dog that work as a team. [Editors' note: *Ruff and Reddy* was the studio's first series.]

Television has to have commercials, of course, and in the *Huck* show the principal characters also appear in the commercials. Audiences don't find this objectionable at all, mainly because the characters retain their identities and continue to entertain.

Just like the rest of Hollywood, the animators are finding that they have fan mail and "star" problems. Yogi Bear, one of the main characters in the Huck presentation, has become so popular that he is being considered for a star part in his own show. And sometimes a character that is used once or twice and then dropped has to be returned. Fan mail demands it.

With their new techniques, Hanna and Barbera have also made a return to theater cartooning. Now being distributed by Columbia is their Loopy de Loop series that is designed for theater audiences.

Also new this fall is *The Flintstones*, the continuing story of the trials and tribulations of a prehistoric family. The Flintstones live in a cave and carry clubs, but it turns out that they have all the problems and anxieties of modern civilized life. Starting in late September, *The Flintstones* will be on the air for half an hour, beginning at 8:30 every Friday evening. This is prime time on television, time for which a cartoon never before was even considered.

"It's a show intended for grownups," muses Bill Hanna, "but I suppose the kids will be pushing their parents away from in front of the screen so that they can watch it too!"

Close-Up on Huck and Yogi: Hanna and Barbera with Antoinette Bower

ANTOINETTE BOWER / 1961

Transcript of a segment of the Canadian Broadcasting Corporation (CBC) television show *Close-Up*, July 4, 1961. Printed with permission of CBC Licensing.

James Frank Willis: In Hollywood, Bill Hanna and Joe Barbera talk with Antoinette Bower for *Close-Up*.

Joe Barbera: [*Inside the Hanna-Barbera studio, Joe Barbera shows Antoinette Bower to a chair in an office.*] Just a second—right here.

Antoinette Bower: You mean, I could have my favorite chair? I've been looking at this all day.

Barbera: Your favorite chair? That's my chair.

Bower: [*Looking around*] I love this.

Barbera: You mean our office?

Bower: I love the chair, best of all. But I must compliment you on the office. Yes, it's wonderful.

Barbera: How do you like our doodad there? [*Points to Emmy Award for* The Huckleberry Hound Show.]

Bower: Very much. As far as I can gather now, you are actually producing more animated comedy than any other studio in the world, I should think. And it's only started four years ago. How did it start?

Hanna: Well, it all started, I guess, back at MGM. They had decided that they didn't want any more of the Tom and Jerry cartoons. And Joe and I had to have something to do. There was quite a staff of people there, sixty or seventy. And this is the beginning. We came up with a format that would work for TV, and we went out and sold it.

Bower: But how long were you both at MGM?

Barbera: Twenty years. I was about three years old when I started. [*Antoinette Bower laughs.*]

What I wanted to mention is that it wasn't all this easy. Here we are sitting—working full speed, full production—in what was then the most successful series in animation. Suddenly, the phone rings, and they say "Stop making cartoons." And we're out of business.

This is after winning seven Academy Awards and operating the most successful department at MGM—we were just out of work. Now, what we did then was go to a number of top television studios, who turned us down immediately. I could name them all—I mean, it would make you shudder. Bill and I trotted into office after office. And they said, "Sorry—We can't use cartoons for television. They're too expensive." And we would say, "Well, we have a new secret way of doing it." And they said, "Oh yes, indeed. Everybody has that." So, out we went.

But I will say that Screen Gems, who were at this time our partners and distributors—it took them exactly five minutes to make a deal with us. And from then on, the deals have been running like this: We would sell a show, step off the plane. They said, "I understand you sold the show." "Yes." "Start another one." And we start that, sell that, start another one. By telephone—that's the way these orders are going. It's been unbelievable.

Bower: I understand that your own operations here are very much run along very much the same lines.

Barbera: Well, we never close the door. And we never send a memo. And I mean, right now, if any one of our employees wanted to talk to us, right in the middle of this conference, they would walk in—because this has to stop. I mean, production comes first. I hope no one walks in. Everybody out!

Bower: How do you get everything done? This is the point.

Hanna: Well, we do not have any executives. Everyone in the plant is a productive person.

Barbera: Well, that's what I want to be. I don't want to sit at this desk . . .

Hanna: No, we can't permit that at all. Everyone has to work. And I think the fact that both Joe and I do spend a lot of . . .

Barbera: Seven days and seven nights a week.

Bower: What did you originally intend to do?

Hanna: Well, originally, I was studying to be a structural engineer. I never did finish the course, however. But, in my early experience in building construction, which is what I was interested in—I was a very awkward kid, and I was continually tripping over the scaffolding or falling off or something—So, I finally decided if I was going to be long for this world, I had better change professions. And I had also studied some journalism. I had the opportunity to move into this cartoon studio. I was still just a kid, and I took it.

Bower: And you, Joe?

Barbera: I started out as a banker. I was promptly, well, I wasn't fired right away. They didn't get on to me for about six years. But, you see, things were kind of bad in those days, so I took up cartooning, which I love. Oh, acting at one time, but I quickly dropped that.

Bower: Heaven forbid it.

Barbera: Yeah. But the cartooning, yes—I began to draw these cartoons at night. And sometimes I would work until about four or five in the morning, and then get into work. I worked in Wall Street—Irving Trust Company. It was a bank. And I can't add—I used to add with my hand under the table using my fingers. In a bank, you know. Well, so what used to happen was I would do these cartoons, and at 12 o'clock sharp, I would run down the stairs, get into a subway, go up to Grand Central Station—that's in New York—run to four magazines, submit cartoons, pick up the rejects—and they were always rejected—get on the train, get back again. And we'll do this all in one hour, because we were on a time clock. And this was my lunchtime career and my nighttime career. Well, then finally they decided that this finger adding wasn't quite right for Wall Street, so they dropped me. And I went into cartooning. And quite by accident, I got into the animated end of it, which I always wanted to do. And that was the start of my entry into the business.

Bower: But, do you manage to separate in any way your—I realize that you're working seven days and seven nights, as you say. Doesn't that leave you absolutely nothing outside? I mean, you live with each other, sort of thing?

Hanna: Well, no, it really isn't—it really isn't that bad. We do put in a lot of time, but we do have time for our individual lives. We'll admit it isn't a great deal. But we do have our own individual . . .

Barbera: That's news to me. He must be resting somewhere along the line.

Hanna: I got somebody over there doing my work for me.

Bower: So what have you got coming up next?

Barbera: Well, I tell you . . . as you know, our shows. We have *Huckleberry Hound*, *Yogi Bear*.

Bower: I know them well.

Barbera: *Quick Draw McGraw*, the fastest horse in the West. We have *The Flintstones*. And now we've come up with another group that we call *Top Cat*.

Hanna: Joe, I think you should take Antoinette in and show her *Top Cat*. Go over the story with her.

Barbera: You want me to go over the whole story for her?

Hanna: Take the whole thing.

Bower: I'd love it. I'm willing.

[*Walking down the hallway*] I want to congratulate you on your miles of corridor. It's like a labyrinth.

Barbera: [*Joe, without Bill, shows Antoinette to a new room.*] And the miles of walking that we do all day long. That's everyone around here.

Now, here is the storyboard that I was telling you about. This is the way *Top Cat*, our new show, comes to life. [*Shows her the large storyboard of drawings, covering much of a wall.*] And actually, this is the way we did *The Flintstones*. It was presented the same way. What I did was take sketches, a storyboard like this, go back to the client, and just run through a story. For instance, now I'll do the same thing for you.

Well, let me give you a little brief rundown here. Top Cat, who is, let's say, for association of mine, like Bilko and his group—Top Cat and his group—and that is Benny; the Spook; Fancy-Fancy, that likes the girls. And then we have the Brain, who is not too bright. And then we have Choo-Choo. These are the cats. And Top Cat and his group originate in this alley.

Now the way he calls his group together is that he picks up two lids of these trash cans, crashes them together like cymbals, and wherever they are, they hear this. Like, when we see Fancy-Fancy [*points to the storyboard*] he's talking to a girl. And he says, "The minute I saw you, I said to myself, 'I gotta meet her.' And you hear this crash. And he goes, "TC!"—well, that's Top Cat's initials, that's the way they call him—and he zips off. Dodo is sleeping under a welcome mat, and when he hears the crash, he zips off. The Brain comes up from behind the fence, he zips off. And as they come in, he's timing them with his wristwatch. He's saying, "Five, four, three, two, one . . ." He says, "Where are you boysie boys? You're a little sluggish," he says. "Where's the nimble, where's the quick?"

[Top Cat] says, "Now listen, there's something big—big—big." And what happens is that he reads in the paper that an eccentric millionaire has left a fortune to a missing pet. You know how people, eccentric recluses, leave fortunes to their cat or their dog or their butler? Well, he has left a fortune to this missing pet, and they decide to find him and get the reward.

Now, in reading it, they want to know what he looks like. He says—here's the way it goes, it's in the description—he says, "Short, like Benny here." That's the little fat cat. He says, "Not too bright, just like Benny." He says, "And he has a birthmark on his foot," he says, "like Benny." And he lifts up his foot. "Now," he says, "I want you to spread out." He says, "Mingle with the crowds and bring me back—" And he lifts [Benny's] foot up again and says, "Benny!" In other words, they think they have the heir right in their midst, and that's the way the story goes.

Bower: Well, I was just going to ask you about your characters. I never think of your things as being things for children.

Barbera: Well, let me try to answer our thinking on children. I just don't think that we should ever—this is a cliché in a way—play down to children. I think television itself has removed the child's show, except for, let's say, two and three years old. I've seen—let's say from five years on—they watch things like *Bob Hope*. And they watch things like *Jack Benny*. They watch *The Honeymooners*. They watch *I Love Lucy*. And kids are very sharp.

Bower: I was going to ask you about your code of ethics for your characters—how you keep them within certain limits or boundaries.

Barbera: We never have a real bad villain. This is taboo. They frown or they pout but they never have teeth and are never vicious. The villain is a real good guy. The worst of things is a bad villain. And I think this is the key to everything we do, is that everyone enjoys them.

Bower: *The Flintstones* has very personal things to say about what we're living in.

Barbera: Well, that's satire. That's something else that we try to get into the shows with the characters. It's just kidding—in a good way. I mean, we kid TV westerns, we kid TV producers, directors, writers.

Bower: If people—I don't know, does this ever happen?—Does somebody walk up to you in the street, for instance, and say, 'What about the social significance of all this?' What would you answer?

Barbera: Well, believe me, we never stopped to write that in. Now, they read this into the material later on. Those bold strokes, the satire, the social significance. And we go, 'What?' Because we just don't think that way. We think of one thing as entertainment, and not to hurt anybody. And this has worked very well so far.

Bower: You talk about loving what you're doing, and what you're turning out, too. And I simply wonder, you know, I'm beginning to believe that you live in a world of your own.

Barbera: Well, you may call it that, but I sure know all the characters. I can name them off, as fast as you'd like to hear them, you know. And we have them in the hundreds.

Now you see, as far as knowing the characters, when we do a story and when we do a recording, I have to go over the story with our talent. So, in doing that, I usually take the voices of all the characters myself, and interpret their thinking, and the actors get the feeling . . .

Bower: Exactly the way you did now, with the storyboards.

Barbera: Well, those were quite rough. But that's the way you do it. I do Yogi Bear, as [*in Yogi's voice*], "How do you do, Boo Boo?" And then when you have Quick Draw McGraw, he says, [*as Quick Draw*], "Uh—just a minute here!" You know, we get into this Western thing. And then we have Boo Boo [*as Boo Boo*], "Yogi—"

And we also have to figure their personality. Like, for instance, Boo Boo is Yogi Bear's conscience. Then, as an agency man said, "Huckleberry Hound is so pure. He can never do anything wrong." And this begins to kind of guide our own thinking, as people begin to read into the characters these things, you know.

Bower: Who gets the first ideas? How do they come?

Barbera: Almost from anywhere. I mean, we stop and chat with writers while you're having coffee. That is, in anticipation of something new.

They'll say, "What do you think we could make a new series on—what kind of characters?" I can certainly—on *Top Cat*, we found out that actually the most popular character of all the cartoon characters are cats. Warren Foster, for instance, is the man that writes all the Yogi Bear stories, the Jinxes, the Huckleberry Hounds, and has made Yogi Bear what he is today. Now, Warren is, at this moment, trying to analyze these six cats, and find out how they think, how they talk. If I can get him—[*calls down the hallway*]—Warren?

Bower: [*Joins in*] Warren?

Barbera: Warren Foster?

Warren Foster: [*Walks in, chuckles*] Hi, Joe.

Barbera: Hi, Warren.

Bower: I am beginning to see how things work in here: you just shout.

Foster: Well, good. Let me know.

Barbera: This is Warren Foster. This is Toni.

Bower: Hello.

Barbera: I know his problems right now. He's trying to find out how Top Cat thinks, and how the other five cats think. But you know how this all started . . .

Foster: Well, it is a problem. . . . When we start putting human characteristics within animal bodies, we have to be very careful that we retain the—that they are really an animal. Like, Yogi Bear is not a man in a bear suit. He's a living, actual animal. And that is our going problem now.

Barbera: Well, Warren, you started this thing! You know, with Yogi Bear's association with the Ranger.

Foster: And, I'm having a little difficulty here, holding the same relationship with Top Cat. I was just working on this— [*points to the paper he's holding.*]

Barbera: We don't have to go into that here—we haven't got time. You've got to go—go—go! [*Gestures to Warren.*] Here's a man that used to do eight cartoons a year. Now, he does sixteen half-hour shows last year, plus another eighty cartoons on top of that. And what are you doing in here?

Foster: I don't know. I should be . . .

Bower: It's only because I wanted to ask you: How Top Cat, for instance, or Yogi Bear, for instance, was born?

Foster: Well, Top Cat—I guess that Joe has briefed you on this—would ordinarily be an alley cat. But he is going to be a person, as far as we're concerned.

Just the very thing I'm working on now, he's just been using the police officer's police phone to call up his cronies. And the officer comes in. The attitude of Top Cat is not one of "run away" like an ordinary cat. He starts to bluff it out. He says, "Pardon me, I'll have to hang up now because somebody is waiting to use the phone."

He says, "Well, Officer Dribble, and I wish it weren't." And then the officer starts threatening him with a club. He says, "Now, you wouldn't want to do that on Be Kind to Animals Week, would you? Especially since you're working for Sergeant." So he fast-talks the officer out of imminent disaster for himself.

Barbera: And that's his character.

Bower: Well, Top Cat's here now. But how does he become transferred? Now, how do I put this properly . . . How does he get to be [*laughs*] an animated cartoon?

Barbera: Well, quite simply. You want me to run down the various aspects?

Bower: I do. I want you to become technical for a minute.

[*Foster politely acknowledges Antoinette and turns to walk out.*]

Barbera: Are you going to go, Warren?

Foster: Oh, yes.

Barbera: Back to the grindstone.

Foster: Yes, indeed.

Barbera: We've lost him on half a picture, you know. So long, Warren.

No, actually, it works in these steps. From the idea, and the story, we then move into layout.

[*Joe begins a voice-over. Elsewhere in the studio, layout artist Alex Lovy takes a drag on a cigarette, then draws characters into a storyboard.*] Now, layout is where we take these drawings, sketch 'em up larger, so that the artists can work on them, and begin to move the characters around. Now, the layout man "keys" each scene with a background drawing—a setting, that is, the same as a set, as I imagine, and the key drawing. Now he, in other words, keys the mood of each scene.

Your next step is animation. [*A male animator sketches and flips several distinct drawings of Yogi's head, back and forth.*] This is the artist—and this is quite a job. And, each artist is like an actor. One can do running better than talking, and one can do music better than the next fella. That's our next step: animation. He's the fellow that moves the characters.

From there we go into checking. The checker is someone that checks every drawing that's been made. [*A female checker looks through a stack of cels and takes some out from the stack.*] Because, with thousands of drawings, quite often they leave out an eye, an arm, a leg—and you'll see this on a finished production.

And from there, of course, we go into inking and painting. [*A female inker finely inks lines on a cel to create a partial image of Barney Rubble.*] Every drawing is inked by a girl. And the inking is a tracing of the pencil drawing on a piece of celluloid. Now, you take the celluloid, you turn it over, and another girl moves in, and she fills it in with color. [*The picture cuts to Joe and Antoinette.*] It's about the same as when you used to do color books. If you ever were a child? Oh, you were. So was I. [*She laughs coyly.*] You do—you fill in [like] color books. [*Cuts *back to the painting department.*] And this is painting. They have a group of jars of different color paints, which are pre-mixed. And they just follow the chart, and they fill in these characters—we have thousands of those.

Now, a man is making the background, in color. [*A background painter paints on a wide background.*] See, we do everything in color. One of these days we are going to see everything that we've done in color, and I think it is going to be quite exciting.

Now, these drawings, these colored celluloids, and the background, move into our camera department. Now, in the camera department, they put down the background. And then they begin to put drawings down on top of the background, one by one. As they shoot this on film, they take it off, put the next one on. [*A camera operator lays down separate cels of Fred Flintstone's head and body over a landscape, lowers a glass panel, takes a photograph, and then moves the character cels to a side stack.*] And they photograph the next step. Take this off, put the next step on. That's what your camera does.

Now, this film is developed, and taken into our sound department, where they are working out the sound tracks, the dialogue tracks, the music tracks. [*Sound editor Ken Spears operates parallel reels of a wide audio tape, locates specific points, and makes marks on the tape for use with syncing.*]

And from this point we move into a Moviola. Now, on a Moviola is where this thing begins to come together. [*An operator manipulates film on a Moviola.*]

Hanna: [*Bill returns and shows Antoinette a demonstration of a Moviola.*] Now, in this particular side, we have the picture. We usually have our music, in here, our sound effects, here. We can move these films backward and forward. And we can adjust the voice so that it matches the picture and the sound effects, where someone is clobbered on the head. Why, it will all synchronize.

Then, when we have all of these tracks fixed, so that they synchronize with a picture, we go to what we call a dubbing session, and everything is transferred onto one single strip of film, which would be our sound. Then, we have our music. It moves into the laboratory. The two things are put on—I should say that the soundtrack is combined with the picture, and we have what we call a composite print. And that's what you see on the TV in your home. That's the whole story. [*Bill smiles proudly at Antoinette.*]

Bower: Tell me now, how many countries in the world are your productions shown in?

Hanna: We make what we call the Spanish version. These films are now being shown throughout all of South America. Then we—in New York—we make a French version, a German version, an Italian version. And, I thought . . . I can't remember them all. I know there's a Japanese version.

[*Over a period of four minutes, cartoon scenes of Yogi Bear and Huckleberry Hound on* The Huckleberry Hound Show *play in a series of languages: English, Spanish, German, French, and Japanese.*]

Hanna: Well, they seem to have done a very fine job in dubbing them for our foreign versions. But, Antoinette, that I think just about winds up, you know, our whole operation here. I think that we have covered almost every phase of it. [*He smiles impatiently.*]

Bower: Which means that you want to go back to work. [*She puts her hand on his arm and laughs.*]

Hanna: No, that's true . . . I should get back. But it has been very wonderful, and I have enjoyed going over it with you.

Bower: Well, I'm not finished, as far as I'm concerned! I'm still wandering through your corridors from earlier in the day. [*She stands up and walks out of the room.*]

Hanna: You have—I'll follow you. All right. [*He gets up and follows her out.*]

Willis: [*Returns to host James Frank Willis.*] Huck and Yogi and their creators, Hanna and Barbera.

TV without Terror

JANE KESNER ARDMORE / 1962

From *Parents Magazine & Better Homemaking*, July 1962, 42–43, 82. Provided courtesy of Meredith Corporation, *Parents*, 1962.

Five nights a week, across the country, one hundred and forty-seven million youngsters are spellbound watching a series of unique television cartoons. What fascinates these child viewers are the adventures of Huckleberry Hound, Yogi Bear, Quick Draw McGraw and Top Cat, a group of cartoons as far removed from the old animated cartoons of pre–World War II vintage as today's car is from a Model T. Parents and educators are delighted, too, for these new cartoons emphasize character rather than sadistic action. The humor is more sophisticated, and the adventures sustain excitement without horror. All of which goes to prove that youngsters can be entertained without violence, mayhem, or villains.

Hanna-Barbera Productions, the parents of this cast of cartoon characters (they also create *The Flintstones*, aimed primarily at adults), entered television with *The Huckleberry Hound Show*—the first animated show written specifically for TV. [Editors' note: Actually, several preceded this.] Daws Butler, an actor with a gift for creating different accents and voices, inspired Bill Hanna and Joe Barbera with his imitation of a languid North Carolina drawl. To fit this voice, they dreamed up a slow-moving, persevering little blue dog, a homespun character who sees only the good in life, never the bad. He is blown up in rockets; trees fall on him; drawbridges collapse under him. Whatever happens, he picks himself up, undaunted, and drawls, "Man, that was a right heavy tree," or some other masterpiece of understatement, and perseveres with whatever he is doing. Soon after Huckleberry Hound was created, Yogi Bear appeared. A gentle, friendly soul, Yogi is the number-one citizen of Jellystone National Park. He is also a nonconformist and tries to uphold the spirit of his forebears (literally) who roamed the area before the advent of rules-conscious humans. To the authorities' wish that he become a good, timid bear, Yogi's comment is, "Never!" He does more than his bit to avoid forest fires, and sometimes he's punished for wrongdoing—he may end in the brig for stealing picnic food. But he isn't always caught.

Although there is considerable action in the Hanna-Barbera scripts, they are not frightening. They never use a vicious character, not even for purposes of villainy. They never use violence for the sake of violence, and the element of pure horror is entirely absent from their shows.

"We use witches in our cartoons," says Joe Barbera, "but strictly for laughs. In a recent episode spoofing a fairy tale, the witch looks in the mirror chanting, 'Mirror, mirror, on the wall, who is the loveliest of all?' And before the mirror gives an answer, she says, 'You don't have to answer that; I know . . .'"

The two producers personally invent each character, personally supervise each character, personally supervise each script—a cat face drawn too fierce could ruin a child's joy—and they have certain definite taboos: no vulgarity, cruelty, or maliciousness.

"We've never tried to educate children. We've never tried to preach to them. We've just tried to entertain them," is the way Bill Hanna explains the appeal of the series. Both he and his partner feel that children are subjected to tremendous pressures these days—schoolwork and Sunday school, dancing lessons, music lessons, French lessons, and swimming lessons. All this education needs to be tempered with fun, some free time for relaxation without any educational message or moral—if children are to grow up into well-balanced adults.

To create such entertainment for youngsters, Bill Hanna explains, "You need all the talent you can find. You have to think of children as human beings. And today's small human beings don't go for the too-sweet, too-cute, too-soft approach. A cartoon story with tiny elves dancing and singing in childlike voices while leaves float away into the waters and bunnies hop about with twitchy noses might have been all right once, but no longer. In the area of comedy, today's child has a taste as sharp as his parents'."

A large part of the Hanna-Barbera humor depends on word usage. Unlike the writer whose vocabulary is limited to what children can read, the creator of animated cartoons has almost no limitations. Children can understand words they couldn't possibly read, and even when they don't get all the meaning, they get enough to comprehend what is happening. Most kids love words, and the producers provide their cartoon friends with an extensive vocabulary. Words such as anonymous, humiliate, churlish, exorbitant, reverberate, colleague, allusions to the Audubon Society and sports car rallies at Monte Carlo are casually included in the day's film. This sophistication colors the treatment of a number of sacred old favorites with agreeable results. Huckleberry Hound as the "Purple Pumpernickel," for example, was a take-off on the days when tyrants persecuted their subjects, and avengers came in assorted colors: the White Crusader, the Green Gadfly, the Scarlet Pimpernel. The Purple Pumpernickel appears in full regalia and modestly mutters, "You can call me Purp."

He has come to the aid of the people who are unjustly taxed. He rights the wrongs and routs the king and the first thing he does when he is proclaimed king is—announce new taxes! Whereupon another defender shows up.

The Hanna-Barbera Cinderella becomes a slick chick with a glass sneaker who doesn't just fall into the prince's arms, but thinks it over. And the father-son relationship takes on a new dimension in Augie Doggie and Doggie Daddy by the use of ridiculous, flowery language ("Dear old, house-builder Dad," "Yes, Auggie, my son?"), through which father and son try to overcome the self-consciousness that sometimes develops during a boy's adolescence.

As is the case with Dr. Seuss, today's most successful writer of juvenile fiction, neither Hanna nor Barbera was trained to work with children. Hanna started out as a structural engineer, who had also studied journalism, and who found himself in depressed 1930 without a job.

Barbera was an income-tax man, "the only guy ever working for a bank whose accounts never proved at the end of the day," because his head was filled with cartoon ideas.

The two men met in [1937] in MGM's cartoon department, where Bill Hanna had been hired as a director and story man, and Joe Barbera was an animator and writer. Working side by side, they tried one or two fairy tales that were moderately successful, then came up with a couple of pantomime characters in the form of a rowdy cat plagued by a clever little mouse—Tom and Jerry—a series that won seven Academy Awards. In Tom and Jerry, they were creating characters, as they are today, for a family audience composed of children and adults. To fulfill their responsibility to the youngsters, big Tom always started off by taking advantage of Jerry, so that the little mouse's acts of retaliation were justified, but this was accomplished without pointing out morals or teaching lessons.

When, after twenty years, MGM decided to bow out of the cartoon field, Hanna and Barbera began dreaming up ideas for television productions. Until then, animation, although used extensively in TV commercials, had rarely been used for programming. What animated material there was consisted of old theatrical cartoons, much of it from the silent screen era. According to Hanna, the techniques were all wrong for television.

"The emphasis in cartoon movie making had been on action," Hanna explains. "For television, you needed the characters brought up closer, you needed more dialogue, more characterization, less action. We devised what we called planned animation, forgoing some of the steps used in previous cartooning without sacrificing quality. We discovered that a character didn't have to move, move, move to make a point. And it's a good thing we did, for each half hour of *The Flintstones* consists of over twelve thousand individual drawings and requires the skill of fifteen skilled artists, layout men, editors, inkers, and painters. Each small gesture—'Good morning, how are you?'—requires more than twenty-four drawings. And where for movies, we did eight cartoons a year, we now do five cartoons a week, or about seventy-eight cartoons a year."

One indication that Hanna-Barbera Productions is on the right track is the quantity and quality of mail that comes in every week. A twelve-year-old writes, "I'm enclosing a short play I've written which might be good for the series."

An eleven-year-old sends twenty thumbnail sketches of *The Flintstones* to illustrate her original story, "Ladies on Strike."

A twelve-year-old writes, "My friend David and I are in the same room at school. We like your shows and your characters so much we have made up some new characters and shows of our own. When we grow up, we want to be cartoonists and work together. Can we work for you when we grow up?"

An elementary teacher from Chicago writes, "May I have pictures of Huckleberry Hound for use in our fourth-grade classroom? The children in my class are all avid fans of Huckleberry and his cronies, and we will use the pictures as a springboard for creating new adventures of our own and drawing characters to illustrate those adventures."

The significant difference between these and most fan letters is that the cartoon series has sparked the kids to produce something themselves. Dramas, stories, and drawings flower, and the artists want the world to know. These youngsters are not sitting passively in front of the magic screen, absorbing whatever appears without thought; their imaginations have been stimulated, and they are responding creatively.

Perhaps it is this quality above all, regarding Huckleberry Hound and his cohorts—the fact that they have demonstrated that television can entertain without either stifling or terrifying young minds—which gives them their most important value. Other television producers can do worse than to remember Hanna and Barbera's basic credo: "We've never tried to preach to children; we've just tried to entertain them."

Doug Wildey on *Jonny Quest*

DAVID W. OLBRICH / 1986

Edited from "Doug Wildey '86," *Amazing Heroes* 95, May 15, 1986. Interview courtesy of Fantagraphics Books, (www.fantagraphics.com).

David W. Olbrich: Can you go through the creation process of *Jonny Quest*? Now, Hanna-Barbera had found a way to get *The Flintstones* on primetime TV, on ABC. What happened next that inspired them to try *Jonny Quest*?

Doug Wildey: I was looking for a job [around 1962–63]. I was coming from another studio [Cambria Productions] where I'd worked for about twelve or fourteen weeks under Alex Toth, on a thing called *Space Angel*. I had applied to Universal as sort of a storyboard/production designer. [Director and producer] Stanley Kramer's office got interested in my stuff, so I figured, rather than move back to Arizona, where my family lives, maybe I could latch onto Stanley Kramer. Hanna-Barbera was up the street from there, so I simply crossed the street, went up to Hanna-Barbera, and said, "Look, I'm an artist," and so forth. A couple of people there had read some of my comic strips and comic books, so they said, "Come in and see [Joe] Barbera." The following day, or maybe even the same day, Barbera called me up and said, "Can you design, in your style, a show: *Jack Armstrong*?"

Olbrich: This is the radio character, right?

Wildey: Right. I said "Yeah." So I storyboarded one, wrote some dialogue, wrote a little script, and then I did a kind of a presentation, showing a little continuity, a little color, and what the characters looked like. I worked on that thing for I guess three months, and listened to tapes of guys auditioning for a whole day.

Now that I think of it—and I never honestly thought about it before—you had almost the *Jonny Quest* setup in *Jack Armstrong*. It had Jack Armstrong, a young guy, about seventeen; Uncle Frank or Uncle Jack, I'm not sure; a sidekick; and a girl, and they went around having adventures.

Again, referring to *Jonny Quest*, it was a sort of global adventure type of thing, so I put them in Africa. I wanted to get into science, so I read *Popular*

Science, Popular Mechanics, Science Digest, all that stuff, trying to project what would be happening ten years hence.

By the way, that's how *Jonny Quest* was set up. We figured it might run for years, so I wanted to keep it current for ten years. As it worked out, the things I came up with were all out of my head, other than projections from *Scientific American* and the like. We had one show where they went to the South Pole. I needed a vehicle, so I invented a thing which I called a "snowskimmer." Now in retrospect, why didn't I think of "snowmobile"? A simple thing like that, right? There was no snowmobile at the time, so I patterned the thing after those swamp buggies in Louisiana that had the big propeller on the back and would go stomping through the water—they're nice visual things anyway. That's what I came up with, this vehicle that would ride on the snow, and I called it a snowskimmer. I was *projecting*, okay? Now, of course, snowmobiles are everyday things.

I would read about things like hydrofoils. I had hydrofoils only because I thought America, with all its waterways, would be inundated by hydrofoils like they are with snowmobiles. I had a hovercraft.

Olbrich: The hovercraft that natives were throwing spears at in the credits.

Wildey: Right. That is all stuff we did for *Jack Armstrong*; none of that was from *Jonny Quest*. Now, the rights to Jack Armstrong were owned by someone, and Hanna-Barbera, I presume, after watching what I had been doing on *Jack Armstrong*, said "Why do we need Jack Armstrong?"

Olbrich: Why license it? Why not just create something you could own?

Wildey: At which point [Joe] Barbera came and said, "Can you create a show for us?" I said, "Yeah!" and went home and wrote *Jonny Quest* that night—which was not that tough.

Olbrich: Well, not after all the research you'd done.

Wildey: Not just that. I had a lot to draw on. I drew on Jackie Cooper's movies, his relationship to, let us say, George Raft or Wallace Beery—that type of relationship. I drew upon some of the Frankie Darrow movies—there's a name you never heard. Frankie Darrow was always the misunderstood kid—still a good guy, but nobody understood him. But he worked with a male lead in most cases; I had him to draw from. And then of course I had, let's face it, [the comic] *Terry and the Pirates*. Not only do I think [Milton] Caniff is still the greatest storyteller in the business, but after I worked for him and got to know the guy . . . I mean, they say imitation is the sincerest form of flattery. [*Laughs*] So, drawing upon all of those, it was not all that tough.

The Barbera influence was felt there because he had gone to see a movie called *Dr. No* and wanted to get in stuff like "007"—numbers. Which we included, by the way, in the first *Jonny Quest*. It was called "Jonny Quest: File 037" or something. We dropped that later; it didn't work. But that was his father's code name as he worked for the government as a scientist, and that kind of thing. That influence was felt.

The actual putting together of the kid and his father and the bodyguard was no big thing. Couple of hours' work and I had the outline. And I believe the following day I wrote the first premise, which was the Sargasso Sea. I wanted a mysterious element. The Sargasso Sea exists—not quite as strongly as I had it—but it was at one time called the Sea of Dead Ships, or whatever the heck it was. It seemed like a good setting for adventure. And then, of course, I wanted a real plausible adventure—if you could call it plausible—in the sense that things were being manipulated by real people. [In other stories,] it wasn't really happening and it had to be explained at the end. This is the part of some of the writing that I didn't like—where they'd come in with the "monster-of-the-week" type of thing, mostly rip-offs. . . .

What I tried to concentrate on were the characters and the relationships between the characters, not just talking heads. By and large it seems to me that the show worked as a whole only because of the way the relationships between the characters themselves worked—incidentals, villains, whatever. . . .

Olbrich: . . . I remember a lot of the characters, and the episodes.

Wildey: But they don't mean much if they are not put together in the context of a show, which they haven't been at all in the shows I've worked on recently. The last two shows I've been responsible for are *Godzilla* and *Jana of the Jungle*. There wasn't enough attention given to the writers. I did some rewriting myself on occasion, to keep the things alive, but they didn't have the same kind of . . . *integrity*, I guess you would call it, writing integrity that *Jonny Quest* did—I guess because *Jonny Quest* was the first show of its type on network: the first animated adventure show.

Shows like this, when they're listed in *TV Guide* or written up in newspaper articles, are simply called cartoons, but I don't call them that. The pure cartoons, which everybody loves, the old Bugs Bunny and Sylvester cartoons, were masterpieces of their type. They were pure cartoons. I don't like to put the two together.

Which we did in *Jonny Quest*, actually, because Bandit was a cartoon dog. A guy named Dick Bickenbach designed the dog. Prior to the designing of the dog, Joe Barbera and I had talked about a pet for Jonny, and somehow a dog didn't seem all that adventurous to me. I happen to like dog shows, *Lassie* and whatever, but they'd pretty much been done. *Lassie* had been a TV show and a series of movies. I believe Bandit was a suggestion on the part of a toy manufacturer to get a saleable stuffed toy. Because I had designed a whole gang of other pets for Jonny.

Olbrich: Other than dogs.

Wildey: I had a small white cheetah and a monkey. Of course, I liked the idea of the monkey, only because of the story possibilities—what a monkey could do that a dog couldn't do, realistically. I thought that would work a little better. But the dog is the thing we went with. Bickenbach did a nice job, but he was a *Flintstones*-type of designer. Somehow the dog worked, though I thought it was probably the weakest part of the show from that standpoint. . . .

And Hadji. We worked it out, not all that cleverly, that Hadji was supposed to be a child of the street in India, and [that] he saved Race's life from an assassin, who threw a knife at him. Then Hadji, the poor child of the street, was picked up and adopted by our group, [and] became part of the cast. People later have asked, if he was a child of the street, where did he get all this magic knowledge and all these nice suits? I pass . . . I don't know.

I've got pictures here of Hadji, the child of the street, in a turban and a loin cloth, which is nice if you are in your own environment, but somehow, I couldn't see him traveling around with this group with just his loin cloth. It just didn't work. It was one of those things where you figure no matter what kind of cartoon or animated show this is it simply won't wash, so I simply re-costumed him.

I wanted a minority character who would work other than just a black kid from the ghetto, which was the usual thing. Which brings us to the other thing: through the years, I've gone to the networks or production studios with various show ideas.

I had one with an Indian kid and an eagle, which was a period piece where this Indian kid worked with the US cavalry. It would have been kind of a showy thing and a little tough to make. But the idea was [that] the kid would hold the bow, hold onto the bowstrings, and the eagle would grab the bow and fly the kid from place to place. It was a little kid [*laughs*] and not too heavy. But it was a big eagle [*laughs*].

Anyway, the phrase that stands out in my mind from the network people that I talked to was, flat, "Indians don't go!" Period. I translated this to mean that there is not that much interest in Indians—which to me is a complete surprise because I thought regardless of what the character was, if the character did interesting things, that would do it. But the word was "Indians don't go," so the show never got anyplace. It was called "Little Bow," and he had contact with bears and outlaws and the whole schtick.

And based on that, I guess there were some objections to Hadji. I had heard this, but I couldn't pin it down as to who said what or how official it was. But I felt there was enough disparity between these two kids, who were roughly the same age—rather than have two twins or two kids who came from the same lifestyle.

I figured Hadji would work better. The magic he could perform, I believe, was a little overdone. I did a bunch of promotional stuff on Hadji, once I had the character incorporated into the cast. Then we did the old rope trick where he climbed up the rope. The cobras. That stuff I figured, okay, I'll go that far. I let him crawl up a rope no one is holding. However, it went a little too far with the disappearing act that was in show two or three, with the mummy, where he jumps from one water jug to another. Which we later saw in Mr. Spielberg's film, *Raiders of the Lost Ark*. We also saw the snake pit in *Raiders*. Maybe that's why I liked that picture so much—I was saying, "Boy what great writing . . . wait a minute, *I* wrote that."

Olbrich: Spielberg's the right age to have been heavily influenced by *Jonny Quest*.

Wildey: And also Mr. Lucas. In fact, when this article comes out, I'd like to send a copy to each of these guys.

The serial thing—I was always hooked on serials when I was a kid going to black and white movies in the local theater. For fifteen cents, you would see two features, a trailer, and a serial. I tried to incorporate the serial approach to *Jonny Quest* in that, yes, it was bigger than life, yes, it can't actually happen, but if it's done properly, you'll believe it. That was the philosophy behind it. There is a line that I never like to go beyond, because it goes from semibelievable high-adventure to straight-out garbage. When scripts would come in, I would read the material. There were things I would simply cross out, when the writer had overstepped the bounds. The first writers were cartoon writers, and at the beginning, nobody in the studio—the writers or the animators or the layout people, none of them—understood exactly how this show was to be projected. Later, they got some heavyweight writers that came in out of live action and novels, and they understood it, so it wasn't quite as tough.

Olbrich: Who was doing the writing? You had control over script approval.

Wildey: I hesitate to use the word "control." If there was a script that came in that I didn't like, I would make it known, and it would be changed. In that way I had control. However, in many instances, myself and Barbera, or Barbera and the writer, would work together and one way or another, it would be straightened out. At which point, if I had a storyboard that I felt could be jazzed up from a visual standpoint and still keep the flavor of the writing, I would do it—there was also some control there.

When a situation happened in the show, I would simply, as I did with a comic strip or a comic book or whatever, sit back for a moment and say, "Am I going to buy this thing?" And if I don't buy it, that's it. I think in today's Saturday morning television, no one cares whether or not an audience has any particular intelligence. I had a horror of an eight-year-old kid sitting in front of *Jonny Quest* and going, "Gee, that's terrible." . . .

The other thing was that early in the game, after *Jonny Quest* was sold, they had a problem getting sponsors.

Olbrich: Why?

Wildey: It was brand-new and had never been tried. It was not *The Flintstones*; it was not anything that anyone had ever seen before. At that time, sponsors were not exactly lined up, knocking on the door. As a matter of fact, [the] show went on the air with two or three sustaining sponsors for three or four weeks.

Olbrich: Do you remember who those sponsors were?

Wildey: I can remember some of them. Skippy Peanut Butter, various toothpastes, the brand of which I forget. I was told they were having trouble getting sponsors, which is not exactly a hilarious way to get a show off the ground. I think it strengthened in its eighth or tenth week. The show had a reasonably good appeal. . . .

What I wanted was a moving comic strip, with the blacks and the shadows. If you look at the show, you can see certain parts where I got mixed up working with the animators. But when you get a whole studio full of people working on a show—Hanna-Barbera had two shows on the air, *The Flintstones* and *Jonny Quest*—and with a huge studio and a whole gang of people working on it, there is no way you can control everything. Things just slip on by.

When I did the pilot film to sell the show, I'd written the sequence and set it up dramatically and even indicated where I wanted the music. At that point I had the best animator in Hollywood, a guy named Irv Spence, and in that sequence the shadows were carried through. Later, of course, in some cases they were added, and in some cases they were dropped.

Olbrich: How was the writing on *Jonny Quest* assigned?

Wildey: Joe Barbera was basically the guy who contacted the writers, talked to them about the show, gave them the flavor, gave them my drawings. And in many cases, I'd work up characters for every show and give them to the actors.

Olbrich: So they could see what the characters looked like.

Wildey: Yeah. Voice actors are incredible. I never had a problem working with an actor. . . .

Olbrich: Seems to me that I remember as a child that Race's voice seemed to pop up in a lot of other cartoons at the time.

Wildey: As a matter of fact, he also popped up in *Jonny Quest* as other voices. In most cases on an animated show, we take what was called a multiple voice actor. "Multiple," meaning [that] under the union rules, one actor could give you three voices for whatever the agreed-upon, going rate is for actors for a day. Theoretically, when you get an actor, you can get his body in the studio for recording for eight hours. Which of course is ridiculous, because you can get the whole show recorded in an hour, with lots of people working. But the theory is, you can actually have them there for eight hours, and you can get three voices from them.

When a script comes in, the writer has somebody in a crowd someplace saying, "Hey, look at that." As a producer, I always have the choice: Do I need this line? Because if I do, I'll either go in and do it myself or I will then pay an actor double rates to say one line. In most cases the line isn't needed. . . .

I'll tell ya something that hasn't been said before. Screen Gems backed this series. They were a partner with Hanna-Barbera financially. I didn't know they were going to get into it creatively, but once the deal was set, a guy came over from Screen Gems and proceeded to tell me his idea of how *Jonny Quest* was going to work. I'm not sure whether this was a suggestion or an order or whatever, but I just simply flipped out. I could not believe it, after all this work had gone into it. This guy had ideas like: "Okay, they're trapped down in this hole, see. It's a hundred feet deep." I was following him, so far: place your character in jeopardy and get him out. This guy says, "Jonny reaches in his pocket and takes out this little ladder, see, and unreels it and they all run up the ladder" [*laughs*]. Then he says, "By the way, I like the name 'Race' but I don't like 'Quest.' Let's call the show 'Race Chase.'" I just couldn't believe it. Barbera's in the office, and I used every four-letter word that I ever thought possible about his ideas. I figured this is about the time I'm gonna get canned. Anyway, somehow it worked out.

Olbrich: Screen Gems eventually backed off, or this guy came around . . . ?

Wildey: I don't recall, exactly. Somehow this meeting, if you can call it that, ended. I don't believe anybody ever mentioned this again. I'm sure I didn't bring it up. . . . At that time, by the way, John Kennedy was assassinated—as the show goes into New York, selling the show and working out the contracts and whatnot. So there was a couple of weeks hold up before we really got back on track again.

I pulled "Quest" out of the LA phone book. And Joe contributed "Jonny," without the "h"—in other words, Jonathan. I liked that. It worked well in the title: the letters kind of came together. And that was acceptable to all hands.

The monsters that were appearing in the show were largely, at the beginning, due to me thinking, "Well, maybe we can pump this thing up." And monsters are okay, but I still wanted monsters that had some sort of Machiavellian hand behind them, or somewhere there's a greater gain on the part of the villain. The Dr. Zin thing was always kind of a cheap shot, in a way, because comic books for thousands of centuries had the mad guy that wants to control the world. Yet, it's still not all that totally unbelievable to me, even now. Because there are still people out there someplace that want to do that. So I felt, okay, it's a little weak but I think by and large it oughta play if we don't milk it to death.

I felt we did that with the dog. We milked the dog too much. Once you use an easy ploy, one writer sees the other writer's stuff and says, "He did it. Why can't I do it?" And then you'd get innumerable scripts where the dog gets into trouble, the kid tries to save the dog, and we're back on the same number again. So, I would put in monsters there, and then I realized we were getting awfully heavy on monsters. We can't make each show nothing but a monster. I wanted a little love interest, so I finally got Race to kiss the girl in one. I liked that one, too, because the animator came down and said, "I'm not sure how we're going to do this" [*laughs*]. So I made the drawings.

Olbrich: With Hanna-Barbera doing two shows that were so different in style, what was it like working with the animators? There had to have been some carry-over—[some] guys had to be working on more than one show.

Wildey: As I said, that was the tough part in the beginning. It was not only with the animation—it was also with the music, and it was with the writing. Everything had to be coordinated. We would get a script in where the writer, who had written many live-actions, now thinks he's writing for a cartoon studio. So he changes his style of writing. One guy came in with a sequence with Jonny Quest and his jet-powered swim fins [*laughs*]. I looked at it and he says, "Well, isn't that the type of thing you're doing? You went into this thing with the hovercraft . . ." I said "Yes, but jet-powered swim fins are beyond the line. It's unacceptable. You can't do that." I took the guy's idea and incorporated it into hydrofoil water skis. I'm not sure whether or not it would work, but somehow, to me, it was believable, whereas jet-powered swim fins were not. It's that line where you say no. . . .

So I lived in fear of scripts—once the show starts and the machine starts running, oh, that stuff piles up. And everybody's hurrying. You've gotta make airdates and the pressure's on. A couple of these scripts I'm not gonna see, and they're gonna go through, and boy are we gonna be in *trouble*. Because I've got a whole realistic adventure attitude. And all of a sudden in comes something that's incongruous. Again, back to my eight-year-old kid sitting there, and the kid says, "Bullshit," and tunes in to an *I Love Lucy* rerun. . . .

Olbrich: On *Quest*, the Bandit sequences often seemed to have been done separately from the rest of the show.

Wildey: One thing I stress highly when I'm working with board people, people who do [story]boards with me, is that it's an acceptably contrived motion picture illusion to do things in cutaways. Therefore, in the Bandit sequences, as much as possible, after a quick shot of Bandit in the group, in someone's arms or in his pocket, I would then cut away to a line of dialogue said by someone else, and then when we got back to Bandit, Bandit was no longer with the group, he was by himself. The Bandit stuff was shot separately.

I can give you a scene in a show, my favorite show, "Shadow of the Condor." Bandit's running along in this courtyard, and the condor swoops down and picks him up and drops him into a pond. This is easily handled by the cartoon guys, the guys who can draw funny dogs, because it's Bandit, he's in motion, and there's no one else in the scene. If any so-called "funny dog"–type artist had trouble with the condor, then one of the layout artists, who can draw realistically, would work on that condor; we could bring him down [and shoot] on a vertical panel, and the dog would take care of itself.

I was working on titles that I wanted to use as main titles, and one thing and another happened—various pressures from all sides, long hours, and the thing just fell through. So I guess the animation department selected stock animation and included them in those titles—where they're riding the plane and Jonny turns his head and the dog turns his head and someone else does something else—which I didn't like at all. That was stock at the time, and they used it. I didn't care for that. But it was a title, it was put together, it was there, and they used it. Now, the end titles, which were taken out of the *Jack Armstrong* footage we had, seemed okay; it seemed a little more in line with adventure thinking, let's say, than the other. But Bandit was included, by the way; in those titles, he was on somebody's lap.

Olbrich: I think he was just sitting there, looking out the window.

Wildey: Yeah. It would work. It didn't work all that well, but I'd use a cutaway at all times.

The realistic stuff was a little tougher, even when Irv started on the thing. The sequence on the Sargasso Sea, as they rose up out of the water, I noticed that the heads were too big, almost like *Flintstones* things. So I said, "Look, Irv"—I drew the water line, and then drew the rest of the bodies to fit the heads that he had animated, and then it worked. It just gets real tough to explain in the beginning. . . .

These guys were used to drawing cartoon-type characters, and they'd come in and they were at a loss. They couldn't handle adventure stuff. Boy, did I get calls at night! From guys who somehow thought that they were failures, simply because they couldn't handle something like this. Which of course was crazy . . . but these guys would keep saying, "I'm not really that much up on anatomy. I haven't had anatomy in quite a while. I can't seem to handle . . . I mean, the artwork doesn't look right." I'd look at it and say, "Yeah, it sure doesn't look right. It doesn't work." In the beginning, I was the only straight man in the entire organization that could draw a reasonably decent-looking human figure. Then, as we added to them, the heavy hitters came in . . .

Olbrich: Warren [Tufts] and Alex [Toth] . . .

Wildey: Warren and Alex, people of their stripe, there was no problem. You could get a group scene of seven people sitting around an office at an angle, with props and the whole thing, and it would work out beautifully.

Hanna-Barbera and Taft Broadcasting

LAWRENCE H. ROGERS II / 2000

Edited from *History of U.S. Television: A Personal Reminiscence* (Bloomington, IN: 1st Books Library, 2000), 443–47, 449–55, 459–64. Reprinted with permission of the Rogers family.

ACQUISITION OF HANNA-BARBERA

Having completed the contract for the acquisition of Transcontinent Television Corporation in the third quarter of 1963, the FCC acted with astonishing promptness by granting the transfer of all the licenses early in 1964.

About a year after this enormous increase in the size of Taft Broadcasting Company (net stockholders' equity just about doubled with the Transcontinent purchase), Lloyd Taft came up with another candidate for acquisition: the Hanna-Barbera cartoon studio in Hollywood. Operated by its two founders, William Hanna and Joseph Barbera, it had already achieved fame in the world of TV by producing the first-ever prime time cartoon series on one of the networks: ABC-TV's *The Flintstones*. . . .

By 1965, Hanna and Barbera were sufficiently well-known in their own right that they decided to try to raise working capital with a public stock issue. Their business agent at A. Morgan Maree Company, Jess S. Morgan, took their notion to Wall Street, where he ended up in the offices of Carl M. Loeb–Rhoades & Company. There Lloyd Taft, with one eye on his own huge stake in Taft Broadcasting Company, suggested to Morgan that perhaps a private sale to Taft would be more advantageous to his clients than a public stock issue. So the negotiations began.

[Taft Broadcasting president and chairman] Hub Taft was rather lukewarm to the idea of the Hanna-Barbera acquisition, but I [president and chief operating officer Lawrence Rogers II] was agog with enthusiasm. We would not be allowed by the FCC to have any more TV stations, except by upgrading our existing seven markets, but the FCC had recently made that nearly impossible by requiring that a licensee sell a station before replacing it. In almost all major market situations, we thought that would be entirely too risky.

But the future of TV programming I believed to be virtually limitless; and the idea of programs that would last forever was even more appealing. It was immediately apparent to me that no matter how often these cartoon series were run, there would be a whole new set of viewers every few years as new children came along. And, it seemed to me, the sale of world-wide licensing and merchandising rights would be a potential revenue bonanza to boggle the mind.

But nothing is ever simple, and this turned into a veritable snake pit. Harry Cohn had died and his wife Joan claimed that she and her two sons owned something like 18 percent of Hanna-Barbera Productions, and that therefore Bill and Joe couldn't sell without the Cohns' participation. This resulted in threatened litigation, and the ensuing wrangle took over a year to straighten out.

Finally, in December 1966, Taft acquired all the stock of Hanna-Barbera Productions, Inc., including its real estate, studios and offices, and the ten-year production output of the studio, for $12 million in Taft Broadcasting Company stock. The management would continue to be in the hands of the company's founders, William D. Hanna and Joseph R. Barbera. . . .

But shortly after Hanna-Barbera became part of the Taft Broadcasting Group, Wall Street expressed its displeasure by severely depressing the price of Taft stock.

Hub Taft and I had already made several appearances before the New York Society of Security Analysts, as well as various private banking houses, such as Jerry Tsai's. We were mystified as to why our stock was being savaged by the Street, so I called and asked for a date to address the analysts again.

We quickly got to the bottom of the analysts' disenchantment with Taft. No sooner had my short, prepared address on the glorious future of Hanna-Barbera come to an end, when one of these fellows—it was doubtless Harvey Sandler, the brilliant young analyst of Goldman Sachs—asked me a question.

"Bud, when you made this deal to buy Hanna-Barbera, didn't you guys know you don't own any of the distribution rights to any of the shows? They're all under exclusive distribution contracts to Screen Gems; and Screen Gems also has all the licensing and merchandising rights as well!

"So it seems to us you fellows bought a company that can't make you any profit, because there isn't any profit in making shows and selling them to the networks. All the profits are in syndicated distribution and licensing, and you don't even own any of those rights!"

Well, Harvey was right. Screen Gems owned all the rights. But not in perpetuity. The calming down process got under way when I explained that of course we knew about the Screen Gems contracts. That was the very reason we were able to buy the whole kit and kaboodle for such a ridiculously low price as $12 million. But what we were counting on was that the contracts, all of which were of seven years' duration, on all ten years' worth of production, would begin expiring by the end of 1967. At that time, it was our plan to initiate our own in-house Hanna-Barbera distribution company. By the time the last seven-year contract with Screen Gems had expired, we would have recaptured everything the studio had ever produced, which would by that time be eighteen years' worth.

There were still many unanswered questions: where were we going to find the people to do the sales and distribution; how were we going to finance new production; what would we do about competing with Screen Gems on the packages they still had under contract; and on and on?

"These are all minor details," I assured them, and we left on a much more positive note than when we arrived. But some damage had been done to our credibility in the marketplace that would take a number of years to overcome....

[A] festival atmosphere prevailed when we flew to Los Angeles in the summer of 1967 for our first Hanna-Barbera board of directors meeting. Hub Taft became chairman, I was vice-chairman, and Joe Barbera and Bill Hanna traded off being president every other year. To give us a numerical quorum on the Hanna-Barbera board from the home office, to the Cincinnati contingent we added the head of our FM stations division, John T. Lawrence Jr., and the corporate secretary, Charles S. Mechem Jr., who had replaced Bob Taft when he got himself elected to Congress. The seventh member of the board was the resident business manager, Jess Morgan.

To add to the merriment of the occasion, this first board meeting was held on the fantail of Bill Hanna's yacht: a commodious sixty-three-foot trawler, which Bill had helped build himself, with Finnish shipwrights, at a yard in Santa Barbara. It was a swell craft, fully equipped for Pacific Ocean cruising and very comfortable.

However, all the jollity went out of the occasion when we got a look at the first quarter results of Taft's new wholly owned subsidiary. Hub Taft very nearly jumped overboard when he discovered that our new pride and joy had actually lost a couple of hundred thousand dollars during our first three months of ownership! It became immediately apparent that these near geniuses, who had the best-selling animation programs in all television, were purely and simply artists of great talent, with no conception whatsoever of how to run a business. The fact that they had Jess Morgan as "business manager" was a very quick clue, because Jess, an excellent fellow, was a talent agent and business advisor. He was in charge of Bill and Joe's personal investment portfolios, and I have no reason to question his abilities in that direction. He was also an impeccable gentleman of no known bad habits. But as for operating a highly labor-intensive business in a competitive snake-pit such as Hollywood, I knew from day one that Jess was a lost ball in the high weeds.

After some desultory discussion of how we might get a handle on cost control, and where we might find a day-to-day business manager who would be a true comptroller, we adjourned to admire the workings of the studio. We were spellbound by Joe Barbera's ability to dream up a scenario for a new animation series right out of thin air, and spin a yarn to go with it that made it seem already in production and ready to go on the air. It seemed to me then, and ever since, that they were a perfect pair, because he was a consummate salesman and idea generator, while Bill was quiet, reserved, and a consummate technician. Between them they could turn out anything that their fertile imaginations could dream up. And they had both come out of Wall Street banking during the Depression! [Editors' note: This was true only for Joe.]

Reflecting on this unsettling first experience on the West Coast, I suggested to Hub on the way back to Cincinnati that we send Sam Johnston to Hollywood as general manager of Hanna-Barbera, exactly as if it were one of our broadcasting properties.

He exploded.

"What the hell does Sam Johnston know about Hollywood, for Christ's sake? And what the hell do you think you know about it," he erupted all over me. "What we need is a smart business manager who knows what it costs to do what these guys do and how to do it cheaper. Then we need a sales force to go out and sell it. How the hell do you suppose a TV manager from Cincinnati can do all that in a strange town full of creeps and weirdos?"

"Sam is exactly the one to do it," I replied, convinced I was right just because of what Hub had said. "Sam has a cash register for a brain—better yet, he has a computer inside his head. He is the most meticulously cost-conscious guy in our entire broadcasting division. Witness what he has been able to do with that can of worms we turned over to him in Cincinnati!" I said, conscious that Hub was still, seven years later, smarting over his "automation" disaster.

"As for selling," I continued, "that outfit needs a sales force like it needs a hole in the head. Joe Barbera is the greatest salesman I have ever heard in my life, including Ollie Treyz. The biggest difference is that Joe is charming and a gentleman, and Ollie is a liar and a cheat."

"Yeah, but Joe doesn't think he can sell the networks and the agencies," Hub replied. "He's completely hung up on the need for agents." And future events were to prove him correct.

In any event, whether Hub liked it or not, we were in the program production and distribution business, which I was convinced would be the future profit center of the television world. But we had a long way to go to get this situation under control, and a great deal further to go before we were actually in command of our own distribution.

As for my notion of sending Sam Johnston to Hollywood, I pressed it again and again. But Hub vetoed it and said we would just have to find out what Jess Morgan could do.

"We'll wait for the next quarterly report in September," he said. And I had no choice but to go along.

THE END OF AN ERA

Come October 1968, and things had gone from bad to worse. Hanna-Barbera showed an even bigger loss in the third quarter than in the second. It was apparent now, even to Hub Taft, that Jess Morgan was totally unfit to be a business manager, let alone the CEO of an operation as complex as the Hanna-Barbera animation studio. Sales of new product not only did not reflect increased revenues, they only showed vastly increased expenses. To me the answer was obvious: Let Bill and Joe do what they know how to do better than anyone else, but let an experienced business operator hold the purse strings and enforce the budgets.

About the end of the month, Hub Taft and I repaired to the Queen City Club for a quiet lunch to discuss seriously this situation at Hanna-Barbera. For the first time since I had known him, he did not order a martini, to be followed by at least one, and usually two, more. Instead, he ordered lunch and asked for iced tea!

In a state of near shock, I did the same. "Buster," he started out, "you and I have not exactly been on the same wavelength recently. You're always up to your neck in operational matters, when I think you should be thinking more along the lines of long-range financial strategy."

"Which is precisely why I insisted on buying Hanna-Barbera in the first place," I broke in before he could continue. "The demand for programming can only explode as more and more stations come into existence, not to mention whatever new methods of transmission will come along to compete with stations.

"In my opinion, the long-range outlook for Hanna-Barbera is for profits from worldwide program distribution and character merchandising sales to be even bigger than all our TV stations put together!"

"I've heard you say that before, and I think you're nuts!" he continued. "But the important thing is right now. We've got to stop the arterial bleeding from this outfit before it does us some real damage. And I'll admit my idea of how to run the place clearly isn't working, so I'm ready to try yours.

"What makes you think Sam Johnston can do any better at running Bill and Joe at a profit than the guys already there? Jess is a recognized Hollywood agent, and his agency Morgan Maree is one of the biggest in the business. And their business manager, what's his name, Buddy Getzler? He seems savvy enough and he's been around a long time."

"Forget Buddy Getzler, Hub," I said. "If he's any good, Sam'll find out in a big hurry and keep him. If not, he'll replace him. What we have to do is get Jess Morgan the hell out of there because he simply doesn't know the first thing about running a business. He is, as you already said, an agent, which means he gets paid a percentage of what other people earn. But that does not qualify him to make business judgments. I don't deny Jess is a nice fellow; a gentleman, if you will. But what we need is a tough son-of-a-bitch who controls the purse strings and calls the shots."

"And why is Sam, that tough son-of-a-bitch, in a business he doesn't know anything about either?" Hub replied.

"Because he has already proved it," was my response. "When I put him in charge of WTVN-TV, he had never seen the inside of a TV station; but he had already made TVN-Radio our most profitable radio station. Then, when I turned over that disaster at WKRC-TV to him, it took him less than a year to make it the most profitable station in the market.

"Hub, it's simple: Sam merely knows that the way you run a business is you spend less money than you take in. In Hollywood nobody gives a good goddamn. They spend money like drunken sailors because it's always somebody else's money and there's nobody to say 'No!' If I ask Sam to take this on, he will stop the bleeding at once. Then he will learn where the bodies are buried, what are the ropes to pull, and which of the projects that Bill and Joe bring up are most likely to be productive. I am not at all intimidated by the prospect of deciding what the studio should or should not undertake on our money; and I don't think Sam will be either. But it's a damn cinch nobody is making those judgments now because Jess Morgan is unqualified, Buddy Getzler has no authority, and Bill Hanna and Joe Barbera are artists. They need our help, and Sam is my choice to give it to them."

"Okay, buster, you win," said Hub, obviously anxious to get away from a table with nothing stronger on it than iced tea. "My system didn't work, so let's try yours. How do you want to do it?"

"I have an Association of Maximum Service Telecasters (AMST) board meeting at the Arizona Biltmore the week after next. Why don't I fly from Phoenix to Hollywood, have dinner with Joe and Bill, and tell them that they are going to have a new boss? Sam's job as VP and general manager of H-B Productions will really be that of CEO, but neither Bill nor Joe is interested in that sort of nitty-gritty. What they want is to make programs that will sell and make us all money. What I will tell them is that Sam's job will be to see that they have all the help they need to get that done. We get along very well, personally. and I don't think there will be any problem at all with the transition."

With that, we shook hands on the deal and Hub ended the conversation with, "Well, buster, you'd better be right!"

Less than two weeks later, I was just finishing the front nine on the Arizona Biltmore golf course, when the assistant pro arrived at the green in a golf cart and said that Mr. Rogers's presence was required at the pro shop for an urgent phone call.

In less time than it takes to tell it, the bottom fell out of my world.

It was John McClay on the other end with the laconic message: "Hub Taft was killed this morning in an accidental explosion at his home. I have already undertaken to get you and [wife] Suzanne seats on American Airlines, leaving Phoenix about three o'clock this afternoon. Is there anything else you need, or anything else I can do?"

Obviously, there was nothing. . . .

HANNA-BARBERA AND THE NEW TAFT BROADCASTING

. . . Absent Hub Taft's iron rule, the board of directors took on a new life of its own and attempted to insinuate itself into operational problems. All at once, I felt as if every day I was under a microscope. The first thing the board wanted to know in intimate detail was what were we going to do about the Hanna-Barbera situation.

Not having been privy to my agreement with Hub Taft to send Sam Johnston off to clean out the Augean Stables of Hollywood, the board was reluctant to approve what they looked upon as a radical departure in an area with which they had no acquaintance whatsoever. When I said it was purely a management decision which Hub Taft and I had already made, the board asked for Charlie's opinion. Since he was very reluctant to take a position, I had to start the project off all over again.

If I have a jaundiced view of lawyers in general, it probably stems from the fact that it took me the best part of a year to convince Charlie Mechem that changing managers in Hollywood was a management prerogative, the same as changing a TV station manager in Kansas City or Buffalo, and none of the board's damn business. Finally, we went ahead and did what Hub and I had already decided to do the previous fall.

Meantime, of course, the problems had become much more severe than they were the year before. Suffice to say, when it finally did get done, Sam Johnston turned out to be just as tough and just as observant as I had known he would. He turned Hanna-Barbera around, and put it on the path to profitable operation, but in a much longer time than would have been necessary, had we not had that year's delay.

Among the things that had to be accomplished were the creation of a marketing arm to sell Hanna-Barbera's output to the networks and in syndication to as many as possible of the four hundred-odd TV stations.

As pointed out at the beginning of the Hanna-Barbera story, all of the studio's output until the purchase by Taft was under exclusive distribution contract to Columbia Pictures' TV subsidiary Screen Gems. The only product to which we had both syndication and merchandising rights were the few shows that had been sold to the networks since we had owned the studio. And that was precious few.

Fortunately, Screen Gems' exclusivity contracts were for each individual series, rather than a term of years, else we would have had hell to pay to get them back. As it was, all the contracts being for seven years, we would begin recovery with *Heckle and Jeckle* the end of this year; and it was only another three years before we would recover full rights to *The Flintstones*. [Editors' note: Columbia Pictures owned *Heckle and Jeckle*; Rogers likely instead meant *Ruff and Reddy*.]

The president of Screen Gems, John Mitchell, I had known since he was a film salesman who called on me in Huntington, West Virginia. John was a big, bluff, black-haired, handsome fellow, with whom I got along as well as with any film salesman. But they all knew I didn't trust any of them as far as I could throw them. John's salesman sold all the off-network Hanna-Barbera shows to the individual stations in syndication—and at horrendous prices that somehow were never reflected in the settlement checks when they finally reached Hanna-Barbera. It usually took them a year or more to pay up, and we all knew they were stealing us blind.

All the merchandising rights were under the control of a wiry little rascal named Eddie Justin [head of merchandising for Screen Gems], whose offices were in the Screen Gems New York headquarters on Fifth Avenue, directly across Fifty-Fifth Street from the St. Regis Hotel, where I habitually stayed when in Manhattan.

Eddie called himself "Honest Eddie," but he was a thief at heart. He did his best to make a pal of me, in order to convince me how foolish it would be to change our sales rep from Screen Gems to our own organization. He did everything he could think of to scare me into thinking we couldn't handle this mysterious market in which they were the past masters. But he did succeed in scaring the hell out of Joe Barbera, who had been convinced that no one other than Sy Fischer, Screen Gems' number one agent, could ever sell a Hanna-Barbera cartoon show to one of the network bosses.

The fact that I was on a first-name basis with all the levels of bosses at all three networks cut no ice with Joe. He was convinced that without Sy Fischer, we'd never sell another program.

I have already said that I thought Barbera was the most scintillating salesman I had ever seen, including the young Oliver Treyz. I knew we didn't even need a sales agent. Joe could do the whole job better than anyone; and getting him in to see the proper person at ABC, CBS, or NBC was about as difficult as hitting the floor with my hat. But Joe didn't know that, and when Sam Johnston and I told him we were going to replace Screen Gems with ourselves, I thought he'd have a terminal seizure. Bill Hanna was not quite hysterical, but it was obvious his confidence was shaky at best without Sy Fischer. There was no other answer. I had no other choice. Sy Fischer was Joe's security blanket, and Bill agreed with him. So I simply had to get him Sy Fischer; which meant I had to hire him away from Screen Gems and big John Mitchell.

I knew Sy, and liked him. . . . I met Sy for lunch at the King Cole Bar, and who should we see across the room but Eddie Justin. He immediately came over to make a pest of himself, and make it utterly impossible to broach the subject of our lunch meeting. We could hardly go across the street to Screen Gems, from whom I was plotting to steal Sy, so we went upstairs to my room to escape Justin.

I laid out the proposition that Sy would become vice president of sales of Hanna-Barbera Productions, and much as I would prefer he operate out of Hollywood, I would hold still for a New York office if he thought it was absolutely essential. After all, it's where virtually 100 percent of the TV network program decisions and purchases were made, as well as upwards of 90 percent of the advertiser or agency program buys.

Sy listened attentively, and made no comment other than to confirm what I suspected would be his insistence on maintaining his office in New York. So I knew I didn't have half a chance on that one. The sales office would be here in New York.

He didn't seem to bat an eye on the subject of quitting Columbia Pictures, and he was supremely confident that sales would easily justify whatever I had in mind. But when we got to the matter of compensation, Sy took my breath away.

"I'll have to have a minimum salary of $125,000," he said, very matter-of-factly, "and to insure a smooth-running office, I'll have to have my number two man at Screen Gems, Karl Honeystein."

Before I could recover enough to ask, he added: "It'll take another hundred to bring Karl over." "Ye Gods, Sy!" was my immediate reaction. "Charlie Mechem and I together don't make that much money and we're the two top officers of the parent company!

"We've got TV managers out there who make half what you're talking about and they're bringing in millions in profits while Hanna-Barbera is still in the red!"

"Well, that's not my problem, bud," he said. "I know what you're paying Bill and Joe is not in the league with those modest figures, and I just have to tell you that's what it takes in this market."

"How about a commission deal?" I tried, as if dipping my big toe in ice water.

"Oh, that's okay. I don't care how you want to do it. It's just that the figure I stated is the floor; and the same for Karl Honeystein."

"Couldn't you get a less expensive helper?"

"That's not the point. Without Karl, there can't be any deal. I'll have to stay where I am."

He didn't apologize or get up to leave, or anything. He just sat there; I knew the ball was in my court. As I reflected on the session I had had with Joe and Bill and Sam the past week, it was clear to me that there really wasn't any alternative. I had the key to what the studio needed and the artists were demanding, and Sy seemed perfectly agreeable to doing what needed to be done.

But how the hell was I going to pay for it without having my head handed to me on a platter, or having half the TV managers quit on me for discriminating against them? It was bad enough that they knew the studio was losing its ass, while they were bringing in all the bacon, without their finding out that I was giving away the company store for a couple of what they referred to as "sprocket-hole salesmen."

We sat there for what seemed an eternity, when I had an idea.

"Sy, how would you like to have your own business, with your own name on it, with an exclusive contract to represent Hanna-Barbera in markets worldwide, as well as open season to steal any other clients you can land anywhere?"

"You've got to be kidding me," Sy said, "or else you've been smoking something when I wasn't watching."

"No, I'm not kidding. I'm perfectly serious," I responded. "What I have in mind is this: we set up a new sales agency, called The Sy Fischer Agency. You are the 60 percent majority owner of it, and Taft is the 40 percent owner. We decide on a figure which represents capitalization cost, which Taft will pay. Then based on a yearly operating budget, which you will prepare, we figure out how much more capital you'll need before you become self-supporting. Taft will supply that in the form of a loan, or loans, to be repaid with interest.

"When Taft has recovered its investment, whenever that is, you will be entitled to buy back Taft's 40 percent at what we will devise as a sweetheart price.

"This way, you can pay yourself whatever you think the traffic will bear. You can hire Karl Honeystein, or whoever else you need, at whatever it takes. And I don't have to report on a Taft proxy, or a Hanna-Barbera proxy, for that matter, what your earnings are, or what you're paying your help.

"If it works, hooray! We don't give a damn what it costs. If it doesn't, then buying the studio was a disaster and we all deserve to get fired.

"Since this is your ball in your name, I'm willing to bet it will work."

It did.

The Sy Fischer Company went into business, and Hanna-Barbera took off.

Not just in the US market. Everything we had, from Yogi Bear and Fred Flintstone to the newest characters such as Scooby-Doo, were syndicated on TV in virtually every country in the world, even China and Bulgaria.

Only the USSR cheated on us. They recorded the H-B shows off the Finns' Helsinki station, then ran them on all their own stations in Leningrad, Moscow, and wherever. But they never paid a dime in royalties, because they said the Soviet Union had never recognized property rights under the International Copyright Convention!

Before I left the company about seven years later, I had told the board on several occasions that when we were in full control of all our properties, the revenues from worldwide merchandising rights and syndication of Hanna-Barbera cartoon characters would outstrip the total earnings from Taft's whole broadcasting division, including its seven TV stations.

Shortly after my departure that prediction came true.

It'll Cost $40 to $50 a Day to Enjoy Area's New Park

GEORGE PALMER / 1969

From *Cincinnati Enquirer*, May 31, 1969, 9. Copyright © Cincinnati Enquirer–USA TODAY NETWORK. Reprinted with permission.

The tab will be "$40 to $50" a day for a family outing at Greater Cincinnati's new planned amusement park, where "swinging, top 40, wholesome entertainment" will be the theme.

The 1,200-acre amusement park and recreation area is still a couple of years away—"1971 or 1972"—and will be located near Kings Mills, Warren County. That's about twenty miles northeast of Cincinnati, along I-71 [Interstate 71].

The park will be built by the Taft Broadcasting Co., and operated by the Coney Island management here. Taft announced in April that the firm had reached a preliminary agreement to purchase Coney for $6.5 million in Taft common stock.

Hanna-Barbera, a totally owned Taft subsidiary operating out of Hollywood, would move in as the creative developers. Bill Hanna and Joe Barbera were in Cincinnati last week to have a look at Coney.

In December 1966, Taft bought 100 percent of Hanna-Barbera—lock, stock, barrel, and Flintstones. It cost a pretty penny. About $12 million.

Hanna and Barbera are the personification of humility. They are obviously immune to their own greatness as creators of popular TV fare.

"Everything we've done for the past twenty-odd years has been for family entertainment," Barbera said, "so we'll try to direct all our creative thinking to that direction—working, of course, with the Coney Island people, who are very familiar with the management and operation of a park."

Lawrence H. Rogers II, president of Taft, justified the multimillion Hanna-Barbera purchase in stating, "Our first diversification was from straight broadcasting into the creation of a product, or program production, for broadcasting in the future.

"And it's a very natural tie-in, to reach the public by direct confrontation (the new planned park), rather than through broadcasting. Everything that we create to put on radio or TV has an application to a family amusement park.

"So that we don't think there is any real diversification—it's merely an expansion in the field of leisure time activity—[the park] will be adjunctive to our broadcast activities, and complementary to them," Rogers said.

There was an indication at the press luncheon that there will be no war rides in the new amusement park. It was equally apparent that some of the famous Hanna-Barbera characters will make up much of the motif, or decorations, in the park.

And that amounts to a wealth of characters for the motif—the Flintstones, Ruff and Reddy, Huckleberry Hound, Quick Draw McGraw, the Jetsons, Top Cat, Space Ghost, Jonny Quest, Lippy the Lion, Wally Gator, Atom Ant, and on and on and on. All were TV hits, to a greater or lesser degree.

"Joe and I first joined forces in 1939," Hanna said, "and produced the first Tom and Jerry [cartoon] for MGM. I think we spent the next twenty years of our lives at MGM, producing the Tom and Jerry series."

Tom, a cat, and Jerry, a mouse, wowed movie theater audiences all those years.

"We started Hanna-Barbera in July 1957," Barbera said. "You see, Tom and Jerry had won [seven] Academy Awards, in theater only. Then we moved into TV. Our first was a series called *Ruff and Reddy*, for NBC.

"We created *The Flintstones* in 1960," he said. "They're still running in eighty countries."

Bill and Joe had somewhat mundane backgrounds for their eventual success as cartoon-makers. Hanna is the story man, Barbera the cartoon man.

"My studies in school had to do with the field of engineering—as a structural engineer," Hanna said in Cincinnati. "I moved from that into the cartoon field as a writer in 1930. Before I met Joe in 1937, when he came to Hollywood, I was with the Looney Toon–Merrie Melody operation."

"I was in the banking business, originally," Barbera said. "With the Irving Trust Co., on Wall Street. I never really belonged there, I can tell you. I was free-lancing cartoons for magazines—the *New Yorker*, the *Saturday Evening Post*, for example—while I earned a living at the bank."

Noting that the H-B combo has had as many as seventeen half-hour shows running at one time, Barbera said, "We're not going to ease out of TV by this union with Taft in the amusement park idea.

"In fact, in our plans with Taft, we'd like to double the production, going into every phase of TV," he said.

Asked why the highly successful H-B operation sold out totally to Taft, Barbera said, "Today's strategy seems to be to pick up capital gains, then continue. But we made the sale for further expansion."

Rogers denied that Taft is a holding company, declaring that's "the last thing Taft is. We're an operating company. We're dedicated against becoming a holding company, or a conglomerate."

He noted that Taft has recently acquired Fuad Said Productions, developed by a "young, thirty-six-year-old Egyptian fellow, who graduated in cinematography from UCLA.

"We feel this acquisition will importantly contribute to the new era of the manufacture of theatrical motion pictures," he said. "Said invented a method of cramming all the gear it takes to make a movie into one self-contained mobile unit that supplies its own power and contains all its own equipment.

"This supplies the live-action capability to make any kind of television show or movie, over and above Hanna-Barbera's capability as an animation studio," Rogers said.

"We've added Said's techniques to Hanna-Barbera's. We've added Said to this mix in order to be instantly in a position to have a complete capability to do live-action filming anywhere in the world.

"Said started for TV, but his technique will make its major expansion area in theatrical pictures," the executive said.

Rogers, Hanna, and Barbera commented on the establishing of a new amusement park in an age of unrest among young people, whose interests seem far afield from those of their elders.

"I think we have an element now that does not conform to the accepted norm," Hanna said. "I think they are a minority, and they are nothing new.

"I think we have had this historically, not only in our country but also throughout the world. I think today we may have a phase that may be a little more than the average, but I don't think it is any worse than it has been."

Hanna said, "I think a wholesome park will attract both elements of society. We feel the park will attract the twenty-five-year-olds and younger because we will have built into sections of the park those elements which will play to that age bracket."

"If you want a pretty good yardstick as to the success of today's paying attractions," Rogers said, "*2001* and *Romeo and Juliet* are the top attractions today in movie theaters, closely followed by *Funny Girl* and *Bullitt*.

"If you look at the dollar returns on things like *Hair* and *I Am Curious (Yellow)* that get all the headlines—there just aren't that many people who show up . . . and pay their dollars to get into them," he said.

"The overwhelming bulk of people want wholesome family entertainment. Walt Disney has proved this, generation after generation," Rogers said.

"*2001* represents today's interest in astronauts—reaching for new goals, not dirty goals," he added.

Barbera said, "I would say our new park relates to the times in that kids today are still going out to see what we would call clean entertainment. They don't all have long hair and go barefooted.

"Millions of young people go to Disneyland today, and are hearing the swing music and the top 40 sound and the latest groups," he said, "and they don't necessarily go into the park to start fires and create problems.

"We're going to be as updated as we can be, in doing the park. We don't want to say we're going back to a nostalgic, old-time type of entertainment," he said. "This is going to be today, and swinging, and it's going to be attractive to everybody. 'Going back' are two words we're not using."

"The park will be an enormous contribution to the economic development of the whole area," Rogers commented. "And to social development. I wouldn't say we're going to bring back a wholesome society, because I don't agree we've lost a wholesome society."

"If we do this park right," Hanna added, "I think you will see the people there who are now running around acting weird."

Rogers noted that the new park, which does not yet have a name, will not replace Coney Island, which will remain as is in most aspects. [Editors' note: The park would be called Kings Island.] He noted that the giant Sunlight Pool could not be moved feasibly, for instance.

Commenting on the cost of family entertaining today, Rogers said, "I can tell you that on the basis of the experience of the existing great parks, which include Coney Island, Disneyland, and Six Flags Over Texas, that an average family now approaches the $40 to $50 area for the day."

The Improbable World of Hanna-Barbera

BILL HANNA AND JOE BARBERA / 1967

From *The Hanna-Barbera Exposure Sheet* 1, no. 1, July 1967, 8. All Hanna-Barbera characters and elements © & ™ Hanna-Barbera. (s20). Reprinted with permission of Warner Bros. Consumer Products, Inc.

During our thirty-year partnership, which began in 1937 at Metro-Goldwyn-Mayer with the Tom and Jerry series, we have made hound dogs sing, bears play pinochle, alley cats graduate from drama school, and prehistoric man live again in Fred Flintstone and his rock-headed pals.

Out of our inkpots have been born more than one thousand characters. Some have had "walk-on" parts; others in the two-dimensional world of length and width which exists on the drawing board have become stars. The percentage is better for the cartoon folk than for real life actors and actresses—ninety of the characters from the inkpots have captured top billing in some twenty-seven series.

And for the 1967 season alone, we developed twenty-nine new cartoon stars and costars. These creations for the ever-never land of the home screen will appear in seven new shows.

Over the years, as we created our animated menagerie, we have discovered that the quest for the impossible and improbable often results in fantastic situations for the cartoonist. To continually amuse and intrigue youngsters, we've had to develop fresh characters and series.

Tasks such as this would fluster a single producer of live-action entertainment, but in the world of animation, limitations of space and time are nonexistent. Our preoccupation—or shall we say occupation—with fantasy allows us to people the world with talking dogs, chattering bears, voluble ducks, and superhumans.

FUN AND FRUSTRATIONS

And believe us, along with our creative staff, we've had our share of fun and frustrations coming up with the Yogi Bears, the Fred Flintstones, and the Huckleberry Hounds.

Shortly after the incorporation of Hanna-Barbera Productions in 1957, we had an idea for a series about a boastful bear. We had more than one hundred possible names for our unborn hero, running from Abby Bear to Zippy Bear. Someplace in the middle of the list was Huckleberry Bear. Then toward the end was Willy Bear, Yocca Bear, and finally, Yogi Bear.

Everybody liked our creation except the sponsor. He contended that Yogi might be confused with a couple of other popular characters, such as one being used to fight forest fires.

The lead went to a lovable, lethargic little hound dog named Huckleberry Hound. Yogi Bear was given featured billing. And by the way, Yogi's name had nothing to do with the major league catcher. The combination just sounded right.

After two seasons of *The Huckleberry Hound Show*, we suspected that Yogi was at least as popular as the hound. When the sponsor decided that he wanted another animated show, there was little question that Yogi would be its star, one of the few instances in TV in which a supporting player was promoted to a lead.

Personally, we liked Yogi. And it was a pleasure to give his budding career a boost.

When viewing the antics of a warmhearted guy such as Mr. Bear, or with any of our stable of ink and paint stars, the audience can always expect the unexpected. We can sketch Yogi being chased by a mad hunter over, under, and through pine trees. The hunter can fill Yogi's furry hide with enough buckshot to sink a battleship, but our hero always flips around, and once the black smoke clears, laughs in the hunter's face.

NEW HEROES

Among our new heroes of the 1967–68 season will be Atom Ant, who is the mascot for the nuclear-powered aircraft carrier USS *Enterprise*. He is a tiny fellow with the strength of an atom bomb and defeats the biggest villains with indefatigable ease.

We also have a super sleuth, Secret Squirrel, who encounters tougher situations than the average 007 agent. SS and his faithful assistant, Morocco Mole, foil the forces of evil in what can only be termed satire-fantasy on the world's secret agents. [Editors' note: Atom Ant and Secret Squirrel debuted together in the 1965–66 season.]

Our stories travel in either direction in history. A typical cartoon opening from *The Huckleberry Hound Show* might begin with the narrator saying, "Throughout the ages, lone men have appeared to protect the innocent. Brave men like the Green Gadfly, the Blue Crusader, and the Scarlet Pumpernickel...."

Then we would have Huck appear in an outrageous scarlet costume.

The narrator continues: "Scarlet Pumpernickel, how do you keep your identity a secret?"

"I do my own laundry," Huck replies.

"And how does that help?"

"Man, you bring in scarlet laundry long enough, and people are going to start talking." The result is a satire on all of the fanciful adventures of swashbuckling fiction.

PHILOSOPHY OF WARMTH

If there is an underlying philosophy about our cartoons, it is to project warmth and good feeling. We spoof lots of things—Hollywood, cars, television, and even our own animated commercials. However, we don't see anything funny in violence or sin. Even our villains are nice guys.

We have never attempted to educate youngsters nor preach to them. We have just tried to entertain.

To accomplish that, we have needed and continued to need all the talent and instinct of creative people around Hollywood. Today's children are far more sophisticated than the generations of twenty or thirty years ago. Kids don't go for the too-sweet, too-cute, too-soft approach as they used to.

Developing story lines often has us following rather odd hours and procedures. When the ideas seem to lack their usual warmth and feeling, we know we are entering a danger period. To discover fresh material, we sometimes find it necessary to leave the studio behind, even to forget it exists for a couple of hours, and relax in the world of reality.

WRITERS AND IDEAS

Many an evening when our studio was very small, we would take our writing staff out to a restaurant on the Sunset Strip. After dinner, we wander into a couple of the clubs, listen to some music and to the conversations around us.

About midnight we returned to the studio and held a story conference on the floor of one of our offices. These meetings, which can become a little wild, often continued until dawn.

We fired ideas at each other, then react.

"What kind of piano would a Stone Age man play? What kind of environment will our new gorilla character best be placed—a pet shop? household? or a jungle?"

Everybody had a turn. The results were usually a composite of three or four ideas from which we made a selection.

If anyone happened past our offices during those midnight meetings, seeing grown men on the carpeted floor, laughing at their own goofy jokes and ideas, they would think Hanna-Barbera was populated with lunatics.

However, it all worked.

The love for fantasy has no age. Everyone would like to fly, to travel back in time, to defeat a bully twice his size, or take everything in stride without temper or panic like Yogi Bear.

One part of Hanna-Barbera's personal story is the personalities of our cartoonists. They are adults who never grow old.

Last week one of our writers created a particularly mean villain. This bad guy was so terrible—a mean-looking, fat, grumpy, old bulldog with a big black, waxed moustache—we called the writer in to ask him where he had gotten the idea.

He admitted he once had a teacher in grade school whose appearance and nature fitted that bulldog.

We often wonder where the thin line between real and unreal is drawn, and by whom. . . .

The Purveyor of Saturday's Fare

JOHN STANLEY / 1968

From the *San Francisco Examiner*, April 14, 1968, datebook section, 12. Reprinted with permission.

"Saturday morning is no longer the junkyard. When you talk about a half-hour cartoon show you're talking about as many as one hundred thousand clams laid end to end. Show me the kid's stuff in that."

Joe Barbera is forty-five, a sporty dresser, and usually just about that subtle when he discusses the cartoon-producing business.

But maybe he has that right. With William Hanna, he runs a subtle animation factory in Hollywood. One of the biggest in the world. And for that reason, he talks to animals.

This year there are eleven half-hour cartoon series on the Saturday morning tube bearing the Hanna-Barbera imprint. They range from reruns of *The Flintstones* to such newfangled offerings as *Birdman and the Galaxy Trio, Samson & Goliath, Atom Ant, Secret Squirrel, Fantastic Four, Space Ghost and Dino Boy, Moby Dick and Mighty Mightor, Shazzan, The Herculoids, Jonny Quest,* and *Frankenstein Jr. and The Impossibles.*

Next fall many of these shows will be making the rerun circuit, not to mention four brand-new cartoon series: *The New Adventures of Huckleberry Finn* (in prime time on NBC), *The Hanna-Barbera Hour* [Editors' note: Soon retitled *The Banana Splits Adventure Hour*], consisting of half-animation, half-live action (these are costing $135,000 per episode), *Wacky Races,* and *The Adventures of Gulliver.*

It might also be said of Joe Barbera that he looks haggard midway through one of his working days. It is already 6 p.m. in his Hollywood office—a spacious affair that is not gaudily plush—but chances are he won't get away from his desk until 10 p.m. With luck.

At this moment he is gazing at a large drawing of a riverboat. Behind him stands the artist—young, nervous, lacking confidence.

Barbera glances up from the watercolor drawing to explain this is for *The New Adventures of Huckleberry Finn*. *Finn*, he elaborates, is the most preferred of all classics. Or so extensive ratings and testing have decided. *Robinson Crusoe* is next, then *Ivanhoe*. Those might be considered for later series. He examines the scene again, giving his full attention to the apprehensive artist.

"Looks kind of grim," he muses. "Colors are grim. What I'd do is start with more white, give it more tone. More shadows here." He points. "This looks too much like steel. Riverboats are made of wood. Throw more shadow across here and it'll start to look like a riverboat. Who told you to do it this way?" The artist, fidgeting, mentions a name. Barbera laughs boisterously. "What do Puerto Ricans know about riverboats?" He gives the artist a light slap on his shoulder. The artist's mood brightens. He'll try again. This time with the shadow.

Barbera watches him leave, then swings around in his swivel chair. "I have a hundred meetings like this every day. And with four new shows . . . I talk to animals."

It wasn't always this hectic for Barbera and partner. He can remember the day when they couldn't find a single market for their first freelance collaboration. But that's getting ahead of the story.

It started at MGM one morning in [1957]. Barbera and Hanna had spent twenty years with that factory, producing Tom and Jerry. They had seven Academy Awards to show for their artistic labors, but the soaring cost of animation had placed their jobs in jeopardy. The phone rang and thirty seconds later they no longer had an employer.

The pair turned to television, but the cartoon field was just as vast a graveyard in that medium. Perhaps they could cut exorbitant costs with the use of limited animation. How about strong character, contemporary satire? Material that functioned on one level for kids, on another for adults. Hey. . . . So they made *Huckleberry Hound*. Would Kellogg's be interested? Maybe, maybe not. It seemed Kellogg's was also considering a package deal with MGM. For old Tom and Jerry cartoons.

The irony of that was almost enough to make them seek jobs as cereal box writers. But somehow *Huckleberry Hound* was purchased and Hanna-Barbera Productions Inc. was formed. And born was a whole new attitude toward cartoon animation.

Barbera recalls those days with a certain respect: They could have spelled total disaster. And from their experience they learned there was more to their trade than a paw-clutched wooden mallet descending toward a mouse's head. They saw now that TV was producing a much sharper level of youthful audience to which they could cater.

"What the adults want for the kids is education now. Good moral material. But you can't present it as education. It has to be translated into entertainment.

And that's what we're here to do. What I personally prefer is what we've always tried to stress—series that have characters the kids can identify with. Characters they can imitate.

"That's why I'm not a fan of the superhero—they're all cut from the same cloth and you can't warm up to a superhero like you can to Yogi Bear or Fred Flintstone.

"But I don't worry about that. Superheroes are a fad on the way out."

And the trend right now? "Toward—and I'm glad to see it—humor and personality. No, not Mickey Mouse. A return to humor that is far more sophisticated . . . no, make that contemporary. It's not even a *Flintstones* humor, *Honeymooner* humor, or *Bilko* humor. Now the humor is going to be a *Mary Poppins* kind of whimsy, fantasy, magic. People wiggle noses and drawers open and things fly across the room. This is the trend you'll be seeing.

"Oh, we're not abandoning adventure. Adventure is always a good staple. And we're going back to animals. Not the animals we've done in the past. Think of it in terms of *Doctor Dolittle*. Talking to animals. That incorporates the whimsy and still gives us what we want . . . not what we want, what THEY want."

There has been much criticism of late about violence in cartoons. Does it apply to Hanna-Barbera? "Certainly. We make a majority of the cartoons so the majority of the complaints apply to us. I can't really defend it but to say it's part of a trend. This entire business consists of trends. Every couple of years we go through major changes. All I can promise is, violence is on the way out. It'll soon be a thing of the past in our cartoons."

(The official statement on violence from the Hanna-Barbera publicity office: "Today's fantastic communications system has painted a realistic picture that children and adults must live with. Hanna-Barbera merely reflects this trend toward realism.")

Another knock on Barbera's office door. The producer sighs under the pending burden of another session with an artist. This time it is an older man. With a sample of a character called Dr. Jungle. He talks to animals.

"Now, if you'll excuse me . . . I can't hold up production. One of these days"—and he pretends to pull his hair from his head—"I'm gonna get out of here before dark."

Joe Barbera. A man who talks to animals.

Hanna-Barbera Presents Saturday Morning and Comedy

HANNA-BARBERA / 1969

From Hanna-Barbera's press kit for the fall 1969 broadcast schedule. Prepared by McFadden, Strauss, Eddy & Irwin, Inc.—Public Relations.

EXCLUSIVE TO YOU IN YOUR CITY FOR IMMEDIATE RELEASE

Hanna-Barbera Productions, television's largest source of animated cartoon shows telecast especially for youngsters on Saturday morning, is reflecting the current shift away from action-adventure to comedy programs.

Producer Joseph Barbera says the nearest thing to violence viewers we will see on Saturday mornings will be "fun-violence."

"Animated cartoons are traditionally action-oriented," said Barbera. "A cat chasing a mouse is comically violent because of the action of the chase. If we eliminate too much of the action, we are going to lose our young viewers.

"If the cat rams into a wall while chasing the mouse and shatters into a million pieces, the fantasy of animation quickly restores the feline, and the cat-and-mouse game continues. No one really gets hurt.

"You have to make a distinction in violence. Comedy slapstick isn't violence.

"For example, you can run a steam roller over a cat and flatten him," Barbera remarks, "and he jumps right up without a scratch.

"But we've learned that you can't do that with human beings. And that's one of the principal differences between slapstick comedy and nonviolence.

"When animals take on human qualities and start waving knives and shooting guns—that's violence.

"It's easy for writers to allow a cat to escape a pursuing bulldog by whipping out a gun and shooting a hole in the dog, but it takes creative thinking for writers to come up with a unique escape plan free of weapons and violent acts.

"The return to comedy is perfect for us. It's something we've been doing for thirty years. This fall we are presenting five new comedy shows along with five returning shows," he says, "and all are certainly nonviolent."

Newcomers for Hanna-Barbera's 1969–70 production include *Scooby-Doo, Where Are You!* (CBS); *The Perils of Penelope Pitstop* (CBS); *Dastardly and Muttley in Their Flying Machines* (CBS); *The Banana Splits Adventure Hour* (NBC); and *Cattanooga Cats* (ABC).

The Men behind Dastardly and Muttley

JOHN CULHANE / 1969

From the *New York Times*, November 23, 1969, Section SM, 50ff. Reprinted with permission of Hind Rassam Culhane.

In a New York suburban household one recent Saturday morning, a father stopped to look at the television screen being watched by his sons, Hank, seven, and Pinky, eight. Cartoon characters called Dick Dastardly and his unfaithful dog Muttley were chasing a pigeon in an airplane, fancifully armed with anvil and hammer.

Father: Why are they chasing that pigeon?
Pinky: 'Cause that's the general's orders.
Father: Why does the general want the pigeon stopped?
Pinky: I don't know. He's delivering mail to somebody, I think.
Father: Which side are you on?
Hank: Muttley's. We want him to win at least one time, 'cause he's funny.
Father: Are Dastardly and Muttley bad guys or good guys?
Pinky: Bad guys. At least, they were the bad guys in *Wacky Races*. 'Cause they cheated.
Father: Then the pigeon works for the good guys. But you say you're not on the pigeon's side.
Pinky: We're not. We're on Muttley's side. And I guess we're on Dastardly's side, 'cause he's on Muttley's side. Anyway, how do you know they're bad guys? Maybe they're good. In wars, everybody thinks they're on the good side, so how can you say who's bad or good? It depends on which side you're on.

The conversation is true. It is also rare, because most parents apparently never see, let alone discuss with their children, the animated cartoons that have practically taken over the Saturday morning TV shows for kids. But an awful lot of kids see them. On a typical Saturday morning in November, the Nielsen ratings people say, 12.2 million homes will be tuned in to network shows. That is about one-fifth of all the TV households in the country. During the morning, some 9 million youngsters between the ages of six and eleven, and 6.6 million youngsters aged two to five, are watching what ABC, CBS, and NBC provide for them.

And what the networks provide is overwhelmingly cartoons. CBS this season serves them five and one-half hours of animated cartoons, interrupted briefly by a rerun of the live-action rock-music show *The Monkees*. On ABC, they can see nothing but cartoons for four and one-half hours. On NBC, they get a three-hour slug of straight animation, plus *The Banana Splits Adventure Hour*, which combines animation and live action. In other words, more than two-thirds of all the Saturday "morning" time on the three major networks—thirteen and a half out of a combined total of eighteen hours between 8 a.m. and 2 p.m.—is occupied by drawings that move (more or less).

The Kings of Saturday Morning are William Hanna and Joseph Barbera, who created Tom and Jerry for the movies and Huckleberry Hound and Yogi Bear for television. This season, Hanna-Barbera Productions fill one-third of the networks' eighteen Saturday children's hours with eight half-hour and two hour-long series. For CBS, they have produced three new cartoon comedies: *Scooby-Doo, Where Are You!*, a comedy-mystery with a chickenhearted Great Dane; *The Perils of Penelope Pitstop*, a hybrid blending silent serials with Mack Sennett slapstick and a noisy soundtrack; and the aforementioned aerial adventures, circa World War I, of *Dastardly and Muttley in Their Flying Machines*, a sort of "Malevolent Men in Their Flying Machines," which surely owes something to the success of Snoopy and the Red Baron. CBS also shows reruns of *The Jetsons*, *Jonny Quest*, and *Wacky Races*. (A disconcerting sign of flagging inventiveness is that Penelope, Dastardly, and Muttley were all characters in *Wacky Races*.) NBC renewed *Banana Splits*, and shows reruns of *The Flintstones*, which ABC ran as the first animated series in prime time back in 1960. ABC has renewed the hour-long *Cattanooga Cats* and reruns *The Adventures of Gulliver*. Hanna and Barbera dominate animation for television as Walt Disney once dominated animation for the movies. "Our big problem is," says Joe Barbera, "we compete with ourselves."

So why do the three competing networks all hire Hanna-Barbera? "We have dealt primarily with Hanna-Barbera and Filmation," says Fred Silverman, vice president of daytime programs for CBS-TV, "because these studios have consistently delivered hit shows for us." Indeed, in Nielsen's first listing of the top ten Saturday morning shows this season, all were aired by CBS, and half of those were made by Hanna-Barbera. (Filmation Associates produces two of the ten, *The New Adventures of Superman* and *The Archie Show*.) "Everyone wants to win, but on a network they don't dare lose," said a rival producer, "so they all grab onto the winner." Unfortunately, as they used to say in high-school talent shows, not everyone can be the winner—even with a Hanna-Barbera product. NBC's Hanna-Barbera *Banana Splits*, which was the top-rated show for its time period last year, lost out in the first ratings this season to CBS's Hanna-Barbera *Scooby-Doo*—with a whopping 11.6 rating.

But it is not only that Hanna and Barbera have consistently delivered hits. They have proved themselves hitmakers while meeting the networks' goat-like appetite for low-cost Saturday morning television. Saturday morning is important to the networks' balance sheets. The gross annual revenue from advertisers to the three major networks is now about $90 million. "Four or five years ago," says Silverman, "it was about $40 million." Revenues are greater for prime time, but so are production expenses. By keeping costs down on Saturday morning, the networks stand to realize a total of $20 million in profits. It works out fine for Hanna-Barbera Productions, too. Last year, the firm had the best year in its twelve-year history—gross revenues in excess of $10 million.

"Really, it's done on an assembly-line basis," concedes Silverman, "but there are ways to get good results by reuse of material and judicious editing." A competitor, Bill Scott, writer-creator of Jay Ward Productions' *George of the Jungle*, describes Hanna-Barbera as "an enormously efficient operation that can produce an enormous amount of footage at low cost." He adds: "I wouldn't want to work there." (*George* was of higher quality than any of Hanna-Barbera's shows, but it got too expensive for ABC and was not renewed.) How do they do it? And who are the dwarfs in the goldmine? And how pure is the gold in those Hollywood hills?

My guide to the mysteries of the craft was one of the greatest artists in the sixty-three-year history of film animation, Arthur Babbitt, sixty-two. Indeed, Robert D. Feild, the Harvard professor of art who wrote *The Art of Walt Disney* back in 1942, called Babbitt "the greatest animator of them all." A precise, silver-haired man who wears a stopwatch on his bony wrist, Babbitt is known for animating movement as if it were ballet. From a tiny Chinese toadstool trying to get in step with his elders (in Disney's *Fantasia*), to a grizzly bear golfing with dandelion fluff (in a Mr. Magoo cartoon called *Grizzly Golfer*), Art Babbitt's animation is what ambitious animators study. At Hanna-Barbera, he is the director in charge of commercials.

We crossed a bridge that can't draw over the small moat that surrounds the three-story, $1,250,000 Hanna-Barbera building. ("We encourage people to throw money in the moat and wish for ratings," Joe Barbera was to tell me.) It was peak season in the animation industry, which is geared to the networks' seasons, when about six hundred people "keep busy" (in the words of a press release) in that funny factory located on two and a half acres of property on Cahuenga Boulevard, near the Hollywood Freeway entrance to the San Fernando Valley. Business was good: A planned $1-million addition will almost double the plant's size, to seventy-five thousand square feet.

The pay is reasonable. "The minimum now is $250 a week, if you're a journeyman animator," said Babbitt. "Tops here is about $350. At Disney's, I was getting $300 in the Depression, but another guy, who did a lot of animation on *Dance of the Hours* in *Fantasia*, got $35 a week. But in a studio like this, where there isn't much difference in quality, a guy usually gets more because he's able to turn the stuff out."

At Disney's in the 1930s, animators could throw away a whole day's work if they weren't satisfied, and Disney would not complain. What Disney did demand was that each piece of animation the artist considered good enough to show the boss be better than the last piece he showed. Unfortunately, those who were not good enough, either at animating or at catching Walt's eye, were barely able to feed their kids. Babbitt was one of the leaders of the 1941 Disney strike that resulted in recognition of the Screen Cartoonists Guild and the immediate raising of base pay for animators to $85. But the strike was the beginning of the end of his career at Disney's.

"This place is not a sweatshop in the sense that somebody stands over you with a whip," said Babbitt of Hanna-Barbera, "but you better get your footage out. They keep very close track of everything you turn out on a picture."

"If you don't turn it out?"

"You're fired."

Babbitt introduced John Michaeli, the publicity manager, who attributed Hanna-Barbera's success to "the use of a realistic production schedule. It's one thing to go to New York and sell a cartoon. It's another thing to deliver it. We say we'll put so many series in production on such-and-such a date, and by such-and-such a date they roll off like an assembly line."

"When you see his visitors walk out, you walk in," directs Bill Hanna's secretary. "We have half an hour," reminds Michaeli. Ben Franklin didn't remember that "time is money" one-twenty-fourth as well as Bill Hanna does. Split-second timing is his trade.

Exit: old appointment. Enter: new appointment. Hanna, fifty-nine, is working in his shirtsleeves at his desk. His hair is white, his face is square, his chin is cleft, his speech is measured.

"When Joe and I made Tom and Jerry, we made about eight six-minute cartoons a year," he said. "That's about forty-eight minutes of animation a year. Now we're turning out 120 minutes a week. In other words, we're doing more than twice as much here every week as we used to do in a year at MGM."

The way Hanna and Barbera have brought it off is through the use of limited animation. For example, think of the full animation in Disney's *Peter Pan*, where Captain Hook catches a chill trying to drown Tiger Lily. Animator Frank Thomas exaggerated the pirate's shiver for comic effect: No live actor could shake, rattle, and roll as elaborately as Hook; yet the shiver takes off from an exact observation of the way people actually tremble—first one part of the body, then another part; not all at once.

"They might take sixty-four drawings to get that elaborate shiver," said Hanna. "I would take four drawings, go into a four-drawing cycle and create a better effect. It takes the animator an hour's time to do the four drawings. It would take him two days to do the sixty-four drawings.

"When we first started the limited animation, it disturbed me," Hanna went on. "And then, when I saw some of the old cartoons on TV, I saw that, actually, limited animation came off better on the dimly lit television screen than the old fully animated things. But the degree of limited animation has changed in the past ten years. Today, limited animation is a lot less limited than it was ten years ago. TV seemed to demand a little bit more than we were giving it. In the beginning, we would put a character into the pose and animate the mouth only. Now we animate the entire head. We also change the body position more."

It was the Depression that sent Hanna, Barbera, Babbitt, and many other top men into the animation business. Hanna was studying engineering at Compton College in California but had to quit school when the stock market crashed. Barbera was an accountant at the Irving Trust Company in New York, but got laid off with all the rest of the unmarried employees. Babbitt wanted to be a psychiatrist but had to go to work to support his family. *Steamboat Willie*, Disney's first Mickey Mouse, had brought sound to cartoons the year before there were jobs for bright young men who could make frightened America laugh and sing.

"Basically," said Bill Hanna, "I started in writing—jingles and things done with songs for Looney Tunes and Merrie Melodies. I work more in production now than in the creative end, but I still do some of the writing. For example, I wrote the title song and lyrics for *Dastardly*."

In his office, Joe Barbera was energetically flipping drawings all over the carpet the way he does when he's selling a show to the networks for next year—which is what he does in October and November. Barbera is fifty-seven, but looks younger with his curly black hair, flashing eyes under thick black brows, and trim body in a navy blazer over a white turtleneck sweater.

"I haven't got time to get fat," he said. "We have the largest animation studios in the world. It's a little sad. Other cartoon studios, in their anxiety to grow, love to run us down, to call us a factory, or a sweatshop. But when Bill and I started, in 1957, our industry was finished. Disney wasn't making any shorts. We had been together at MGM for eighteen years, making Tom and Jerry, when they closed their doors. The 'factory' reputation came about because we employed different methods of production. We never belittle our competitors, but a competitor who makes only five cartoons a year and calls us a factory is forgetting how many people we give work to."

I reminded Barbera of a lovely sequence called "The King Who Couldn't Dance" that he and Hanna did at MGM for a 1944 Gene Kelly musical called *Anchors Aweigh*. A live-action Kelly danced with a fully animated King Jerry the Mouse all over a painted kingdom. "There's a difference in time and a difference in money," said Barbera—and suddenly their problem was clear: Hanna and Barbera have become the kings who won't dance—because dancing takes so many drawings, and animator hours are still the greatest cost factor in the "different" production methods they have decreed.

Barbera began flipping the drawings again. "For *Dastardly*, our designer, Iwao Takamoto, created 100 to 150 airplanes, each with a different function, just as we created brightly colored cars for *Wacky Races*, the year before. I flipped them on the floor, and that's the way we sold the shows. When the network people come in, they walk on a carpet of eye-catching art. This plane, for instance, is a flying vacuum cleaner...."

(CBS's Silverman says it was not quite that simple: "Our dealings with the studios in California are cooperative efforts. For instance, *Dastardly and Muttley* was originally called "Stop the Pigeon." Just in looking at it, I saw that it needed a little more top spin. The network came up with the idea of substituting Dastardly and Muttley, the stars of *Wacky Races*, for two other characters that Hanna-Barbera showed us.")

"The idea for a cartoon is conceived by a writer—or writers," said Babbitt. At Hanna-Barbera, the top writers are a team: Ken Spears and Joe Ruby. They write *The Perils of Penelope Pitstop* and *Scooby-Doo*. Spears, who looks like a live-action Jonny Quest, is only thirty-one.

"I was twenty-one when I started at this place," he said. "My partner and I were film editors here. On the side, we were doing a bit of writing for the bridges—show openers and closers. Two years ago, Bill Hanna gave me a break. He said: 'Why not try writing full time?' We knew this place, and our timing was perfect. The timing's the thing: You can't dawdle. Anything from comedy to drama here is mainly rapid-fire attack. Otherwise, the kids'll turn the channel on you."

Did Ruby and Spears ever write the superhero type of show that has been condemned by the National Commission on the Causes and Prevention of Violence as encouraging real violence?

"Oh, yes," said Spears. "But we never killed anybody. We never destroyed cities, either. That was wrong for cartoons—too impersonal. We destroyed machines like crazy, though.

"The network was the dictator. They said: 'We're going to buy superheroes this year. If you don't make them, you're out of the game.' The public appetite for this kind of thing came from James Bond and it lasted until Robert Kennedy was assassinated. After that, the networks said: 'The mothers are writing in.' Now there's no more fighting, as such, on TV." Spears shrugged.

"To do adventure without violence is very tough. They not only cracked down on violence, they cracked down on confrontations. So there's no threat. Take *The Adventures of Gulliver*. An evil sea captain is after a map. He's the only heavy on the show. Last year, they said, 'Take away his knife.' He didn't ever *use* his knife. It was there as a threat. But they said, 'No type of weapons whatsoever.' So we had the sea captain kidnap the dog and say to the boy, 'Give me the map or you'll never see your dog again.' We leave it to the kids' imaginations what he's going to do with the dog.

"Joe and I have adapted. We can write adventure or go funny. We've just finished seventeen *Penelope Pitstops*. Actually, the traps in *Penelope* are more violent than anything we had in *Gulliver*—but in comedy you take it with a grain of salt. If it's adventure, you accept it as real, even though it's a cartoon.

"We write the *Penelope*s and the *Scooby*s out in story form. Then a story director translates our idea into a storyboard. . . ."

The written script doesn't mean much in cartoon making. The printed word can't convey the fast action and fantastic visual effects that can be achieved. So the storyboard evolved. The first real storyboard was created by Webb Smith, a cartoonist who sketched out gag ideas on sheets of paper at Disney's in the thirties. When he began to pin all the sketches on corkboards in sequence, the storyboard was born.

"After the story is sketched into storyboard form," said Babbitt, "a script of the characters' lines is prepared. Actors are called and the dialogue is recorded onto quarter-inch magnetic tape. Then a [sound] track reader listens to the dialogue, which has been transferred to 35-mm. magnetic film, and he measures each vowel and consonant of every word. These words are written on 'exposure sheets,' where each space corresponds to a frame on the magnetic film. This is now a visual record of dialogue, so that action can be synchronized with sound.

"Next comes the layout man," Babbitt went on. "Utilizing the storyboards, the layout man is the member of the group who actually stages the scenes. He is responsible for how the cartoon looks. He also moves the characters around, placing them in key positions and action poses."

Babbitt introduced Dick Bickenbach, who studied art at Chouniard Art School in Los Angeles but "learned animation during thirty-nine years in the field." The field included MGM, where he worked on Hanna-Barbera's seven Oscar-winning Tom and Jerrys.

On this day, Bickenbach was laying out a sequence from *Scooby-Doo* in which "we've got this guy in the galley of an old ship. He's supposed to be stirring broth. Now, I'll sketch in the background. It's up to the background painter to interpret my sketch. But it's up to me to make sure something isn't pushing in the way when that guy goes to stir the broth."

The rough layout sketch was on his drawing board. It was a black and white rendering which determined the basic composition of the scene. The key positions of the cook as he stirs the broth were traced in blue pencil, so he could check the size and perspective of the character in all his moves. Architecture, costumes, furniture, props—all are in the layout man's domain.

The animation director controls the overall tempo of the cartoon. As Babbitt explained: "He times it out, gives the assignments to the animators, and then double-checks to make sure the animator interpreted the action right and there are no mechanical mistakes. At Disney's, it was not unusual to have seven or eight pencil tests, refining and refining a sequence before it was inked. On commercials, I use very much the same process. But a one-minute commercial sells for $14,000 to $16,000. We can't afford to be as liberal on the entertainment shows. It's very costly. It holds up production. The animation director would have to find a very serious mistake for it to be done over. An animator is fired if he makes very many of those mistakes."

(Says Bill Scott of Jay Ward, which may have priced *George* out of the jungle but keeps profitably busy doing commercials for Cap'n Crunch, Quake, and Quisp [cereals]: "If we were to get the budget we use for a commercial for the entertainment shows, it would mean a quarter of a million dollars for a half-hour show. The reason they can reap those big profits is that they don't put very much money into animated cartoons." Networks pay producers from $48,000 to $62,000 for a half-hour Saturday morning show. "But the money is paid only if you'll permit networks to run it two or three times," says Scott.)

The animator is the man who brings the layouts to life, simulating motion by means of slight progressive changes in a series of drawings. Babbitt introduced Dick Lundy, who has been an animator for forty years. He went from high school to Disney's, where he animated the early Donald Duck.

"Dick Lundy *was* Donald Duck," says a Disney veteran. "Irascible, raging in incoherent squawks. His own personality animated the duck." Indeed, animators often get their characters' expressions by drawing what they find in the mirror.

Lundy lowered his pencil arm awhile to reminisce that he and Babbitt had animated *The Three Little Pigs* for Disney in 1933. "I did the dance of the pig with the fiddle and the pig with the fife to 'Who's Afraid of the Big Bad Wolf?'" Lundy said fondly. It was at about that time, Babbitt recalled, that Disney began to pay for the art education of his animators. None of his competitors were willing or able to train their men. "I decided," Disney said later, "to step out of their class by setting up my own training school. We had enough revenue coming in so we could plan ahead, and I laid out a schedule of what I wanted to accomplish over the years. . . . It was costly, but I had to have the men ready for the things we would eventually do."

Today, Hanna and Barbera face a similar problem. "A training program is a must," said Barbera. "We're still depending on the guys we used twenty years ago. But nobody is equipped to set up a department where you spend money training people."

"Twenty years from now, whom will you hire?" asks Shamus Culhane, teacher of advanced animation at the School of Visual Arts in New York, and the animator who made the dwarfs march home in *Snow White*. "They hire all the years a man spent learning how to make a figure move, and then have him do skeletal animation—no bones, no meat, no blood. So the young animators learn only what is cheap and fast. This is the way an art form dies."

"Seventy-five percent of the people in animation are tired out, anyway," said Bill Hurtz, animation director for Jay Ward, at the first world retrospective of animation cinema at Expo 67. "They don't give a damn about advancing the medium. Hanna-Barbera are the real-estate agents. They move animation like real estate. It's very competent. Very professional. But somehow or other, there's the odor of death about it."

While the animators are at work, another department is turning out color background paintings based on the pencil layout drawings (like the drawing of the ship's galley that Dick Bickenbach had been working on). "We key the environment to the story and the personality of the characters," said Walt Peregoy, forty-three, a handsome man with a Latin mustache and long sideburns, who heads Hanna-Barbera's background department. "We create a mood and an attitude consistent with the characters. For example, Penelope Pitstop has a fresh, direct charm, so that's the quality you try to get into the backgrounds."

Peregoy held up a drawing in which Penelope simpered under the gimlet eye of her evil guardian. The background was a Victorian parlor. From the throw rug to the love seat, it did, indeed, have a fresh, direct charm.

Peregoy studied art with Fernand Léger in Paris, then spent fourteen of his twenty years in the animation industry with Disney. "I keyed *101 Dalmatians* and *The Sword in the Stone*," said Peregoy. "Walt didn't like *Dalmatians*. He felt it wasn't Walt Disney." Indeed, it was because Disney's artists became prisoners of Disney's "house style" that artistic experiment all but stopped at that studio.

I asked Peregoy about a haunting painting in a corner of his office in which Don Quixote and Sancho Panza ride through a forest of muted green. "Oh, that's my own," he said. "I still dream of doing a really good animated *Don Quixote* one day."

Formerly, at this stage, the animators' original drawings were traced by hand onto cellulose sheets (cels) by specialists called "inkers," but now a crew duplicates the drawings on the cels with a Xerox machine. Xeroxing instead of inking a one-minute commercial saves between $700 and $900.

In the camera department, a cameraman was photographing each cel over the correct background. A single frame of film was exposed at a time. A scene of only a few seconds' screen time was taking hours to photograph.

"Now we animate the entire head," Hanna had told me earlier, but here were the mouth and eyes on separate cels—the head remained stationary. The camera clicked away: the eyes blinked; the mouth moved up and down. Babbitt scowled.

"In full animation, the mouth does not behave as a separate entity," he said. "When the mouth opens, it will affect the cheeks and jaw. When a character talks, he breathes, and when he breathes, his chest expands. As his chest expands, his waist grows smaller.

"In animation here, certain drawings work for a situation, so they repeat them. But they've emasculated them. There's no vitality. Also, most of these guys haven't hefted a book or looked at good contemporary drawing in twenty years. They've stopped growing."

Finally, in the dubbing department, dialogue, music, and sound effects are rerecorded from as many as eleven separate tracks onto one balanced track. We found Joe Barbera himself at work, sitting at a huge console with Alex Lovy, a story man, as they watched a screen on which Pockets, a member of the Ant Hill Mob, Penelope's constant rescuers, answered the phone.

"Hello, Penelope," said Pockets. "You don't say? . . . You don't say? . . . You don't say?"

"Where is she?" asked another member of the mob.

"She didn't say."

"Is it too late to save Penelope?" shouted the narrator. Now, Chugaboom, the Mob's all-purpose limousine, drove onto a dock and lowered its buzzsaw wheels as Snoozy shouted: "Okay, Chugaboom, make with the fancy wheels!"

"We have to bring up the saw sound," said Barbera. "If you get a loud sawmill sound, it's gonna help the gag. Maybe we're going to have to lose the line of dialogue. The saw sound isn't up enough to get across the idea that the wheels become a saw blade."

Will Joe Barbera bring up the saw sound? Will Hanna-Barbera lose a line of dialogue? Don't tune in tomorrow for the answer: The answer is yes. "Nothing's going to happen on a Hanna-Barbera show that you haven't seen before," said Bill Scott. "Their style of humor is about 1950 Warner Bros.: entirely predictable. As a result, their techniques of animation can be done at an enormous saving. But the limited action cartoon is essentially a story medium. It has to be written richly—with lots of scenes, lots of jokes, lots of plots, and really funny dialogue. Because when an animated cartoon is thin in animation, it has to be fat somewhere. But nothing happens verbally on any Hanna-Barbera show." [Editors' note: We think Scott means "visually."]

Yet, because they can meet the networks' price, and still turn out a professional-looking product on time, they get more time to entertain our children than any other studio. And what do our children get out of it?

"There have been two different Saturday mornings on which I've observed some of the new fare," said Fred Rogers, who won a Peabody Award for excellence in children's programing this year for National Educational Television's *Mister Rogers' Neighborhood*. "Out of one hour I watched, the first half seemed to be two men in a flying machine trying to catch a pigeon. The child with whom I was watching turned to me fifteen minutes into the program and said, 'Why are they chasing the pigeon?' This seven-year-old boy had already watched two shows without understanding why they were chasing the pigeon. The next half-hour had to do with a young maiden called Penelope Pitstop, whose guardian was trying in every imaginable way to do away with her because he wants her inheritance.

"We're presenting to the children what they must think is the adult way of problem solving. The adults are the men in the flying machines: always bumbling. In *Penelope*, the adult is the guardian who wants to kill her. My objection to this is that there's no interpreter—unless the parent is sitting beside the child—and I would imagine that there are very few who can do that. So the message that comes across is that big people are incompetent and go after little people for no good reason—and if this is the adult world, why should we make an effort to join it?"

Mister Rogers's comments will pain Bill Hanna, who said: "I am glad we are moving away from the realistic adventure cartoon that was filled with violence. We as a studio have always been specialists in comedy and satire.... The hits in Tom and Jerry were played for comedy. The harder the cat got hit, the harder they laughed and laughed. The way it was staged was for comedy—like the old slapstick comedy. It's the spirit in which it was done that made it nonviolent. Immediately preceding the hit, Tom would have done something that made him deserve it—so the audience delights in seeing the mouse triumph, because he's a small, defenseless character."

In point of fact, many of the Tom and Jerry cartoons *were* sadistic—in the sense of delighting in cruelty. But one typical eight-year-old boy insisted that cartoons are not violent because, "In cartoons, they never have the character die. He just gets all black and blown up—and they make like it doesn't hurt." To be sure, the bam-pow-sock violence of "hits" has largely been eliminated this season, but the threat of violence—to kill a pigeon, to pulverize Penelope—is bred in the bones of Hanna-Barbera's television shows. They are heavy years away from the nonviolent charm of "The King Who Couldn't Dance."

Dr. Margaret McFarland, director of the Arsenal Family and Children Center in Pittsburgh, and psychological consultant for *Mister Rogers' Neighborhood*, says bluntly: "Saturday morning television isn't designed to educate children, or even to give them pleasure," she says. "It is designed to sell products. And part of the technique is to hold the child out of fear. You can't do away with violence. It's part of human nature. But it shouldn't be so gross that it's way beyond a child's ability to master it. The things in these programs may fit right into the child's deepest fears. If a show evokes mild fear, mastering that fear can be a real pleasure for the child. But where the fear is beyond the child's mastery, he might be overwhelmed. But many of these cartoon makers don't really know anything about children."

Violence aside, it is a safe bet that no cartoon on Saturday morning today is going to enchant a child the way Hanna and Barbera charmed this writer twenty-five years ago by letting King Jerry learn from Gene Kelly to "be a pleasanter guy." Nor is any child's esthetic sense going to be awakened by so much as Dick Lundy's little pig dance.

Dastardly and Muttley, The Perils of Penelope Pitstop, and *Scooby-Doo, Where Are You!* are relatively harmless chapters, but Saturday morning TV is an American tragedy. Part of the tragedy is that creative men who began their careers making *The Three Little Pigs* and "The King Who Couldn't Dance" should end them turning out artistic pitches for breakfast food and very limited animation for those illustrated radio programs that the networks insist are television. Part is that networks, sponsors, and producers are season-wise and childhood-foolish. "If you create something which has lasting value—even by spending more money, your audience is completely changed in five years," said David D. Connell, who produced *Captain Kangaroo* before becoming executive producer of NET's *Sesame Street*. "So there are some arguments for spending money toward the future."

But the saddest part is that parents act as if Saturday's child will always be there to share an experience with—if ever we should want to. We are wasting the fleeting time of childhood and men's talents, acting as if we, like Tom and Jerry, can never die.

Iwao Takamoto

AMID AMIDI / 1999

Edited from *Animation Blast* no. 3 (Spring 1999), 5–7. Reprinted with permission.

Iwao Takamoto: Around the [time of Disney's] *The Sword in the Stone* [1963], the animation industry was beginning to have a down period caused by a variety of factors, including the death of the theatrical short biz. I looked around Disney and saw this group of the best, especially as a group, and they were at the peak of their careers. I realized I didn't have much of a chance of making a dent in that place. In the meantime, all of these really good short subject animators that were laid off had been picked up by Bill Hanna to work at Hanna-Barbera. Some were calling me, saying "Why don't you come over here?" I eventually decided to make the move to TV. . . .

Amid Amidi: Post-*Flintstones*?

Takamoto: Well, post–first season of *The Flintstones*. This was after they had gone through their first set of classic characters. According to Jerry Eisenberg, he and I started about the same time, and he insists that it was in the summer of 1961.

Amidi: What sort of a transition was there, coming to television from feature [animation]?

Takamoto: It was rather comfortable for me to move from the actual process of animation to layout. The characters had to be staged graphically so that they read quickly, because you had a much smaller screen. Because they were so dependent on strong graphic statements, it became important that layout people not only blocked out scenes in its structure but also did the best they could in posing characters for the animators, so that you got the best possible staging and drawing of these characters. The adjustment was especially fascinating in the design area, because you had certain limitations placed on you that you never worried about at Disney. At Disney, you had to have your designs and characters structured in a fashion that could have movement shadings and be subtly animated. You could keep characters moving to keep them alive, but you also had to design for it.

You can't take a character like Yogi and do that with him as easily, because of his design. But I also found that there was suddenly that liberty, where you could get interesting designs because of the fact that you didn't have to move them around as much. Designers like Ed Benedict took full advantage of that and really set a great pace stylistically. And then somebody like Bick [Dick Bickenbach] had to take that and find ways of adapting these designs to make them animatable. People like Harvey Eisenberg, Gene Hazelton, and Joe [Barbera] himself added to this part of the process.

Amidi: Did you stay in layout?

Takamoto: Yeah, but in those days there wasn't any delineation between any of this stuff. Sometimes you'd move over to do a scene of animation. Sometimes you'd design characters or do a storyboard section just because you could. I did that for several years. What happened over time was a gradual expansion of my responsibilities. By the time we had gone into *The Jetsons*, I had the chance to design numerous things.

Eventually, they ended up with this show they produced with Gene Kelly—*Jack and the Beanstalk* (1967)—and predicated upon that, Joe got a chance to produce a series called *The New Adventures of Huckleberry Finn* (1968–69), with three live kids moving around in an animated world. Consistent with that time, I guess things were ripe for them to let me take charge of the design and layout part of this studio, because it was exploding and [Bill and Joe] didn't have time to cover all of this [due to] their other responsibilities. As a result, a great deal of the visual presentation material and that sort of thing came under this department.

Amidi: Did you actually design a lot of the characters, or did they come through you?

Takamoto: If you take out that first era of the Yogis, Hucks, Quick Draws, Flintstones, and most of the lead characters on *The Jetsons*, I think it'd be safe to say that I was responsible for 75–80 percent of Hanna-Barbera's output. In other words, I either designed them myself or worked directly with the people who designed [them]. Sometimes it was no more than assigning something and then critiquing it. I would say that anywhere around 40 percent of the stuff I had to design myself. The major part of what I didn't really have to touch were in the hands of two guys that turned the TV industry around: Doug Wildey and Alex Toth.

Amidi: What is the general process for designing a show from scratch?

Takamoto: It happened in a lot of different ways. Take a character like Penelope Pitstop, who came out of *Wacky Races*. Now, there's a show that had primarily four designers: a couple artists did one or two characters on that; Jerry Eisenberg and I did the balance. Jerry did a hell of a lot of good work on that show. As we were working on it, Joe comes in and says, "I'm in a meeting with the people that are sponsoring this show and they asked a question: 'Don't we need a female in this group?' And I agree with them." So he asked if I could just cook up something—a sketch that was as feminine as I could get it with a dash of color—and he'd come back soon to get it because he was still in the meeting. So I sit down and just put the kitchen sink in there. I thought, what do race car drivers wear? I put in helmets and scarves. Then I put a parasol on her car, and made the car sort of Disney-esque with eyelashes and lips. I figured if he wanted feminine, I'd give him feminine, so I put in lavender and shocking pinks and all that stuff. He comes in and grabs the thing, runs back into the meeting, and a character has been designed.

The reason I bring her up is that it worked there: everybody said it was terrific. She actually spun off into a show of her own. I modified her costuming for her own show [*The Perils of Penelope Pitstop*, 1969–71], turning her from a competitive race car driver to a Perils of Pauline–type heroine. That's just one way a particular show happened.

Sometimes a name, like *The Beverly Hillbillies*, would start a design. Joe comes up with this great title: "Hillbilly Bears." Everybody loves it. So he comes in and says he's going to New York, and asks if I can give him a family of bears—a mother, a father, and this time, a teenage girl and a little kid brother—which sounds like *The Jetsons*. Anyway, all I know is that they're bears and they're hillbillies. So I do a lineup on that, and he grabs it and takes it to New York. [He comes] back and says, "I'm in trouble." I ask, "Why?" and he says, "Because they loved it. They loved the title, concept, and designs. And we got the show. Now I don't know what the hell to do with it." [*Laughs*] So it works like that sometimes.

Scooby-Doo, Where Are You! (1969–71) was a process, and it came in stages. It was supposed to be current, so we went with a sixties look. Fred Silverman, working with Joe and the two writers, Ruby and Spears, wanted a teenage mystery. He wanted a full, half-hour Saturday morning show where, for the first time, he could tell a true story with an actual plot. They came up with the names and type of people, and I did the designs, but something was still missing. So Joe [Barbera], who's had so much success with animals, suggested a dog. He did the same thing with *Jonny Quest* by adding Bandit, which really rounded that show up. Everybody said it makes sense, and I just wanted to do a big dog for a change, because all the other dogs were cute and little. So that's how that happened; the characters came in stages.

Amidi: What shows did you design that never got done?

Takamoto: There were so many of them. For every one that we got on the air, there must have been five or six that never made it. We presented a whole bunch of cartoons about bands—Western, rock and roll, gospel—travelling through the world doing good. Typical shows like that. We tried to put together classic stories like *Man in the Iron Mask* and *Robinson Crusoe*. In the early days, they were tinkering with Cantinflas and a show about the Marx Brothers. All types of things.

Amidi: Going into the seventies and eighties, were you still doing this sort of thing—staying on top of things and overseeing the shows?

Takamoto: Well, that was supposed to be my priority area. In other words, I couldn't turn my back on it. In the meantime, I did other things, like help direct the feature *Charlotte's Web* (1973), or I did a full-blown animatic for a show called *Where's Huddles?* (1970). That turned out better than the final version, because it had the attraction of having that quick-moving, quick-cutting, very graphic type of presentation. I also worked on *Wait Till Your Father Gets Home* [1972–74].

Amidi: You designed that?

Takamoto: No, the designs were done by Marty Murphy. What I did was produce model sheets, trying to stay as close as I could to what he designed, and Marty seemed quite happy with it. Again, you're sort of a jack-of-all-trades, so I also ended up helping direct the show.

Amidi: From your experience, what is it that makes a good character design?

Takamoto: In animation, you have an advantage over live action, because you can do anything you want; yet at the same time, you want to study the potential that lies in a character, in the way that he's able to visually express emotion and so on. This, of course, works in conjunction with the type of character they [the writers and voice talent] picture. A good place to start building your design is from what the writer writes, in terms of the business between characters, and how characters respond to certain situations. Taking it all into consideration, I like the idea of trying to design a character that answers dimensionally to these sorts of issues. If you look at successfully designed characters, you'll find [this] is fairly consistent. I think today *The Simpsons* have that. It's not just the way they look, it's what they're able to do, and the way that they can do it, with the expressions and body language. They have the tools built into the design of the characters that brings them alive and gives them a brain and a heart. And essentially that's the fascination of characters in animation; even moreso than the fact that you can create such tremendous effects, especially now with computers and so on. To me, my love, and where I'm most impressed, is that thing with the characters: in taking what is essentially a still, two-dimensional piece of art, and through the wedding of sound, music, and especially voice, and then timing and movement, create an actual living thing.

Joe Ruby and Ken Spears on *Scooby-Doo, Where Are You!*

STU SHOSTAK / 2012

Edited from the transcript of the internet radio program *Stu's Show*, Program 276, May 2, 2012. Printed with permission.

Stu Shostak: Let's talk about how you made the jump back from [Twentieth Century-] Fox to Hanna-Barbera. Was it only on the condition that you became writers—Ken?

Ken Spears: . . . Actually, we started when we freelanced. We did a spec script on *Voyage to the Bottom of the Sea* at Fox. Which never got made, but it was kicking around there for the longest time. We really desperately wanted to be writers. And of course, to be a writer, you couldn't walk into a place and talk to them unless you had an agent. And, of course, you couldn't get an agent unless you had a track record.

Shostak: Chicken and the egg.

Spears: Catch-22. So I called Hanna-Barbera and talked to Joe Barbera. [Probably in 1967.] I said, "Joe, do you remember Joe Ruby?" And he goes, "Yeah, I remember Joe." I said, "Well, he and I are writers now." Which we weren't. We were editors. And I said, "We were wondering if you have anything going on we could help you with?" And he goes, "When can you get over here?"

Shostak: Wow, timing. Timing is everything.

Spears: So we go over to Hanna-Barbera. And this is when they started the Saturday morning stuff: *Space Ghost*, *Herculoids*, and [*Mighty*] *Mightor*.

Shostak: *Space Kidettes*. I remember. *Frankenstein Jr.*

Spears: All that stuff was going on. And they were having terrible trouble with it, because the animation writers were all the guys that were doing Bugs Bunny. It was Warren Foster and Mike Maltese, and those guys who knew funny. They didn't know science-fiction and action-adventure. Well, we came out of Fox doing *Lost in Space*, *Batman*. My show was *Green Hornet*.

Shostak: Oh, my god, this all just came into focus.

Spears: We had all this background going on. And the guys that they hired were terrible. They were all these live-action writers. . . . So, we came up with some ideas for one *Mightor* and one *Herculoids* and turned them in, and Joe Barbera liked the ideas. Then we went back to write them. And we did it at Fox while we were cutting music. One of us would be writing, and they had a secretary in there typing for us, and so forth. Anyway, Barbera would be calling: "When am I going to get the script? When am I going to get the script?"

Shostak: Sounds like Yogi Bear: "When am I gonna get the script? Hey-ay-ay."

Spears: We went over there [to Joe's house]—pitch-black at night at 10 o'clock—slipped it under his mat at the front door. Anyways, he got his two scripts. I don't think he made any changes in them—sent them off to CBS, and the word came back from CBS [that] they loved them. Fred Silverman was the head guy, and he says, "I want these guys to write all our shows." Which was physically impossible. . . .

Shostak: It would seem to me that Barbera's attitude probably at that point would have been: "Fine—as long as we get work out of them."

Spears: Yeah, he was very happy. We saved their lives in a sense.

Shostak: Wow, so that's it. That's what started you off.

Spears: That's what started us off and that's when we became Freddy's boys. . . . In terms of *Scooby-Doo*, the whole thing was that we were pulled into Joe's office. Sy Fischer, who was their head agent, was in the office—We went in for the [*Perils of*] *Penelope Pitstop* show. . . . Joe said to us, "This is what we want to do. So, do all this stuff." We said, "Okay, we'll get busy on it right away." And we walk out of the office.

As we walked out, we run right into . . . sorry, Sy Fischer was walking in. He says, "Hold it, guys. Did Joe tell you about the mystery show that Freddy Silverman wants?" And we went, "No." He goes, "Get back inside here." So he shoves us back in the office, and Barbera is on the phone, and Sy says, "Joe, tell the guys about the mystery show that Silverman wants." And Joe says, "You tell them."

Joe Ruby: That was it.

Spears: [Sy] says he [Silverman] wants a show that is a combination of *House of Mystery* or *I Love a Mystery* and something else, but with kids.

Ruby: [Barbera was already] working on his own version, which was *House of Mystery*.

Shostak: What I had heard was that Joe wanted an *Archies* clone, because *The Archies* had done so well.

Spears: He wanted a combination of *Archies* and a mystery show, and all this other stuff.

Ruby: *I Love a Mystery*.

Spears: School and kids.

Shostak: The old-fashioned, who-done-it type of mystery. Whose concept was it to have teenagers involved—was that Barbera's?

Ruby: No, no, he had nothing to do with [that concept].

Spears: Yeah, that came down from Silverman. We just said, "All right. We'll come up with something."

Shostak: And there wasn't even a dog at this point.

Ruby: No, no dog.

Spears: . . . We walk out of the office, but Joe [Ruby] sticks his head back in and says, "Oh, Joe, is it okay if we put a dog in it? We know Freddy likes dogs." And Barbera goes, "Ahh, whatever you want." . . .

Shostak: From my understanding, from what I've read, the dog went through several different morphs. It wasn't supposed to look like Astro from *The Jetsons* in the beginning.

Spears: Yes and no.

Ruby: This is something I can tell. . . . We were talking, and we said, "Let's have a Great Dane." You can have a little feisty one or a big lovable one. You want a lovable one, because the kids would like it better.

Shostak: You don't want Muttley, though. You don't want that "He-he-he" [*Muttley's snicker*].

Ruby: No, no, no, no. We just wanted a big, goofy dog. A big, goofy, funny dog. . . . I said to Ken, . . . "Oh, shit. Maybe we'd get sued because there's a [Great Dane in the comic strip] *Marmaduke*." And I thought, maybe we should change it. Ken listened to me . . . [*laughter*]. So, we changed it to a big shaggy dog and called him Too Much.

Shostak: Too Much.

Ruby: That was the only change in the dog that took place. And that was between ourselves, nobody else. When that was submitted, Fred, for some reason, hated it. Didn't like a shaggy dog. So we went back into Joe's office, and we told him the story. And he says, "Use a Great Dane—don't worry about the lawsuits." So that's what happened.

Shostak: The teenage kids kind of morphed a little bit too, right?

Ruby: I got original copies of the stuff that we wrote, and the notes they gave us. Originally, we took *The Archies*. There was *Dobie Gillis*, and *The Archies*—we went *The Archies* way. [Joe Barbera] didn't like our Archies concept, even though it was his recommendation.

Shostak: He always liked to base—and you kind of learned from him on this, too—he always liked to base cartoons on things that are happening around . . .

Ruby: That's what we learned. Even when we pitched story ideas to Joe, we had to tell him we took it from somebody else, even if it wasn't true. Because he always wanted it if it had been something before.

Shostak: And if it worked for him, it would work for you guys, when you went out on your own.

Ruby: So, we changed it from the Archies to Dobie Gillis, and modified it somewhat. When we wrote the script—this is even in Joe's autobiography—that's when it took shape. Because when we wrote the script, we automatically teamed Shaggy and Scooby. They seemed to glue. It was something that you feel. It's a writing thing. . . . Shaggy was originally Maynard, you know . . .

Shostak: Maynard G. Krebs. . . .

I have a question from Brandon from Washington on various subjects. He says, "Please put this to bed for Scooby-Doo fans. Was Shaggy intended to be a stoner, or not?"

Spears: No, it never even crossed our minds. I took umbrage that you see [that in the 2002 *Scooby-Doo*] movie, when they came out of the back of the van, and smoke is flowing. They always thought that the quest for food was because they had the munchies all the time. But we never used that. Never.

Shostak: That's funny, because [19]69 is when that was created, and that was the big thing back then.

Ruby: We didn't do it.

Shostak: You were just nice, wholesome guys trying to earn a living. . . . Now this thing gets on the air. It's like ultrapopular—it turned everything around. It was as big for Hanna-Barbera as *The Flintstones* was, ten years earlier.

Roundtable Discussion with Mike Maltese

DARRELL VAN CITTERS / 1977

Edited from the transcript of an event organized by Darrell Van Citters at the California Institute of the Arts on March 14, 1977. Printed with permission.

Mike Maltese: In 1958, I went to work for Hanna-Barbera. I quit in 1971 because the network boys were telling me how to write cartoons, and this I didn't want. . . .

The cartoon business is a good business to be in, but rough today. They've got to pull out of those Saturday-morning, kiddie-cartoon show things—if they can do it. Get the hell away from that. And you have to fight the network boys. . . . And, of course, the animators have to fight this cutthroat animation in Australia and other foreign countries, where they'll work for peanuts. . . .

At times, a story man worked in tandem with another story man. At other times, he could be working in a group. As for myself, I preferred working alone as much as possible, and with directors who gave me that freedom. In that way, a future audience could say, hopefully, "That was a Mike Maltese story; those were Mike Maltese gags." In that respect, I was fortunate to spend many happy years working with good directors, chief among whom were Chuck Jones at the Merrie Melodies/Looney Tunes fun factory and, later, Joe Barbera at the Hanna-Barbera nut farm.

They gave me as much freedom as my ego—or whatever prompted me—required. Their guidance and particular talents helped me tremendously. I'm happy to say I enjoyed the good years of animation. Unfortunately, the days of the big studios and theatrical cartoons are all but dead. The big market today is in television. Let's not be satisfied with just Saturday morning kiddie cartoons. Perhaps we should go after primetime audiences—with the audience values of a *Mary Tyler Moore* show, or an *All in the Family*.

At any rate, new avenues of advancement for the animated cartoon must be explored in order to assure its future as an audience medium. It's a beautiful challenge. I can't do it. I've done my part. I'm going to be seventy years old. . . .

Darrell Van Citters: Did you find that any particular characters were more difficult to write than others?

Maltese: Yeah—the Hanna-Barbera characters like the Harlem Globetrotters and the Wacky Racers, because we were working under the conditions set up by the network bosses. They thought [that] the more characters [there were] in a story, the better it was. Trying to make that stuff funny was impossible. For instance, I went in one day (this was later on); before I tell my story to Joe Barbera, he says, "Great—Do another one."

At Warners, I did one a month, twelve a year, sometimes one every two weeks. At [first at] Hanna-Barbera, I did two a week, then three a week. One hundred and fifty stories a year—we went like *that* (snaps his fingers several times). One right after another. [Hanna and Barbera] moved from three rooms in the old Chaplin Studios on La Brea to where they are now, [in their new studio] on Cahuenga. And then the network boys took over. [Another day I went in] to tell Joe my story, and he said, "I like it, but you'll have to tell the story crew." They told me, "Drop it on the desk, we'll call you and let you know." Boy, those were rough times.

There was a series I refused to do completely. One day, Joe Barbera says, "The head man (I won't mention his name) at CBS got a helluva idea, he thinks, for an animated series he wants you to work on." I go, "What is it?" and he says, "It's a secret fighter for justice—a whaaaale. And what a name he's got for it—Moby Dick!" [*Laughter*] "And he's got all this here sparkling electric stuff: 'Beep-beep-beep'—'Trouble in Morocco!'—'Beep-beep-beep'—'The whale is off!'" Who cares? I told him, I says, "Forget it!" He says, "Please." I say, "NO!" . . .

So, I refused. But there was other stuff I *had* to work on. Finally, I said, "No more. I quit." If we had had to do the cartoons at the old Warner Bros. studio, with the pressure put on us by the network boys, we wouldn't get a Bugs Bunny done. We wouldn't get *anything* finished. . . . We discovered at Warner Bros. many years ago, that if we write a cartoon for the kids, the grownups aren't going to like it. But if we write our cartoons for the grownups, the kids are gonna like it. They're gonna like it anyway.

Now, many of the Merrie Melodies I wrote some twenty-five years ago, that you see on television, still hold up in time. Because I learned long ago to try to write cartoon stories that would hold up in time, like Laurel and Hardy, or Chaplin. Abbott and Costello today look real corny. . . . [T]hey don't hold up as well as Laurel and Hardy. So I tried to learn *that* much about a cartoon, to write stories that aren't hurt by time, if possible.

But the kiddie cartoons done later by Hanna-Barbera, they're—[*snaps fingers*]—quick, quick—get 'em out. Which is all right, but then you have these bosses from the networks telling you how to write them, locate 'em, and all that. Not only that, you are not allowed to have a cartoon character crash into a wall. "Ummm. Just missed that wall." [And they] told us, "No machine guns. No machine-gun bullets." We had a bunch of these tough little guys with the black shorts and white ties and all [the Ant Hill Mob on *The Perils of Penelope Pitstop*]—they all jump like the Keystone Cops. And, of course, there's foul-ups—and BANG-BANG-BANG-BANG-BANG with the machine guns. But [now] they don't want us to use them, even though the machine guns *miss*. So, I go, "What are we supposed to do?" Joe Barbera says, "I don't know . . . we'll use . . . cream pies." So what I did was have 'em shoot chocolate syrup, and they say, "Here comes the fudge!" Those were the rough cartoons to make. . . .

Brad Bird: I was wondering if it was easier to think up gags for full animation rather than limited animation.

Maltese: There is a difference, but the amount of work is almost the same. You can do a storyboard for full animation, and what they do with it is up to them. You can get a director who'll say, "Well, I can cut this down to limited animation." Now, the way we used to do that was we'd have Quick Draw McGraw go off-screen; we'd set up the thing that was going to happen to him off-screen. That would require good sound effects. "Hold on thar!" He'd walk off-screen, and we'd hear this BOOM—CRASH—BANG—and then you'd cut over and you'd see the result. . . .

Chuck [Jones] won't touch limited animation. Limited animation to us [when I was at Warner Bros.] was always a test reel. We'd always do limited animation test reels for the animator. Then the directors find out where he could improve on it, and they'd say, "Fill in the drawings," and all that.

No, there isn't a helluva lot of difference. The amount of work in writing a story—it's there. You think of the idea. The only thing you show is maybe a few little drawings of the thing happening to the guy. But you had to *think* about what was happening to him, and then cut it down to fit the limited animation method. That kind of explains it. . . .

It's a great business, and I hope that someday you'll be able to take it out of the kiddie matinee thing, and bring it up to something better, because it's going to die otherwise. There's just so much time on Saturday morning, and you know what they do to make way for the new stuff on Saturday morning—it's to move this kiddie crap to *Sunday*.

Now, Hanna-Barbera tried unsuccessfully for primetime with *Wait Till Your Father Gets Home*. Prime time. I know the writers, and we were hamstrung. They were stopped. Experienced writers who know the cartoon business were stopped by the network boys. They'd say, "We want this, that, and the other thing. I'd say, "Wait a minute. We know what we're talking about."

Joe Barbera was a great salesman. He could sell anything to the networks. I heard that CBS was going to build a cartoon studio in California and compete, and hire, if necessary, the talent from the other studios, and put their boys in charge. What they did was they went down to the other studios and would pit one producer against another—"You do it our way, the way *we* want, or we'll give it to DePatie-Freleng, or Filmation, or whoever!" The result was [that] the producers, who never said anything before, shoulda got together and said, "The hell with *you* guys. You do it *our* way or we don't wanna play with you guys at all, 'cause we've got the sponsors, the advertisers. Without them, you can't live!" But they got chicken. They got chicken and did it *their* way. The result was [that] great talents like Joe Barbera and the rest of them backed off and made room for these boys put in by the network. . . .

John Musker: Has Chuck Jones ever approached you on doing stories on his TV specials? It seems like there's a pretty noticeable decline in the story content once you left his unit at Warner's.

Maltese: Yes, he wanted me to come back. But I wouldn't leave Hanna-Barbera, because I didn't want to go back to work for Warners. I knew Warners was on the way out. Because Warner Bros., unlike MGM, who publicized Tom and Jerry, never publicized Bugs Bunny or any of the cartoons. Any publicity on the Warner cartoons was done by word of mouth. The only time I went back to work for Chuck was when I had a hiatus at Hanna-Barbera, and Joe Barbera says, "Well, I'll call you." It was the end of '63. I waited about two or three weeks. Chuck called and says, "I got a chance to get the MGM release, but I have to do a couple of Tom and Jerrys." [Editors' note: Jones's subsequent MGM releases would include *How the Grinch Stole Christmas* (1966).] "Will you write them for me?" I say, "Sure. I'm not working." . . .

I did the Tom and Jerry—I think I called it *The Cat Above and the Mouse Below* [*laughter*]. The first Tom and Jerry I ever wrote. They couldn't be as good as Joe Barbera's Tom and Jerrys, because Joe had, from the beginning, that something—he couldn't explain it—that thing inside him that made him do Tom and Jerrys the way only Joe Barbera could do them. My Tom and Jerrys were only passable. I told Joe—"What did you ever do? You did ten thousand feet of a cat chasing a mouse!"

So the result was these two Tom and Jerry cartoons. Chuck got the MGM release, and they set him up at Tower 12, on Sunset. He says, "You want to work for me?" I said, "Sure." I did about fourteen Tom and Jerrys for him. [Then] Joe Barbera called me up and he says, "How much is Chuck paying you?" I say, "$250 a week." He says, "I'll give you $500." I say, "I'll be in in the morning!" [*Laughter*]. . . .

I went back [to Hanna-Barbera] in 1965, and I worked on a whole bunch of different things, writing various types of cartoons . . . that was the whole secret of it. Fred Silverman, who was the head of children's programming at CBS, had three or four crazy characters—Wireman, and all those. (Who remembers? This was twelve years ago.) He says, "Could you get a couple of ideas?" I said, "Sure." I went home and wrote fifteen story ideas. And I knew the villains in each one had to be strong enough to challenge the talents of these four "super-guys." I had Paper-Man, who could fold himself up and fly like a paper airplane. This one [villain], Electro-Man, could appear on a TV screen at some home, step out and rob the place, jump back into the TV screen, jump in a car, and zoom off. Now, it was up to these [super-]guys to get him. They trapped him in a phone booth, and he disappeared through the wire. They trapped him in the wire, and they tied the wire in a square knot! [*Laughter*]

I had fifteen ideas like this, and I called them "The Impossibles." Joe Barbera says, "The Impossibles?" I say, "Yeah, call them the Impossibles." So he told the ideas to Fred Silverman, and he says, "Unless Mike Maltese writes these things, you're not gonna get the show." Joe says, "I'll give you another $100, Mike." Like, stupid. I coulda asked for another two or three hundred. I was always eager to work. I say, "Yeah, yeah, yeah!" . . .

The thing is, you go along, and you try to make your buck. I never made the big money, because I never had the opportunity to go into live-action. I'll tell you one thing: Joe Barbera got fooled by a lot of live-action writers who tried to write cartoons. He found out that a cartoon writer could write live-action stories—they write *Phyllis* and a few other TV shows—the transition from cartoon writing to live-action writing is easier than the other way around. Because live-action guys come in and say, "A guy comes in here—and he has a damn funny walk. And the way he walks funny—you know how you guys draw it. He meets this other funny character here—could be an aardvark or a lion, and . . . oh well, *you* know how you guys do it. I don't care, if it's funny—ha ha" [*laughter*]. . . .

I had a lot of fun doing the [*Quick Draw*] *McGraw* show, and I also used Snagglepuss—I don't know if any of you remember him—the guy who talked like Bert Lahr. . . . I made sure not to use any of the real Bert Lahr material, [but] I added my own Bert Lahr-isms, as it were: "Exit—stage left!" "I'll be with you in a forthwith—in a fifth-with, ee-vun." All that stuff. But we had to stop because [Bert Lahr] threatened to sue. . . .

Well, that's all, fellows.

Hanna-Barbera Australia

DAN TORRE AND LIENORS TORRE / 2018

From *Australian Animation: An International History* (London: Palgrave Macmillan, 2018), 161–78. Reprinted with permission of the authors and SNCSC.

> I actually had an argument with a cab driver coming back from the Sydney airport once. I told him I was working for Hanna-Barbera doing a Fred Flintstone special at the time, and he just flatly refused to believe me, totally convinced that I was telling a pack of fibs. "I thought that was all done in America." "No, it's not all done in America, it's done here." After a while, I thought, I'm not going to try anymore. So, in future, if someone asked me what I did for a living, I said I sold real estate!
> —DIANNE COLMAN, AUSTRALIAN ANIMATION DIRECTOR[1]

Unknown to many, Hanna-Barbera established a large animation studio in Sydney that operated from approximately 1972 to 1988. The formation and rise of Hanna-Barbera Australia represent a colorful narrative and a previously unpublished segment of both Australian animation history and that of the Hanna-Barbera studio.

OVERSEAS EXPANSION

Bill Hanna and Joe Barbera had left MGM after winning a number of Academy Awards for Tom and Jerry and other animated films for the cinema, and had opened the Hanna-Barbera studio in Los Angeles in 1957. The commencement of television had created an almost insatiable demand for animated films at minimal cost. Hanna-Barbera responded by developing and exploiting a uniquely limited style of animation, costing only a fraction of that of the cinema shorts. Early productions included *The Flintstones*, *The Jetsons*, *Yogi Bear*, and *Top Cat*.

In 1966, after a steady stream of hit shows, Hanna and Barbera sold their animation studio to the Taft Broadcasting Company, but stayed on to run the studio, overseeing a number of further successful series. But cost increases and competition from other television animation studios prompted Hanna-Barbera to look offshore to find more cost-effective places in which to produce their animation. Having a low exchange rate in relation to the American dollar, and generally lower labor costs, Australia appeared to be a promising market. In his autobiography, Bill Hanna describes:

> After an initial evaluation of prospective locations for such expansion, we concluded that Australia would be a good place to start. Although we were prepared to work with any communication problems that might arise from language differences, it was just common sense to launch the organization of our first foreign studio in a country that spoke English. I was absolutely confident of my ability and experience in putting a cartoon studio together, but assimilating people of different cultures to the logistics of our American operations would still be a trial-and-error process. If I was going to break ground in this region of business development, I preferred to do it without an interpreter.[2]

Hanna-Barbera's link with Australia actually spanned back to the mid-1960s, when Eric Porter Productions was first commissioned to produce the *Abbott and Costello* animated series (which aired in 1967). In 1970, Hanna-Barbera asked Porter to produce a further series under a contract that was reported to be worth AU $670,000.[3] But Porter, who had just begun production on the feature film *Marco Polo Junior*, had to turn down this proposition since his studio was already working at full capacity.

Hanna-Barbera subsequently contracted with Sydney-based API (Air Programs International) in 1971 to produce the animated television series *The Funky Phantom*. At that time, API was working simultaneously on a number of feature-length animated specials, including *The Legend of Robin Hood*. Consequently, they soon fell behind in their production of the Hanna-Barbera commission. Bill Hanna used this as a pretext for travelling to Australia, where he could then supervise the production. He also, it would appear, had a further motive, which was to set up a Hanna-Barbera studio in Australia. Zoran Janjic, who was animation director at API, describes Bill Hanna's arrival:

> He subcontracted *The Funky Phantom* to API, a thirteen-part half-hour series, and supervised the work on it. The owner of the studio stuck Bill Hanna into a pokey little office, partitioned off by himself, no phone or anything. I had a big corner office; so I went to Bill Hanna, said, "Would you like to move in with me?" And he said, "You sure?" I said, "Yeah!

We're working together; you're doing the timing: I'm storyboarding and doing this and that." He replied, "Oh, I'd love to. There's only one thing: I really like to go out for lunch." After a while it became routine; he'd say "Let's go!" As we were going past the paint department, he would look in: "OK, this row of girls, come with me; we're going to lunch!" He would take out the whole row of girls, twelve or more of them! "You are next day!" he'd say to the others. He was terrific fun to work with, and very good with people.[4]

Margaret Parkes, who began working as an animator soon before Hanna arrived at API, also noted Bill Hanna's gregarious nature:

He was in his sixties, just the most amazing man, energetic, a person who works beautifully with people. He wants you to work hard, but he really appreciates his staff. He'd bring in whole bowls of chilli, put them on the up-side radiator and serve everybody in the studio lunch. Then, if you're working back late, he'd walk around the studio and buy everyone there a hamburger. Or he'd say, "Come on—let's all go out to dinner."[5]

Ultimately, API became the channel through which the Los Angeles Hanna-Barbera studios expanded into Australia. During the time that Bill Hanna was supervising the production of *The Funky Phantom*, he was also quietly laying the groundwork for setting up a studio in Sydney, scouting out locations and making note of useful contacts. After API's completion of *The Funky Phantom*, he returned to Los Angeles. But soon after, he contacted Zoran Janjic, inviting him to fly to Los Angeles to meet with both himself and Joe Barbera. It was then that they offered Janjic the top job of managing their Australian studio. In his autobiography, Bill Hanna recounted these events in a rather abbreviated manner (leaving out the essential details about the API studio): "I booked a flight to Sydney to scout out the various facilities and meet some of the folks currently involved in Australian animation production. During this reconnaissance, I became impressed with some layouts by a talented animator named Zoran Janjic. After some discussion with Zoran, I was convinced that I had found the right guy to function as manager of the Australian studio—to be called Hanna-Barbera Australia."[6] However, Hanna-Barbera's plan to open a studio in Sydney was met with a great deal of resistance—on both sides of the world.

In America, the animation unions were already angered by the fact that Hanna-Barbera had taken *The Funky Phantom* series to API for production (instead of undertaking it at the LA studio where preproduction work had begun). They claimed that Hanna-Barbera had "breached its pact by failing to notify the union" of its plan "to finish films in preproduction in Hollywood, in a foreign country (Australia)." In protest, the union had ordered its Los Angeles animators to stop all work on *The Funky Phantom* series.[7] The news that Hanna-Barbera was about to open a full production studio in Australia greatly compounded their frustration.

In Australia, the imminent opening of a foreign studio was also worrisome to many. API and other local studios had been striving for a long time to set up a viable animation industry in Australia. By 1971, things were finally looking quite positive. Walt Hucker observed: "All the ingredients for a successful animation industry have been here for a long time but they have only just gelled."[8] But then this optimistic mood was all but dashed when it was announced that Hanna-Barbera was to set up shop in Sydney. From API's point of view, they had welcomed Mr. Hanna into their studio, but they had also unwittingly let in a Trojan horse of competition.

Subsequently, Walt Hucker attempted to block the arrival of the Hanna-Barbera studio. Eric Porter, who also saw the threat that Hanna-Barbera posed, joined in the calls for government intervention. Hucker and Porter held a meeting with a local senator, who admitted that nothing could be done "under the present system," but that "perhaps the government could impose a very heavy tax on the American company."[9] Encouraged by this prospect, both Hucker and Porter then travelled to Canberra for a meeting with the Federal Minister for the Arts, Peter Howson. Although the minister offered his sympathy, nothing concrete eventuated from this meeting.

On the other hand, not everyone feared the arrival of Hanna-Barbera, certainly not most of the Australian animators. Bill Hanna had garnered a very positive reputation among the local animation community while he was embedded at the API studio. And although many newspaper articles accurately expressed the fears of the local studio directors, these articles also inadvertently expressed the hopes of many local animators: "Hanna-Barbera Productions Pty. Ltd. is a multimillion-dollar company with large distribution outlets available to it. The company would be able to offer to Australian animators a substantial increase on their present salaries. It is possible that the large Hanna-Barbera company could acquire the total work force of Australian animators and this could mean the end of the Australian animation film industry."[10] For the local studio management, the key point from this article was *the end of the Australian animation industry*. However, to the local animator, the indisputable key points would have been interpreted to be: *higher wages* and *jobs for everyone*.

Eventually, API managed, through the courts, to get a temporary injunction placed on the new Hanna-Barbera studio, which they hoped would lead to a further "twelve to eighteen months breathing space to enable them to consolidate their positions."[11] The actual court case lasted several weeks. In the meantime, both Bill Hanna and the Australian studio heads were frequently in both the local and international press. US *Variety* magazine reported:

Bill Hanna, sitting in his new office in the inner Sydney suburb of St. Leonards, told *Variety* that on legal advice he was unable to discuss the structure of the subsidiary company or his future plans until the court case had been disposed of. He did say that in future, he expected to spend much of his time in Australia. However, he has already advertised in the *Sydney Morning Herald* for application from animators, layout artists, assistant animators, background artists, Xerox technicians, camera women, and cartoon painters.[12]

Unfortunately for both Hucker and Porter, the judge ruled in favour of Mr. Hanna. It seems that, even though Bill Hanna had successfully lured away the best local animators, he had done so legally—most of API's employees were employed on a casual basis and were therefore essentially free agents.[13] Hanna-Barbera was found not to have broken any laws, but their move to Sydney unquestionably caused a significant disruption to the local animation industry which, although apparently booming in 1972, had been operating on fairly thin margins. With Hanna-Barbera's large foreign capital reserves, it would be virtually impossible for a small company, bound solely to the local economy, to compete.

Hanna-Barbera wasted no time in scooping up the cream of the animation industry talent. Bill Hanna also exploited many of the useful contacts that API had previously established. For example, in the first months of Hanna-Barbera Australia, he recruited Australian musician and composer John Sangster (who had composed the score for a number of feature-length animated specials for API) to compose the music for several of his shows. Sangster recalls his initial meeting with Bill Hanna:

> Over luncheon, the first day we met, Bill asked me whether musicians in Australia were eligible for residual royalties from film music they'd played on. It was his one and only query. I answered him that no, they weren't, but that a few of the studio musos were agitating their union to this end. "How long do you reckon before that happens?" As truthfully as I could, I explained to him the speed at which the Australian Professional Musicians Union works. He said, "OK, then we'll go ahead." Later on over coffee I asked Bill, "What would you have done if I'd said yes?" In reply, he pulled out of his pocket a long list of countries, beginning with Guatemala. Seems the main reason he'd come out here was that the American studio musos, along with the American animators, had priced themselves out of the game, on the basis of residuals.[14]

Clearly, Hanna-Barbera's move to Sydney, although encouraged by a significant pool of talented animators, was motivated primarily by a desire to significantly cut production costs.

In an interesting twist, just three months after the conclusion of the court case, Eric Porter accepted a commission from Hanna-Barbera to produce an animated series based on the detective Charlie Chan, called *The Amazing Chan and the Chan Clan*. The initial contract was worth a reported $400,000. The following year, Porter signed another deal with Hanna-Barbera to produce the first season of the superhero-themed *Super Friends*. Although it might seem surprising that Porter would have accepted these contracts (after attempting to block Hanna-Barbera's arrival), his own studio was suffering greatly from the heavy losses resulting from the *Marco Polo* feature film: the arrangement with Hanna-Barbera would ensure the continuation of his animation studio for at least a couple more years. One magazine article viewed this in a positive light, noting: "When Hanna-Barbera Productions first set up in Australia many people expressed the fear that the Australian animation industry would be pushed out. This fear now seems unfounded."[15] However, at this point in time, Hanna-Barbera Australia was still very much in its infancy, and considerable growth and expansion would soon take place.

BUILDING THE STUDIO

Bill Hanna was very hands-on in his involvement in the setting up of the Australian studio. He recalls:

> Setting up our first major production facility there proved to be an entirely novel adventure. The core staff we recruited was a group of about sixty young people who were as congenial a gathering of folks you'd ever want to meet. They were a fun bunch of kids, and Vi [Bill's wife Violet] and I had good times hosting a series of in-house picnics and get-togethers during the weeks we all spent working together to set up their studio. Despite their youth, all of these people were experienced in animation production—respective of their abilities, of course—and the initial organization of the studio was a fairly seamless operation. By [late 1972], we were up to speed and production was underway.[16]

In general, Hanna-Barbera did pay better than the Australian studios and also provided more modern and better working conditions. One animation director noted that before Hanna-Barbera moved into town, many of the local studios were comparable to sweatshops: "But that changed with Hanna-Barbera: air-conditioning was improved; we were given drawing classes; it became altogether more professional."[17] But, rather than earning a weekly salary as before, most animators at Hanna-Barbera were paid by the foot. So, those that worked hard (and learned to use plenty of short cuts) could earn a very substantial salary. Gairden Cooke reminisces: "That was the heyday for earning capacity! Everybody will tell you that. We were earning so much money we hardly knew what to do with it! Blokes said, 'I'm making more money than the prime minister!'"[18] But this "heyday" was short-lived, admitted Cooke: "When you think back, it didn't last that long." One complicating issue was that Hanna-Barbera Australia was geared primarily toward the seasonal demands of the American television market. In 1977, the estimate was that "For eight months of the year Hanna-Barbera [Australia] employs one hundred and forty people to rush material through for the peak US production period; this drops to twenty workers between January and April."[19]

For those first few years that Bill Hanna lived in Sydney, he was described as being very personable and fostering a very egalitarian working environment (which was said to be quite different from his Los Angeles studio). He continued, for example, routinely to take his staff out to lunch (groups of twenty or more at a time), and he would happily drop in on employees who lived in shared flats and cook them up one of his famous chilli dinners. This comradery with the Australian animators extended even to the Los Angeles facility; if anyone from the Australian studio were to drop in, Bill Hanna would make time for them.[20] On one occasion an animator from Australia, being in Los Angeles, decided to drop in (without an appointment) to the Hanna-Barbera studios. He went up to the receptionist and said, "G'day, I'm here to see Bill." The receptionist stiffened and replied, "You mean *Mr.* Hanna!" "Yeah, yeah, that's the bloke, Bill Hanna." The receptionist was in the process of turning him away, but just then Mr. Hanna happened to walk by; he immediately and warmly greeted the animator. Then, to everyone's disbelief, Bill took him out to lunch.[21]

EXPANSION

The studio began by producing the animated series *Wait Till Your Father Gets Home*, and was soon making *Scooby-Doo* and many other established Hanna-Barbera shows. In these early years, the work was, in the opinion of some, "really churned out," regardless of quality.[22] Zoran Janjic remembers how Bill Hanna was usually quite happy with their work; but in contrast, "Joe Barbera wasn't so fond of us. I met him a couple of times. I went over there, and he said 'Oh, yeah, yeah, you're from Australia; you're delivering us tripe!'—or something like that."[23] But as the studio matured, its output attained a higher level of quality, and for nearly a decade they were producing a substantial portion of the company's total animation output.

At this time, all of the animation produced in the Sydney studio was contracted work from the main American studio. In an interview many years later, Zoran Janjic noted that one of the things that had convinced him to join Hanna-Barbera was the assurance that the studio would also be able to produce original Australian-generated series and specials. In the first several years many different ideas were pitched to the parent company, both by himself and by other directors; but in the end not one of these proposals ever saw the light of day. This was a big disappointment to Zoran and was one of the reasons why he left the studio in the mid-1970s to start up his own animation company, Zap Productions.[24]

Around this same time (in 1974) the Australian publishing group Paul Hamlyn purchased a 51 percent share of Hanna-Barbera Australia. The deal was spearheaded by Paul Hamlyn executive Neil Balnaves, who saw it as an excellent opportunity to capitalize on the Hanna-Barbera licensing potential. This acquisition, in a sense, "Australianised" the studio. Soon, books and other items were produced locally, based on just about every Hanna-Barbera property. Balnaves pointed out, "It always felt good when you had books, or you had videotapes, or dolls, or games with a character base." However, he conceded that "It was never a big money spinner; we only owned the rights in Australasia and our local market was only twelve to fourteen million people."[25]

As Hanna-Barbera Australia was now, at least in part, an "Australian" company, the studio also moved into local television advertising production. In 1975, a commercials division was formed. Everything was produced at the Sydney studio: "the original storyboards and voice recording, through the whole animation process, up to the video transfer."[26] As with other studios in Australia, this proved to be very lucrative. The division was initially headed by Robbert Smit, along with Dianne Colman as the lead animator. They produced a wide variety of advertisements, but most of the time the client would want to use a Hanna-Barbera character—such as Yogi Bear [for] ice creams. "Major accounts handled included Weston's (the biscuit people), Scotties (the tissues people), AGL, NRMA, Streets, Pauls, Arnott's, and many others."[27]

INTERNATIONAL IMPEDIMENTS

By the late 1970s, Hanna-Barbera had also set up sizeable studios in Brazil, Spain, Taiwan, and South Korea, creating a worldwide network of animation studios. This allowed for Hanna-Barbera to greatly expand its output of animation; but at the same time, it was noticeably decreasing its production schedule at its Los Angeles studio. This, understandably, upset the American animation union further. Things came to a head in 1979 with a large Hollywood strike in which "more than 800 members of the Motion Picture Cartoonists Guild walked out . . . in protest at work being taken overseas."[28] However, the Australian press was not overly sympathetic to the American animators, describing their plight somewhat patronisingly: "Australian artists are being blamed for a strike in America. Hollywood artists claim the Australians are doing work which rightfully belongs to Americans. They're demanding that cartoon characters like Fred Flintstone and the Pink Panther come to life on their drawing boards."[29]

Bill Hanna describes the unrest, also from a rather understated perspective:

> From the viewpoint of management, it should be realized that none of us ever intended or believed that expanding our operations abroad would deprive our own people here in the U.S. of a livelihood. Business was flourishing at that time here, and there was more than enough work for everyone, not only at Hanna-Barbera but within the entire cartoon industry itself. . . . On the other side of the coin and for that matter the ocean, we had been receiving for years overtures from numerous foreign animation studios who were crying for work, as well as offering attractive costs. It seemed a fair and effective alternative.[30]

Of course, his concluding comment about "foreign animation studios who were crying for work" was, in fact, a request to take on subcontracted work so that the struggling local studios could maintain continuity of employment for their staff. It was clearly not a cry for Hanna-Barbera (or any other foreign studio) to move in, take away their employees, and ultimately become their competition.

There were other challenges that Hanna-Barbera faced through being such a large company with studios worldwide. The Australian studio needed to produce a minimum of two episodes per week to be profitable. Thus, approximately every two days, the Los Angeles studio would send over a packet of storyboards with audio tapes of the character dialogue, to which the animators would listen, working out the lip-synching of the characters. By this time, the work on a single series might be divided up among several studio locations: "Bill Hanna used to have this nightmare where shows would go missing. If Sydney were making the key animation on certain shows, for which the layouts were being done in Brazil, the storyboards being done in Spain; the show being conceived in L.A., you would have the show being fabricated in five or six countries."[31] And, on occasion, things would get lost in transport, grinding the whole series to a halt. "You'd have bits of shows all 'round the world which you could not complete!"[32] Zoran Janjic remembers on several occasions "going on my motorbike with my editor on the back, holding two cases of film." Upon arriving at the airport, they would then have to convince the customs officer that they were doing "nothing illegal" but that the reels absolutely had to go on the next plane.[33]

The cultural differences between America and Australia were relatively small, but subtle variances would become apparent from time to time. One such instance occurred in the production of a baseball-themed Flintstones special. Not being familiar with the predominantly American sport of baseball, the Australians animated the characters running around the baseball diamond in a clockwise direction (rather than the correct counterclockwise path). It had seemed a logical thing to do since that was the direction that the horses would run around the local Australian racetracks. But to correct this error, many of the scenes had to be completely reanimated.[34]

Being a large studio staffed mostly by young people, a number of animator hijinks also took place. Margaret Parkes recalls one incident where, while working on the production of the *Berenstain Bears* series, a background artist mischievously painted some underwear on the floor of the bears' bathroom. It was returned from America with a stern note saying, "Remove the bra!"[35] Another more serious incident was described by Neil Balnaves regarding the production of *The All-New Popeye Hour* series (1978). It seems that a number of the animators surreptitiously inserted periodic nude drawings of the character Olive Oyl, which were only noticeable when viewed at a very slow speed. Thus, the various "offending" scenes were repeatedly aired on American television, the prank only discovered when someone at the television network viewed one of the episodes on a Moviola. To their disbelief, they saw "running across the screen every eighth drawing, or so, a naked Olive Oyl." A furor ensued and "the network screamed!" Balnaves, who was manager of the Australian studio, was then forced to review, virtually frame-by-frame, nearly seven hours of footage. Offending images were found in virtually every episode; finally it all had to be discarded![36]

A CHANGING LANDSCAPE

As mentioned earlier, Hanna-Barbera's Australian studio went through several different ownership arrangements. When first opened in 1972, the Australian studio was set up as a subsidiary of the American studio (at that time owned by Taft Broadcasting, but managed by Bill Hanna and Joe Barbera). In late 1974, Paul Hamlyn Publishing purchased a 51 percent share of the Australian studio, which they sold in 1978 to James Hardie Industries (historically, Australia's largest producer of asbestos products), who were keen to diversify their holdings.

However, one of the most interesting developments occurred in 1984, when Hanna-Barbera Australia set up a small studio in Los Angeles that was independent of (and would prove to be in competition with) the American parent company. This new studio was given the very Australian name of Southern Star Productions (referencing the prominent star constellation which is most visible from Australia). As a further symbolic move, the studio was set up in the office space located on the floor directly above Olivia Newton-John's boutique retail outlet, Koala Blue. This facility was primarily a development studio that would devise original projects, then to be produced at the Sydney studio. The finished products were wholly owned by the Australian Hanna-Barbera division and were sold directly to American television networks, circumventing the parent Hanna-Barbera company. It was a curious arrangement, but it allowed for the Australian studio to maintain a healthier financial position and to provide relatively stable employment for its staff. This became increasingly important as the parent company over the next few years began to shift more of its work to the lower-cost Asian studios.

One of the first animated projects that Southern Star/Hanna-Barbera Australia produced was a series based on the Berenstain Bears (1985). The local press detailed the significance of this production:

> The Hanna-Barbera studio [in Sydney] produces principally for Saturday morning television in the US. Most of the work it does is subcontracted, that is, work passed on from the parent company in the US. But recently Hanna-Barbera in Australia has taken a history-making step by developing its own cartoon series for the American market. It's *Berenstain Bears*, based on books by Stan and Jan Berenstain, a husband-and-wife team who have been writing and drawing books about bears for twenty years. Thirteen half-hour episodes have been sold to the CBS network. The target audience is four-to-seven-year-olds and it will go to air in September. The production costs of *Berenstain Bears* are astronomical. The Australian side will cost more than $100,000 to make each half-hour episode. Still, it is a coup for Salter. "This really is an extraordinary thing for us," he says. "We own it, we developed it, we did all the original work. I'm convinced that the long-term health of the studio down here depends on us actually owning a series. What's good for us is to keep doing the subcontracting but also to have our own ideas. We have gone out on a limb to the tune of $500,000 in setting up a development studio of our own in Los Angeles. We did that about nine months ago and it has taken a bit of careful nurturing but it's paid off, and now we've got this series."[37]

The next major show that the studio developed and produced independently was a two-season run of the animated series *Teen Wolf* (1986–87), which was based on the live action Michael J. Fox movie of the same name (1985).

Around this time (1985), Australia's Wonderland theme park (partially funded by the Australian Hanna-Barbera studio's half-owner, James Hardie Industries) was opened in Sydney. This large theme park prominently featured Hanna-Barbera Land, which was described as "a colourful cartoon village which features Yogi Bear, Fred Flintstone, and many other favourite cartoon characters."[38] It included such Hanna-Barbera themed rides as Dino's Derby, Fred Flintstone's Splashdown, Magilla Gorilla's Flotilla, and The Beastie.

Unfortunately for the Australian studio, the American studio had discovered by now that there were much cheaper places in the world to produce animation. This led to an expansion into South Korea, Taiwan, and the Philippines. Thus, Hanna-Barbera Australia began receiving less work from America and, as a result, the parent company began to contemplate divesting the Sydney studio altogether. Simultaneously, the Australian owner, James Hardie Industries, was being forced to pay compensations to the families of those who had died from asbestos poisoning; it too was seeking to shed its investment in Hanna-Barbera. Thus, in 1986, Neil Balnaves led an MBO (management buyout) and purchased both the American (Taft Broadcasting) and the Australian (James Hardie) portions of the company—which also included the Southern Star studio in Los Angeles, and all the merchandising and distribution rights of the Hanna-Barbera catalogue for Australasia.[39]

Soon after this transfer, however, there was a further shift in the sales and marketing of television animation in America. Almost overnight, the networks significantly reduced the amount that they were willing to pay for an animated show. This forced the producers to recoup their investments through licensing and toy sales instead of network sales, which left the Hanna-Barbera Sydney studio and its approximately 120 employees in a very precarious position. Balnaves recalls, "So out of desperation I did a deal to sell the company to Disney, who came down and put up a reasonable offer for the business."[40] However, at the last minute Disney was prepared to offer only a fraction of the previously discussed amount. Knowing that he had little choice, Balnaves was forced to accept: "I took the view that, whatever I can do to save my employees' work and keep the creative, intellectual thing alive, we owe that to the industry, and I just couldn't face closing it. Plus, there was a lot of desks, equipment, computers, and cameras. I thought if I could sell the whole thing, lock, stock, and barrel, as a going concern, to Disney, I'd save everyone's jobs."[41] So, in a sense, Hanna-Barbera Australia was transformed into Walt Disney Australia. The new Disney studio flourished and would soon become one of the most significant of the Disney animation studios.

After transferring the studio to Disney, Balnaves and his business partners still retained ownership of the Los Angeles Southern Star studio and, most significantly, they still owned the Australian and Asian rights to the Hanna-Barbera catalogue (including licensing rights). Neil Balnaves then relocated the small Southern Star office from Los Angeles to Sydney, and the newly formed Southern Star studio successfully set about producing animation and live-action programming for more than two decades.

CONCLUSION

Over the years, the Hanna-Barbera Australia studio created hundreds of hours of animation. They produced dozens of television series ranging from Yogi

Bear and Scooby-Doo to *Wait Till Your Father Comes Home*, many hundreds of animated advertisements, a large number of animated title sequences, as well as numerous feature-length animated specials. During this time, they trained hundreds of Australian animators, many of whom then went on to work either overseas or for other studios in Australia (bringing their newly learned expertise with them); some even set up their own studios. "They gradually became fingers that went out into the animation industry," Robbert Smit says.[42] Although the studio officially closed in 1988, Hanna-Barbera continued for several years to have work produced in Australia on a freelance contract basis with various small local studios. When Hanna-Barbera set up a studio in the Philippines, it was initially run by a contingent of Australian animators and directors. In 1989, Margaret Parkes relocated to the new studio in Manila to work as a director. She recalls: "The Hanna-Barbera studio in the Philippines had nine hundred employees. You'd never seen anything like it in your life—it was just massive! We worked on a lot of productions: Jonny Quest, The Addams Family, Yogi Bear, Flintstones Christmas and Easter specials, Paddington Bear."[43] Parkes stayed at the Manila studio for only a few years, but a number of other Australians remained for over a decade.

Bill Hanna's presence in Sydney is remembered fondly by nearly all who worked with him which, as the years progressed, reached an almost legendary status. [Balnaves recalls]:

> He made such an impression down here because it was very rare that a person of that caliber and reputation had ever actually taken the art department, thirty inkers and painters, out to dinner. He would flood restaurants, take the whole paint department out, might be fifty or sixty people. He was lovely with these people. I think it broke everyone's heart when he moved on and did exactly the same thing with the Taiwanese. They adopted him, and he fell in love with all of them, too.[44]

Unquestionably, Hanna-Barbera provided work for hundreds of Australians in the animation industry—at an above-average wage (relative to local wages)—and in doing so he also provided a training ground for many who would have never had an opportunity to work in animation. In fact, Hanna-Barbera provided work for many thousands of animators across the world; but as the studios would shift to progressively lower-cost markets, they also, in a sense, took away work from thousands of animators. In the Australian experience, as the studios relocated from Sydney to Taiwan and Manila, the Australians found themselves in much the same situation that the American animators had faced a decade before—wishing that "Fred Flintstone would come to life on *their* drawing boards."[45]

Notes

1. Dianne Colman, interview with Dan Torre and Lienors Torre, May 5, 2004.
2. Bill Hanna with Tom Ito, *A Cast of Friends* (New York: Da Capo Press, 2000), 198.
3. "Cartoon Characters March into a Gold-Plated Future," Sydney *Sunday Telegraph*, July 18, 1971, 74.
4. Zoran Janjic, interview with Dan Torre and Lienors Torre, January 19, 2005.
5. Margaret Parkes, interview with Dan Torre and Lienors Torre, April 24, 2004.
6. Hanna, *A Cast of Friends*, 198.
7. "Australian Animation Industry Fears American Company," *Film Weekly*, April 3, 1972.
8. "Cartoon Characters," *Sunday Telegraph*, 74.
9. "Australian Animation Industry Fears," *Film Weekly*.
10. "Australian Animation Industry Fears," *Film Weekly*.
11. "Australian Animation Firms Fear Hanna-Barbera Will Crush Them," *Variety*, May 9, 1972, 44.
12. "Australian Animation Firms Fear Hanna-Barbera," *Variety*.
13. Janjic, 2005.
14. John Sangster, *Seeing the Rafters: The Life and Times of an Australian Jazz Musician* (Melbourne: Penguin, 1988), 181.
15. "Eric Porter Gains Hanna-Barbera Contract," *Film Weekly*, September 4, 1972.
16. Hanna, *A Cast of Friends*, 198.
17. Robbert Smit, interview with Dan Torre and Lienors Torre, January 12, 2005.
18. Gairden Cooke, interview with Dan Torre and Lienors Torre, January 24, 2005.
19. Humphrey McQueen, *Australia's Media Monopolies* (Melbourne: Widescope, 1977), 155.
20. Neil Balnaves, interview with Dan Torre and Lienors Torre, February 14, 2007.
21. Cooke, 2005.
22. Colman, 2004.
23. Janjic, 2005.
24. Craig Monahan, *Animated* [short film], 1989.
25. Balnaves, 2007.
26. Colman, 2004.
27. Colman, 2004.
28. "Cartoon Row No Laughing Matter," *The Australian*, August 16, 1979.
29. "Cartoon Row No Laughing Matter," *The Australian*.
30. Hanna, *A Cast of Friends*, 201.
31. Balnaves, 2007.
32. Balnaves, 2007.
33. Janjic, 2005.
34. Balnaves, 2007.
35. Parkes, 2004.
36. Balnaves, 2007.
37. Bronwyn Watson, "Animation Moves a Winner—Sydney Animators Have Cracked the US Market with a Homegrown Product," *The Advertiser*, August 9, 1985.
38. Australia Wonderland promotional brochure (Sydney, 1985).
39. Balnaves, 2007.
40. Balnaves, 2007.

41. Balnaves, 2007.
42. Smit, 2005.
43. Parkes, 2004.
44. Balnaves, 2007.
45. "Cartoon Row No Laughing Matter," *The Australian*.

Darrell McNeil on *Super Friends*

MARC TYLER NOBLEMAN / 2011

Edited from "Super '70s and '80s: *Super Friends*—Darrell McNeil, Animator," from the blog *Noblemania*, July 29, 2011. Reprinted with permission.

Marc Tyler Nobleman: How did you get the job on *Super Friends*?

Darrell McNeil: Before getting the *Super Friends* job, I was, among other things, just getting out of Westchester High School in 1975, then attending two classes at Cal State Long Beach and one at UCLA. The main Cal State class I took was an animation class taught by Hanna-Barbera veteran producer (and future *All-New Super Friends Hour* producer) Art Scott; the UCLA class was on the history of Saturday morning television, taught by future ABC Saturday morning standards and practices [S&P] ace Bonny Dare, where I met Bill Hanna and Joe Barbera.

Mr. Barbera invited eighteen-year-old *moi* to pitch several animated series concepts of mine to Hanna-Barbera's then-directors of development, Duane Poole and Dick Robbins. Mr. Hanna encouraged me to enter his studio's training program, to supply Hanna-Barbera with the next generation of animators. Despite the *dis*couraging efforts of program administrator and all-around rat's ass Harry Love, ([overruled] by both Mr. Hanna and Mr. Scott), I entered the training program and, while I was still eighteen, was hired by Hanna-Barbera as an inbetweener (early-level animator). *First* show? Guess!

Nobleman: What were your responsibilities?

McNeil: I was a *Super Friends* layout/assistant animator [on and off] from 1976–83. I started as an inbetweener, then breakdown artist on all the series Hanna-Barbera produced in-house that season (1976–77). But because of my speed, my near-fanatic love of the characters and knowledge of same, and the importance that ABC placed on this show, it was decided after a few weeks that I be solely assigned to *Super Friends*. I cleaned up almost every scene in *The All-New Super Friends Hour* opening title, and ended up cleaning up and finishing the famous group shot of the Super Friends in the final scene of the title sequence. . . .

[Bill Hanna] and I had an interesting relationship, employer-employee wise, which I shall go into thusly. . . . I was the first *fan* of Hanna-Barbera that Hanna-Barbera had ever hired. Most of its animators, who were Disney/ Warner Bros./MGM "full" animation vets, hated the place, or saw it just as a job. To most vets' chagrin, I would, whenever I got my daily quota of footage done early (which was often—I was the fastest breakdown/inbetweener they had), knock on Bill's door and, if he wasn't busy, just go right in and jaw with him. (Sometimes Alex [Toth]'d come in, too . . . and man, if I'd had a tape recorder *then* . . .). We all also shared the second floor bathroom, where I'd see Bill frequently. (Joe's first floor office had its own toilet.)

It was a shame that Bill wasn't *my* boss, however. That distinction went to a man of dubious character, and the closest I dealt with in terms of bigotry that I (naïve, cartoon-loving *moi*) had thought I'd deal with in my first year of employ in my dream profession. Meet my actual boss, Southern redneck/ Boss Hogg–wannabe John Boersema, whose license plate was actually "Big Bwana" . . . and who ran the in-between breakdown department like a Southern plantation.

Now, those who've seen me in previous stories/articles/columns know that I'm Black. If we had [then] the type of publicity we have now, the fact that an eighteen-year-old Black kid had 1) sold three animation ideas to the thenbiggest animation producer in the world, then 2) became the youngest artist ever hired by them at that time, would've made a little bit o' news. The fact is, during the next four years working in-house for three different studios (Hanna-Barbera, Filmation, Ruby-Spears), I was either the first or second Black person hired in whatever artistic position I performed at said studio. In Hanna-Barbera's case, I was the first Black inbetweener the studio had hired. In our department, I was the first Black person; one other, who was also gay, came in after me. Neither of our hirings made Big Bwana happy . . . but because gay Black guy was somewhat docile and I wasn't, I tended to get the bulk of his subliminal "massa" rages. The fact that I had fun, *loved* my job, *and* was friends with most of the studio higher-ups *really* teed him off.

Nobleman: How long did you have the job on *SF*?

McNeil: I worked in-house for Hanna-Barbera from October 1976 to November 1977, [then got] laid off two days after my birthday. Was hired back a month later, after *All-New Super Friends Hour* was finished, left soon after to become a staff layout artist (what I *really* wanted to be) for *Tarzan and the Super 7* and *The Fabulous Funnies*, at crosstown rival studio Filmation Associates. While there, I discovered that union studio Hanna-Barbera used a number of nonunion subcontractors in town to facilitate show production.

The most prolific local one was Love, Hutten, & Love [LHL], headed by veteran animators Bill Hutten, Ed Love, and son Tony Love. We in the biz used to have a running joke about LHL: They would always get to lay out/animate the series Hanna-Barbera's in-house [staff] *least* wanted to do . . . either due to the show's complexity (read: number of characters) or the [studio's] inability to produce major chunks of animation footage in our network-mandated limited time (read: number of characters). The show LHL was assigned that season (1978–79) was *Challenge of the Superfriends*. (Note that this was when "Super Friends" became "Superfriends"—one word.)

A fellow Filmation layout person who had worked on *Challenge of the Superfriends* for a week found the show too daunting (read: number of characters), wanted to switch to another Hanna-Barbera show LHL was doing, and offered to recommend that I take *his Super Friends* slot. Now, because I was a union employee and the union frowned upon union 'toonists doing freelance, nonunion work, I'd get no screen credit, but to work again on my favorite DC superheroes *plus* their greatest villains . . . well, no freakin' duh!

And partly due to my layout speed (even while working a full-time Filmation gig), partly due to my previous *All-New Super Friends [Hour]* association with *Super Friends* visual creator/model designer Alex Toth, and partly being flat out from Planet Crazy, Bill Hutten gave me all of the Alex Toth–boarded *Challenge of the Superfriends* and *Super Friends* acts to lay out . . . which I did until that part of the show finished production that summer (1978). Continued picking up freelance in-betweening/assistant animation work (*still* uncredited, natch) on *Super Friends* until 1982–83.

Nobleman: What do you know about the creation of the Wonder Twins, Apache Chief, Black Vulcan, Samurai, and El Dorado?

McNeil: [The Wonder Twins] were created by Norman Maurer, series developer then story editor of *The All-New Super Friends Show* (it hadn't become an all-new "Hour" yet) and father of next story editor Jeff Scott (Maurer), as allnew, super-powered "junior Super Friends" to replace the nonpowered Wendy, Marvin, and Wonder Dog of the first series. . . .

As for said guest heroes, the original, multiethnic ones (Apache Chief, Black Vulcan, Samurai, and '81–'82's El Dorado) were created by people at the network, partly as a desire to bring racial diversity in a kinda/sorta stereotypical fashion to the show, and partly as a reaction to Filmation "running the races" with their in-production *Young Sentinels* for NBC, which featured a Black heroine and Asian hero as leads. . . .

Nobleman: What do you know about the origins of the Hall of Justice and the Hall of Doom?

McNeil: The former's my all-time fave headquarters building. As you might've guessed, [the Hall of Doom's] resemblance to a certain bad guys' helmet in a certain movie that premiered the year before (1977) is merely . . . coincidental. The day *Star Wars* premiered, the entire studio took off . . . including Bill Hanna! I think Joe was the only one who stayed at work that day.

The next day, we got a "blast memo" from Hanna, basically hinting that, if we in creative were to "borrow" anything from *Star Wars* and incorporate it into our shows, neither he nor the network would have a problem with it. I had the bar scene from "Time Rescue" [a short featuring Superman, Hawkman, and Hawkgirl] on my desk to clean up, and all the aliens in said scene looked like cowboys in space suits. Two days later, Bob Singer plopped a bunch of quickly designed *Star Wars*–ish creatures, with the instructions "Change those into these." And next year, *every* show had a C-3PO character in it . . . even *Archie*!

So combine *that* kind of thought with a dollop of Alex Toth genius and . . . *voilà*—one Hall of Doom coming up! My only problem with it: we had to keep cheating sizes, since it had to be big enough to house thirteen supervillains, living spaces, equipment, etc., yet [also] be plausible that it could fly around like a . . . massive building that flew around. That's Saturday morning physics for ya!

Nobleman: How much involvement did the network have in shaping scripts?

McNeil: If there's one thing I have to smile about in my doting old age (not that, at fifty-two, I am that old), it's how both fans and creatives (at least when it comes to adventure-oriented toons) like to mock or at least make fun of the restrictive atmosphere we produced our toons in, versus the relatively unrestricted one they're currently in.

We had just gone through a roughly four-year period (1969–73) where, after the MLK and RFK assassinations, and the rising outcry against violence on TV in general and in kids' cartoons in particular, we weren't doing superhero cartoons *at all*. (And not that many funny animal toons, either.) The nets (remember when you could only see new cartoons, for the most part, *only* on ABC, CBS, and NBC, and only during a designated five-hour period *one* day a week? Cartoon Net-what?) felt because of the success of such shows as *Scooby-Doo* and *Josie* that their kid viewers (two to eleven) wanted to watch toons featuring older versions of themselves . . . until, having run almost all the variations of same into the ground, they had to try something else.

Now, the trick was: Could we do violent superheroes without said violence and get kids to watch? The answer, judging by the *Super Friends* ratings (high thirties/low forties shares) was *yes*!

One of the compromises we as toon producers had to make was to add pro-social/teaching messages to our shows, as well as to do actions that weren't seen as "imitable" by our audience. That meant no punching, no guns, etc. That lent rise to what we called "cheekensheets" from ABC, listing the various "offenses" in our scripts/boards/finished animation and asking us for possible alternatives.

Was this annoying? Lots of times, yeah! Would *you* have seen a Super Friends series (or any other superhero/adventure show) on *any* air without said restrictions? Flat out . . . *no*. So we had to make do. And admittedly, it *was* fun finding ways of creatively bending the rules every now and then.

Example: the opening *All-New Super Friends [Hour]* titles. As I hinted earlier, when Alex Toth laid out the opening title, he added three still shots of Batman and Robin that weren't indicated in the storyboard . . . including one of Robin tied to a pole by gangsters, as Bats jumped into the shot to rescue him. The net wasn't too happy when they saw those shots, but in those predigital editing days, it would've been too costly to edit the scenes out, so ABC kept 'em in, hoping that no one'd notice.

Another example: ABC wanted to axe the last episode of *Challenge of the Superfriends*, "History of Doom" (which *really* should've been the episode we called "Doomsday"), because someone at S&P truly thought that "destroying the world" was an imitable act. We convinced them that "No, no one right now (in 1978) could single-handedly destroy the world." ABC agreed and relented.

[That same year, a] girl in Ohio, I think, saved her sister from choking with [the Heimlich] maneuver, which she learned from watching Batman and Robin do it on *The All-New Super Friends [Hour]*. Since I did all the cleanup animation on that sequence, well, it's one of the prouder moments of my career.

Hanna-Barbera School to Keep an Art Alive

LEE MARGULIES / 1977

From the *Los Angeles Times*, September 1, 1977, H20. Copyright © 1977 *Los Angeles Times*. Reprinted with permission.

Animation, says Joe Barbera, is the last of the great hand arts in the movie and TV industries—a talent that can be mastered only with years of painstaking practice, apprentice working alongside journeyman.

But the training of young people in this art "came to a screaming, roaring halt about twenty years ago," he says, when the studios stopped producing theatrical cartoons and, with the exception of Disney, closed their animation shops.

Barbera and his partner, William Hanna, getting the boot from MGM, where they had created Tom and Jerry, went on to establish their own animation company in 1957 for the production of TV cartoon series such as *The Flintstones*. Their success spawned other TV animation studios.

Together, they provided work for the existing cartoon craftsmen. Still, Barbera recalls, training young people, or even giving jobs to graduates of the animation programs at universities such as UCLA and Cal Arts, was extremely difficult, because the production season lasted only about six months. Of course, that wasn't a big problem until the last few years, when many of the animators who had started back in the 1930s and '40s began dying or retiring.

"We have to train people if the industry is going to continue," Barbera finally said. So, last October, Hanna-Barbera Productions launched what it calls a college of animation at its plant in Hollywood. So far, 103 men and women have gone into the training program and been given jobs at Hanna-Barbera.

The secret, Barbera explained in an interview, was finding other work for them once production for the new TV season was concluded. What he did was convince Hanna-Barbera's parent firm, Taft Broadcasting Co., to put up money for four animated feature films, to be made over at least the next five years. "We had to build a steady flow of work," he said, noting that employees will move back and forth between TV and features, as the demands of the TV production season dictate.

DEPRESSED, PROUD, DRUNK

The animation college is run four nights a week by Harry Love, a veteran animator, writer, and director who screens job applicants and invites those who show promise to attend the classes. Some are given apprentice jobs right away, with the understanding that they will participate in the training program, too.

The classes, offered at no cost to the students, feature lectures by top craftsmen from every production department, and lots of practice at drawing and animating. On a recent evening, for example, layout designer Bob Singer talked about the importance of putting personality and attitude into not only characters but also inanimate objects; he used the blackboard to illustrate with his version of a depressed, then proud, then drunken brick. Afterwards, the students sat at their own drawing boards and worked on individual projects, with Love and Singer moving among them to answer questions and offer advice.

Some of the people in the program are working during the day on storyboards or backgrounds, but their purpose at night is to learn how to animate—that is, create the illusion of movement with still drawings. "What we're trying not to do," Barbera says, "is to train them in the television technique of limited animation. We're teaching them the feature technique (full animation) that we were trained on, which means teaching them motion, style, and design."

"It's the best job I've ever had," reports Warren Greenwood, who entered the program in February and was hired by Hanna-Barbera in April. "I'm learning and I'm getting paid at the same time. It's great."

Greenwood, twenty-four, was a self-proclaimed underground cartoonist for five years, publishing a series of comic books with some friends. Later he worked at Marvel Comics, but then moved here in hopes of landing a studio job. There was nothing until this program started, he says; now he hopes to learn enough to make his own films one day.

CAN'T BE TOO CREATIVE

Another employee and student, Mark Kirkland, twenty, says the Hanna-Barbera college doesn't measure up against the training he received in three years at the Cal Arts animation program, but acknowledges that it covers the basics well enough for people to perform on the job. "We're actually lucky to have a place like this for young people who are still learning and yet are being paid for it," he said.

Love says his program is not like one at a university because he has a very practical goal of training people to do a job. "Young people in art school want to do their own thing; they want to be creative," he said. "An animator here can't be too creative; he's working with a character someone else has created and someone else is directing. And he's got to work fast."

What Love looks for in an applicant's portfolio is good life drawings. "The day of a guy drawing funny figures is over. You've got to be a good artist," he said. "The name of the game is anatomy figure drawing. If they know construction, we can teach them to animate people or animals."

Disney Studios says it, too, is interested in bringing more young people into the animation field. Since it isn't producing cartoons for television, however, its needs are much smaller. A talent search in 1971 turned up thirty young artists who were hired full-time; nine of them have advanced to animator status, a studio spokesman says. Further influx of new talent is expected, he added.

Sums up Barbera with considerable pride: "We're keeping the art going. No computer will ever replace it."

My Adventure in the Hanna-Barbera Animation Training Program

TOM MINTON / 2024

Original essay written for this volume. Copyright © 2024 Tom Minton.

My name is Tom Minton—I'm generally known as a writer/producer who began in the industry as a storyboard artist. Prior to that beginning, I experienced an earlier start, not long after moving to Los Angeles from my native Illinois in September 1977. I first heard about the Hanna-Barbera animation training program from Lew Irwin, who then headed the assistant animation department at the Filmation studio in Reseda, California. I had been cold calling anyone at any animation studio who'd pick up, and early on happened to connect with Lew, who gave me excellent advice. I exclaimed to him, "Hanna-Barbera has a training program?" Lew replied, "Yes, they do. A very extensive one." So I quickly called Hanna-Barbera and was promptly connected to animation training program director Harry Love, who told me to present my portfolio and he'd gladly take a look. I also figured I'd bring a Super 8 projector to show Harry one of the short, fully animated films I'd made in Illinois.

I had graduated in June 1976 with a BA in Fine Art from Southern Illinois University at Carbondale, which in those days offered but one animation-related class, a decent animation history course taught by live-action filmmaker Frank Paine. Absolutely no animation production classes were offered by SIU at that time. Outside of the California Institute of the Arts, New York City's School of Visual Arts, or Toronto's Sheridan College, no academic institution then offered a real nuts-and-bolts, four-year animation production curriculum. Largely, the only people who really understood the craft were a dwindling band of highly skilled, aging animators still around from the Golden Age of animation, none of whom lived anywhere near me.

I graduated and continued in my small hometown to make short animated Super 8 films on my own. By mid-1977 I concluded that one could only get so far working in the dark, far apart from a major urban media center. I craved regular access to seasoned animation professionals, for whom making animated film was a normal, daily activity, not a once-per-decade specialty. The only spots in the United States such people called home were New York City and Los Angeles, and the craft was already seriously dying out on the East Coast, so to LA I drove as soon as the possibility materialized. I did not expect to linger in Los Angeles and enjoy a thirty-seven-year career in the Hollywood animation industry, which is how things eventually came to pass.

The Hanna-Barbera animation training program turned out to be my portal into the professional Hollywood animation industry, and it was a rare open door, indeed. Prior to that opportunity, large groups of young artists had been actively discouraged from entering the cartoon studio ranks since the 1930s by the old guard of entrenched seasoned pros, an arrangement that worked out very well for them. One of the finest 1940s studio animators still in demand three decades later was fond of telling younger people, "It's a one-generation business, kid!"—meaning HIS generation. There was also a potent catch-22 situation that then existed in the closed cartoon shops in Los Angeles. One could generally not get hired at a union studio unless one was a member of what was then called The Motion Picture Screen Cartoonists Local 839, and one could not become a member of that Hollywood trade union unless one had a certain number of hours of union work experience under one's belt!

Staring down unrelenting production schedules, Hanna-Barbera was bending these standard hiring rules by creating their training program for good reason. By the late 1970s, the valued members of the old guard had begun dying out, leaving no group of up-and-coming animation artists ready to replace them. Joe Barbera mentioned in a 1977 *Los Angeles Times* article that all training had ceased about twenty years earlier in the animated cartoon business, around the time theatrical production ended and television animation took over. [Editors' note: "Hanna-Barbera School to Keep an Art Alive," reprinted in this volume.] The old guys relied on their vintage skill sets, developed and finely honed in the era of fully animated theatrical shorts, which they modified into a specific shorthand, tailored to whatever limited animation TV cartoon shop they worked for. Was it even possible for green, talented, and very young people brought in literally off the street to pick up that rarefied skill level without years of apprenticeship experience? Hanna-Barbera was about to find out!

I showed up early for my Harry Love interview at Hanna-Barbera. Harry had a fairly small, gray-walled office at H-B, and was on the phone about half the time he met with me. He nodded his approval as he perused my portfolio, then I ran one of my brief animated films. Somehow, Harry got the wrong idea watching that movie. After it was done, he tersely snapped, "So, by showing me this, you're tellin' me ya wanna be a producer? Listen, we got two producers here already. Their names are Bill Hanna and Joe Barbera!" The phone rang and Harry spoke a few words to the caller, then slammed the receiver down.

"Ya know who that was, kid? That was Joe Barbera!" Harry was letting me know that he was a big shot at the studio. I reined in his fiery mood with the words "No, Mr. Love. I didn't come here to be a producer. I want to be an inbetweener!" Harry continued his minirant about five seconds more, until what I just said registered. Then he grinned broadly and with deep satisfaction told me, "Young fella, you just said something very intelligent. You said you want to be an inbetweener!" Harry's mood lightened as he revealed to me that his "real job" at H-B was "to keep long-haired people carrying guitar cases the hell out of this building!" To call that landscape a generation gap would be incorrect. It was closer to a canyon.

The Hanna-Barbera animation training program was a tuition-free night school, taught after regular working hours right in the studio. My first session in September 1977 was memorable, for it was the final day at the studio for Jerry Eisenberg, who had been there forever. Jerry was a top character designer and was departing to join the newly announced Ruby-Spears studio, headed by Joe Ruby and Ken Spears, former writers and story editors at H-B, best known today for having created Scooby-Doo. Jerry was the guest speaker in the class that night and it was a wonderful experience for all of the students. On other nights, we would glean priceless professional tips from staff legends such as Bob Singer, an ace character and model designer known for his strong design sense, or the distinctive graphic stylist Marty Murphy, who enjoyed a whole side career as a *Playboy* cartoonist while he was working at UPA. There was also H-B animator Ed Solomon, who patiently explained exposure sheets and things about limited animation then not found in books. On one evening, layout supervisor John Ahern went over the fine points of his production classification. During other sessions, H-B staff animation camera operators would show us the stark difference between animation charted and photographed one frame per drawing versus two. We eager students ate it all up, because we knew it was such a rare, coveted trade to learn at that time. A creatively energized feeling was palpable in every class session. That group of young kids had one thing in common: raw talent. I'd been in art classes at the college level where only two or three students could really draw, art majors or not. Here, in this one room at Hanna-Barbera, were about thirty-five young people from all over the country who shared a similar backstory: they had all been "the kid who drew" in every grade of their education.

The class itself had begun in June 1977, and I quickly learned that the students were steadily working on their very own pencil tests, to be forty-five feet in length, exactly thirty seconds. Students were told to pick any Hanna-Barbera character and animate a test using that character. I chose a fairly new one, "Big H," from the then-current H-B series *Heyyy, It's the King!*, which was an unofficial animated takeoff on *Happy Days* starring an animal cast. Big H was a hippopotamus; and I picked him because I was thinking how much fun it would be to animate a hulking mass in an absurd situation where he became weightless. These were to be silent film tests, so everything had to be visual and make clever use of the medium. I was also aware of a quote from Max Fleischer from around sixty years earlier: "If it can be done in live-action, it isn't animation!"

In my personal pencil test, I was determined to showcase utterly full animation in the longest scene, with several shorter scenes done in limited animation before and after. I designed my film to reach a key shot where my hippo character would be sailing through the air in that condition, his arms and legs flailing gracefully, as a repeat pan of billowy cumulus clouds panned in the background. I animated that long scene mostly on ones, meaning one drawing per frame of film, which then went against the way Hanna-Barbera, or any television animation studio in the United States of America, did things. But I knew that animation looked smoother and better on ones, despite the extra effort, and so I charged ahead. One night our guest speaker was seasoned animator and director Dave Tendlar, whose storied career included many years on staff at the Fleischer Studio in the 1930s. Dave saw me working on ones, flipped some of my drawings, and shook his head in disapproval. He told me, "Aw, we don't put this much work into 'em anymore, son!" I told Dave that I was aware of limited animation, but I did want this one shot to be as fluid as possible. Dave just shrugged and went on to the next student. He wasn't wrong, but I was young. I wanted to get animation back to where it had been at its Golden Age peak and that, to me, meant animating on ones. On another evening I was animating breaking glass, as my hippo character had to fall through a skylight in his trajectory back to earth, and, once more, the number of drawings I was doing caught an instructor's eye, this time none other than that of Harry Love. Harry's animation experience stretched to the early 1930s, but he had also been an effects animator during the 1950s at Warner Bros. in the Chuck Jones unit, providing stylized, adroit effects animation for several now-classic shorts, including the 1953 *Duck Dodgers in the 24½ Century*. Harry said to me, "No! Breaking glass shatters and gets the hell out of a shot fast!" Harry had a point. I watched him scribble three very rough key effects drawings over my background layout, indicating exactly how that skylight should disintegrate. I appreciated the difference and did it his way. That quality is what separated the old-timers from the novices—the seasoned animators had been at it long enough to know what NOT to draw!

When it came to the physical act of drawing in that class, the studio was then experimenting with a carved pencil line done by the assistant animators for their camera-ready artwork, with thick-and-thin segments that resembled hand-inking, without resorting to actual hand inking on cels, which H-B halted on their series work around 1967 in favor of a faster, cheaper Xeroxed line. This new carved line approach was unusual for television animation, but

Hanna-Barbera attempted it for a brief interlude on a couple of their series, *Jana of the Jungle* and *Godzilla*. It had to be dropped because of the difficulty of getting a uniform level of decent thick-and-thin line work for more than a few scenes in film continuity.

We finished our pencil tests, which were then shot on 35mm motion picture film by the studio camera crew. All of our films were screened on a December evening in the studio's theater, with Joe Barbera in attendance. I suppose that Bill Hanna might have done the honors, but for whatever reason just Joe was there that night, and Joe certainly knew good animation from bad. Like many people, I seldom saw both Hanna and Barbera together at the time when they ran their own studio. My test came out well, as did many from our group. The studio was not yet ready to hire us *en masse*, but they would bring on as many of us as they could as soon as it was doable, we were told. Class members who had been there longest had already been hired to work in the layout department and some as assistant animators. Meanwhile, I had a day job at a Sunset Boulevard ad agency, but was poised to quit the moment some momentum occurred at Hanna-Barbera. I had already made up my mind that while working in both small- and large-market advertising was interesting, I didn't want to spend my life in that trade. There was an ad agency in nearly every good-sized town on earth, but the unique craft of animation was then in real danger of going away forever, and I wanted to be a part of keeping that from happening.

Harry Love called me not long after our screening and told me out of the blue that H-B wanted me to go overseas and supervise crews at their Taiwan studio! One can imagine my utter shock. I was twenty-three years old, spoke only English, and had never been a supervisor in any line of work nor traveled beyond the USA. I had no idea why on earth, other than having made a decent-looking pencil test, Hanna-Barbera imagined that I should take on such a key overseas straw boss role. About a week went by before someone at the studio realized that they actually needed a person with previous overseas crew supervision (and foreign language) skills instead, and it was, frankly, a big relief that that person wasn't me. In retrospect, I must assume that Harry somehow pushed someone at the studio to give me a position, and the Taiwan gig was offered without due diligence in terms of who I was, and several other details, which must have fallen through the proverbial cracks.

Then, one evening a week or two later, Harry introduced our class to the night's guest instructor, a rare middle-aged animator named Mark Glamack, who had come up through the industry ranks, starting at Disney as an inbetweener and assistant on films such as *The Jungle Book*, before moving into animation at Hanna-Barbera. Mark, Harry told us, was about to head a new unit of assistant animators, and this very night he would help select which students would make his team. Harry was ready to show Mark the fine thick-and-thin, carved line assistant work done by the few students who had mastered that peculiar technique. Then Mark pulled a switch that Harry didn't see coming. Mark handed out his own assistant animation test—partly consisting of key drawings of a pith helmet-wearing character waving a large butterfly net. The key drawings had been done not in the thick-and-thin carved line technique that H-B and Harry had been championing but in the sketchy Disney feature animation style, used since 1961 and intentionally a bit rough, to better capture the feel of kinetic motion than had been the case with stiffer hand inking. At first Harry objected, but Mark insisted on letting everyone perform his test. Mark's point wasn't to make everyone at H-B try to draw like Disney but to get the students to fully appreciate that it was the solid mass of the people, animals, or objects being animated that mattered, much more than line quality. Of course, he was correct. I had been animating in that looser, scratchier line on my own stuff, so it was no problem to do inbetweens using it on this test that evening. I was one of those chosen to join Mark's new assistant animation department, which would come to be known as the "overflow unit."

We newbies were surprisingly told to report to work not at the main Cahuenga Boulevard H-B studio but to an address on north Radford Avenue, in the run-down industrial section of North Hollywood the next Monday morning. To our amazement, the location was a former Jantzen swimsuit factory, with no heat, and holes in the arched, rusty roof. Hanna-Barbera had sublet this dive to house their overflow unit, and brought in about a dozen vintage cast-iron Acme animation camera rigs owned by the Take One Camera Service, with which H-B had contracted to shoot all the footage that their regular camera department could not accommodate. We went to work immediately, as animation desks and chairs had been set into place, and our group happily assisted animation on virtually everything that the main studio tossed our way. The shows then in production were the 1978 season of *Challenge of the Superfriends*, an iteration of the Flintstones called *The New Fred and Barney Show*, as well as *Scooby's All-Star Laff-A-Lympics*, a programming block that included *The Scooby-Doo Show* and *Captain Caveman and the Teen Angels*. The only challenge for me was the lack of heat in that gaping factory space, which would occasionally cause my drawing hand to stiffen, and I'm sure I wasn't alone in that experience. I would watch the Take One camera crews shooting painted animation cels, as quickly as humanly possible, during our daily union breaks, at 10:30 a.m. and 3:30 p.m. One morning break during a downpour, I noticed a vertical stream of water flooding in from a roof hole and splattering directly onto a stack of painted backgrounds. I alerted a camera person to the situation—he just moved the stack over about three feet and sponged off the top acrylic background painting, until it was dry enough to photograph. Not even that year's El Niño flood could halt production!

All of us youngsters had a grand adventure, churning out the required forty feet per week, or about the equivalent of thirty-five to forty camera-ready drawings of assistant animation per day in a real studio, regardless of our spartan working conditions. It was a marvelous experience, until one morning a few weeks after we were hired, Bill Hanna and studio H-B creative producer Iwao Takamoto suddenly appeared, both wearing metal construction hard hats. I figured that they knew something about that leaky roof that we didn't, and wondered why we all hadn't been issued the same protective headgear. Murmurs went up around me: "What the hell are Bill and Iwao doing here?" It was unusual, but there was no time for speculation, as we were all hustled into a cavernous conference room area of the old swimsuit plant—except for two members of our youthful crew, who I noticed being quietly escorted outside in the other direction.

Bill let the diplomatic Iwao do the talking. "We have unfortunately overestimated our employment needs for the year." He paused. "We're gonna need you young people so bad in two years!" And with that, we were all laid off! I suspect that the 1978 opening of the outsourcing studio Wang Film Productions in Taipei might have presented the irresistible economic opportunity for Hanna-Barbera to ship our assistant work overseas—it then cost pennies on the dollar to perform labor-intensive tasks internationally, with nonunion wages. There was also then no "runaway clause" in effect in Local 839's contract, but situations like this helped bring one into existence just one year later. Once Hanna-Barbera sent our remaining work overseas, they no longer needed an overflow unit, so it was disbanded. Those two crew members who were led away as we were about to be laid off turned out to be Canadian citizens, in this country on what were known as "sweetheart" work visas; since these were apparently not so easy to terminate, they were taken to the main Cahuenga Boulevard H-B studio and handed work.

I can speak only for myself here. Others who were involved likely have their own perceptions and memories of their time in the Hanna-Barbera animation training program. In my case, I was very glad to get the chance to get a foot in the door of the closed Hollywood animation industry. Despite what Hanna-Barbera pulled, I wasn't about to leave the business, having gotten a real taste. In fact, not long after that, I went right back to the nightly, unpaid H-B training program to help Harry run it! Those who'd been aiding him had moved on, and there were still new young people joining the class. Mark Glamack, after getting his department yanked out from under him, grudgingly returned to being an H-B staff animator. Harry Love wasn't happy about the way the studio had treated several of his students, but remained a good company soldier and kept it largely to himself. He didn't tip his hand to me until he got a call from none other than Lew Irwin at Filmation, who asked Harry if he had any young person in his class who could work as a staff assistant animator, while also taking on a special side task that Filmation needed done immediately. I happened to be standing nearby when Harry took that call. He glanced over to me and said, with a wink, "Lew, I got just the person!"

I was immediately hired at Filmation in March 1978 and learned that their "side task" involved shooting pencil test animation with their then-new Lyon-Lamb video system for their new animated feature, *Flash Gordon: The Greatest Adventure of All*. Unlike Hanna-Barbera, Filmation kept their word: they told me that if I worked out doing what I was hired to do, they'd try to move me up. In about three months, I was promoted into what became the very first "young" storyboard unit in the Los Angeles television animation industry. In those days, "young" meant "under age sixty."

I never worked on staff at H-B again (partly due to the bad taste their mass layoff left in my mouth), but I did pick up freelance storyboard work from them over the years. I was a staff storyboard artist at Filmation for nearly three years, then freelanced for both Ruby-Spears Enterprises and Hanna-Barbera, until joining the Ruby-Spears staff as a storyboard artist in 1983; there I also participated in painting large pieces of presentation artwork drawn by comic book legends Jack Kirby and Gil Kane. In 1987, I became head writer on Ralph Bakshi's *Mighty Mouse: The New Adventures*. This was a seminal cartoon series that restored actual humor to Saturday morning animated shows and shook up the industry in the process. I joined the fledgling Warner Bros. Television Animation crew in 1989 as a staff writer/story editor, early in the development of *Tiny Toon Adventures*. I spent 1990–92 at Walt Disney Television Animation, initially as a *Darkwing Duck* story editor. I subsequently earned an Emmy nomination for writing and story-editing on their experimental series *Disney's Raw Toonage*. After writing one half-hour of their series *Aladdin*, I returned to Warners, where I worked on various animated series over fourteen straight years, receiving nine more Emmy nominations in the process. One might argue that my career path came full circle after Hanna-Barbera was absorbed into Warner Bros., for then I ended up writing one episode of *What's New, Scooby-Doo?* entitled "Homeward Hound," a unique half-hour airing in 2003, which I partially fashioned from a few pages of unfinished material intended for a feature written years earlier by Joe Barbera and beautifully drawn in rough storyboard form by Iwao Takamoto.

One day during the late 1980s, I ran into the elderly Harry Love at a Burbank restaurant. He grumbled that most of the kids who'd gone through his late 1970s H-B training program had long since scattered all over the industry, seemingly working for and bettering every studio except Hanna-Barbera. Somehow, Harry was missing the program's broader positive effect. Various alumni of the H-B training program went on to become leading lights at esteemed animation studios in the following years, making key contributions to major animated television and feature film projects.

I witnessed a tsunami of technological and creative change in the animation industry during my thirty-seven years of professional cartoon-making experience, ending with my 2014 retirement from the industry. Animation was literally dying when my generation was fortunate enough to gain entry; working together, over time, we were able to actually turn the tide. The gradual improvement in the state of the craft led to what is today regarded as the Silver Age of animation, encompassing both theatrical and television work. The 1990s were the pinnacle of that moment in time and, again speaking for myself, without the portal that was the Hanna-Barbera animation training program, many of the individuals who made it possible might never have gotten past the gatekeepers of an enfeebled system.

Tom Sito on Hanna-Barbera

KEVIN SANDLER AND TYLER SOLON WILLIAMS / 2021

Edited from the transcript of an original interview for this volume, conducted May 21, 2021. Published with permission of Tom Sito.

Tyler Williams: How did you arrive at Hanna-Barbera?

Tom Sito: I started there a bit in 1977, and then in '78. When I started, I think I was on like the ninth season of Scooby-Doo, and I was a professional assistant. I hadn't really reached the rank of full animator yet. . . .

Hanna-Barbera in '77–'78 was the largest animation studio in Hollywood, maybe the world. It was something like two thousand employees. And it was like a factory. For a long time, there was a time clock and you clocked in. Although when I was working there, the time clock wasn't working anymore. It kept having accidents. People accidentally poured Super Glue into it. "Oops—oh, no! Sorry." . . .

Work began at 8:30 in the morning. And even though the time clock would break frequently, they had a thing called the "late book." A minute after 8:30, they'd lock the door. And there was a security guard. If you showed up after 8:30, you had to sign in to the late book. Supposedly Jayne Barbera, who was Joe's daughter and a head of personnel, would read the book at the end of the month to see who was late. Everybody dreaded that—Don't be in the late book!

I used to take the bus to Hanna-Barbera; I didn't own a car yet. After I got off and was walking to the studio, you could literally see people, even old people, running up the hill. We all had to get there by 8:30 to be on time. And we adhered to strict union rules. From 10:00 to 10:15 was a morning coffee break. Lunch, I think, was 12:30 to 1:30. Afternoon break was from 3:00 to 3:15. During this, you could see the elderly MGM animators, the old duffers, walking up to the Oak Crest Market, which was like this little supermarket up the block, to get a pint of bourbon for their desk. Quitting time was 5:30, something like that.

Williams: What were Bill and Joe like, at the studio?

Sito: The thing I admired about Bill and Joe, especially in our current, sort of colder, corporate environment, was that Bill and Joe were very loyal to the people who were loyal to them—so, their old guys, the folks from back in the 1940s, from the Tom and Jerry/MGM era, that had come out and stuck with them, through everything. So, when one or two of the old guys used to go up to the Oak Crest Market to get their pint, Joe Barbera told the manager: "Don't charge him—just keep a tab. At the end of the month, send me the bill." And he would pay it! . . .

Williams: They employed a lot of people from the early days . . .

Sito: These guys had been in the business for forty, fifty years. They were the veterans of Hollywood's Golden Age. Bill and Joe relied on those guys. They were their elite group. What was great about Hanna-Barbera was that they were like a lifeboat for the rest of old Hollywood animation. You'd walk around the studio and go, "Oh, there's Dave Tendlar, who was a lead animator on Betty Boop and Popeye in the 1930s. And there's Coz Anzilotti, who was Ralph Bakshi's right hand on *Heavy Traffic* and *Fritz the Cat*, and there's Nick Nichols, who was a sequence director on *Bambi*. There's Hal Ambro, who was a top Disney animator—and Charlie Downs, he was another top Disney animator."

These were the guys who never broke into Nine Old Men-dom. They got very close to the top at Disney. Some were part of Ward Kimball's television unit. But they couldn't break into that Nine Old Men kind of strata. The Nine Old Men could be very political when they wanted to. So, these guys got fed up and left, and then Bill and Joe would be there to get them. Tex Avery was working there for a while, and Art Babbitt. And actually, even when Friz closed DePatie-Freleng, before he retired, he worked for Bill and Joe for a little bit, producing a show. The anecdote I always like to use is when I was working on the *Godzilla* show (1978–80), there was an animator named Ken Muse. Kenny Muse was a top animator at MGM, basically like the Milt Kahl of MGM. He was really the best animator. He did a lot of the animation in *Anchors Aweigh*, of Gene Kelly dancing with Jerry the Mouse.

Williams: Wow—a total showcase for MGM's talent.

Sito: One of the finest pieces of American animation ever done. It's just so beautiful, his work. But, when I knew Kenny, he seemed burned out. He had two canes, and he'd hobble around on these canes, and just sit at his desk and draw. He looked very feeble. I heard he really wasn't that old—he just lived really hard. He was a workaholic, and an alcoholic, you know, burning the candle at three ends. [Editors' note: Muse was sixty-eight in 1978.]

Anyway, I was working on a scene from *SuperFriends*—it was Superman, flying. And his hair was supposed to be fluttering from the wind in his face. Kenny had animated the [key drawings] as if Superman was going backwards, the hair going the other way. So I went over to him, very furtively, and said, "Um, Kenny? . . ." He had two hearing aids. "Kenny?" He didn't say anything.

"Kenny?" Nothing. So, I went over to the side: "Kenny!" He jumped. "Ahhhh! . . . What?" I showed it to him. Hoarsely, he hollered at me, "Just follow the roughs—just follow the roughs!"

So, I went to the head of the clean-up department, Jay Sarbry, and I explained to him the problem. Jay goes, "That stupid old man—gimme that." And he started redrawing it, right in front of me. And I said, "Why doesn't Kenny retire, if he can't do it anymore?" Jay suddenly stiffened up, like Thumper being admonished by his mother. "Mr. Hanna says Kenny is one of the people who made this company. So, as long as Kenny wants to work, Kenny can work." Yeah—I was like, "Wow." Now that I'm at retirement age, I respect that.

Williams: So, after quitting time, would you freelance?

Sito: At Disney, you got your scenes, you did your stuff, and you went home at 5:00 p.m., whatever. At Hanna-Barbera, besides the work that you were doing in front of you, this eighty feet a week quota, you could pick up in-house freelance. You could take extra work home with you. Sometimes I used to pick up work from Ron Campbell [Films] or Ruby-Spears, which were their outsource studios. So I'm still working on Hanna-Barbera stuff, although it's outside the company.

One thing Bill Hanna created was the bonus system. For every foot you went over eighty feet, you got like $10. So, if you did one hundred feet, you got that much more money. I remember when we were working on the *Godzilla* show, we had fallen behind in production. To Bill what really mattered was the airdates. In September, we've got to have the first three shows ready—we've got to make our airdates. And, so, Bill had a big meeting of us all together—all the assistants, and all the animators. He goes, "Well, *Godzilla* is this monster that's killing us. We're gonna have to do something here. So, I'm going to lower the quota and raise the bonus. And I hope you all get rich." That's the way he thought! To him, hitting the airdates was more important than pinching a penny here and there, because the shows are already cheap. . . .

Kevin Sandler: And the bonus footage . . . was a way Bill Hanna got around paying overtime, right?

Sito: Yeah, basically. Because, when you're on the clock, overtime would have been time and a half after eight hours. . . . Disney then rarely paid overtime. You worked for straight salary. And actually, one of the things you were told when you started at [Walt] Disney [Feature Animation] was to slow down, to stop turning out so much stuff, because you're so used to cranking a lot of footage out. Sometimes, you might redo the same scene up to six times. Our quota as an animator was three feet a week. Three feet is about two seconds. At Hanna-Barbera, your quota was 80 feet a week, which is like thirty seconds. Although most of it was simple dialogue.

Williams: Like the head with only the mouth moving.

Sito: Yes. Bill and Joe had worked out a system called the A to F mouth system. You draw a head, and you would just expose these mouths: The "A" mouth is a closed thing. The "D" mouth is wide open. "B" is all teeth. "C" is halfway between "B" and "D." And the "F" mouth is an "oo," like if you're saying "boot." "E" is halfway between "C" and "F." So, you would just list all the letters, and that would be your talking head. You'd put in an eye blink; about every three to four seconds, you have a character blink. These libraries of mouths and eyes are now standard in many modern digital 2D animation shows. . . .

Sandler: What was Hanna-Barbera's role in the two strikes, in the late 1970s and early 1980s?

Sito: The thing is, Bill especially was always trying to figure out a way to get stuff done cheaper. He was sort of the prime mover towards this idea of outsourcing.

Jay Ward had started outsourcing in 1959 for *Rocky and His Friends*. He had Gamma Productions in Mexico City. And they were banging stuff out, cheap. Which is interesting, because Jay himself not being an animator, he expected the work to come back looking like Bugs Bunny. When it came back, it was not that level of quality. Very simplistic. But, with good writing, it could pass. If you put on Rocky and Bullwinkle, turn off the sound—it's not really well-animated. They didn't have any Ken Muse or Iwao Takamoto, any top guys like that. . . .

So, Hanna-Barbera started this subcontracting system, of sending stuff overseas. . . . The studio first started with Australia, because of the corresponding language and entertainment cultures. They then turned to Taipei, Taiwan, then Seoul, South Korea, Japan, and others. . . . We used to joke about it in the 1970s, saying, "You know, Bill and Joe are staying up nights trying to figure out a way to get rid of all of us. Someday they're going to figure it out."

At the time that I was at Hanna-Barbera, even though we had twelve series, only three of them were actually in-house. The rest were all being done in other parts of the world. . . . In 1979, The Animation Guild, Local 839, which is the animators' union, was trying to get nativist legislation, which was to say that a certain amount of the production had to stay in town, before you send other stuff overseas. . . . The interesting thing was that other countries like Canada had that all along. When *Heavy Metal* (1981) was being done, the deal they had was that 30 percent of it had to be done in Canada, with local talent, before they can outsource anything. Here, we were in the age of Reagan, which threw all those rules out. You know, businessmen *über alles*. . . .

Sandler: Is it true that Bill tried to stifle the union demands by conspiring with the studio's ink and paint employees?

Sito: Yes. H-B management tried to drive a wedge between the animators and what we call the back end of production. So, the front end is storyboard, layout, animators. The back end is clean-up, paint, and checking. In a lot of companies, the largest number of employees would be the painters. Because it's a very painstaking job; it takes a long time to do. The management would basically talk to them and say, "Why should you strike to make more money for the animators? They're not going to do nothing for you. Why risk your jobs for the sake of them?" They were very good at playing sides off one another.

Sandler: Was that a legitimate argument he was making to them, in some ways?

Sito: Well, it gets down to the debate of, you know, "Are everybody's lives going to be made better, or just certain parts of everybody's jobs?" When I was union president, I really tried to make sure that everybody, across the board, did better. Of course, if we were able to enact some sort of nativist legislation, like "So much work had to stay in-house," certainly a lot more people would still be working today. After the '82 strike, there were people bagging groceries. Basically, people were doing all these kind of menial, local jobs, when they used to have really good jobs at H and B. So, it was bad for everybody, all around.

Sandler: What was H and B's role in leading you toward being the president of the union?

Sito: I always felt that part of the problem with the '82 strike was that it was really an argument between members of the older [Golden Age] generation, and they didn't really kind of explain it correctly to my [baby boomer] generation. I noticed that there was a definite lack of understanding between all of us. The older generation remembered the bad old days of six-day work weeks, and no benefits. They fought tooth and nail to build our union. Our generation, in the main, was ignorant of that. (It wasn't like you could reference a book on Hollywood animation labor history. I had to write the first one in 2006 [*Drawing the Line*].) In 1982, we young animators just felt that Mo Gollub and Bud Hester, who were the business agent and the president of The Animation Guild then, just had a feud with Bill Hanna, and they were dragging us all into it. . . .

From my vantage point, I couldn't really understand what was happening. All I knew was that my savings account was drying up, and that I was asking my old man for a loan. . . . You can't go on unemployment while you're on strike. So, you're not getting anything. That's a tactic that bosses do, basically to starve everybody back to work. . . .

When the '79 strike happened, it was over in a week. Bill and Joe were unprepared for it—they couldn't afford to lose the time. They caved because they couldn't have the production schedule be stalled like that. With the '82 strike, they had three years to prepare. So when the strike did happen, they were all set up for it. I think they prepared meticulously, just for this eventuality, because they contacted studios in other countries, and prepared to send stuff away. I remember friends of mine in Canada were saying, "Boy, we sure hope you guys strike, because we've been promised a lot of work if you do." I said, "Don't worry, we're going in with all flags flying."

And that year, the approval of the new shows was later than usual. The networks put off the green light, instead of April, until almost June, because they knew the strike was coming. When it came, it lasted over sixteen weeks, and many of the rank and file were forced to go back to work . . . It all fell apart.

Margaret Loesch and Joe Barbera

SONNY FOX / 1979

> Edited from "Children's Television: Margaret Loesch and Joe Barbera," from *Inside the TV Business*, edited by Steve Morgenstern (New York: Sterling, 1979), 135–48, 153.

Sonny Fox: To start out, we should ask Margaret Loesch to explain where NBC is currently, at the end of March, in the process of buying, scheduling, and developing shows.

Margaret Loesch: We have just announced our schedule of new shows that start in September—on September 9 to be exact. Traditionally, at this time of year we have just closed our development season and are starting production on the shows we selected. Children's programming at the network level has been very seasonal, with commitments made to programs for the full year. As a matter of fact, only in the past two years have we gotten into midseason new production for midseason shows. Traditionally, the schedule has been that from September through February, we develop product with the major houses, like Hanna-Barbera. At the end of February or the first of March, we make up our schedule by selecting from the shows we have developed. From that point on, March through September, we are in production. Then the cycle repeats itself. As I mentioned, the networks have just recently started developing new product for midseason, so the very strict season that I've just explained is changing. As a matter of fact, we are just now negotiating a deal with Hanna-Barbera to start developing a midseason series for January or February of next year, so that during the summer, while attending to production of current shows, we will also be developing a series for midseason.

THE BIRTH OF *GODZILLA*

Fox: Joe, I know that your company right now is dealing with ABC and NBC. Are you doing anything for CBS this year?

Joe Barbera: Yes, we have an hour, and we've resurrected Popeye. And why do you resurrect Popeye? Saleswise, when you walk in somewhere and say, "I have a new series with a green elephant, and I have Popeye," they always seem to go for Popeye. They're not going to buy anything new if they can help it. It's show biz. For instance, you're thinking what NBC might want, what CBS might want, and you try to come up with something, and you wake up one morning and think, "God, no one has touched Godzilla." Now, you know it would have been death to mention that three or four years ago. So I call the man who controls the property—he's involved with Toho in Japan—and I say "What are you doing with it? Why don't we take a run at it for Saturday morning?"

You have to keep thinking of these kinds of projects, or someone else will beat you to it. Then, after you think of it, you know something like *Godzilla* is going to be a tough sell. So, how do you handle it? First, he's a superhero, second, he's going to help the environment, third he's going to come to rescue us from incredible menaces that are going to ruin the Earth, and fourth, we include a new character that's a small version of him, which was once used in the movies, called Godzooky. He's an eager beaver, who wants to become like Godzilla, who blows out smoke and flame, but when Godzooky tries, he just comes out with smoke rings. In this way I'm getting around the programs and practices departments, who will stop everything you do that's violent. I can assure you that we've been on a nonviolent kick for over ten years, no matter what anybody says. If there's any violence, it's an old product. Certainly nothing we've done over the last ten years.

Fox: Let's stay with *Godzilla*, and track that project as a case history of how something gets put on the air. I can start the story, because it actually started when, many, many months ago, a man named Hank Saperstein, who owns UPA, came to me in New York and said, "What about doing Godzilla on Saturday morning?" Now, I remember Godzilla from the Japanese movie *Godzilla*, and I said, "You've got to be kidding, Hank—they'll hang me by my thumbs. Godzilla is everything that everybody says we can't do for kids any longer. If I walked into my management and said, 'Let's do Godzilla,' they'd throw me out." So Hank picked up his bag and walked out. Many moons later, Joe says, "What about Godzilla?" But Joe then said, "Wait a minute, what if we turn him around and make him a hero figure?" as Joe just explained. So then I began to see a way around it, and I said, "Terrific." I wanted it, because my instinct was that *Godzilla* would be a very big hit, and God knows, NBC was looking for big hits. Anyway, I left NBC.

Loesch: And Sonny's instincts were right. It has all the makings of a big hit. We at NBC actually got into a bidding war with ABC, both wanting the property, which happens very often. Normally on Saturday morning television, NBC will purchase thirteen episodes of a project over one year, and repeat it so it plays a total of four times, totaling fifty-two weeks. We are an exception—ABC and CBS purchase product over two years for their Saturday morning schedule. They buy sixteen episodes and run them over two years, playing them each six times. The reason for the difference is that ABC and CBS have Sunday morning network programming, which allows them to play off shows that cannot function competitively on Saturday morning. NBC does not have that. Our Sunday morning belongs to network sports and to local affiliated stations. So we have only Saturday morning, and if something doesn't work for us competitively, we don't have somewhere else to play it off. Therefore, we make one-year deals.

The way NBC worked out acquiring *Godzilla* from Hanna-Barbera was simply that we broke tradition and made a two-year deal, buying twenty-six episodes to play over two years. This also is an extraordinary situation because it is a deal that was worked out first with Hanna-Barbera, Toho Japan, and UPA, who work in conjunction with Toho. We have our contract with Hanna-Barbera.

We have had, surprisingly enough, very few problems with our broadcast standards department, which monitors everything we do in programming, thanks to the twist in the concept, making Godzilla a hero. We also have a social science advisory panel that was commissioned a number of years ago, who review all of our material, and they also have had no problems. We have still been able to create a very exciting episode, and the Godzooky character that Joe described serves very well for comic relief. The show has a great deal of comedy in it.

Barbera: This is an hour show, but Godzilla himself comes up in only one segment, and then he only comes in at the end, when the big deal and the big problem comes up. We don't stay with him and fire breathing. We have a segment with a Cousteau-type hero traveling around the world, environmentally trying to straighten things out, and he's a humorous character. That with *Godzilla* makes up a half hour of an hour segment. We still are working on two more segments that will make up the entire hour.

Loesch: We're going to sandwich two eleven-minute segments on either side. Right now, we're trying to decide on those segments.

Two weeks ago, we announced that we acquired the show, and finally put it on our schedule, which is now complete. We are now at the script-writing stage, and have started the storyboards, and Joe is working very diligently to get the kind of look we want. We have just finished auditioning voices and recording the first show. So you can see where our schedule stands in March. It's a very time-consuming process, and we probably will be producing this series right on through November.

Fox: Joe, what's the lead time? When is the first time you will see a first finished episode of *Godzilla*?

Barbera: Well, if it's normal, it will be one minute before it goes on the air. You get on the plane at 11 o'clock the night before and fly it into New York. That's how desperate these things are.

But, actually, yesterday we were testing voices for Godzilla and Godzooky. You have to see this to believe it, because here's Ted Cassidy, who's a huge giant of a man, and he's roaring, and then Don Messick is answering him as the small one. We have to get personality and fun into it. Now, we live and die on the pick of the voices. As Margaret knows, I've been running up and down that studio, dumping voices, canceling voices, picking up new voices. We look desperately for new voices. I was trying to get a personality with the little one, and I tried to get some words out of him. Well, he came out sounding like an idiot. So now we got two actors in a room and they began to communicate with sounds, and we were getting some laughs out of it.

DEFICIT FINANCING

Fox: What are the economics inside Hanna-Barbera on a show like *Godzilla*? NBC pays what seems like a lot of money. You apparently have to give some of it to Toho.

Barbera: We have a license fee with Toho. We have a man here who's kind of guarding the property, so we meet with him once in a while, as little as possible. He reads the script and tries to give us some advice. Then we pay a license fee to him, and there are merchandising rights, which sometimes he controls and sometimes we control. Then there are foreign distribution rights, which are split sometimes. It's a lot of juggling around to see who ends up with any money. We happened to get the highest fee in the history of Saturday morning programming on this property. To explain that, you've got to go back to my original statement. It's only there because Godzilla is a known commodity. An article in the *Wall Street Journal* six or eight months ago mentioned that Godzilla has never lost money in the theater. Every single picture that's been made, and at this moment they're starting to make another one and have asked us to participate. So then when I say, "Let's do Godzilla," I find a receptive ear.

Fox: There's another factor in the high payment NBC is willing to give you, Joe, and that's your own past success. Because your shows were so strong on ABC, and of course Hanna-Barbera down through the years has such a fine reputation, that they would be much more willing to reach to meet your fee than they would for somebody else, who doesn't have that track record. That might make a difference of $5,000 an episode on a licensing fee, to give you an arbitrary figure. There are factors in there that the network would consider, that you have to be aware of if you're selling a show or making a deal with a network. There really is a reward for success, over a long period of time, a proven track record.

But getting back to the economics. Most of the time when you do a show for NBC or CBS or ABC, whether it's a half-hour or an hour, whether the license fee is $100,000 or $500,000, whatever it is, you actually lose money—do you not, on producing that show?

Barbera: Quite often, yes. One of the reasons that we hang in there with red deficit figures, which no one seems to understand, is that we have built up a backlog over the years, which is out working for us today, still being sold in various ways. Almost everything we've made over the last twenty years is at this point running somewhere for some reason, for fifteen cents here or two cents over there. That's what keeps us going. It's the income from merchandise, any income from foreign sources, and the fact that sometimes a network will buy a rerun of one of our products to fill a hole when something else drops out of the schedule.

Once you have your studio set up, you're ahead of the game. I can give you some quick figures. When Warner Bros. tried to start their own studio, about eight or ten years ago, they figured out it would take them about $800,000 to crank up—which means people, staff, bookkeepers, unions, and all that. If they sold one show they would be in the red; if they sold two shows, they would break even. That's starting from scratch.

I have to admit, frankly, that in 1957 my partner and I started completely from scratch, with $4,000 each. You're going to ask, "How did you manage that?" And it's quite a story, but we did. We were lucky. We did Tom and Jerry cartoons until 1957, and I'll give you my tale of woe on that count. Bill Hanna and I did every single one of them, wrote them, produced them, directed them, and finally left MGM. They're still running them. They might make $20 million this year in syndication with the same things that we did, and Bill and I don't get one dime out of that. It's like movie stars who see their pictures at night on the late show, and they don't get a dime, and they're starving.

From that we went into our own studio and hit with *Huckleberry Hound* and *Yogi Bear*, which by the way we're doing again for NBC as *Yogi's Space Race*. Those characters are like owning a TV star. If we keep them going, we're lucky. That's how we can exist.

Fox: Put another way, in terms of the deficit financing, if it costs Hanna-Barbera $110,000 to produce a half-hour show, and they're getting $100,000 from NBC, they are deficit financing $10,000 a week. On the other hand, they're using $100,000 of NBC's money to create a property that will be owned, after the first year, unless options are exercised, by Hanna-Barbera. So, for $10,000 a week, or $130,000 all together, they have now created equity for themselves, they have created a property. And animation has an incredible shelf life, doesn't it?

Barbera: Yes, but there's one more thing to keep in mind. If I do a show like *Popeye* or *Godzilla*, we don't own that outright. We participate with many partners. On *Popeye*, we have the toughest partners in the world, King Features. That's why we prefer to do something original.

Scooby-Doo, for instance, happened to become a gold mine. Don't ask me how it happened—nobody figured the dog would become a star, but he has. He's been on the air over nine years, and he'll be on about four more years. Like anyone who's creative, you'd much rather get your own character out there and make a success out of it, but the kids will keep turning to Superman, Batman, whatever.

You never know when an idea will present itself—you have to be open to those ideas all the time. I met a fellow at breakfast one time who was the head of King Features, and I said to him, "What are you doing with Popeye?" and out of that came the deal to do *Popeye*. They weren't doing anything, but they were thinking of doing something. *Godzilla* was just waking up one morning with an idea and calling the guy. We work with DC Comics, and one day I picked up a cover and there were two long rows of characters, on one side were the superheroes, and on the other side were all their super enemies. Each one had a special enemy, like Superman has Lex Luthor, Batwoman has Cheetah, and so forth. And I looked at it, because I'd been watching the *Battle of the Network Stars* and all that on television, and I said, "Holy mackerel. The Battle of the Superheroes!" So I made a call, and we had a deal on it in about two seconds. Now we have to negotiate with that company, and they get a nice piece of that. But you're only as good as your ideas.

TRAINING ANIMATORS

Fox: True—ideas and execution. Let's go to execution. You made a deal with NBC to deliver a property called *Godzilla*. Do you have to go out and hire people now, in addition to the people you have in house to do this? How much of an operation is involved? I mean, your organization works like an accordion, doesn't it?

Barbera: We've instituted some policies in the last two years which have changed that a little. I'll backtrack a bit. When we were doing motion picture cartoons, we worked a full year. It was a steady job. Disney was steady, Warners was steady, and the people who were being trained were just super people. Suddenly, it all stopped, because they stopped making movies and started going into television, which was seasonal. For eighteen or twenty years, we had almost no new talent. We couldn't train anybody, because if a young aspiring artist walked in the door, we would say "Terrific, look at these samples—but we've got to tell you, you only have a six-month job, and then we have to lay you off."

What we've done lately, and with the fact that you have midseason buys now, [is that] we're able to keep people working all year. We used to fire everybody just before Christmas. But now we're making animated features, which is a company policy, through which we are training people. We have a school. We have 134 people that we put on and trained last year. We're now training writers, and we're the only ones who have started to do that seriously, because the talent has just been disappearing. When people came into our studio, they'd see our staff with seeing eye dogs, in wheelchairs. We've been having a terrible time producing the amount of work that we are lucky enough to sell. Selling it, creating it, and thinking of it is one thing. Now comes that big production machine which has to be going, and you have to try to keep the quality up.

In the last few years we've overcome some very strong resistance and started to do some of the animation abroad. We opened a studio in Australia, started right from scratch, and then, to be smart about it, we sold half of it to an Australian company, because it's very tough to operate down there without an Australian partner. That is normal all over the world—they all move in as your partner.

We did train a group, and they're excellent animators now. They're technically super. The one thing they can't do is create ideas that will sell in America. That's their ambition. They want to come in and cut our throats (this is our own company). And we have a group in Spain that is very good. We have a group in Mexico, another in Yugoslavia, and we're talking to a group in Taiwan that's very good, but mainly for one thing—animation. All the stories, the layouts, the storyboards, the creation of the characters, the voices, are all started in our studio. None of them seem to have the knack, fortunately for us, of creating subjects that will sell to networks.

FOREIGN ANIMATION

Fox: The foreign animation work has gotten so good that last year CBS insisted that some of their shows be done abroad, and NBC got to that point too. I was very suspicious of it. There had been, some years ago, an attempt to do it there, and it was not done well. The control was a big problem. So we proceeded gingerly and insisted on having some tests made abroad, but they turned out to be good. As a matter of fact, Margaret was convinced that the stuff coming from abroad was superior to what we were getting done here.

Loesch: It was. We found that during the crunch, the part of the season when the pool of talent is being strained, certain types of comedy animation are done better out of the country, and NBC has requested that some of our animation be done in Spain and Australia. As a matter of fact, we've approved some of it to go to Mexico City, to try it out and see how it looks.

ANIMATION ON A TV BUDGET

Fox: The normal way of doing a storyboard is to tell a story frame by frame, writing out the script and including enough pictures so you can follow the script and get a sense of how the animators intend to direct the sequence. Then we can look and see if there's enough action, if there's too much talk, or too many head shots. Now, we may ask for things the animators can't give us. It may simply be too expensive to do what we want to do for the price. There's always that little argument that goes on between the network and the animator. The network says, "Why can't we have more of this and do this a different way?" and the animator says, "Because you're not paying us enough."

Loesch: We work very closely with the animators, going over original storyboards and revised storyboards, until we agree on the way a sequence is to be done. To give you an example, in a fight sequence between Godzilla and the Firebird, which is a pterodactyl type of monster, we have a staging of a scene where Godzilla and his adversary are clutching and fighting, and there's a shot indicated where they fall offscreen, down into the water. Now, my note was that I'd like to see a dramatic shot. I'd like to see it from above, and look down and watch them plunging into the water, instead of having them just slide off camera, and in the next shot show a splash of water. Those are the types of things I'm always looking for, and that's one of my notes on this board.

Fox: All right, let's use that example. Joe, you're the practical guy, because this means dollars and cents for you. What is the difference to you between two monsters falling offscreen and dropping, and watching them from above getting smaller as they fall?

Barbera: It so happens, I think I told the animators to do the scene this way for that very reason, because they fall offscreen this way. Margaret would like to watch them fall, which means we have to cut back, do a longer shot to see them fall, and they're going to hit into the water and splash. Well, that means a lot of drawings of very complicated prehistoric characters, and a lot of water animation. You may have seen slow motion films of a drop of water hitting. First it hits, then it begins to come up, and then another drop comes out, and then it hits, and then it bubbles, and then it spreads. That's eight billion drawings. That's one of the things that gave Disney some of his biggest problems in his time, by the way. He used to think that that was important. Well, we have found out that that isn't important, but Margaret would not concede that. My effect would be that they drop off, there would be a tremendous splash, and then we would cut to the water bubbling and boiling and steam coming up—we'd give you a terrific effect. But she's the boss!

Loesch: You see, this is exactly the type of thing we have to concern ourselves with. He has to worry both dramatically and economically about what it is we're requesting, and we worry about it dramatically. One of the things that we can do which does not require a great deal more animation, and it's something that Joe is a master at doing, is drawing a scene so that it's dramatically staged. It's very exciting, even if it is a still shot and there is no animation in it, if the camera angle is a dramatic camera angle. We've been discussing *Godzilla*. Instead of using a shot of Godzilla just coming up out of the water in a long shot, we would have the shot designed so that it will look as if the camera were under him, looking up, or, as another possibility, as if the camera were over his shoulder, looking down into the water. Designing a board and staging it that way does not necessarily require more animation, but more imagination. Joe gives us those touches.

Barbera: More imagination, and a certain specialized type of artist, of which possibly on the West Coast there are two or three, and in New York maybe three. That's the difficulty with this type of product. We happen to have a super artist for *Godzilla*, but I just wanted to make one thing clear. We are talking about Saturday morning or semilimited type of animation, and not theatrical animation. If you do theatrical animation, you're going to talk about five or six times the money. So that's the difference. You have a budget, and you have to stay within it, and you have to do footwork, and tricks to come out with an effect. That's where we started twenty-odd years ago, with what you call "limited animation," and without it we would never have gotten to television. . . .

On Saturday morning, you must give kids action and entertainment, and noise. There's no doubt that a lot of people say, "Oh, look at that junk. And "We could do better." We've suffered, we've burned on all that stuff. We did a show called *These Are the Days*, for which we received nothing but kudos, handshakes, and pats on the head from all the organizations. It was a family show like *The Waltons*, [but] the kids are switching to *Batman*. We got all the good notices, but we didn't get the rating points. And if you don't get the rating points, all that work goes down the tubes: Goodbye—cancel the show. . . .

MONEY FOR PRODUCTION

Fox: Hanna-Barbera is now owned by Taft Broadcasting. How does that work to your advantage?

Barbera: Actually, if you have a business of your own, and it's working fairly well, it's very hard to get any money out of it unless you sell it and get a capital gain. It's an odd statement, but that's the only way for a small company like us. DePatie-Freleng is trying to do the same thing. Eventually, if you build an asset like we did with this company, you find another company that is looking to diversify. We had three [groups] interested in it: Universal, Columbia, and Taft Broadcasting, which eventually bought us. In a sense, it gives you a money base that takes care of some of your deficit. They have money, and will back you in projects. For instance, Taft is backing us in making [the] three or four motion picture features that we're working on now. Without Taft putting up the money, we wouldn't be doing them, and it took three years to talk Taft into that expenditure.

I'll tell you something strange, on the Wall Street side of it. If our company announced that we were going into motion picture production, the analysts on Wall Street would be terrified, because it's possibly the trickiest business in the world, and you can lose everything. But if we announced we were doing an animated feature, they'd be delighted. Now, what is the reason for that? If you do an animated feature that works, it's a lifetime asset. It will run forever. That's how Walt Disney built up his library, and his studio's still holding most of those films. You have to remember there were times when Walt Disney was so broke, after *Fantasia* and some of the others, that he hocked his 16-mm library for a million dollars, to raise money. That's how tough things were. They were received well, they were masterpieces, but they just didn't make it financially on the first time around. Since then, they keep making more on reruns. Every time they bring *Fantasia* out, they make more money than when Walt first started. So that's how I convinced Taft Broadcasting, and that's why Wall Street backs us in that kind of thinking. You have a lifetime asset if you make an animated feature.

Squire Rushnell at ABC

KEVIN SANDLER / 2021

Edited from the transcript of an original interview for this volume, conducted May 31, 2021. Published with permission of Squire Rushnell.

Kevin Sandler: How did you find your way to the ABC television network? And what was your role there prior to meeting Joe Barbera?

Squire Rushnell: . . . I became vice-president of children's television at ABC in 1973. . . . That's how I got to know Joe Barbera, because [the studio heads] all wanted to come and meet the new network guy and sell the new network guy a show. I loved Joe, and I loved Bill, too. But I didn't see Bill much. It was only when there were very special occasions where he would come out and put on a tie and a jacket and do things like that.

But Joe and I became very, very good friends. And I found that the creative process worked really quite delightfully with him. We could kind of bim-bam on ideas. And I loved Joe's style. I really didn't know a lot about him before I took that job. . . . In my twenty years at ABC, I spent a lot of time with Joe, because he recommended that I be his successor at Hanna-Barbera.

Sandler: That would have been in 1989, when Great American Broadcasting searched for a new president and CEO of Hanna-Barbera Productions to replace Bill and Joe.

Rushnell: Yes. I went through an interview process, as it was a period of my life when I thought, "Gee, you know, this would be really cool, to do that and work with Joe and Bill on a consulting basis." . . . I didn't get the job, anyway. They hired somebody else. And it was a younger guy. Joe called him a flash dancer.

Sandler: That would be David Kirschner. . . . Bill and Joe probably didn't have the choice who to hire.

Rushnell: In the final analysis, no, they didn't. They recommended, but somebody at [Great American Broadcasting] did that. Kirschner was marketed, probably by himself, as the young Steven Spielberg. And so that's what they bought into. . . .

Sandler: Why was it such a pleasure to work with Joe? How did he work?

Rushnell: Well, I didn't realize that my way of being a network executive was not the typical way. I took a lot of chances. It was more like Fred Silverman. Joe and I got along very, very well, because we were kindred spirits. You see a great idea, you see great characters, and you take chances with people and things. Joe was highly creative. And I was very creative. I didn't know it at the time. I only found that out later, that I could feed off of somebody else's creativity, particularly at that time: spotting creative things and then building upon them.

And so that's where Joe and I would sit down at dinner. I can remember a lot of white tablecloths, red wine, and bread being served. And at the end of the evening, there were a lot of red stains on the white tablecloth and a lot of breadcrumbs. We moved our arms a lot, made a lot of gestures, but it was always very creative and very productive. I just enjoyed that. I actually tapped into [some examples] that I think are representative of how that creative process took place, and how our relationship took place.

Sandler: What's your first example?

Rushnell: There was one very big acquisition that Hanna-Barbera got, which was Pound Puppies [in 1985]. You may remember that Pound Puppies was a hugely successful toy product. It was puppies that came in a little cage that had something about the pound on it. And it was just hugely successful. That was Joe and Bill's knack: they would take something that was popular, like Jackie Gleason and Art Carney [on *The Honeymooners*], and say, "How can we turn this into a cartoon?" And then you get Fred Flintstone and Barney Rubble. They did that all the time. We called it, "Joe ripped off this, or ripped off that," but it was a creative kind of a rip-off, where he would take a great personality, and then build a character around that personality. . . . So, Joe came into the pitch meeting, which was either in LA or in New York. He always had a bunch of guys around—the writers—and big cards with the drawings, and all that kind of thing. They were selling me on how successful Pound Puppies was. I nodded, and nodded. I said, "What's the show?" And then they started pitching the show. . . .

But the characters that they were pitching for *Pound Puppies* were awful. . . . So I said so. I said, "I think it's a great brand. It'd be very attractive. We'd get a great tune-in on Saturday morning, but I don't think the kids would stay. I think you need better characters." So I sent them away. Over the next month and a half or two—usually these development seasons were between February and March of the new year—Joe kept pitching this show and the characters just kept being so-so. I said, "I don't want to be disrespectful but these characters aren't the Hanna-Barbera kind of characters. We were almost at the end of the development season when Joe called and said, "I want to come into New York and talk to you, okay?" I said, "Sure." So we had dinner at one of those Italian restaurants: white tablecloths, the bread, the wine. I pretty much knew he was going to pitch me *Pound Puppies* again. I was surprised but not surprised that he had also not sold it to any of the other networks. I presumed that [Hanna-Barbera] had put up a pretty penny—or a lot of pounds—for the Pound Puppies, and that they had to make back their investment.

Somewhere over dinner, he said, "You know, there's a great character on *Saturday Night Live*—I'm sure you've seen him. This character, he comes out, and he tells a little lie. Then, you know, he moves to another lie and, and then to a bigger lie. And then a big, big, bigger lie. And it's a very interesting character." And so I'm thinking, we got this show that takes place in a puppy pound. And it's kind of run like [*Hogan's Heroes*]. . . . "And so you got this one character, Little Whopper, and he tells little whoppers. He'll tell a story and then all of a sudden, it'll come [true]." . . . Well, I had never seen the *Saturday Night Live* character.

Sandler: It's Tommy Flanagan, the pathological liar, played by Jon Lovitz.

Rushnell: Lovitz. Yes, indeed. That was it. Joe stole that too, by the way. So anyway, we rolled up our sleeves, made more breadcrumbs, and more wine stains. And by the time we had a call for the check, we pretty much had the three or four main characters, and I had a pretty darn good idea. I would have given him the order right then and there. But I made him go back and write it up, and draw some pictures, and things like that. *Pound Puppies* launched and it was a huge success. Big, big, big success. So that was a story . . . that describes how Joe had such talents of pursuit. I mean, dogged pursuit for the *Pound Puppies*. And to just to keep going and keep going. . . .

Sandler: Can you share another story about Joe Barbera?

Rushnell: Scooby had been on [CBS since 1969]. Fred Silverman had [become head of all programming at CBS in 1970], and whoever succeeded him [in charge of daytime] was not protecting the property of Scooby-Doo. Fred would have fiercely protected that because he was part of the creative process of that birth. But we got Scooby-Doo back [after Fred became president of ABC Entertainment in 1975]. . . . I thought that we needed to put in some new characters or a new character. Just something to kind of give it a new flavor.

One of my favorite all-time characters was the chicken hawk, Henery Hawk, from the Looney Tunes cartoons. A little character that was tough as nails. A Jimmy Cagney kind of character that was afraid of nobody. . . . And I felt with Scooby-Doo being a huge dog, that it would be great to have a little dog for him to play off of. So I kind of threw that idea out with Joe. And he was ruminating and so forth. I was out [in Los Angeles] doing some pitch meetings, and Joe had invited me to come out to his Palm Springs house to spend the weekend.

Sandler: Was it typical for a network exec to go to the home of the producer of the cartoons that they work with?

Rushnell: I think it was Joe's way of doing business, but I think it was the same with each of those guys that I worked with. . . . I would have gone to Lou Scheimer's house [of Filmation], although we didn't have that same kind of personal relationship, that kind of friendship relationship. . . . Friz Freleng, I never went to his house, but we did go to dinner and that kind of thing. And Marty Krofft—I went to his house a lot of times. They knew that the selling process is a relationship process. And their success was how good their relationship is with the people that they're trying to sell to. It isn't just because you're going to get favors, or Squire is going to give you a deal because he's my buddy, or he's been to my house. . . .

And so there's Joe's place [in Palm Springs] and a pool. . . . Joe and I spent that, probably Saturday afternoon, taking a swim in the pool. Now, in the pool of a Hanna-Barbera executive, like you would expect, you'd be floating around on a Yogi Bear inflated inner tube or a Fred Flintstone something or another or a Scooby thing around your waist. And so these two grown men are paddling around. . . . Anyway, we had this issue of who the new character is going to be. . . . Joe says, "I'm kind of thinking of . . . a smaller character. I think he ought to be his nephew. And so he looks up at Uncle Scooby, and he calls him Uncle Scooby. And, you know, he's just a nice little character. But like you say, Squire, he's like the chicken hawk. He's tough as nails. He's not afraid of anything." And I'm now picturing Scooby in the chandelier and the chandelier shaking because the ghost is coming, and then Joe says, "Yeah, yeah. And this little character is, you know, really scrappy. He looks up and says, "Good idea, Uncle Scoob! You're going to jump on the ghost when he comes in!" So Joe adds to the dynamic of this, where Scooby is afraid of his shadow and this little character is not, [but] he never sees any of Scooby's faults. . . . Then somewhere in there, it becomes Scrappy, and then Scrappy-Doo. Scrappy-Doo was born while we were paddling around on Yogi Bear inflatables. But that was how the creative process kind of evolved with Joe Barbera. I don't know if Fred Silverman operated that way because I never went paddling around with him. But Joe and I had that kind of a relationship. . . .

Sandler: Did you feel that Hanna-Barbera was the top studio producing cartoons at the time? Were they the go-to studio?

Rushnell: In my view, Hanna-Barbera was the premier producer of Saturday morning television cartoons. I never even considered Disney in that category, because they wouldn't deign to do Saturday morning cartoons for a long time. . . . My end game was to get hits—I just wanted hits. I didn't want Hanna-Barbera to create a series that was going to be a hit for the other networks. I wanted them to create hits for ABC.

Sandler: Do you have any stories involving Bill?

Rushnell: . . . There was one time where I had a summit meeting [outside of Boston in August 1974]. It was part of my diplomatic initiative with

Action for Children's Television. I had invited all of the studio heads to a very auspicious place, the Concord Colonial Inn, where the Revolutionary War started, right outside or down the street. The summit meeting was with Joe Barbera and Bill Hanna. Lou Scheimer, Friz Freleng, and David DePatie were there too, these legends of children's television. And here they were coming to this meeting that Squire was dragging them along to, to meet those terrible women from Boston who were causing such *havoc* with our Saturday morning programming. . . . [T]hat was the most time that I ever spent with Bill. I got to know Bill, talk about him and his family, and about the days of Tom and Jerry. We just had a lot of downtime where we could talk about those kinds of things. . . . We had that on that Saturday afternoon when we were doing our summit meeting.

It started out like a seventh-grade prom, with the boys over here, and the girls over there. Right? You got the cartoonists over here and the witches from Boston over there. Pretty soon, as the time went on, Joe was romancing them with his stories and so forth. Everybody thought that Friz Freleng was charming, even though he was scared to death. . . . At about the midpoint in that day, we all stopped and turned on the TV, and watched Nixon resign. Somehow, [there was] the divine alignment of all of those events, the "shot heard around the world," right there in the neighborhood, and we're having this experience of watching Nixon resign at the same moment. We all had a very memorable weekend that we went away with. From that point on, I knew that Peggy Charren looked upon those people with a lot more respect and admiration, because she had met them. And they had a lot more respect and admiration for what she was doing. So anyway, we coexisted with them for a long time. . . .

Sandler: Do you feel that summit might have been a turning point in children's television?

Rushnell: I do believe that Joe Barbera and Bill Hanna went back with a sensibility about what [ACT was] talking about, what they were looking for. [Bill and Joe] had now gone and met the enemy and the enemy wasn't such a bad enemy after all. They were just a grumpy neighbor down the street, like that grumpy neighbor on your paper route that you finally won over. And then he came to your baseball games, that kind of thing. . . .

Sandler: When you look back at your relationship with Hanna and Barbera, what would you say they should be remembered for?

Rushnell: I really appreciated both Joe and Bill, and Friz Freleng . . . [W]hen I was interviewed by the [Great American Broadcasting] executives, they asked, "What would you do with Bill and Joe, if you were the CEO?" Now, I figured that was probably a trick question. It was probably like if I said, "Well, I'd put them out to pasture or something," then that would cost me the job. But I didn't have any hesitancy at all. I said, "I would treat them like the legends that they are. I would respect them for the wealth of knowledge that they have. I would use them until I couldn't use them anymore." [*He starts to cry.*] They weren't treated with respect by the network executives [after me]. We called them snot-nosed network executives. Most of them were younger than thirty-three by the time I was leaving. . . . And I don't think Turner treated them with respect either. I don't know about [Great American Broadcasting], but I got the feeling that [Great American Broadcasting] . . . knew who they were and treated them with value.

Hanna-Barbera:
The Cartoonists Who Own Saturday Morning

JOHN MARIANI / 1979

From *Saturday Review*, November 24, 1979, 24ff.

One hour out of every twenty-four, a Hanna-Barbera cartoon entertains some segment of the world's population, capturing an international audience Walt Disney never even dreamed of. Yogi Bear, Fred Flintstone, Huckleberry Hound, and Scooby-Doo are embraced by five hundred million people in eighty countries. Hanna-Barbera's parent company, Taft Broadcasting Company, manages the largest merchandising operation of its kind in the world, with more than 1,500 licensed manufacturers turning out some 4,500 different products based on Hanna-Barbera characters, including everything from Fred Flintstone window shades to Banana Splits bubble bath.

Were you to turn on the tube on a Saturday morning this winter, you would be hard put to escape "The Funtastic World of Hanna-Barbera" created by the studio, which this season has sold the networks seven hours of children's programming over a four-and-a-half-hour schedule. Hanna-Barbera cartoons run the gamut of children's fare, from lovable-dopey animal characters like Scooby-Doo and his "rascal side-kick" Scrappy-Doo to classic epic heroes like Superman and Wonder Woman. There are Black characters (the Super Globetrotters), and monster characters (Godzilla), and supernatural characters aided by liberated females (Casper and the Angels). Most of these shows are interrupted by drop-in safety tips and educational admonishments, and for those children who are too dumb to know when to respond to a joke, there are laugh tracks. The CBS network bought Hanna-Barbera's *The All-New Popeye Hour,* while ABC has *The World's Greatest Superfriends* and *Scooby and Scrappy-Doo.* NBC is filling out its entire 7:30 to noon slot with Hanna-Barberisms: *Casper and the Angels, Fred and Barney Meet the Thing, The Super Globetrotters, The New Shmoo, Godzilla, Jonny Quest,* and *The Jetsons.*

Every Saturday, Bill Hanna and Joe Barbera babysit for an audience of twenty-five million American children, a situation some would call a stranglehold. As babysitters, Hanna and Barbera would claim a benign influence on the children, who sit mesmerized by their cartoons from dawn to noon, but the total command Hanna-Barbera has over the networks at those impressionable hours troubles the people who see themselves as guardians of the children during that four-and-a-half-hour period. Peggy Charren, president of Action for Children's Television (ACT), argues, "Our organization has always been against censorship of any kind, and for all kinds of diversity in children's programming. But if you want diversity, you don't hire Hanna-Barbera to produce 77 percent of your children's schedule, as NBC has done. The networks have all that money, and they could be making the finest children's programs in the world. Yet they come up with a schedule that in its entirety—not in any individual show—is an insult to children."

Joe Barbera, who is generally credited with being the creative member of the Hanna-Barbera team, responds to such citizens' group criticism by saying, "The networks themselves have killed all the creativity in Saturday morning animation. They won't make a decision on the fall schedule until late in the spring, and then they send down directives that force us to alter the characters we've created, even down to their voices. Bill Hanna and I were the first to do Tom and Jerry, back at MGM in the forties—we won seven Academy Awards for those cartoons. Now we're told those Tom and Jerry shorts are too violent, even though in syndication on local channels they've scored very high ratings. We can't do slapstick anymore. Every year the network tells us what we can and can't do. This year Popeye can't hit Bluto with his fist. Characters may not use guns, but they may use lasers. It's crazy—you simply can't plan a character that way. We haven't had real violence in our cartoons for a decade, but the networks still find something to complain about."

ACT's Peggy Charren shakes her head at such statements: "For Joe Barbera—whom I know very well—to say he's not allowed to be creative anymore, just because he can't show killings, is a cop-out of the first order. We've never asked the networks or Joe to cut out violence in cartoons. All great fairy tales have violence in them. But when I turn on the first episode of *Jabberjaw* [a 1976 Hanna-Barbera series about a talking great white shark that walks on its tail] and see an Oriental villain drawn like a Fu Manchu stereotype right out of my own childhood, well, I wonder if that's what Joe is trying to justify as creativity."

The networks' defensiveness about Saturday morning cartoon shows borders on paranoia, and they bristle at the charge that the shows are not diverse, or that they stifle creativity. NBC's vice-president of children's programs, Mary Alice Dwyer, insists that the cartoon characters do in fact differ from one another, and that NBC does other kinds of children's programs at other hours. "We find we can better capture children's attention with live-action characters at other times in the schedule, and we do drop *Ask NBC News* into the cartoon shows." Miss Dwyer explains that the network has a "panel of social scientists" who advise producers how to make animated shows more educational. After Hanna-Barbera made the Harlem Globetrotters into superheroes with individual powers in their *The Super Globetrotters* show, the panel suggested that stories be developed in which the Globetrotters "help each other to solve problems," a swell lesson for the children to pick up between the super antics. "So, rather than putting a lid on creativity," says Dwyer, "we are really asking Hanna-Barbera to perform the difficult task of coming up with more interesting characters and story lines, instead of just going with the first thought that comes to mind."

ABC's vice-president of children's and early morning programming, Squire Rushnell, sides with Joe Barbera, but he puts the blame on his own network's Broadcasting Standards and Practices department for what he calls a "sanitizing" of Saturday morning cartoons. "I'm continually fighting alongside Joe Barbera on this issue," says Rushnell. "Organizations like ACT and the PTA caused an awakening at the networks some years back, and they've made a positive contribution. We had been inattentive. Recently, we turned down the Road Runner series [produced by DePatie-Freleng Enterprises] because the main characters are always trying to kill each other. Nevertheless, I think we've gone too far if we begin to question whether Scooby-Doo getting hit by a wave at the beach is an act of violence. TV doesn't turn out criminals. But if you take a rotten kid and put him in front of a rotten TV show, maybe he'll be more rotten."

The storm over the effects of TV violence on children has raged for more than a decade ("Ever since Bobby Kennedy was shot," says Barbera), but none of the numerous studies on the subject has come up with anything approaching hard evidence against it, especially with regard to animated cartoons.

This past spring, the University of Pennsylvania's Annenberg School of Communications released its annual Violence Profile, of trends in network television from 1967 to 1978. The study contended that violence on television during weekend children's programming was way up in 1978. But the statistical tally of violent acts made no distinction between Fred Flintstone tripping over a dinosaur bone and Superman blowing up an alien spaceship. (The study argued that accidents in scripts "victimize characters who fall prey to them, and the message of victimization is one significant aspect of exposure to violence.")

Such arguments make Joe Barbera do a double take, followed by a slow burn of the type that has made Popeye so often turn to spinach.

Barbera is one of the cuddlier studio tycoons you'll ever meet. He is a big man, though not tall, given to white shoes, shiny shirts open at the neck, and dark glasses—which he wears even in dark Italian restaurants of the kind he frequents near the two-and-a-half-acre Hanna-Barbera studios in North Hollywood, where I met with him recently to discuss the past, present, and future of Saturday morning TV.

"Y'know, Frank Sinatra comes to this restaurant," he said. "Try the veal something-or-other, with the artichokes on top. The chef'll make it special for me. It isn't on the menu."

Joe Barbera has lost most of his original New York accent. Second-generation Italian, he grew up in New York, attended New York University, and took some banking courses, worked for the Irving Trust Company and, in his free hours, hawked cartoons to magazines. After a modest success selling cartoons to *Collier's* and other journals, he sent off a batch to Walt Disney and requested a job. That was in the thirties, when animation at the Disney studios was burgeoning into a remarkable art form at a thousand drawings per minute. Disney's hallmarks were perfection and experimentation. The studio drew the finest talent and most dedicated animators in the world, and plowed its profits back into new animation techniques. Joe Barbera never even got an interview, but found work at Metro-Goldwyn-Mayer, where he met Bill Hanna, an engineer from New Mexico, in 1937. At MGM, the two animators developed the Tom and Jerry cartoon series, which usually played with the studio's double-feature programs, at a time when the big studios owned the theaters.

The Tom and Jerry cartoons were based on the theme of cat meets mouse, cat chases mouse, cat gets blown to smithereens. But the animation was excellent, the characters were well-delineated, and the slapstick was inventive, if sometimes a bit grisly, as when the cat was sliced into salami sections after hitting a wire fence. No matter. He was back together in the next scene, ready to be hit by a truck.

In the early 1950s, the studio system broke down, and the antitrust laws dissolved their hold on distribution and theaters. Short animated cartoons were among the first casualties. Only Disney continued to make animated shorts throughout the fifties. [Editors' note: Actually, a number of animation studios were still producing animated shorts at this time.] Hanna and Barbera were let go by MGM, with no financial claim on Tom and Jerry.

Meanwhile, Disney was moving into television—producing the *Disneyland* series of live shows, including *Davy Crockett*, as well as animated speculations on the future of space travel, and *The Mickey Mouse Club*—and was continuing to make feature-length cartoons like *Lady and the Tramp* and *Sleeping Beauty*. But Hanna and Barbera realized Disney had not conceived of an animated TV series specifically tailored to the economy and pressures of getting a show on the air weekly. (Disney's own TV shows were either live-action or reruns of old animated shows.)

Using the newly developed technique of "limited animation" (invented by United Productions of America, a cartoon factory), in which only certain simplified movements are animated, thereby giving the characters a more stilted, less lifelike action—Hanna and Barbera could cut down the number of drawings shot per minute from one thousand to about three hundred or less. By

1959, Disney animator Ub Iwerks had also developed a more practical method of turning out cartoons: a Xerox process for copying animators' original drawings onto transparencies called "cels." Although this technique compromised the line and modeling of the figures, it eliminated a costly, laborious, separate inking process.

These two techniques allowed Hanna and Barbera to produce animated television series on a weekly basis, first for children's shows, then for prime-time television. "Our first prime-time series, *The Flintstones*," says Barbera, "was about a caveman, his family, and friends. We had all this clever stuff, with dinosaurs and everyday objects made out of stone, and it wasn't violent either. Well, I took it around to the networks and they thought I was nuts—a cartoon show in prime time? I told them this was an *adult* cartoon show. I must have told the story line five times a day. Finally, ABC took a chance for the fall schedule of 1960. The show was a smash. It won an Emmy."

The Flintstones was innovative insofar as the characters were human beings rather than animals; in fact, they were modeled on the Jackie Gleason–Art Carney series *The Honeymooners* (which had gone off the air in 1956), and plots involved Fred Flintstone's struggle to make ends meet in the Stone Age town of Bedrock. What started out as an adult show was certainly enjoyed by children, and subsequently *The Flintstones* was tailored for Saturday morning, where it now appears on NBC.

Other animation studios emerged in the sixties and seventies to claim a share of the Saturday morning market, but none even approached the output of Hanna-Barbera, which has produced more than a hundred different animated series to date, among them series based on Laurel and Hardy, the Three Musketeers, and Moby Dick. The studio now also produces live-action shows and movie features, including the Emmy Award–winning *The Gathering*, which starred Maureen Stapleton and Edward Asner. Currently in production are *Jesus at XVI*, about Christ as an adolescent, and the project dearest to Hanna-Barbera's heart, *Heidi's Song*—a full-length animated feature that will depend on animation techniques more reminiscent of the Golden Age of cartoons than of the dreary Saturday mornings of children's programming.

"We're so proud of *Heidi's Song*," says Barbera from behind his sunglasses. "We're really spending our own money on this one—$8 million—to make it truly special and wondrous. The animation will be the finest we can make, sometimes better than the old Disney days, because we know so much more about special effects now. It's the kind of project I'd like to do more of, but the economics are just too rough."

After lunch, Joe Barbera and I returned to the studio, and I was shown around the facilities by master animators Harry Love, Friz Freleng, and other legends of the business. "In the old days," said Love, "an animator would be expected to turn out maybe eight to ten feet of cartoon a week. For this

Saturday morning stuff, we've got to turn out seventy feet a week! Some of the old guys used to have their specialties: They'd only draw one character, or they'd just do water, or fire, or something like that. Now, that's all changed. Animators today just make things move.

"Back in the forties, Warner Bros. would spend $35,000 on a cartoon, while Disney would spend $120,000. And it shows. You can't compare them to the Saturday morning cartoons. Another problem is that there just aren't enough animators around today. We were training two hundred people in a school right here, but we suspended that program because a lot of the graduates were stolen by the other studios."

We walked through the hallways, flanked by small offices full of idea men, story men, master animators, producers, and directors. Then into the cavernous rooms full of background artists, layout artists, inkers, painters, paint checkers, camera operators, Xerox operators, film editors, sound scorers, music scorers and arrangers, dubbing engineers, special-effects people, and then on and on through the labyrinth.

Harry Love pointed out the old-timers who had worked with him at Warners or Disney or MGM. Men who had drawn the original Popeyes, or a sequence in *Fantasia*, or specialized in Daffy Duck. Harry Love himself was one of the original animators of Krazy Kat cartoons, now artifacts in a cinemabilia somewhere. Scholars at the University of California, the American Film Institute, and the French magazine *Cahiers du Cinéma* are cataloguing these men's accomplishments, looking for the story boards used to illustrate an early Mickey Mouse cartoon, plotting the rise and the fall of Gerald McBoing-Boing cartoons, and investigating the sociological significance of Betty Boop in relation to the adolescent sex drive.

Harry Love rambled on: "Y'know, Disney spends $8 million on an animated feature, and takes two and a half years to make it. That's ninety minutes of animation. For the Saturday morning cartoons, Hanna-Barbera turns out *seven* hours of animation every single week. You can't get real quality. But, if the networks said to us, 'Make good cartoons,' we would. We can do it; it just takes time and money. That's why we're all excited about *Heidi's Song*, which won't be ready until 1981. And Disney's making *The Black Hole*—an outer space film combining live action with animation. These things will be beautiful to see."

As we walked through the studio, I wondered if the amount of animation viewed by children on Saturday morning might in fact have dulled their appreciation of the wondrous possibilities of beautifully modulated animation. Do children see the difference between a Hanna-Barbera character done in limited animation and a rounded, shadowed, richly colored Hanna-Barbera Tom and Jerry cartoon from the 1940s? Will these children care very much for *Heidi's Song*?

As I passed by a recording session in which a Black actor was dubbing a voice onto the animated Black Falcon character, I picked up some safety tips in the dialogue. The Black Falcon was telling a little boy (dubbed by a grown woman) about being careful with electric sockets. I was suddenly struck by the facile condescension of the idea that animated cartoons should be educational, that a panel of "social scientists" should force health and nutrition tips out of the mouths of Black Falcon or Superman or Porky Pig. I could only imagine a Pollyanna world in which Pinocchio cannot be swallowed by a whale because such a plot would be a cruel stereotyping of the leviathan.

Later on, I was encouraged to learn that the truly harmful aspect of cartoons—their mass, and unimaginative, production—is perhaps not so bad as I'd thought. Despite Hanna-Barbera's domination of the Saturday morning schedule, despite their ability to churn out seven hours of animation a week, despite all the wringing of hands over citizens' group pressure, the most popular of all the Saturday morning cartoons is still *The Bugs Bunny/Road Runner Hour*—for reasons, I suspect, that have little to do with cannons, pistols, dynamite, and other instruments of animated destruction. Those characters never condescend to children; indeed, Bugs Bunny and Daffy Duck are closer to the Marx Brothers than to Captain Kangaroo.

Children realize at once that Bugs, Daffy, and Wile E. Coyote are playing out their own fantasies of revenge, aggression, and fair play, as opposed to the current crop of cartoons, wherein characters like Casper the Friendly Ghost and Scooby-Doo are reflections of all the imbecilic human characters on prime-time situation comedies. The characters on *The Bugs Bunny/Road Runner Hour* series are sophisticated, but, beyond that, the drawing, the backgrounds, the way a character lifts his foot and casts a shadow still have the ability to rivet the attention of the child and adult, because of the stretch and elasticity invested in the flesh of wisecracking rabbits, daffy ducks, and lisping cats.

Joe Barbera remembers how he used to draw Tom and Jerry back at MGM. "The cat would rig up an anvil over the mouse," he says, "and somehow the cat would get in the way and he'd get hit with the anvil—a ten-thousand-pound anvil!—and the mouse would peel him off the ground, and you'd hear it like a Band-Aid, right? But the cat was in perfect condition in the next sequence. We can't do that stuff anymore. They tell me it's not good for kids to see. I don't understand what they're talking about!"

It occurred to me that the men who own Saturday morning have become too successful at what they once loved best—drawing characters who seem not only lifelike but true to life's complications—and now there's little heart left in them or the characters they create. Which is the definition of television itself: success at the expense of the ineffable quality of true fantasy. For true fantasy, especially in animated terms, gives us the world as it should be, a place where witches get thrown in ovens and cats, just scraped off the sidewalk, bounce back to rounded life again and again and again.

The Smurfs

GERARD BALDWIN / 2015

Edited from *From Mister Magoo to Papa Smurf: A Memoir* (Austin, TX: Neighborhood Publishers, 2015), 153–64, 166–69.

Production meetings [at Hanna-Barbera around 1980–81] were usually held on a Monday morning, in a thickly carpeted conference room at a very long, highly polished, ten-thousand-dollar table that could easily accommodate fifteen or more people. Bill Hanna sat at the head. His secretary, Ginger, sat beside but slightly back, as if she knew her place in this hierarchy of the largest animation studio in the world. This gathering was a mix of line producers, production managers, and department heads. I thought it odd there were no directors. The talk was always about production schedules, deadlines, costs, and pressure. There was pressure to produce more and more, faster and faster, for less and less. As the meeting droned on, some of us, those that could draw, would doodle or make sketches of each other. The problems were serious, but this was not West Point.

I was assigned two shows—*The Herculoids* for CBS [Editors' note: Part of the H-B anthology series *Space Stars*] and *SuperFriends*, for ABC. The line producer had nothing to do with anything that was really creative. My main job was to see that the scripts were not too long. It was okay if a script was too short, you could always add an insert, but Hanna hated shooting footage and then throwing it away. Using a film meter, which is just a stopwatch, and reading the script aloud, playing all the parts and using your own voice for music and sound effects, you could come pretty close to length, within a second or two. I might enact a scene three or four times and choose the average.

"Superman, look out!" Deeedeee da taa taaaaaaaaa BOOM . . . BOOM . . . BOOM . . . ka-RASH.

"Whew! That was a close one, Superman." (Nine seconds.)

The producers did not do this. They just counted script pages. Somewhere between forty and forty-seven pages would be just about right for a twenty-five-minute episode. This approach was almost never accurate.

After a script was storyboarded, it was the producer's job to go over it in detail with the network executive, always a female vice president in charge of children's programming. They were picky, and correctly so. It was their money. But they were also somewhat helpless, as there was never enough time. I would attend to their concerns by changing the storyboard, covering it with little drawings, directorial notes, timing notes, inserting new scenes where needed, and finally, with the exec's approval, I would send it into production. Many weeks later, when the network VP next saw the episode, it was on film, and good or bad, nothing could be done. Air time—FINISHED!

My efforts at improving the quality of the company's product did not endear me to board sluggers, sheet timers, production managers, and other functionaries down the line. My input was crowding their space. I was interfering with their freedom to do as little as possible. My effort made their jobs more difficult. Many of them didn't give a damn about making good films. The pervasive attitude was "It's all shit anyway," and, of course, there was some truth in that. They were tired and cynical. They complained to Hanna about the changes I was making.

The network executives, on the other hand, were very pleased. They could see that someone was trying to make their shows better. They also spoke to Hanna.

At the peak of a production season there was so much work to be done in so little time that just about any twenty-five-cent subcontractor could pick up an episode. Some of their films were atrocious and, standing at a Moviola, I found myself berating, "Hell. You guys are concerned about runaway production, but this stuff is not as good as what we get back from Taiwan—and they're just learning."

Much of the work continued to be poor. Even after Band-Aids, it would be embarrassing to screen an episode with a network VP. They would give a look and the look said, "How can you even show this to me?"

"I'll fix it . . ."

But you couldn't fix everything. The episodes had to air on time. The biggest sin of all was missing an airdate. The next biggest sin, in my opinion, was the poor quality of the studio's product. The cause of these gigantic log jams and the inability to do good work could be traced back to the big three—ABC, CBS, and NBC—who never made up their minds about what shows to buy or when to start production until much of the time needed to produce a decent product was already expended, in indecision.

With little pride in what I was doing, I was coming to the decision that maybe it was time to leave Saturday morning and find something else.

I can't say I ever got to know Joe Barbera or Bill Hanna very well. I can't say I even remember their corporate titles, but Joe was #1 and Bill was #2. Why? Perhaps when they first formed the corporation and offered shares, the board of directors, one being big-time director George Sidney, simply voted Joe top dog.

Joe's office was much bigger than Bill's and might be described as a suite. There was a large bathroom, a conference room, and a large, well-appointed waiting room. Glass cases displayed all of their Oscars, Emmys, gold records, and honorariums. A loud, fading redhead was Joe's secretary and defensive guard.

Bill's office, although still quite large, was more modest, but it too had a private bathroom. Ginger, Bill's secretary, was nothing like her name implied. She was rather motherly and soft-spoken.

I guess I related more to Hanna than to Barbera. Bill's job was to keep the assembly line moving and not exceed budget, while Joe, it seemed, was always off somewhere creating and pitching new shows, and was rarely involved in the daily drudgery.

Did I really know these guys? No. Our conversations were almost always about animation, network concerns, and production problems. They were older than me and had family and friends that went way back to MGM and Tom and Jerry. I think Joe saw himself as the creative force behind the studio, and I sensed Bill Hanna resented this assumption.

Bill frequently ate lunch at the old Smoke House restaurant across the street from Warner Bros. The Smoke House was, and still is, I presume, a very good, typically American establishment serving prime rib, good steaks, fish and chips—a large menu with no surprises. Starting at the cocktail hour, a piano offered favorites into the night. Lunch with Bill was always about production schedules, delivery dates, flow charts, and budgets.

At the peak of a production season and over a weekend, Bill would invite all of the line producers, board sluggers, sheet timers, and assorted helpers aboard his yacht for a big party. This was an all-male event. Of course, the guests brought along animation work to be done—work first—then party. Bill did the cooking. I was never invited, nor would I have gone. I think Bill knew that I, as a former president of the Screen Cartoonists Guild, saw these "parties" as a form of labor exploitation. [Editors' note: We cannot confirm that Baldwin held this position.] We never talked politics.

He had a reputation of being a real tough ogre. . . . Returning to my office from a long lunch, I would frequently shut the door, lay down on the floor, and hypnotize myself to sleep. During one nap, I recall hearing the door open just a bit, and half-opened one eye to see Bill Hanna. I started to jump up as he crossed the room.

"Don't get up. Don't get up." He leaned down over my prone body and proffered a page of a storyboard over my face.

"Do you mean scene 372A to be inserted before or after scene 372? Not clear."

". . . Oh, yeah. Before."

"Okay."

He walked back to the door, and as he closed the door, glanced back at my still prone body.

"Feels good, doesn't it?" Some ogre.

But he could also be extremely forceful. After listening to Bill deliver a long list of "must happens," I replied, "Well Bill, I'll do my best."

"NO! That's not good enough!"

For many years, the Hanna-Barbera studio had a near monopoly on the production of animated films made for television. The three networks—ABC, CBS, and NBC—had a near monopoly on all television entertainment produced for children. TV had a huge appetite. There was little time for creativity and even less for quality.

Design and manufacture a television set and an assembly line can produce one million sets that, at the end of the line, will all work and be of acceptable quality. Design and produce a television show for kids and the assembly line can never guarantee or even anticipate what will come out at the end. There are too many variables. Joe Barbera saw himself as the studio's creative genius, while Bill Hanna figured out, as best anybody could, how to run a cartoon factory.

The Screen Cartoonists Union had a minimum pay scale for directors. The key to any film is the director, but there were no directors, as such, at H and B. Once a network approved a script, it was turned over to a producer (me), who turned it over to a storyboard artist, who turned his work over to a board timer, who turned it over . . . SO, nobody was a director, and the producer had the final cut. None of these people had the credit "directed by" but rather some ignominious title like "sheet timer" or, and this one I really love, "board slugger." By splitting the director's role into its component parts and avoiding the word "director," the studio saved money. For a creative and talented artist to refer to himself as a "board slugger" must have been humiliating. They got used to it. Usually, creative people with robotic jobs are not too happy, and the paradox of doing more and more with less and less created an invisible anxiety that infected the studio. This method of turning out miles and miles of animated film was Bill Hanna's idea—and it worked. All television animation studios were soon using the same system. The only trouble was that, sometimes, what came on the screen was enough to make a sensitive animator throw up.

In 1998, Warner Bros. published a big, overpriced hardcover book titled *Hanna-Barbera Cartoons*. This book tells the reader very little about Bill and Joe. Its sole purpose is to coin money. It is a catalogue of animation cels, none of them original and, therefore, all of them fake. Not a one of these cels was ever under a camera! The book offers no insight into these once famous, now-fading personalities. On page 9, Barbera offers: "People sometimes ask me how Bill Hanna and I managed to work together for more than fifty years without fighting. My answer is always the same. 'We did fight, the first week—and we haven't spoken since.'"

Joe was not invited to attend Bill's funeral service.

Quite often, Joe Barbera ate lunch at an elegant Italian restaurant in old Hollywood. Unlike the Smoke House, this place had a quiet elegance, enhanced by a sparkling fountain. The maître d' always greeted Mr. Barbera as if he were a prince of the Medici, a role Joe accepted with grace. After a couple of glasses of chianti, lunch with Joe was always about ideas, concepts, and imagination.

After one long lunch, Joe was driving us back to the studio when, somehow, the subject of an heir apparent came up. Joe turned ashen. Death? Retire? They never did. Even after the bean counters took over "their" studio, they went to work every day. Neither one of them seemed to have a life beyond cartoons. In a Jungian sense, they were the thing they did. From my observation, they were not much more than that. But I may misjudge.

In 1964 Joe Barbera said: "The days of showing little elves playing around a mushroom are gone forever."

In 1980, out of the blue, came the Smurfs.

Saturday morning children's programming on the NBC television network was not doing well. For whatever reason, kids were not watching NBC. The Nielsen ratings were so low that the network was considering making a big, big change, dropping children's programming altogether and replacing it with news. That was the rumor. Someone else was also making a big change. Fred Silverman, NBC's CEO, was resigning. I heard he was bored. I don't know how anyone could run a television network and be bored. Maybe he just needed a change. Legend has it his daughter returned from a trip to Europe and presented daddy with a couple of little blue figurines. Silverman was soon looking at Smurf hardcover comic books. They were selling well in Europe but [were] unknown in the United States. He thought the books could be the basis for a great show. Before leaving NBC, he made a deal with the creator of the Smurfs, pen name Peyo. He also made a deal with Hanna-Barbera. Done.

Margaret Loesch was Hanna-Barbera's executive vice-president of development and programming. Prominent in her home was a large and imposing portrait of her father who, at one time, had been the youngest general in the United States Air Force. Margaret had inherited all of those qualities one needs to be a general, and she was a good one. She managed people, including me, very well. I don't know why she chose me to be the guardian of *The Smurfs*. Perhaps I got good grades from the networks, or perhaps I let it be known I wasn't too happy working on hopelessly idiotic films that were empty of any meaningful content. I recall her introducing me to someone: "Gerard comes to us from *Bullwinkle*." To me, that was odd. Why not, "He comes to us from Dr. Seuss"?

Many years would pass before I realized that everything "Bullwinkle" had become a cult, with a large US following numbering in the hundreds of thousands. As the children of the early 1980s mature now in their thirties, so too will *The Smurfs* take on a cultlike status; only these happy memories, worldwide, will number in the millions.

I always felt, during my first season producing *The Smurfs*, that Margaret Loesch was my protector and guide. She seemed all business and motherly at the same time. If I had to go to the airport and welcome Peyo, or go out to dinner with someone in product licensing, she would always advise, "Don't drive, Gerard. Feel free to take a limo anytime. That's what they're for." Bill Hanna would never have said that.

The [NBC] children's programming people in New York were not happy with Silverman's decision to air *The Smurfs*. They were not the least bit enthused about *The Smurfs*. [As characters,] they were too soft, too wordy, too old fashioned: "I mean come ON! The Middle Ages?"

Mickey Dwyer, a woman in her fifties, was the NBC vice-president of children's programming. H and B sent a delegation to New York to meet with her, discuss the show, and, of course, for her to meet and become acquainted with its producer.

Since the concept was something "new," she would need to see a pilot film, and test it. I liked Mickey and thought she was an okay gal, even if she did have grave doubts about the appeal of the Smurfs. All I was certain of was that the Smurfs were charming and unlike any of the slam-bam stuff like *SuperFriends* that was being fed to America's children. The folks at NBC were totally convinced the Smurfs had no appeal.

Back in Los Angeles, I made a pilot film about six minutes long. I felt the same way about Peyo's Smurfs as I did about the good doctor's Grinch. In the translation from book to screen, nothing must change or become distorted. Peyo had complete creative control and this little film looked as if Peyo had drawn it himself. It was charming. On the assumption that to children, classical music would sound very old, and thus help them enter the Middle Ages and believe that the stories were about a time long, long ago, I chose music by Beethoven and Vivaldi. At the first screening an NBC exec turned to me and asked: "Who did the music?"

"Vivaldi."

"Nice. Can we get him?"

Len Janson was the story editor on a Hanna-Barbera TV series, *Space Ghost* [also part of *Space Stars*]. He needed a secretary. An attractive young woman by the name of Frances Novier accepted the job, on the condition that she could submit stories. Okay. She had ambition to be a writer. Len made her rewrite her first one-page premise five times. He made her rewrite her five-page outline five times, and rewrite the twelve-page script for an eleven-minute story five times. She finally sold her first *Space Ghost* story, but this guy was also doing his best to discourage her. He probably felt she had no talent. This very talented guy was also destined to be one of the two story editors for *The Smurfs*. . . .

As always, NBC tested the pilot on a focus group in New York and, much to their surprise, the pilot tested off their charts. If a pilot tests well and is still a flop, the exec can always say, "Well, it tested okay." Children's programming gave a reluctant nod. The studio could proceed with production without any more input from the brains at NBC. But I got a phone call from Mickey Dwyer. She grudgingly allowed that the pilot tested rather well, but there would be one change—the classical music would have to go!

"But why? That music reinforces the concept that the Smurfs live in the Middle Ages."

"NO. Got to go."

"I don't understand."

"Kids don't like classical music. They like rock 'n' roll."

"But isn't it absurd to see a knight in armor on horseback and hear rock 'n' roll?"

"Gerard, if you put ANY classical music on that show, I'll break your arm!"

And she meant it. The network is the ultimate boss. I was despondent until suddenly Mickey Dwyer . . . got fired! I don't know why. Perhaps the top network brass saw her as responsible for their low Saturday morning ratings. As NBC searched for a new boss for children's programming, there was a short period of time when the kid department had nobody in charge. The studio already had an okay to proceed with production, so we recorded the entire musical library for the as-yet-unwritten episodes, and pretty much spent the entire budget allowed for music, all classical.

From early storyboards, we already knew that, more than once, we would see a line of happy Smurfs marching along as if on parade. Hoyt Curtin, the studio's music director, was having difficulty finding an old piece of classical music, just the right musical phrase and tempo that would express the "spirit" of the Smurfs. We were talking about it when, suddenly, I had a eureka moment, and offered, how about:

LA LA
LA LA LA LAAAAA
LA LA LA LA LAAAAA . . .

That was it! Too bad I don't own it.

Later, when ratings soared, everybody was singing the LA LA LA song, and the sale of little blue figurines topped hundreds of millions of dollars. *The Smurfs* was the most-watched show on Saturday morning, holding a forty-four Nielsen share, which means that forty-four out of every one hundred TV sets on Saturday morning were tuned to NBC. When *The Smurfs* went from a half-hour show to a one-hour show to a one-and-a-half-hour show and kids stayed glued to their TV sets—when that happened—all of the NBC executives stood up and basked in their collective wisdom.

Joe Barbera said he thought the show was a hit because the Smurfs were blue. Odd. *The Smurfs* were a hit because the concept was great and the stories were good. . . .

In 1984 Margaret Loesch left Hanna-Barbera to head up Marvel Productions and, without her shield, I was open to the snipers.

By the time NBC found a new VP to oversee children's programming, the *Smurfs* show was well into production. Phyllis Tucker Vinson was a tall, striking African American, new to her job and, at first, a bit unsure of herself. She got my admiration when she took me aside and asked me to help her play her part. Smart lady. Phyllis supervised not only *The Smurfs* but all other children's programming for the network; however, *The Smurfs*, being the most demanding, was also the most challenging. NBC had gone from the Saturday morning basement through the skylight. It was now number one, and NBC wanted to keep it that way. Phyllis had to read and make input on every story premise outline, script, storyboard, voice recording, and finally, with a critical eye, view every foot of film. A difficult job. She was good at it and always listened. A ninety-minute show might have three one-half hour stories, and six ten-minute stories, and each one had a beginning, a middle, and an end. This was not soap opera writing, and at the peak, staff and freelance, I am sure we had fourteen writers working. . . .

Preproduction work on *The Smurfs* television series probably started in 1980, although the precise dates, to this historian, are not too important. What is important is that, in the twenty-three years prior to the television premiere of the show, Peyo had written, illustrated, and published many hardcover comic books, and the Smurfs were only the latest in a rather long series, and the most successful. These Smurf books numbered fifteen. At the studio, our two story editors used up a near quarter-century of Peyo's creativity in three weeks. Now it fell to our writing staff to come up with new Smurf stories at a prodigious rate. By 1982 it was a ninety-minute show! This huge success brought much attention to anyone connected to its production and, as we entered the second season, our two story editors quit for opportunity elsewhere.

There was not one writer immersed enough in Smurfland to replace them except, of course, me. With the blessing of Margaret Loesch, I anointed myself supervising story editor, and with her further blessing found myself an associate producer and advanced to supervising producer. Heady stuff. We quickly broke in a new story editing team, but I remained supervising story editor until I walked away. . . .

With animation being so labor-intensive, there was always a search for artists outside of Hollywood where wages were much lower. Bill Hanna found them in Taiwan. The Chinese learned very quickly, and soon Cuckoo's Nest studio was doing most of the *Smurfs* production, [from] animation through camera. This was a company Hanna had nursed from a seedling to a first-class production house and, in appreciation, at the studio in Taiwan, you were greeted in the lobby with a bronze bust of Bill.

James Wang, president of Cuckoo's Nest, wanted me to visit his studio and see how it functioned, and thus solve some serious communication problems, which were considerable. Our man in Taipei, Peter Aries, was doing an excellent job, and he too thought I should visit and see how the place worked.

Hanna, being the shortsighted cheapy he could be, did not want me to go, on the grounds that I was needed at the studio. But actually, he didn't want to spend the money. Finally James Wang paid for my visit. It was first class all the way. . . .

In the second, third, and fourth *Smurf* seasons, we needed at least six stories for a ninety-minute show, plus the scripting of five prime-time specials. Linearly, that's a feature a week. The procedure for creating a story worked like this: Every story premise was translated into French and faxed to Peyo and [his writer] Yvan Delporte. Their input, in French, was faxed to Hollywood and translated into English. This premise would then be sent to NBC. With the network's okay, the premise would be expanded into an outline of perhaps ten pages, translated into French, faxed to Brussels, comments returned in French, translated into English, and then forwarded to NBC. With their nod, the outline would morph into a script of forty or more pages, which would then be translated into French and sent to Peyo, his comments returned in French, translated into English, and then sent to the network for an okay to proceed with recording. More often than not, there would be a second and third draft. This plan did not always work as it was supposed to.

Sergeant-Major John Novier, retired, and his charming wife, Madeleine, took on the near-overwhelming job of not only translating but interpreting all of these many, many stories. They lived in Texas. Literal translations have no poetry. A joke in English may be totally flat in French, and vice-versa. Nuance is everything. Wherever their origination, all words moved through a triangle: Hollywood–Texas–Brussels or Brussels–Texas–Hollywood; and when Taiwan, a subcontractor, became involved, this pathway evolved into a quadrangle. . . .

Imagine an assembly line with over a thousand people all being paid, but they have nothing to do because they are waiting for a story. Very expensive. The show must go on air, on time, no matter what. More than once, a script would be put on the conveyor belt before Peyo ever saw the final. This would really anger him, and he'd throw a tantrum, resulting in the arrival of a long, sometimes angry, diatribe concerning our failings with respect to holding onto the Smurf concept: Smurf characters out of character—story ideas he didn't like—a long, long list of faults and cautions—thirty or forty points to be addressed NOW!

Poor Peyo, far away in Brussels, could only be reactive to the onslaught of stories. Although he had complete creative control, he understood television's gaping maw and was usually cooperative and helpful. Only rarely did he angrily stiffen in defense of his concept. Nothing could be injected into the show that was not Smurfy. Nothing, at least not for the first three years. . . .

Hanna-Barbera: Will *Heidi's Song* Be Its *Snow White*?

JOHN CANEMAKER / 1981

From *Millimeter*, February 1981, 82–93. Reprinted with permission.

Hanna-Barbera Productions, Inc. is such a giant corporate entertainment entity that it prompts the old joke: What does a two-ton canary sing? Any damn thing it wants! This Hollywood "canary" has expanded since 1957 to become the world's largest producer of animated TV series and specials; more recently Hanna-Barbera has become involved in themed amusement parks and live action movies for television.

Now H-B is eager to enter and conquer the sacred Disney domain of fully animated, "quality" feature-length animated films for theatrical release. William Hanna and Joseph R. Barbera hope to do so with an expensive flourish this summer when they will premiere *Heidi's Song*, a $9 million cartoon feature that has been in production for five years. The film's staff of two hundred–plus includes twelve background painters, sixty assistant animators, eight layout people, and eighteen top character animators. All cut their teeth years ago at the Disney studio, or at MGM, working with Hanna and Barbera during their halcyon days in the 1940s and '50s, producing Tom and Jerry shorts and animated segments for live action features such as Jerry the Mouse dancing with Gene Kelly in *Anchors Aweigh*.

Joseph Barbera claims *Heidi's Song* will be "a step forward in animation that's very exciting." But perhaps it will actually be a welcome artistic step back—a comeback of sorts—for Hanna and Barbera, who were once considered by their peers and the public to be superior cartoon craftsmen, winners of seven Academy Awards for two decades of beautifully timed and fully animated Tom and Jerry cartoons. In the twenty-three years since forming their own company—a factory geared to the production of "limited" animation series, a reduced form of animation that, as an H-B publicity release points out, "ignored the time-consuming and expensive detail that would not be visible on the dimly lit video screen"—Hanna and Barbera have produced over twenty TV specials and some sixty series (*Huckleberry Hound, Yogi Bear, The Flintstones, The Jetsons, Scooby-Doo and Scrappy-Doo*, and so on).

In other terms, H-B produces more film footage in a week today than it did in a year at MGM. The principals' choice to, as they say, "exploit a niche Disney had missed in family entertainment with low-cost cartoons for television," has made the two men cartoon tycoons, rich beyond their dreams. They claim "there is not one hour out of every twenty-four that a Hanna-Barbera cartoon is not entertaining some segment of the world's population."

When, in 1967, Taft Broadcasting Company of Cincinnati acquired H-B, the company expanded its operations into five themed amusement parks, including Kings Island (Cincinnati) and Marineland (Los Angeles), where life-sized replicas of H-B characters—Yogi, Huckleberry, et al.—roam about greeting visitors. More than 1,500 licensed manufacturers worldwide turn out 4,500 different products bearing likenesses to H-B characters: for example, Flintstone window shades, Scooby-Doo pajamas.

In 1978, H-B won an Emmy, this time for a live action TV movie, *The Gathering*, starring Ed Asner and Maureen Stapleton; more live action films are planned for theatrical release and TV. With all this success, why would Hanna-Barbera bother pouring money into turf that is traditionally Disney's and has proved to be a producer's graveyard, from *Gulliver's Travels* (1939) to *Raggedy Ann & Andy* (1977)?

COMPANY IS BUILT ON CARTOONS

One should not forget that cartoons are the heart of the H-B corporate structure (as they are at the Disney studio). And it must be noted that as popular as the TV series are with small children, there is, to Hanna and Barbera's distress, a persistently vocal, mostly adult contingent that just plain doesn't like their cartoons! Veteran animator/director Chuck Jones, for instance, dismisses the whole breed of limited animation TV fare as "illustrated radio"! Writer Leonard Maltin once denounced H-B cartoons as "consciously bad: assembly-line shorts grudgingly executed by cartoon veterans who hate what they're doing."

Years of this kind of criticism (and worse from TV critics, parents groups, and, most painfully, professional peers) has hit Hanna and Barbera right in their pride of craftsmanship. Witness Bill Hanna's responses during an interview with Eugene Slafer: "Are you accomplishing what you believe is good TV animation?" asked Slafer. "No, I do not," came Hanna's candid reply. To a further probe, "Have you ever been ashamed of your work, especially since parents have ranted about the general lack of quality on Saturday morning cartoon shows?" Hanna admitted, "Actually, I feel like I should crawl under a seat sometimes."

Joe Barbera recently spoke with *Millimeter* about his partner's abilities to recognize the difference between good and bad quality animation and their alleged lack of craftsmanship. "We had to get that stuff out for Saturday morning," he explains. "That's a budget problem. Believe me, I don't stand still for people saying, 'Oh, they're doing junk! They don't know how to do. . . .' We're not doing that. We only do it because you don't get the money to do it differently. When we get the money—and you're talking about millions—we do a job!"

So perhaps the initial thrust for the *Heidi* feature came from Hanna's and Barbera's desire to prove they haven't forgotten how to produce animation in the "classical" style, or how to create memorable characters that affect more than an audience's funny bone. Of course, Hanna and Barbera are too business-wise to produce a full-animation feature merely to assuage pain dealt to their pride; there also had to be a bedrock of financial motivation behind the move and, sure enough, there was. "The thrust," states Barbera, "was to do one every year and to build a superb perennial library, which Disney had for years."

The Disney animated features, from *Snow White and the Seven Dwarfs* (1937) to *The Rescuers* (1977), are rereleased like clockwork every seven years, just in time to greet a new generation or to remind an older group of their existence. "They are," says Barbera admiringly, "forever pictures"; that is, films that keep the Disney empire well-oiled with money derived from box office returns (pure profit, since there are no production costs on rereleases), and from lucrative merchandising spin-offs, like comic strips, dolls, or themed amusement park rides. This money-making machine depends upon the public's continuing affection for the cartoon characters and their "classic" stories found in the Disney features. Hanna and Barbera have not yet fully entered this profit arena, but they have been working on it.

PREVIOUS ANIMATED FEATURES

Heidi's Song is not H-B's first attempt to produce an animated feature. There was, for example, *Hey There, It's Yogi Bear!* in 1964 and *The Man Called Flintstone* in 1966, both low-cost, limited animation, based on the one-dimensional characters from TV. Neither film was a "forever" picture.

There was, in 1973, an H-B version of E. B. White's book *Charlotte's Web*, but this, too, suffered from the taint of limited animation and questionable production values. Reviewer Vincent Canby of the *New York Times* said of the film, "Parents will survive it, and so will the children." Barbera acknowledges there was "a problem" with *Charlotte's Web*, but to him it was a misjudgment of the financial potential of the material. "*Charlotte's Web*," says Barbera, "is an American classic. It is not an all-world classic. Germany ended up calling it

Zuckermann's Farm—Wilbur im Glück, after the name of the man who owned the pig in the story, because who ever heard of a Charlotte's Web? The film version is recouping some of its money on Home Box Office TV, on video cassettes, and in nontheatrical markets, a fate H-B hopes to avoid for *Heidi's Song*.

While Disney can produce almost any project known or unknown because of the sales value inherent in the name "Disney," Hanna-Barbera is not yet in that sublime position. To the general public, "Disney" means full animation, technological craftsmanship, and beloved characters in stories containing mythic or nostalgic associations. To the same public, "Hanna-Barbera" means limited animation of flat characters on redundant television series. H-B seeks to improve its image with *Heidi's Song*.

Heidi's Song is the story of an orphan girl, based on Johanna Spyri's one-hundred-year-old, internationally known book. The cartoon feature contains a "Broadway" score of sixteen songs by veterans Sammy Cahn (lyrics) and Burton Lane (music). The characters' voices include Lorne Greene as Heidi's reclusive grandfather, Broadway actress Margery Gray as Heidi, and Sammy Davis Jr. as King Rat, leader of a band of rodents. Other characters include a "mean and scary ancient housekeeper," Fraulein Rottenmeier; Sebastian, "the butler who helps Rottenmeier be miserable to Heidi"; Clara, a lonely girl "confined to a wheelchair"; and Peter, "a young goatherd, agile as the animals he tends."

Offsetting the human characters is a gaggle of animals: Spritz, Heidi's "feisty" pet goat; Hooter, a baby owl who "warns Grandfather of Heidi's imprisonment in the cellar"; Gruffle, Grandfather's "gruff old hound"; Schnoodle, a "nasty little dachshund who is rotten like his mistress, Fraulein Rottenmeier." There is also a "crusty" German Schnauzer, a white mare, a white kitten, and the aforementioned royal rat, "the power-loving and peppy leader of the rats in Sebastian's basement, who spurs his clownish rodents into a strong force to attack Heidi."

"We do have our animals," points out Barbera. "My gosh, if we don't have animals, we're in big trouble," he notes with an eye toward audience appeal and merchandising. "But we do have humans and some marvelous dancing," he continues. "We are not rotoscoping," he says, referring to the technique of animators tracing frame-by-frame projections of live-action. "I don't care for rotoscoping at all."

CHOOSING TALENT

Hanna and Barbera have instead hired a team of twenty top character animators. "Let's use the word humbly and respectfully: the old-timers," adds Barbera—people like Hal Ambro and Charlie Downs, both of whom specialize in human figure animation and have worked on films such as Disney's *Peter*

Pan and Richard Williams's *Raggedy Ann & Andy: A Musical Adventure*. There are also master animators of animal caricatures and comic timing, such as Irv Spence and Ed Barge, veterans of the fine Tom and Jerry shorts. The great Disney/MGM animator Preston Blair was also involved with *Heidi* for a time.

One might assume that the difficult task of manipulating the drawn human form in full animation is what kept the film in production for five long years. Barbera, however, offers this explanation: "When we are in the slow season, which happens in television all the time, everybody has to be laid off. We were going to keep people busy on the feature. We found that doesn't work. The kind of people you use on a feature are the old super-pros of our industry, and there are few of them left.

"Secondly, we wanted to use *Heidi's Song* as a training ground for new animators. The first three or four years the picture would go into production and stop, then go back into production and then stop. That was not good for the picture. We were losing momentum, the enthusiasm of the artists, and the excitement we wanted to build up. So finally, about a year and a half ago, we marshaled the last remnants of what we think are the best people in the business. When we brought these people in, we had to change directors. We had a fine guy, but he had forgotten how to go back and really work these old-timers—really get the good animation! We then hired a brilliant young director, Bob Taylor, who is dynamite!"

Prior to rejoining H-B a couple of years ago (he had first worked there in 1966 for one year), Robert Taylor worked for Ralph Bakshi, Steve Krantz, DePatie-Freleng, and Murakami-Wolf. "I always seem to come in on things that are hopeless," he commented recently, "and we try to turn them into hopeful. I think we've done it with this picture. For me and the whole crew, and for Joe and Hanna-Barbera and Taft, this is our entrance into real good quality stuff!"

It has not been a piece of cake for Taylor. When he took on the *Heidi* assignment, the script was written and the tracks were already recorded. "It was a hang-up for me," he admits. "That's the albatross around my neck. The story is episodic. If I had written it, I would have made it a little stronger in terms of her emotions and some of the dialogue. But," he adds brightly, "my whole trip is to keep the audience entertained—get people to go to animated films and make them feel when they come out that they've seen something they can't see anyplace else. It isn't so much the tools; it's what the hell I'm trying to do with it."

Trying to elicit a description of the film's style from both producer and director is difficult. According to Barbera, "The results have been what I call a Hanna-Barbera feature. It is not going to look like a Disney picture, or a *Fritz the Cat* or a *Raggedy Ann & Andy*. We have our own style." When pressed, Barbera cites "some very imaginative pieces of business." Pressed further: "We're not holding back. When they lock Heidi in the cellar, that's a scary place—to be locked in a basement in a house in Frankfurt in the 1880s—that's enough to put you away. We're not holding back, yet we're keeping it in good taste throughout."

NEW WAVE ANIMATION

Taylor was a bit more specific: "I hate to use that word 'Disney-esque,'" he begins. "It certainly has that form of quality to it. But it's really a style unto itself—more like a live action picture in the staging, as opposed to what you'd see in animation." Taylor calls this mysterious style "new wave animation," which he says is "essentially a combination stemming from my pictures with Ralph [Bakshi] and Krantz; that is, trying to update animation, from composition to character design to mental attitudes, psychological insight feelings, to live action cutting techniques."

Taylor was himself an orphan, a battered child with painful memories of Heidi-like humiliations. Doubtless, these life experiences will find their way into the cartoon feature. "When I was nine," he recalls, "I was adopted by a traditional New England couple; they were stuffy and stiff, much like the Sebastian/Rottenmeier characters in the story. Before the adoption at the orphanage, we were regularly put on display for potential parents. We were the 'unadoptables,' because our race was unknown. Several times, I had to remove my clothes so they could see the merchandise. This was happening in this country, in Providence, Rhode Island! It was excruciating!"

Taylor mentions a sequence that is an example of his "psychological thrust" in the film: "We focus on the orphan, what it must be like, what people go through. She's getting run from person to person, and the minute she gets attached, she gets ripped away again. She's brought to the Rottenmeier house. Frau Rottenmeier says she's a nothing. They begin to circle her and it goes into a total fantasy, depicting what it must feel like in the mind."

Heidi literally shrinks into the floor during this "She's a Nothing" musical number. "But," adds Taylor, "we then turn the situation around so that Heidi sees her tormentors as the ugly creatures they are. This is accomplished through some mind-blowing animation. It is an example of using animation to illustrate how a character sees others. Where it's intended with the story to scare, I'm trying to scare. Where it's intended to make you cry, I'm trying to make you cry."

The *Heidi* staff occupies one whole side of the H-B studio, and there is a reported competition to work on the feature among the younger animators and assistants toiling on the Saturday morning TV series. "They all want to join the '*Heidi* club,'" suggests Barbera. "They are the elite and everybody wants to get in." By the end of 1980, the "*Heidi* club" seemed to be a male stronghold; Taylor reports the feature has only one woman animator (Margaret Nichols), who is "doing very well."

"This picture has provided a college, if you will, for full animation, and an opportunity for the guys to get back into what it's really all about. We take as many new animators as we can bear—the ones that have the enthusiasm and are really interested in what we're calling a 'renaissance.' But even more important, we are just interested in making great animated films and updating them into the 1980s."

The *Heidi* unit has already begun production of its next two animated features: *Rock Odyssey* (which Barbera describes as "a marvelous treatment of music from the 1950s, '60s and '70s—a rock-*Fantasia*, if you want to call it that") and *Nessie Come Home*, a tale about the Loch Ness monster. Again, the thinking behind the choice of both projects is carefully calculated toward maximizing box office. "If you are going to do a feature," reasons Barbera, "you must have something people will identify with. You can't do 'Willie the Glowworm'! That's why *Heidi* is so great. It's always a problem finding material. *Watership Down* is a marvelous book, but we would have hesitated to do it because it's just not that well known. It's a gamble. You have to put four to five million dollars into something like that."

MARKETING CONCEPTS FOR ANIMATED FEATURES

At a time when Disney films are attempting to woo an older ("PG") audience, one wonders why Hanna-Barbera appears to be aiming toward a traditional, family-oriented, "G"-rated audience with its animated features. Barbera explains: "First of all, anything that Disney has done is going to play forever, so he will have that constant market in every media. Secondly, the theater audience isn't going to be the only audience. There are going to be cassettes, a perennial that will run forever. And thirdly, we are going to have our own style. We're not going to have a picture that will be only for kids. We will get the adults with this one."

"*Rock Odyssey*," continues Barbera, "will appeal to those between the ages of eighteen and thirty-five, but we will not lose the kids because of the animation. And we will have the adults that remember those 1950s and '60s songs. *Nessie* will have a great, I hate to use the word, 'environmental' appeal, but we will be protecting a character that's getting it. If there are monsters in that lake, they get bothered—by submarines, depth bombs, cameras—more than any character in the world. We have a very unusual twist that will make it appealing."

Asked whether the future might see Hanna-Barbera producing adult-oriented features à la Bakshi, Barbera answers, "Oh yes, very much! We had a recent all-day meeting where the thrust was the fact that we can't depend on the children audiences to pay for these things. We must attract the adults, too. Statistics show there are less children around now. So whatever we do, we must attract the adults." Barbera must have been thinking of a recent Bakshi product, i.e., *Lord of the Rings*, for when asked if he would produce an unquestionably adult cartoon such as *Heavy Traffic* or *Fritz the Cat*, he replied, "No! I don't think we would do *that*! We certainly wouldn't shy away from a gutsy project, but it must bring in the kids, too. So there would be no bad taste."

For the time being, it is significant that Hanna-Barbera is training an enthusiastic crew in the techniques of full character animation, one form of the art that for the last two decades has seemed to teeter constantly on the brink of extinction. It is enough for now that H-B is producing with integrity and care a film like *Heidi's Song*, which will attract and appeal to large audiences.

The success of Hanna-Barbera will keep an avenue open for future animated features, and hold the public's awareness of and interest in the medium of animation itself. With an increase in the number of future animated features will come diversity in form and content. Animation as a vital and viable entertainment medium will then come closer to realizing its potential, as it did in 1968 when George Dunning directed *Yellow Submarine*, and in the early 1970s when Ralph Bakshi excited audiences, and, indeed, as in 1937 when a struggling young producer named Walt Disney redefined the genre.

Yabba Dabba Crew:
Working with Hoyt Curtin at Hanna-Barbera

JEFF BOND / 2001

From *Film Score Monthly*, April/May 2001, 20–23. Copyright © 2001 Jeff Bond. Courtesy of Film Score Monthly. Reprinted with permission.

When Hoyt Curtin died in December of last year, the world lost a cultural icon. But the composer of such instantly recognizable TV show themes as *Jonny Quest*, *The Flintstones*, *The Jetsons*, and *Magilla Gorilla* was largely unknown to audiences. The fact that he was often listed as a music supervisor on the various Hanna-Barbera cartoon series he worked on—making it unclear whether or not he had actually composed music on the shows—didn't help matters.

Curtin did, in fact, compose most of the themes and a great deal of the music for Hanna-Barbera cartoons at the end of the 1950s and throughout the 1960s. Over the years he also pulled into his orbit other composers, musical directors, producers, and a veteran group of musicians to assist him in supplying music for Hanna-Barbera's massive factory of animation. Curtin's training for the world of cartoon theme songs couldn't have been more effective: He came from the world of commercial jingles, eventually becoming perhaps the most successful West Coast producer of catchy advertising songs. Trained to boil down the appeal of a product in thirty seconds, Curtin applied his knack for simple yet indelible melodies to his first cartoon for Hanna-Barbera, 1957's *Ruff and Reddy*.

He went on to provide themes and music for cartoons like *The Huckleberry Hound Show* (1958–61), *The Yogi Bear Show* (1961–62), *Top Cat* (1961–62), *Wally Gator* (1962–63), *The Magilla Gorilla Show* (1964–67), *The Peter Potamus Show* (1964–66), *Frankenstein Jr. and The Impossibles* (1966–68), *The Banana Splits Adventure Hour* (1968–70), *Wacky Races* (1968–70), *Cattanooga Cats* (1969–71), *The Perils of Penelope Pitstop* (1969), and *Hong Kong Phooey* (1974–76).

After a period of semiretirement, Curtin did music supervision and themes for *The Smurfs* (1981–89) and other Hanna-Barbera series. During that period, Curtin worked with such composers as Ron Jones (*Star Trek: The Next Generation, Family Guy*), John Debney (*Spy Kids, Heartbreakers*), Mark Wolfram (*Piercing the Celluloid Veil: An Orchestral Odyssey*), Steve Taylor (*Tiny Toon Adventures*), John Massari (*Killer Klowns from Outer Space, The Ray Bradbury Theater*), and Tom Worrall (*Tom and Jerry Kids, The Wild Women of Chastity Gulch*), among others. For some of these composers, working with Hoyt Curtin was their first major gig. And while they generally did not receive screen credit for their work, the job turned out to be an invaluable training ground for future composing assignments.

Some of the composers knew Curtin's reputation and pursued him for the job, while others just knew they might be able to get a job writing cartoon music. "I was familiar with the shows, but I didn't make the connection between Hoyt and the shows," Ron Jones admits. "I was new to the business, but when you watch all that, you don't really pick up all the names. You pick up all the bigger names and Hoyt's kind of goes right by you."

A TIRELESS CREATOR

John Debney was one who was familiar with Curtin's work. "Hoyt was like a Mike Post," Debney says, relating Curtin to the man who has written countless familiar TV themes and acted as a music supervisor and brand name for their background scores. "You know who he is and you know what he's done—and I worked for Mike Post, too. Hoyt had been around a long, long time by the early 1980s, and by that time he had really retired. I certainly knew who he was."

Ron Jones became one of the mainstays for Curtin in the early 1980s. "I worked on more than a hundred different series with Hoyt," Jones says. "I worked on *The Smurfs, Scooby-Doo, Trollkins, Richie Rich, Pound Puppies*—the list goes on and on. My résumé is so ridiculous with all the listings that people have told me to actually delete stuff—it's like two single-spaced pages of Hanna-Barbera credit. And they're all network shows. The first season I worked for Hoyt, I got a break and went home and was watching TV on a Saturday morning, and I had shows on ABC, CBS, and NBC simultaneously."

Jones was attending a professional arranging school and doing copying to make ends meet when he saw the opportunity to get into animation. "The copyist copied all of Hanna-Barbera's stuff, and I looked at it and thought, I could do that," Jones says. "So I asked if I could deliver it. I cornered Hoyt Curtin and he gave me a shot."

At the time, Curtin was working with producer Paul DeKorte at Group Four Studios. "At Group Four, he'd be on a break and I asked if I could hang out and I'd be asking him little questions. And over a period of sitting there watching, I told him I'd been taking film scoring and orchestration, and that I understood all this," Jones recalls. "I didn't know that everything was scored with storyboards and cassette-slugged dialogue. He told me to come back next Tuesday, and I came back next Tuesday . . . and he said to come back next Thursday, and I came back next Thursday . . . and he told me to come back next Tuesday. The third time, he said, 'Let me go out to my office.' And his office was his Lincoln Continental in the parking lot. He handed me some storyboards and a tape and said, 'Here you go.'"

SCORING BY NUMBERS

Jones quickly discovered that scoring Hanna-Barbera animation involved more work on the composer's part than he'd anticipated. "I got home, and the storyboards from Hanna-Barbera are very cryptic," he notes. "You don't really understand what's going on. I was used to film footage but this was ridiculous. The storyboard would say six feet of somebody swishing by, and then it would go to the next panel and it would say the dialogue, and there was no continuous accounting for that time. So I realized I had to take a stopwatch and time that and add up the footage and make this huge map. It took me about four days to figure out how to do that."

Mark Wolfram found the key to entering the world of Hanna-Barbera literally at his feet. "I sent Paul DeKorte a letter at one point, and on my demonstration tape I put an example of a commercial I had done for a sneaker called Snorks, which just happened to be a Hanna-Barbera character at the time," Wolfram remembers. "It sat on a shelf for a year and eventually Hoyt heard it and called me up. Hoyt said we should meet, and we had a nice breakfast at Smokey Joe's on Riverside and Coldwater. He filled me in on his career, about his early days as one of the biggest jingle guys on the West Coast, and he asked if I wanted to go to work for Hanna-Barbera."

At the time, Curtin and his crew were working on *The New Adventures of Jonny Quest* (1986–87), an updated version of the classic adventure series that had aired in prime time in the 1960s. "The first thing I did was three or four episodes of *Jonny Quest*," Wolfram says. "It was kind of adventure music. There were more modern effects around the edges than in the sixties version, some synth drums just for some touches. Obviously at that point we were using EVI or EWI [a woodwind synthesizer] rather than three or four woodwind players, but that was really the only concession to contemporary."

Wolfram was faced with the same working approach Jones and the other composers met. "We basically had to be our own music editors and make our own cue sheets and from that you try and hit as best you could," he explains. "But you didn't want to get too specific because everything would be used for the library, so you tried to serve the episode as best you could but still keep it broad enough to have multiple uses."

CARTOONS ARE A FUNNY BUSINESS

John Debney likewise fell into the working routine quickly, sharing scoring duties on individual cartoon episodes with the other composers. "There could be anywhere from three to four of us," he says. "Someone would get four minutes, and I'd get three or Ron Jones would get three, and once you had done it for him a number of times, [you] knew what his vocabulary was and knew the kind of endings you had to do. It was very specific, the way Hanna-Barbera did it. They were librarying this music and they would use it on other shows, so every few bars you'd have to put a hole in the music because they could take that and cut to another piece of music. It was very formulaic, but it was really fascinating and I learned a lot by doing it."

The sheer volume of music that needed to be produced made a major impact on most of the composers. "I would try to do a minimum of twenty pages a day, and during the summer I'd end up working six or seven days a week, so it would be 130 pages of finished score every week," Jones recalls. "Mostly you'd get an act to work on, the whole act or sometimes a whole show. Or sometimes it would just be generic themes, like, 'Can you write a bunch of chases? Can you write a bunch of dialogue cues?,' because once they had a few shows scored, they'd track it. That came in handy when I did *DuckTales*, because when I got there, they said, 'How can you score nine shows and track a hundred of them?' and I said, 'Watch.' They'd say, 'Why did you do that Arabian cue?' and 'Why did you do that other cue?' and I'd say, 'Look, trust me, you're gonna need that.' All that training really allowed me to envision what needed to be done."

Jones developed his own system for keeping track of exactly what show he was working on at any given time. "You keep a notebook or a manila folder and put the themes in there," he recalls. "They'd be right there next to the piano, and I'd say, 'What show are we doing?,' and then any shows I'd make up themes [for] I'd put them there too, so there'd be a folder with dialogue themes, one with Hoyt's themes, one with my themes, and so on."

Though Curtin was only writing bits and pieces and providing show themes by the 1980s, Debney notes that Curtin's work during his first decade or so with Hanna-Barbera was far more extensive, and involved a long-standing collaboration with William Hanna, a founding partner of the animation factory with Joseph Barbera. "I was told by Paul DeKorte that Hoyt used to write most of the music himself," Debney explains. "I got to know Bill Hanna really well too, and Bill would really work with Hoyt on those themes and write lyrics for them, even though you might never hear the lyrics. Bill was a musician and an old-school guy, and he knew how to read animation charts. He'd have storyboarded things for a [main title or a] two-minute main title and he'd actually time it out."

Debney notes that Curtin's background in jazz was invaluable both to his jingle work and his fashioning of some of television's snappiest theme songs. "Hoyt was a jazzer," Debney says. "He was a keyboard player for one of the big bands and he was in the service. That's why his music sounds the way it does—he always loved those jazz chords, and they're fabulous."

Even in the eighties when Curtin wasn't writing most of the music, he conducted all the scoring sessions with a group of veteran players with whom he had long-standing relationships. "Hoyt conducted everything and Paul DeKorte was in the booth," Jones says. "Before MIDI [Musical Instrument Digital Interface] stuff came in, he and Paul DeKorte budgeted things so they could have a pretty good-sized band, but we did *The Smurfs* with six violins and a little band, and it was all takedowns of Berlioz and Rachmaninoff and Beethoven. *The Smurfs* gig was about how many classical themes can you use, because the Smurfs were these little characters they did in Europe, and they tracked it all with classical music." Paul DeKorte was also a talented singer who sang on and contracted vocals for all of Curtin's sessions. "As far as musicians, I recall Gene Cipriano on woodwinds, Frank Capp and Steve Schaeffer on drums, Jerry Hey, Chuck Findley, Rick Baptist and Charlie King on trumpets. Lloyd Ulyate on trombone, Tommy Johnson on tuba and bass trombone, Vince DeRosa on horn, Clark Gassman on keyboards, and Chet Record on percussion," Jones says. "The concert master on violin was Sid Sharp."

THE BOYS IN THE BAND

Jones says he learned a great deal of his craft just by talking to Curtin's team members. "We had the best players on Earth and that's how I'd learn," the composer says. "I'd write for them, and then I'd talk to Tommy Johnson and say, 'What did you think of my tuba part?' And he'd say he liked this part and maybe I could do this other part better. Or I'd go sit with Chet Record, who was the percussionist, who had to play like a million instruments, and I'd say, 'How do you get from the timpani over to the xylophone in time?' and he'd say, 'I draw these arrows.' It was like a master orchestration class. I'd work with Lalo Schifrin on these French orchestration books, and then I'd go practice what I learned in terms of transparency and amplitude and intensity with all that writing each week. It was really a school unlike anything I've ever seen. The players were all great sight readers. They all loved the work. He made it fun and musically interesting."

According to the composers, Curtin made the job interesting in other ways as well. "Hoyt used to do certain things," Debney laughs. "I'd finish my allotment for the week, maybe ten minutes of music, and he'd always call me on a Sunday night as I was getting ready to sit down for dinner and say 'Hey, Big John! You think you could squeeze out another two or three minutes of *Pound Puppies?*' I always knew he'd call, too, because Hoyt always intended to do some writing himself at that time, but somehow he never got around to it."

Curtin also reportedly had his own idiosyncratic ideas about Los Angeles geography. "He'd always say, 'John, can you come out and meet me halfway?' I lived in Burbank and he lived in Westwood, and 'halfway' would somehow always mean about three minutes from his house," Debney recalls. "But he knew it—he was just a character."

Ron Jones points out that Curtin had to try to keep his home life and professional life separate. "His wife thought that music was dirty," Jones says. "That somehow it was the red light district. Hoyt wasn't allowed to keep any musical instruments in the house. He kept a beat-up upright piano, where every third note didn't work, in his hall closet. But he had perfect pitch so he wrote everything from perfect pitch. We'd be at Denny's or Jack's Deli, and he would take the napkin, flip it over, write out the clef and say, 'Here's the bad guy theme' or 'Here's the *Smurf* lick,' and then you'd take the boards and that's what you had to go by."

Debney found himself dealing with Curtin's legacy years later when he wrote the score to the feature-length animated version of *The Jetsons*. "When I did *Jetsons: The Movie* (1990), I was in a room with a bunch of suits, and I had gotten the job to score the movie, and it wasn't a great movie, but it was a movie," Debney recalls. "They were in this meeting and they went, 'Now what are we gonna do for the main title?' And they all look at me. And I said, 'I think we should do the *Jetsons* theme.' And they were like, 'I don't know if we really want to do that. I mean, we do have Tiffany.' They were actually proud of that! I said, 'I really think we should do the theme. I mean, I'll use a bigger orchestra and fill it out a bit more, but I think we should stay true to it because when people are in a darkened theater, when this thing comes on, they're going to cheer.' I said, 'If you really want that cheer, you're going to have to play the theme.' They were really fighting me on it. And when I went to the screening and they played the theme, people clapped."

THE UNDYING SPIRIT OF ADVENTURE

Debney says he's even seen Curtin's effect on live-action directors who grew up listening to the composer's themes. "When I got called into work on *Spy Kids*, I was sitting with Robert Rodriguez, talking, and Rodriguez said, 'Maybe we could have kind of a *Jonny Quest* theme,' and my eyes lit up and so did his. He went over to his computer and he had the *Jonny Quest* theme on it. He said he used to listen to that while he was writing *Spy Kids*."

Debney still carries a flame for Curtin's themes. "For my money I think that Hoyt was completely underappreciated for what he's done," the composer says. "*The Jetsons*, *The Flintstones*, *Jonny Quest* . . . plus there are ones that you don't talk about but you'd remember if you heard them, like *Magilla Gorilla*, *Wally Gator*, all that stuff we grew up on. It's so great and so catchy."

"Hoyt was a great communicator," says Ron Jones. "His themes are like *perestroika*—where one word means an entire paragraph. In English we don't have a word for it, so I would say in music it's the musical equivalent of direct communication. He would always tell me to keep it simple and that there's a main thing and another thing and that's it—there's nothing else. I never heard anyone else say that except Lalo Schifrin. He would emphasize a lot of melody and then say, 'What else is left?' I try to be in that mold."

For Mark Wolfram, Curtin's joy in his work made the most lasting impact. "This is a guy who really loved what he did. There were problems on sessions. Things didn't always go the way he wanted them to, and he'd have to make some changes. But most of the time this was a guy who was just having a great time. All the musicians felt the same way."

And for a man who could write music that sent chills down the spine (like *Jonny Quest*) or simply make the viewer bust out into laughter, Curtin's personal sensibility couldn't have been more appropriate. "He truly was loved, and he was just hilariously funny," John Debney says. "The beauty of Hoyt was that he took the music seriously, but he had a great time doing it. He kept it light, and the musicians loved him."

Fred Seibert at Cartoon Network

JESSE KOWALSKI / 2017

Edited from the transcript of "From *Dexter's Laboratory* to *The Powerpuff Girls*: An Evening with Fred Seibert," an event conducted for the exhibit "Hanna-Barbera: The Architects of Saturday Morning" at the Norman Rockwell Museum, March 22, 2017. Copyright © The Norman Rockwell Museum. Printed with permission of Jesse Kowalski, Fred Seibert, and the Norman Rockwell Museum.

Fred Seibert: One day, [MTV Networks CEO] Bob Pittman, my former boss at MTV, called up and said, "Could we hire you as consultants?" [Editors' note: At this time in 1984, Seibert and partner Alan Goodman had a consulting firm called Fred/Alan.] He . . . immediately assigned us to Nickelodeon, which was [Viacom's] family and children's channel. At that point, Nickelodeon was the number-thirty-rated cable channel—and there were only thirty cable channels. It was like the lowest-rated cable channel.

Jesse Kowalski: You noted that it was a kids network that nobody watched—least of all kids.

Seibert: Exactly. . . . [W]e knew nothing about kids. [Nickelodeon was] really upset that we had been hired, because we were the evil people who did that weird rock and roll stuff for teenagers, and we were distorting the minds of youth. And here was a group of people trying to do good things for kids. They said, "Well, the only thing we can figure out is we keep telling kids that we are fun—the problem is we're not." Which is, the shows were really good, but the environment that they put it in was not so good. It was a very . . . what they used to call a "green vegetable environment." Like, this is really good for you kids and, you know, we're lots of fun.

So, Alan and I immediately banned the word "fun" from the vocabulary, and we said that we didn't really know too much about kids programming, but if you say this stuff's good, we will take you at your word. What we have to do is create an environment where kids are happy to be here. . . . So, we went about hiring young, creative people who were wonderful writers, had great senses of humor, didn't really know all that much about television, certainly didn't know anything about emotion. And we gave them the keys to the castle. We sort of set up their bumpers—their bowling lane bumpers—and said, "You need to say these four or five things about Nickelodeon. Other than that, go to town—have a great time through the most creative work you can. If you can't figure out how to do it, we'll help you."

This young team, one by one, would make these little interstitial spots for Nickelodeon that nobody could deny. No kid of any age could deny that it was for them. We basically said that we are going to set up Nickelodeon as the greatest clubhouse for kids in all of television. It was the only place for kids that was on seven days a week. At that point, the architects of Saturday morning, [Bill] Hanna and [Joe] Barbera, had dominated Saturday morning. But it was [just] four hours a week. . . . So, we created this great environment, and a really interesting thing happened. Six months later, Nickelodeon had become the most-watched cable channel in America. It went from worst to first.

Kowalski: Give him a round of applause. [*Audience claps.*]

Seibert: [It] wasn't that we did anything special, other than talk to kids in language they wanted to speak with, and they wanted to hear. And just from a statistical point of view, [before, the network had found that] 44 percent of kids [with cable tuned in weekly but] watched for less than six minutes; now, they were now watching thirty minutes a week. Which is what really put Nickelodeon on the map. . . .

Kowalski: And then in 1992, you got in touch with Ted Turner. He brought you on board to revitalize an animation company that was once monumental, but at that time was kind of running on fumes.

Seibert: It kind of faded, right?

Kowalski: Yeah. So, how were you brought into Hanna-Barbera?

Seibert: . . . [Ted Turner's head of entertainment, Scott Sassa, called me] and said, "Hey, Ted just bought the Hanna-Barbera studio." I said, "Yeah, I know. I saw it in the paper. Good luck." And he said, "Well, there's really a problem. We wanted to buy it for the library. The studio has been losing $10 million a year. They haven't had a hit since *The Smurfs* in 1981. It's a train wreck over there." I said, "Gee, that's too bad. Best of luck." You know, what am I going to say? And he said, "I have this idea: why don't you come out and run the studio?" I paused. He knew then Alan and I were thinking about closing up Fred/Alan. I looked at my watch. Lo and behold, at 12:00 was Scooby-Doo; at 3:00 was Huckleberry Hound; at 6:00 was Fred Flintstone; and at 9:00 was Yogi Bear. Just 10:35 in the morning. It was I think February, something like that. I said, "I can't be there until June." He said, "We'll wait." I said, "What are you talking about?" He goes, "Well, I can't close it. Ted won't let me close the studio. If we have to wait, we'll wait." I said, "I know nothing about cartoons." He goes, "Oh, you do all those logos for Nickelodeon." And I said, "That's ten seconds of wiggling the logo. And I hire animators to do that. I don't know anything about that. I've never seen a storyboard. I've never read an animation script." He said, "Look, it couldn't get worse." So, Alan and I decided to close Fred/Alan. . . . Sadly, in my own life I was getting divorced . . . The idea of moving three thousand miles across the country looked like a pretty good deal. So, I took the job.

I arrived in June of 1992 to three hundred or four hundred employees who had no idea what I was doing there. And truth be told, I had no idea what I was doing there. I was scared to death. I had only driven by the Hanna-Barbera building for twenty years as I was visiting Los Angeles. I would see the sign up on top that said "Hanna-Barbera." I went, "I wonder what it's like in there? It must be amazing—you know, they do Huckleberry Hound." [Now] I walk in for the first time and I'm president of the company. It was, like, a completely surreal experience. They sit me down in what had been Bill Hanna's office, [which they now] said was my office. There was a desk there that was so big; it had been custom-built for Bill in 1961. It looked like it could come from *The Jetsons*. It was sort of a curve. It looked big enough to sleep a family of four. I'm like, "Well, doesn't Bill want this office?" "No, he wants to be as far away from. . . ." He had a little office on the third floor. He was eighty-two years old. Right across the hall was Joe Barbera. They were both signed for life as consultants to the studio.

Kowalski: Yes. What were they doing at the time? Were they just figureheads, or were they still in charge of production?

Seibert: They had actually sold the company to . . . Taft Broadcasting in 1966. They thought that maybe their day was up. They sold it for what we would now think of as a pittance: the whole company for $12 million. And then Taft had blown up in the early 1980s, and it had gone through a whole bunch of machinations, and was now owned by a company called Great American [Broadcasting]. It was run by a guy called Carl Lindner, who was the chairman of Chiquita Banana. . . .

At that point, they had put a very hefty price tag on [Hanna-Barbera]—$350 million—while by traditional showbiz accounting, it was actually worth $175 million. And nobody even wanted to put up the $175 million. Actually, Universal Studios thought they might want to buy it, but they kept holding out for a better price. And Carl kept saying no. Finally, Ted convinced his staff, who had all told him, "No, Ted. We never want to buy Hanna-Barbera. You [should] never pay more than $175 million for it." He had convinced them that 350 was a decent price, and borrowed $300 million of money, put up 50 million of his own dollars, and bought the company outright, solely for the library. Remember, six or seven years before, he had had a disaster buying the MGM studio. It made him bankrupt. He sold the studio back to its original owner, but kept the library and launched TNT off of it. He realized that he could set up Cartoon Network with the same scheme, with the Hanna-Barbera library.

So, long story short, I get there. I don't know anything about cartoons. I call a meeting of the senior staff, and I said, "There's good news and bad news.

The bad news for you is I know nothing about cartoons, and I'm the boss. The good news is you all know about cartoons, so why don't we make a deal? Why don't you tell me what to do, and I will do it." Immediately, about half of them quit. They were used to working under Joe and Bill . . . [A] couple of the [senior staff] came up to me afterward and said, "Look, whatever we can do to help, we'll help." The problem is I didn't know what I wanted them to do, and they didn't know what to do to tell me, because they had run under this dictatorship that Joe and Bill had run for so long that they were used to doing what they were told.

In fact, I went up to the head of production after this meeting, and I said, "So what do we do well? What's the studio good at?" Like I would know what she was talking about. And she said, "We can do anything. Please, just tell us what to do." I was flummoxed, because I didn't know. So, I went into Joe's office, and he said, "I'll do everything, just tell me what. I can do everything." And I thought to myself . . . This is a really tough position to be in. Here were these two men who had basically been part of inventing the cartoon business as we knew it, not just television, but in all their years doing Tom and Jerry at the MGM studio. They were truly part of the innovation that created the animation business. But it was clear that they had lost the mojo, in terms of what to do for the contemporary market. So, I had to quietly back out of Joe's office, sort of nodding my head going, "Great idea, Joe," and go back to my office and be freaked out.

Mike Lazzo was the head of programming at the Cartoon Network. He came to me one day and said, "I think we should put together an advisory group for Cartoon Network. I'd like Joe and Bill to be on it, and I've gotten Friz Freleng and Chuck Jones to be on it. And John Kricfalusi," the creator of *Ren & Stimpy*, a young guy who had sort of helped revitalize the cartoon business. So, we went and we had this meeting. Mike, at one point, said to them, "What made a great cartoon producer?" Joe Barbera always had the best stories, ever. He said, "Well, our producer at MGM, Fred Quimby—he was the greatest producer." Mike and I were both sort of quizzical because we knew that Joe and Bill hated Fred Quimby.

Kowalski: Fred Quimby took . . . they won seven Oscars for Tom and Jerry, Bill and Joe. And Fred Quimby kept them all.

Seibert: Yeah. He took all their awards from them. . . . "So," Joe said, "Fred [Quimby] would come in the morning, and he would have a couple of meetings with people. At 11:00 every day, his barber would come in and give him a shave and a trim. And then, at lunch, he would go to lunch with all the movie stars in the commissary. He'd come back . . . from lunch and call the East Coast distributors to find out what the grosses were from yesterday. And then at 4:00, he'd go home. He was a *fabulous* producer." I thought to myself, "I could do that job—I'd be pretty good at that." And I said, "How did the cartoons get made?" He goes, "Oh, we were off in another building, just doing what we felt like doing." And through this advisory meeting, I heard them say that *they* were the cartoonists, and *they* invented the stuff. They would make something, one by one, put it in the theater, and if it worked, they'd get the order to make another one.

I thought that was a fabulous idea. I said, "Why can't we do that in *television*?" [People responded,] "Well, television isn't made that way." There was some cockamamie way of how television was made. And I realized that exactly the same way they had done it in the 1930s and '40s—we could do it now in the '90s. So I went and I told my boss, Scott Sassa, and he said, "Great, let's call Ted." And I told Ted about it. Ted said to me, "Well, so far you've failed. You've made a couple series, and they haven't worked. What makes you think that you can do it this way?" I said, "Well, if you give me another $10 million, I'll make forty-eight short cartoons. Even not knowing anything, if I do something forty-eight times, don't you think one of them will work?" Ted, being a very natural entrepreneur, went "You're right. That's great. Go—go do it." And that was how we really started reinventing the studio.

Kowalski: That was called *What a Cartoon!*

Seibert: It was called *What a Cartoon!* We made these forty-eight short films, and basically, we did it the way that all the older cartoonists had told us, which was: We went out into the world and said, "What kind of ideas do you all have?" And five thousand people pitched us their cartoons. We had enough money to make forty-eight of them. So, we made [all] forty-eight, and we ran them each as an individual cartoon before a Sunday night animated movie on Cartoon Network. We tried to do it like the old days of the theatricals. I didn't really know what I was doing. Luckily, I had a great team of people around. I didn't even know when people would pitch something whether it was good or not. I had to look around the room and see what they all felt like. And if enough people nodded, I said, "Oh, great, we can do that one." That type of thing.

We literally made shorts with people from Europe, from Asia, but primarily from the young people who were toiling in the studio. They were all part of the factory system within our company—they were doing storyboards for Flintstones specials, they were designing characters for Scooby-Doo specials—whatever it was that they were doing. And one by one, as those young folks came in, we realized that they had this passion for this medium that seemed to have been lost, out of the industry. We gave a lot of them their shots. And out of *What a Cartoon!* came six hit cartoons, after a dry spell of fifteen years, when there was nothing going on with the studio. So, *Dexter's Laboratory, The Powerpuff Girls, Courage the Cowardly Dog, Johnny Bravo, Cow and Chicken, I Am Weasel.* Which are still some of the icons today in the industry. . . .

[*During the subsequent question-and-answer period, an audience member asks Fred a question.*]

Seibert: [The question is,] "What were my major takeaways from working with Joe and Bill?" It's not every day that you get to walk into an office with two legends. . . .

What I learned from Bill is what I learned from my parents: that there's nothing that work won't cure—there's nothing you can do [with] a little more work [that] won't be good for your soul. And sure enough, Bill was one of those guys who just believed in good work and hard work. He was an incredibly modest man. He was living in a house in the San Fernando Valley that was the same house he lived in when he was a contract worker, a daily worker by salary over at MGM, forty years before. He had made millions and millions of dollars. . . . And he was still in that same house, with his wife Violet, thinking of himself as a guy who came to work every day.

Joe was an opposite kind of guy. Joe lived large. He loved Hollywood. He loved telling stories of the movie stars that he knew, of all the people that he had worked with. He drove a fast sports car at eighty years old, but he also loved coming in to work every day. At the time that I started at the studio, he was still producing a show for Fox, which was their top-rated animated show, *Tom and Jerry Kids*. I've got to tell you: If there was ever a horrible idea for a show, it was *Tom and Jerry Kids*—until you watched it . . . it was genuinely funny. You would go into his office with his creative team, and they were a bunch of people, probably in their thirties, maybe early forties, who all were sitting in a circle, around the campfire of a genius. He was sitting there, and as they would throw out a joke, he would improve the joke. You would look at his notes. He was still sketching exactly what the gag would look like when it was put into a storyboard. It was, really, an incredible sight to watch. When I had walked in, and Joe just told me he could do everything, he meant it from the bottom of his heart. . . . And by the way, each of them continued to work until the day they died. They continued to come into the studio every single day.

Brian Levant on *The Flintstones* Movie

KEVIN SANDLER / 2021

Edited from the transcript of an original interview for this volume. Published with permission of Brian Levant.

Kevin Sandler: So, when did you first meet Bill Hanna and Joe Barbera?

Brian Levant: I had been hired to direct *The Flintstones* movie, a million to one shot as far as I was concerned, and got it. We set out to recreate their vision of Bedrock in three dimensions.

Remember, this is 1993 and CGI technology was very young and expensive and difficult to produce. Today, I believe 90 percent of that movie would be CGI. Back then, we built over six thousand sets, props, wardrobe, pieces, cars—everything, down to literally the kitchen sink. And twenty-two animatronic creatures by the Henson Creature Shop. Everything was as accurate as we could humanly make it.

Bill and Joe had blessed the project, with Steven Spielberg having it. I don't believe they'd even seen a script at that point, and we were about a couple months [away from shooting]. We had, I would say, about one hundred thousand square feet of soundstages that were devoted to literally creating Bedrock out of foam—curved foam, and chicken wire, and wood slats, and spray foam—then hard coating it and painting it. An army of technicians, about eight hundred in all.

I picked up Bill and Joe outside Steven's office in the first car that was finished, Barney's double pencil car. It had a back seat, so we could all go in it. Driving over there, they were very solemn, and I really felt that they expected to be disappointed. But once they got inside, and they saw the scale and the detail and the fidelity to their vision, they came alive and were energized and delighted by everything. . . . They were laughing and exchanging looks between each other when they'd see something that they liked, like an old married couple. They understood what the other was thinking very clearly—it was a love fest.

I remember we got to the Flintstones' bathroom and it was almost finished. The striations were painted onto the walls and stuff, and it was really looking pretty good. Bill Hanna goes, "There's no toilet paper." I turned to Russell

Bobbitt, our property manager, and I said, "Russell, why don't you get a roll of birch bark and hang it right next to the toilet?" And Bill liked that very much.

Finally, we stepped out into the daylight again. Joe Barbera just stood there, silent, for like fifteen seconds. I was waiting to ask them, "Okay, what do you think, guys?" They're just quiet. Finally, Joe goes, "Never in my life did I ever expect to see anything like that." I told them, "We're just getting started." And we were.

Sandler: And that was the first time that you had met them?

Levant: Yes. I'm a little young for most of the original Tom and Jerrys in the theaters, but I saw the first episode of *Ruff and Reddy*. I was there on the opening night for Huckleberry Hound and his cartoon pals. And I watched the premiere of *The Flintstones*. Very few things caught my imagination the way that did.

To try and do what they did, and try and set the tone that I believe was the glue behind it, and the positivity of the world they created: man living in utter harmony. A world where man and animal lived with dinosaurs, not in a predatory relationship whatsoever. It was all working towards the common good. It was a happy place. And this is the kind of thing that you have to sew into the entire package to try and meet the huge worldwide audiences' expectations of what this would look like when it was real.

Sandler: Had you known about Hanna and Barbera's involvement, if at all, with *The Flintstones* movie prior to first meeting them?

Levant: I know that they had signed off. I believe, later, Amblin didn't want to give them the script until it was really very, very close. They only had two notes, which were about things that they felt were in questionable taste, and they asked to remove those lines.

Sandler: Do you know what those were?

Levant: I can't remember at this point, they're just a couple. Producer Bruce Cohen and I looked at each other and said, "Well, it's not a bad joke, but we can get another one." We did, and we wanted more than their approval. We wanted them to be part of it.

We had originally wanted both of them to appear in the scene when Fred first comes to the boardroom and the villain, played by Kyle MacLachlan, reveals his whole steam-powered contraption to make Bedrock homes faster. But Joe, as it turned out, was unavailable that day. So Bill did it alone. He had one line: "Steam—He's a madman!" And he really did a very nice reading on the line. It was such a kick to see him in Flintstones clothes, with the cuffs and stuff. And he was very happy all day.

Sandler: How was their health at the time?

Levant: They were not frail. Six years later, when we did [the 2000 sequel,] *Viva Rock Vegas*, Bill had declined. He was having some Alzheimer issues. But physically, he was still pretty good.

Joe was obviously one of the strongest men I've ever met. When I first met him, he was probably eighty-three or eighty-four, and his vitality was shocking. I'd met Groucho Marx, a decade before, when he was eighty-seven and barely breathing, rheumy-eyed and sad and debilitated. And here's Joe Barbera, beautifully dressed. Every time I saw him, a natty dresser, to say the least. Really sharp, really contemporary. He dyed his hair. He was slick. He was like a hipster, a Rat Packer. He was cool. Bill Hanna gave off a very different vibe, of somebody who wasn't dressing to impress somebody, who dressed comfortably, like suitably for his station in life.

So, Joe came in to record his cameo, and we gave him a car to drive. We turned Stonehenge into a nightclub in Bedrock and Joe drove up in our establishing shot. We gave him a hot young girl to sit in the car with him. He liked that very much—he'd toss the keys to the valet, and that was his contribution to the film. But he liked to hang around. He visited the set a couple of times. And it was just such a thrill for everybody to have him and to know that they were into this.

The cast, when they met him, were gushing. These guys, at that time, were more legends than anything else. I think *The Flintstones* movie ushered in the final chapter in their long careers, where they kind of became primarily icons and mascots. Warner Bros. owned their studio. They weren't producing as much, so they were very interested, I think, in their legacy.

Sandler: What else in Hanna-Barbera's legacy attracted you to their vision, and propelled you to make the live-action *Flintstones* movie?

Levant: I wish I could just grab the pulse and hold on to it because it's a little evasive. But basically, I think they reflected very much the entertainment that they grew up with. They insisted to me when I pressed them: "Now come on. This is *The Honeymooners* crossed with Buster Keaton's *Three Ages*, right?" They said, "No, not at all." They copped to *Three Ages*. Buster Keaton is trying to steal the woman back from Wallace Beery. Wallace Beery throws a rock at him. And in the most cartoony moment I've ever seen in a movie, Keaton takes his club and hits the rock back and hits Beery in the forehead, and he goes down. Fifty-eight takes for that, by the way, until they got it.

But they insist that it was Laurel and Hardy. The big man, the little man, the blowhard. They insisted that that was really the genesis of *The Flintstones*. If you apply that silent comedy formula, what is the *Wacky Races* but just one big, long Keystone Cops chase scene, right? And what about Yogi Bear, Pixie and Dixie, Tom and Jerry? The same thing. It's Chaplin in *Modern Times*, right? Man's ability to survive is his ability to feed himself.

So, everything is about finding your next meal, surviving predators. And, who are you going to relate to in those scenarios, the cat? You're the little guy trying to get by. Are you going to relate to Ranger Smith, the authority figure, or the guy who's gonna do anything to get that pic-a-nic basket? I think it's the empathy that they were able to deliver in so many of their leads—not all of them, but certainly the ones that I was really attracted to.

The other thing that I think helped burnish their legacy was that Hanna-Barbera did very little licensing of products, until like 1966. However, Hanna-Barbera had that exclusive sponsorship deal with Kellogg's since the late 1950s, which put Yogi Bear and Huck Hound and Quick Draw McGraw in [as spokes-characters for different Kellogg's cereals]. Not only in the commercials, but also in the opening and closing credits of the shows. It put them on the breakfast table with you.

Hanna-Barbera were big on licensing watches and Flintstones toys, and after like a year, they started doing massive licensing. *The Jetsons* were only on for nine months, but somehow they managed to stick around in our consciousness. And the series didn't appear on a cereal box until 1990.

I think a lot of the problem with *The Jetsons* was, had they put it on after *The Flintstones*, I think it would have been much more successful in a block like *Happy Days* and *Laverne and Shirley*. Somehow ABC ended up putting it on Sunday against *Walt Disney's Wonderful World of Color*. *The Jetsons* couldn't compete. And they didn't get that licensing deal that *The Flintstones* had with Miles Laboratory for Flintstone vitamins in 1968. And *The Jetsons* didn't have the Post cereal deal that *The Flintstones* had since 1971. Two thousand and twenty-one is the fiftieth anniversary of Post's Fruity Pebbles cereal—so, every day, you're sitting at your kitchen table, eating Flintstones cereal, and chewing their vitamins. This builds strong brand identification.

Sandler: What was the main challenge during the production of *The Flintstones*, in terms of channeling the spirit of Hanna-Barbera into live-action form?

Levant: My job was to walk the tightrope between animation and reality, and try and tilt from one side to the other, without falling off that wire. We tried to be really true to them, while at the same time trying to dig a little deeper in the characters and put them into more relatable situations.

For instance, a test of their friendship was the Flintstones and Rubbles living under the same roof, and how success changed Fred, and how that impacted the Rubbles. As well as adopting a kid, getting into the deeper emotions of that, rather than just like, "Hey, look what we got—Bamm-Bamm!" And then having Wilma leave him, or having your kids kidnapped, things that challenge real emotions a little bit. Where it wasn't so cut and dry.

But, at the same time, we really wanted to preserve the satire of the Kennedy era of America in the television series. That the world was changing—you had instant photography and instant coffee, and everybody had vacuum cleaners and washing machines. For the first time, TVs! You had a new middle class that acquired more and more. Air travel. All these things became accessible.

Owning your own car! What family had more than one car until like 1955? And they reflected that beautifully in *The Flintstones*. All those time-saving conveniences, you know, they really added another layer.

Sandler: Did Hanna and Barbera see the finished product? Were they at the premiere?

Levant: Okay, so when we finished the film, Kathy Kennedy, one of the cofounders of Amblin, didn't want them to see the script until it was ready. She didn't want them to see the movie 'til it was done. She didn't want them to, I don't know . . . she was afraid of their input. Or she just didn't want to present it. They didn't like to show anything to anybody. It's kind of their MO.

Bill and Joe came to Amblin together. And I ran the film for them. I'm sitting in the same row with Hoyt Curtin. They sat through the whole thing, and I watched their faces. They were very, very happy. And when the lights came up, though they were well into their eighties, they jumped out of their seats, with tears in their eyes. They grabbed me and hugged me. Like the homecoming scene from *The Best Years of Our Lives*. Honestly, I got very emotional, to please them to that degree. Somebody who you've spent a good part of your life watching, and not even knowing who they were, really. And then to have them recognize our affection in tribute to their work, and to greet it like that, was kind of overwhelming. One of the greatest moments in my life. No shit. It really was.

Their attitude about the sequel was, "Great—Let's do it again!" And they were both in it again. They were in the finale. As I said, Bill was having some Alzheimer issues, and wasn't happy to be there, really. But once the cameras rolled, he was a pro. They sang the song, and they took pictures with everybody. And just to have them there, I can't tell you what it meant to people. I think that that experience kind of shaped how they saw their future as icons. The day-to-day was done and they were free to mine the rewards of their decades of labor.

And, things like Boomerang. Who else had a network? They never dreamed, when they were making six-minute cartoons in the 1940s, that there would be twenty-four hours a day devoted to their work. Joe wanted me to do the *Jetsons* movie, but Warner Bros. never wanted me to do it. . . . Joe was very excited about the *Scooby-Doo* movie, even though he saw problems in the script right away. For Joe, it was like: give me more, give me more—you know, pay more tribute to me. Let us be the source of number one movies. Let our work that we did forty to fifty years ago find new audiences, and shine in ways that we never imagined.

Joseph Barbera: An Animated Life

SCOTT SHAW! / 2007

Excerpt from "Joseph Barbera: An Animated Life," by AWN Staff Editor, *Animation World Network*, April 27, 2007. Reprinted with permission.

I was born in 1951, so I was at Ground Zero for *Ruff and Reddy*, *Huckleberry Hound*, *The Flintstones*, *Quick Draw McGraw*, and all the other early Hanna-Barbera TV cartoon shows—the studio's "good" shows. My generation of kids had been existing on a diet of afternoon marathons at local theaters and telecast hand-me-down cartoons. In the late 1950s, Hanna-Barbera (and Jay Ward) arrived like the cavalry to provide cartoons that were ours. (For many years, a lot of people claimed that Hanna-Barbera destroyed animation, but I always believed that they had saved it!) Sure, [the cartoons] didn't move much when they didn't need to, but H-B's animators knew what to leave out to achieve Bill Hanna's concept of "planned animation." The important thing was: They were hip and funny.

The hipness? That was Joe Barbera's specialty. Mr. B. was primarily in charge of conceiving the cartoons, writing the cartoons, designing the cartoons, voice-casting the cartoons, and selling the cartoons. (Bill Hanna was in charge of making the cartoons, on time and on or under budget.) But it was Joe's hip quotient that was the secret ingredient for H-B's early success. Yogi Bear wasn't the only nonconformist at the studio; he shared that quality with Joe.

Joe Barbera was a real character. He always struck me as being the last of the old-time Hollywood bigshots, with the tanned complexion, the blazers and yachting jackets, the ascots and cravats, the sunglasses, the jet-black hair. I don't think he ever gave thought to the possibility that in Hollywood, animation is waaay down on the list of showbiz greatness. But he was the Sinatra of animation.

At development meetings, he would often ask, to no one in particular, "Am I right? Am I right?" (The original pitch-title of *Top Cat* was "J. B. and Company." Maybe Joe was waiting for someone to answer him by saying, "Right, J. B.!") He once even called me into his office just to show me his listing in *Italian-American Who's Who*. Strangely, I always got the impression that, although they had achieved monumental success with Hanna-Barbera Productions, Joe (and Bill) regarded their studio as merely a necessary step to survival, but that the Tom and Jerrys they made at MGM were their real source of pride.

One thing is for certain—when Joe Barbera died, we lost the last old-time animation studio boss who actually knew how a cartoon was made. I'll always be grateful that I was able to work with Joe and Bill and their cast of classic cartoon characters.

SUGGESTED RESOURCES

CONVERSATIONS WITH HANNA AND BARBERA AND ABOUT HANNA-BARBERA

Books

Adams, T. R. *The Flintstones: A Modern Stone Age Phenomenon*. Atlanta: Turner, 1994.
Adams, T. R. *Tom and Jerry: Fifty Years of Cat and Mouse*. New York: Crescent, 1991.
Barbera, Joseph. *My Life in 'toons: From Flatbush to Bedrock in Under a Century*. Atlanta: Turner, 1994.
Beck, Jerry. *The Hanna-Barbera Treasury: Rare Art & Mementos from Your Favorite Cartoon Classics*. San Rafael, CA: Insight Editions, 2007.
Ehrbar, Greg. *Hanna-Barbera, the Recorded History: From Modern Stone Age to Meddling Kids*. Jackson: University Press of Mississippi, 2024.
Grossman, Gary H. *Saturday Morning TV*. New York: Dell, 1982.
Hanna, Bill, with Tom Ito. *A Cast of Friends*. Dallas: Taylor, 1996.
Lenburg, Jeff. *William Hanna & Joseph Barbera: The Sultans of Saturday Morning*. New York: Chelsea House, 2011.
Mallory, Michael. *Hanna-Barbera Cartoons*. New York: Hugh Lauter Levin Associates, 1998.
Maltin, Leonard. *Of Mice and Magic: A History of American Animated Cartoons*, rev. ed. New York: Plume, 1987. Originally published in 1980 by McGraw-Hill.
Mullaney, Dean, and Bruce Canwell. *Genius, Animated: The Cartoon Art of Alex Toth*. San Diego: IDW Publishing, 2013.
Museum of Television & Radio. *The World of Hanna-Barbera Cartoons*. Atlanta: Hanna-Barbera Cartoons, 1995. Museum catalogue published for exhibit.
Norman Rockwell Museum. *Hanna-Barbera: The Architects of Saturday Morning*. Stockbridge, MA: Norman Rockwell Museum, 2016. Museum catalogue published for exhibit. Excerpts available online: https://www.nrm.org/2017/04/hanna-barbera/.
Ohmart, Ben, and Joe Bevilacqua. *Daws Butler, Characters Actor*. Albany, GA: BearManor Media, 2005.
Sennett, Ted. *The Art of Hanna-Barbera: Fifty Years of Creativity*. New York: Viking Studio, 1989.
Sito, Tom. *Drawing the Line: The Untold Story of the Animation Unions from Bosko to Bart Simpson*. Lexington: University Press of Kentucky, 2006.
Solomon, Charles. *The History of Animation: Enchanted Drawings*, rev. ed. New York: Wings Books, 1994. Originally published in 1989 by Knopf.

Takamoto, Iwao, with Michael Mallory. *Iwao Takamoto: My Life with a Thousand Characters*. Jackson: University Press of Mississippi, 2009.

Articles and Essays

Amidi, Amid. "Analyzing Ed [Benedict]: John Kricfalusi Talks about His Favorite Animation Designer." *Animation Blast* 8 (2002): 38–42.

Anton, Glenn. "Joe Barbera Speaks His Mind." *Animato!* 34 (Spring 1996): 40–42.

Arnold, Mark. "Hanna-Barbera at Marvel Comics." *Back Issue* 59 (September 2012): 19–27.

AWN Staff Editor. "Joseph Barbera: An Animated Life." *Animation World Network*, April 27, 2007. https://www.awn.com/animationworld/joseph-barbera-animated-life.

Cohen, Martin. "The Rocky Road to Success." *TV Radio Mirror* (April 1961): 26–29, 85–86.

Evanier, Mark. "Scrappy Days: The Birth of Scrappy-Doo and What I Had to Do with It." *News from Me* (blog), 2007–2009. https://www.newsfromme.com/articles-such/scrappy-days/.

Fleming, Thomas J. "TV's Most Unexpected Hit." *Saturday Evening Post*, (December 2, 1961): 62–65.

Gill, Alan. "The Wonderful World of 2062." *Cedar Rapids Gazette*, August 23, 1962, 10.

Gross, Ben. "Here's Success Story." *Sunday News* (New York), December 18, 1960, 23. Recounts Bill and Joe's history to 1960.

Gross, Ben. "Seven Months of Work Go into a 30-Minute Cartoon." *Sunday News* (New York), December 25, 1960, 23.

Hanna, Bill. "The Case for Animation." *Business Screen: Tools, Techniques and Ideas for Audiovisual Communication* 30, no. 5 (May 1969): 19, 22, 23.

"Hanna-Barbera 30th Anniversary Salute." *Hollywood Reporter* (December 11, 1987). A sixty-four-page supplement with several pieces on Bill, Joe, and the studio.

Harbert, Ruth. "Mr. Tom and Mr. Jerry." *Good Housekeeping* (March 1956): 344, 168.

Keavy, Hubbard. "New Animated Cartoon Process Proves Entertaining in Hollywood." *The Sun* (Baltimore), May 5, 1940, Sec. 1, 6.

Kisseloff, Jeff. "Kids' Stuff." In *The Box: An Oral History of Television, 1920–1961* (New York: Viking, 1995), 443–64.

Kricfalusi, John. "Ed Benedict Talks with John K." In booklet included with LaserDisc set *The Flintstones Collection*. Warner Bros., 2004. Available at https://johnkstuff.blogspot.com/2008/11/my-interview-with-ed-benedict.html.

Lenburg, Jeff. "Hanna and Barbera." In *The Great Cartoon Directors* (Jefferson, NC: McFarland, 1983), 38–47.

Lewell, John. "Behind the Screen at Hanna-Barbera." *Computer Pictures* (March–April 1985): 14ff. On computer painting software.

Love, Harry. "The H & B Animation Training Program." *Cartoonist PROfiles* 52 (December 1981): 22–28.

Love, Harry. "Harry Love Talks about Hanna-Barbera." *Cartoonist PROfiles* 44 (December 1979): 92–94.

Love, Harry. "Joe Barbera." *Cartoonist PROfiles* 66 (June 1985): 58–61.

Love, Harry. "The Production of Animated Cartoons." *Cartoonist PROfiles* 42 (June 1979): 60–65.
Mayerson, Mark. "The Lion Began with a Frog." *Velvet Light Trap* 18 (Spring 1978): 39–45. Historical discussion of the MGM animation studio.
Miller, Chuck. "Hanna Barbera Records: The Other Side of Bedrock." *Goldmine* 31, no. 11 (May 2005): 19–20, 41, 45.
Shaw!, Scott. "Yabba Dabba Draw! Storyboarding the Flintstones with Scott Shaw!" *The Aspiring Cartoonist* 4 (1995): 4–10.
Slafer, Eugene. "A Conversation with Bill Hanna." In *The American Animated Cartoon: A Critical Anthology*, ed. Danny Peary and Gerald Peary, 287–92. Theme Park Press, 2017. Originally published in 1980 by E. P. Dutton.
Speranza, Ken. "Hanna Barbera: From Cavemen to Computers." *Video Magazine* 8, no. 9 (December 1984): 112–14, 184.
"We Are the Acorn." *Forbes* (May 1, 1971): 40. Hanna and Barbera confirm their influence by Disney.
Witbeck, Charles. "Animated Character No Longer a Problem." *Troy Record* (New York), February 20, 1960, 9.
Zeitlin, Arnold. "TV Goes to the Dogs, with Arf and Aroo-o-o." *Pittsburgh Post-Gazette*, August 9, 1960, 31.

Media

The Animation Guild. *Animation Guild Interviews*. The union's interview subjects include a variety of former Hanna-Barbera employees, including Tony Benedict, Jerry Eisenberg, Willie Ito, Don Jurwich, Floyd Norman, and Walt Peregoy. https://animation-guild.org/about-the-guild/interviews/.
Barbera, Joe. "An Interview with Joe Barbera." Audio interview by Joe Bevilacqua. WNYC Radio, January 1, 1990. https://beta.prx.org/stories/372.
Benedict, Tony, ed. *The Last Cartoonery* (blog). Cartoon blog about Hanna-Barbera. https://lastcartoonery.wordpress.com/.
Burnett, Bill. "Hanna-Barbera Essays." *Bill Burnett* (blog). Sixteen internal memorandums written for Hanna-Barbera employees after the Turner purchase, 1993–96. https://billburnett.wordpress.com/hanna-barbera-essays/.
The Eerie Mystery of Scooby-Doo History. The Scooby-Doo/Dynomutt Hour, The Complete Series DVD. Warner Bros., 2005.
The Flintstones: One Million Years Ahead of Its Time. The Flintstones, The Complete Fourth Season DVD. Warner Bros., 2005.
Hanna-Barbera: From H to B. Scooby-Doo, Where Are You!, The Complete Third Season DVD. Warner Bros., 2006. A history of the studio.
Hanna-Barbera's Legendary Music Director Hoyt Curtin. The Flintstones, The Complete Fourth Season DVD. Warner Bros., 2005.
Hanna-Barbera's Pic-A-Nic Basket of Cartoon Classics. Booklet accompanying 4-CD set of Hanna-Barbera music and sound effects. Contains pieces by Bill Hanna, Hoyt Curtin, Pat Foley, and Greg Watson. Available on Fred Seibert's website. Rhino, 1996.

Here Comes a Star. Documentary television special introducing *The Magilla Gorilla Show*. Syndicated December 1963.

How Bill and Joe Met Tom and Jerry. *Tom and Jerry*, Spotlight Collection [Vol. 1] DVD. Warner Bros., 2004.

Illustrating the Times. Wait Till Your Father Gets Home, The Complete First Season DVD. Warner Bros., 2007.

In Their Own Words. The Scooby-Doo/Dynomutt Hour, The Complete Series DVD. A documentary on voice actors. Warner Bros., 2005.

The Jetsons: The Family of the Future. *The Jetsons*, The Complete First Season DVD. Warner Bros., 2006.

The Jetsons Return to the Future. *The Jetsons*, Season 2, Volume 1 DVD. Warner Bros., 2009. This set collects the 1985–87 series.

Mangini, Mark. "Classic Cartoon Sound Effects!" Audio interview by Dallas Taylor. *Twenty Thousand Hertz* (podcast). October 1, 2018. https://www.20k.org/episodes/cartoon.

Nobleman, Marc Tyler, ed. *Noblemania* (blog). Includes interviews with people associated with Hanna-Barbera. https://www.noblemania.com.

Norman Rockwell Museum. "Media." *Hanna-Barbera: The Architects of Saturday Morning*. Original and archival videos from the museum exhibition. https://www.nrm.org/2017/04/hanna-barbera/#media.

The Phoo-Nomenon. *Hong Kong Phooey*, The Complete Series DVD. Warner Bros., 2008.

Rearview Mirror: A Look Back at Wacky Races. *Wacky Races*, The Complete Series DVD. Warner Bros., 2005.

Seibert, Fred, ed. "My Hanna-Barbera Index, 1992–1996." *Fred Seibert dot com* (blog). A collection of materials from his time at the studio. January 6, 2009. https://fredseibert.com/post/68783118/my-hanna-barbera-index-1992-1996.

Shostak, Stu, ed. *Stu's Show*. 2006–present. Internet audio and video show featuring interviews with former Hanna-Barbera artists. https://www.stusshow.com.

Silverman, Fred. "Fred Silverman, Executive/Producer." Video interview by Dan Pasternack. *The Interviews*. Television Academy Foundation. Academy of Television Arts & Sciences. March 16 and May 29, 2001. https://interviews.televisionacademy.com/interviews/fred-silverman.

"The Sultan of Saturday Morning." *60 Minutes*. CBS. March 30, 1986. An interview with Joe.

Television Academy Foundation. "Joseph Barbera, Animator/Show Creator." Video interview by Leonard Maltin. *The Interviews*. Academy of Television Arts & Sciences. February 26, 1997. https://interviews.televisionacademy.com/interviews/joseph-barbera.

Williams, Tyler Solon. "Understanding the Early Television Cartoon." PhD diss., University of Iowa, 2021. Available open-access at: https://www.proquest.com/openview/a3f8e997e50e56eb4de384560b9b0d1d.

Yowp, ed. *Yowp: Stuff about Early Hanna-Barbera Cartoons* (blog). A voluminous resource reproducing a wide variety of articles and profiles about Hanna-Barbera between about 1958 to 1961. Analyzes early cartoon episodes individually, with original writing by Hanna-Barbera historian Yowp. https://yowpyowp.blogspot.com/.

INDEX

Abbott and Costello, 142
Abbott and Costello Cartoon Show, The, 147
ABC television, xviii, xix, 7–8, 53, 68, 122–23, 161, 164–65, 184–87, 194–99, 202, 204, 208, 210, 226, 241
Academy Award (Oscar), x, xiii, xxiv, 5, 12, 20, 33, 34–35, 76, 86, 109, 117, 127, 146, 201, 217, 235. *See also* Tom and Jerry: Oscar wins
Academy of Television Arts & Sciences, xxii, xxvii, xxviii
action (character movement), 21–22, 27, 30, 31, 35, 36, 40, 70–71, 73, 84, 85, 86, 127–28, 131, 164, 191, 203
action-adventure genre, x, xv–xvii, xxvi, xxviii, 118, 119, 127, 131, 137, 144–45, 164
Action for Children's Television (ACT), xviii, 198, 201, 202
Addams Family, 158
Adventures of Gulliver, The, 116, 122, 127
advertising, 29, 41–42, 56, 59, 60, 65, 70, 73, 105, 123, 128, 130, 132, 144, 153, 158, 225, 227, 241
Ahern, John, 171
Air Programs International (API), 147–50
Allen, Bob, 16–18, 23n4, 26
All in the Family, 141
Amazing Chan and the Chan Clan, The, 151
Amblin Entertainment, xx, xxviii, 13, 239, 242
Ambro, Hal, 179, 220
American Tail, An, xix, xxvii
amusement parks, xi, xvi, xxvi, 8, 13, 108–11, 156, 217–19
Anchors Aweigh, xxiv, 7, 35–36, 126, 179, 217

Anderson, Alex, 37–40
animatic, 136
animation, full: animating on ones, 30, 171–72; as art form, xii, 123, 166, 203; education/training, xviii, xxvii, 127–29, 161, 166–68, 169–77, 189–90, 221; feature films, 4, 28–29, 129, 133, 166, 189, 193, 204, 217–24, 230, 236; gags, 17, 143; movement, 18, 19, 25, 28–29, 81, 96, 123–24, 128, 167, 204; production process, xix, 30–31, 73, 124, 126–27, 130, 148, 162, 167–74, 217–24; short subjects, ix, xiii–xiv, xx, 26, 55, 133, 169, 170, 203; volume, 30, 180
animation, limited: animal characters, 18, 33, 128, 220–21, 224; animating on twos, 30, 171; animation department/stage, 25, 27, 57, 59, 60, 71, 81, 96, 124, 129, 130, 133, 182, 215; animation of movement, xi, 65, 81, 96, 123–24, 128, 134, 155, 167–68, 181, 192, 203; assistant animator, xvii, 35, 59, 72, 161–63, 169, 172–75, 217, 222; cartoon characters, 39, 112, 136, 206; cel technique/cel layering, xiv, 5, 25, 31, 43, 71, 96, 125, 130, 210; children's entertainment, x, xvii, xxvi, 3–4, 53, 78, 85, 87, 111, 114, 131, 142, 192, 198, 200–204, 210–14, 224, 232; clean-up, 64, 164–65, 180, 182; Hanna-Barbera production system, ix–xv, 5, 7, 25, 37–40, 55, 60–69, 70–74, 86, 125, 129–32, 143, 146, 170, 192, 203, 217–19, 243; human characters, 9, 33, 35, 52, 80, 96, 119, 204, 206, 220, 221; inbetweener animator, xii, xv, 27, 30, 35, 58, 59, 72, 161–63, 170–71,

249

INDEX

173–74, 222; key/lead animator, xviii, 35, 59, 72, 124–25, 128, 153–54, 166–67, 169–77, 178–79, 191, 209, 217; mistakes, 128, 155; mouth dialogue system, xv, 25, 31, 71–72, 125, 130, 180–81; perspective/dimension, 72, 112, 128, 136, 238; production process (pipeline), 81, 151–53, 157, 190, 209, 210, 215; satire, 73, 79, 85, 113–14, 117, 131, 241; "semilimited," x, 192; shortcuts/"tricks," 12, 70, 192; stock footage, 38, 96; techniques (methods), xii, xiv, xx, 70–74, 86, 130, 132, 167, 203–4, 224; volume, xi, 67, 72, 124, 126, 151, 153, 157, 163, 180, 205, 206, 210
animation art schools, xvii, 25, 35, 59, 127, 129, 141, 166, 167, 169
Animation Guild, The (IATSE Local 839 animation union), xviii, 148, 153, 181–82
Ant Hill Mob, 130, 143
Anzilotti, Coz, 179
Archie Show, The/The Archies (1968–69 series), 122, 138, 139, 164
Aries, Peter, 215
Arriola, Gus, 17
Ashley, Ted, 8
Atom Ant, 50, 113, 116
Atom Ant/Secret Squirrel Show, The, 113, 116
Augie Doggie and Doggie Daddy, 45, 86
Australia's Wonderland, 156
Avery, Tex: at Hanna-Barbera, 179; influence on Hanna and Barbera, xxiv, 26–27; MGM animation unit and staff, xiii, xxiv, 16, 20, 21–24, 25–27, 41–42, 48, 59; Raid commercials, 42; style, xiii, 16, 27, 38, 40

Babbitt, Art, 123–28, 130, 179
background painting, 35–36, 58, 60–62, 71–72, 82, 129, 155
backgrounds (layouts) xiv, 17, 60–62, 64, 81, 127, 129, 172
Bakshi, Ralph, 176, 179, 221–24
Baldwin, Gerard, xix, 207–16
Balnaves, Neil, 153, 155, 157
Banana Splits Adventure Hour, The, 116, 120, 122, 123

Barbera, Jayne, xxiii, 178
Barbera, Joe: as artist/animator, xi, xii, xxiv, 5, 11, 15, 17, 21, 25, 125, 134, 176, 192, 206, 237; autobiography, xi, xx, xxviii, 139; banking job, 3, 77, 86, 100, 109, 125, 203; childhood, xxiii, 4, 59, 203; creative roles, ix–xi, xv, xviii–xxiv, xxvi, 4–7, 16, 21, 25, 52, 60, 63, 65, 70, 86, 93, 102, 108, 130, 134, 138, 142, 201, 209–10; as Hanna-Barbera copresident, xvi–xx, xxv, xxvii, 99, 101, 106, 155, 208; imitative creative approach, 46, 52, 64, 122, 139, 195–96; office at Hanna-Barbera studio, 10, 61, 63–64, 162, 209, 234–35, 243; Palm Springs residence, 196–97; personality, xiii, 5, 10, 33, 100, 116, 125, 198, 202–3, 237, 240, 243; as sales pitchman, xi, xv, xx, 4, 6, 8, 44, 65, 66, 67, 77–78, 100, 105, 134–35, 143, 209; as story writer ("story man"), xii, 10–13, 26, 29, 52, 57, 61, 65, 73, 77–81, 85, 88–90, 92, 94, 100, 135, 138–40, 142–45, 185, 186, 194–97, 214, 237
Barge, Ed, 21, 221
Barney Bear, 25
Barrier, Michael, x, xiii, 15–24
bar sheet, xxiv, 16
Batman: *Batman* (1966–68 live-action series), 137; character, 165, 189, 192
Battle of the Network Stars, 189
Beery, Wallace, 89, 240
Beethoven, Ludwig van, 212, 229
Beiman, Nancy, 25
Benedict, Ed, xiv, 41–44, 134
Benny, Jack, 4
Berenstain Bears, The, 155–56
Bergen, Edgar, 50
Berra, Yogi, 65
Best Years of Our Lives, The, 242
Betty Boop, 179, 205
Beverly Hillbillies, The, 135
Bewitched, xxiv
Bickenbach, Dick (Bick), 19, 21, 24, 29, 57, 60–61, 63, 65, 90–91, 127, 129, 134
Big H, 171
Bird, Brad, 143

Black Falcon, 206
Black Hole, The (1979 film), 205
Blaine, Jimmy, xxv
Blair, Preston, 221
Blanc, Mel, 48, 50
Bliss, Lucille, 37–39, 40n5
Blitz Wolf, 20
board slugging, 208–10, 227
Bonsall, Shull, xxiv, 38–39, 40n4
bonus system, 180
Bradley, Scott, 18, 22, 29
budgeting, production, xiv, xvi–xviii, 6, 39, 40, 43, 51, 54–56, 58, 70, 91, 100–101, 106, 116, 117, 123, 126–29, 146–47, 150, 154–58, 165, 175, 188, 191–93, 204, 207–9, 213, 218–19, 229, 243
Bugs Bunny, 11, 90, 137, 142, 144, 181, 206, 241
Bugs Bunny/Road Runner Hour, The, 206
Butler, Daws, xiv, 37–39, 45–52, 71, 84

Cagney, Jimmy, 196
California Institute of the Arts (CalArts), xvii, 25, 141, 169
Cambria Productions, 88
camera department, 17, 36, 60, 67, 71–72, 82, 130, 171–75
Canby, Vincent, 219
Caniff, Milton, 89
Cap'n Crunch, 45, 128
Captain and the Kids, 15, 24, 26. See also *Katzenjammer Kids, The*
Captain Caveman and the Teen Angels, 57, 174
Captain Kangaroo, 132, 206
Carney, Art, 46, 195, 204
cartoon. See animation, full; animation, limited
Cartoon Network, xix–xx, xxvii–xxviii, 232–37
Cascade Studios, 42
Casper and the Angels, 200, 206
Cassidy, Ted, 187
Cat Ballou, 65
Cattanooga Cats, 120, 122, 225

CBS television, xix, 8, 122–23, 126, 138, 142, 143, 144, 184–86, 190, 196, 200, 208
Chaplin, Charlie, 25, 27, 142, 240
character animation. See animation, full; animation, limited
character design, xiv, xvii, 18, 42–43, 57, 60, 65, 66, 69, 133–36, 167, 171, 222
Charlotte's Web (1973 film), xxvii, 28, 136, 219–20
Charren, Peggy, xviii, 198, 201. See also Action for Children's Television (ACT)
checking animation, xi, 37–38, 81, 128, 182
Chilly Willy (Walter Lantz character), 48
Clinton, Walt, 60
Cohen, Bruce, 239
Cohn, Harry, xxv, 25, 66, 98
Collier's magazine, xxiii, 34, 203
Colman, Dianne, 146, 153
Columbia Pictures: animated shorts, xxv, 39, 74; film studio, xxvi, 66, 192. See also Screen Gems
comic books, xvi, 62, 88, 92, 94, 167, 176
comic strips, xvi, xxvii, 11, 68, 88–89, 92–93, 139, 189, 211, 214, 219
"Comic Strips of Television, The," 40n2
commercial advertisements, animated. See advertising
Coney Island, 108, 111
Connell, David, 132
Cooke, Gairden, 151–52
Cooper, Gary, 48
Cooper, Jackie, 89
counterculture, 110–11
Crusader Rabbit: failed reboot, 37–40; original series (1950–52), xxiv, 37; successful color reboot (1956–59), 39
Cuckoo's Nest studio (Wang Film Productions, Taiwan), xviii, xxvi, 153, 157–58, 173–75, 181, 190, 208, 215. See also Wang, James
cue sheet, 228
Culhane, Shamus, 129
Curtin, Hoyt, xix, 213, 225–31, 242

Daffy Duck, 205–6, 241
Dangerous When Wet, xxiv, 7

252 INDEX

Darrow, Frankie, 89
Dastardly and Muttley in Their Flying Machines, 65, 120, 121–22, 125–26, 131–32
Davy Crockett (1954–55 series), 203
Delporte, Yvan, 215
department head, 67, 207
DePatie, David, 198
DePatie-Freleng Enterprises, 143, 179, 192, 202, 221
detail sheet, 35
development, xv, xviii, xix, 6, 15, 37–40, 60, 65, 66, 68, 155–56, 163, 184–87, 194–99, 202, 212–13
Dick Dastardly, 65, 121, 122, 126
Dinehart, Alan, 62, 64
Disney, Walt, 124, 129, 191, 193, 203, 224
Disney animation. *See* Walt Disney Studios
Disneyland (amusement park), xxvi, 111
Disneyland (1954–58 anthology series), 203
Disney's Raw Toonage, 176
Doctor Dolittle (1967 film), 118
Donald Duck, 128
Don Quixote, 129
Downs, Charlie, 179, 220
Driscoll, Don, 38
Droopy, 13
Dr. Seuss, 86, 211
dubbing (international language vocal recording), 13, 56, 82, 83, 130, 205–6
Duck Dodgers in the 24½ Century, 172
Dumbo (1941 film), 29
Dwyer, Mary Alice "Mickey," 201–2, 212–13

effects animation, 124–25, 127, 136, 172, 191–92, 204–5
Eisenberg, Harvey, 17, 19, 21, 59, 134
Eisenberg, Jerry, xv, 59–69, 133, 134, 171
Emmy Award, xxv, xxvi, xxvii, 7, 73, 75, 176, 204, 209, 218
Eric Porter Productions, 147, 149–51
exposure sheet, 21, 31, 62, 171

Fairbanks Productions, 38–38, 40n1
fan letters, 87
Fantasia, 30, 123, 124, 193, 205, 223

Federal Communications Commission (FCC), xix, 97
Feild, Robert, 123
Filmation studio, 122, 143, 162–63, 169, 175–76, 197
Fischer, Sy, 104–6, 138
Flash Gordon: The Greatest Adventure of All, 176
Flintstones, the: in amusement parks, 156; characters, 9–10, 107, 108–9, 112–13, 116, 118, 134, 140, 154, 195, 200–202; development, 62–64; *The Flintstones* (1960–66 series), ix–xii, xv, xxi, xxv, 7–8, 13, 54, 57, 62–64, 74, 77, 79, 82, 84, 86–87, 88, 91–93, 96, 97, 104, 107, 118, 122, 133, 146, 166, 204, 218, 225, 231, 243; *The Flintstones* (1994 live-action movie), xx, xxviii, 13, 238–42; *The Flintstones in Viva Rock Vegas*, xxviii, 239; *The Flintstones Kids*, xxvii, 10; franchise, 158, 236; *The Man Called Flintstone* (1966 film), xxvi, 219; merchandise, 104, 156, 197, 200, 218, 233; *The New Fred and Barney Show*, 57–58, 174; original sale, 62, 77
Foster, Warren, 31, 61, 80–81, 137
Frankenstein Jr. and The Impossibles, 116, 137, 145, 225
Freberg, Stan, 46, 48
Freleng, Friz, 11, 15, 19, 26, 179, 197, 198, 204, 235
Fritz the Cat, 179, 221, 224
Funky Phantom, The, 147–49
funny animal characters, 33, 52–53, 80, 116–18, 135, 164, 168, 171, 204, 220–21
"Funtastic World of Hanna-Barbera, The," 200

gags, animated, 15–23, 27, 130, 141–43, 237
Gallopin' Gals, 16
Gamma Productions studio, 181
Gathering, The (1977 telefilm), xxi, xxvii, 204, 218
Gaumont Animation, 30
Gentle, Bob, 60
George of the Jungle (1967–68 series), 123, 128

INDEX 253

Getzler, Buddy, 102
Glamack, Mark, 173, 175
Gleason, Jackie, 195, 204
Godzilla: character, 185–87, 191–92, 200; *Godzilla* (1978–81 series), 57, 90, 173, 179, 180, 184–92; Godzooky character, 185–87
Golden Age of animation (1930s–50s), 15–24, 169, 172, 179, 182, 204
Goodman, Alan, 232
Goodman, John, 14
Good Will to Men, xiii, xxiv
Goose Goes South, The, 16
Gordon, Dan, 62
Gordon, George, 31
Grantray-Lawrence Animation studio, 28–30
Great American Broadcasting, xix, xxvii, 8, 194, 198–99, 234. *See also* Taft Broadcasting
Greatest Adventure, The, xxi
Green Hornet, The (1966–67 series), 137
Greenwood, Warren, 167
Gulliver's Travels (1726 novel), 218

Hand, David, 30
Hanna, Bill: Alzheimer's, xx, 239, 242; autobiography, xi, xiv, xx, xxviii, 147–48, 151, 154, 159; Boy Scouts, xxiii; childhood, xxiii, 4, 109; creative and technical roles, xii–xiii, xv, xx, xxv–xxvi, 4, 11, 21, 26–27, 29, 31–32, 60, 70, 74, 86, 102, 125, 131, 163, 188, 195, 238, 239; as director and producer, xi, xii–xiv, xx, xxiii–xxiv, xxv–xxvi, 4–6, 11, 15, 17, 21, 26–27, 28–31, 37–40, 41, 57, 59, 71, 82, 85, 100, 109, 126, 133, 170, 188, 195, 198; economization, ix, xiv, xvii, xviii, xix, 31, 51, 100, 129, 181, 210, 218, 243; engineering training, xxiii, 3, 76, 86, 109, 125, 203; financial efficiencies, 60, 66, 100, 124, 149–50, 175, 180–81, 210, 212, 215; international activities, xvii, xxvi, 67, 146–60, 215; labor tensions, xviii, xxvii, 57, 63, 154, 173–75, 180–83, 212; marketing, 104–6, 223–24; music involvement, xix, 228–29; office at Hanna-Barbera studio, 6, 209, 234; personality, xi, xiii–xiv, 4–5, 9, 33, 67, 100, 148, 152, 158, 162, 209–10, 237, 238–40; press shyness, xii, 218; as production manager, xi, xiv, xx, xxv–xxvi, 5–6, 26–27, 28–31, 34, 37, 59, 60, 67, 82, 101, 105, 124, 133, 147–54, 170, 175, 179, 188, 207–10, 218, 234, 238, 243; Shield Productions collaboration with Mike Lah, xiv, xxiv, 25, 27, 37–40; wife (Violet Wogatzke), xxiii, 9, 151, 237; yacht (*Gallatea*), 31, 99, 209
Hanna and Barbera collaboration: animation unit at MGM and production process, xiii–xiv, xx, xxiv, 5–6, 11, 15–24, 25–27, 28–31, 41, 51, 59–60, 67, 75, 109, 117; anonymity at MGM under Fred Quimby, x, xiii, 15–16, 20, 26, 33, 235; awards and recognitions, x, xiii, xxiv, xxv–xxviii, 3, 5, 7, 12, 20, 33, 34–35, 73, 75, 127, 131, 204, 209, 218, 235; Cartoon Network shorts, xx; cinema views, 56, 73–74, 167; closure of MGM studio, xxv, 7, 12, 41, 51, 55, 76, 146; George Sidney relationship, xxiv, xxv, 7, 8, 25, 38, 56, 66, 208; as Hanna-Barbera copresidents, xvi–xx, xxv–xxviii, 6, 99, 101, 106, 112–15, 155, 179, 194, 207, 208, 233, 238, 244; as joint producers, xxiv, 5, 17, 20–21, 31, 33, 42, 59, 60, 70, 75–83, 112–15, 122–32, 134, 141, 170, 172, 184–93; legacy and influence, ix, xx–xxi, xxviii, 3–4, 122, 132, 198–200, 238–42, 243–44; limited animation production process (*see* animation, limited); loyalty to employees, 179; moonlighting on television credit sequences, xxiv, 29; non-Tom and Jerry cartoon shorts, xx, xxiv, 12, 16; press relationship, x–xi; relationship, 4, 6, 21, 36, 210–11; reputation, ix–xi, xvii, xxi, 125, 130–31, 187, 197–98, 201, 218, 220; retirement views, xiv, xviii, 9, 115, 211; roles in collaboration, xii, xxiv, 5, 6, 11, 15, 26, 29, 57, 60, 109, 125; television

views, 12, 55–56, 72, 75, 203; work culture, 30, 32, 62–68, 76, 141, 162, 178–79, 235, 237; work ethic, 4, 9, 32, 76, 77, 83, 211, 235–37
Hanna-Barbera Australia, 146–60
Hanna-Barbera Cartoons (1998 book), 210
Hanna-Barbera New Cartoon Series, The, xv, 61
Hanna-Barbera Records, xvi, xxvi
Hanna-Barbera's Marineland, 218
Hanna-Barbera Studios Europe, xxviii
Hanna-Barbera television studio: action-adventure style, xv, 88–96, 113, 119, 131, 162; at Chaplin Studios, xxv, 7, 30, 38, 63, 64, 142; comic house style, xiii, xv, xxiii, 4, 16–19, 22, 27, 54, 58, 73, 79, 84–87, 91–92, 95–96, 99, 108–15, 119, 131, 190, 195; dependence on studio-era animators, xviii, xix, xxvii, 166, 169, 179, 204; distribution, xvi, 6, 73, 76, 98–101, 104, 149, 157, 187, 218; entertainment philosophy, xii, 84–87, 112–15; *Exposure Sheet* newsletter, xvi; finances, 8, 64, 94, 97–107, 110, 187–89, 218–19; founding, x, xiv, xxv, 7, 12, 13, 25, 37, 38, 39, 55–56, 63, 75, 109, 117, 146; freelancing, 25, 59, 65, 67–68, 117, 137, 158, 163, 176, 180, 214; hiring, xiv, xxv, 60–62, 68–69, 88, 137, 144–45, 179; industry competition, ix, 122–23; intellectual property library, xix, xxvii, 7, 193, 219, 233–34; lack of overtime, 180; late book, 178; low morale of artists (reputed), x, 162, 208, 218; overflow unit, xviii, 174–75; pay, 60, 124, 151; production pressures, 58–62, 68, 70, 124; production schedule, xiv, xviii, 67, 124, 170, 182, 184–93, 207–16; quantity vs. quality debate, ix–xi, xvi–xx, xxv–xxvii, 4, 7, 23, 32, 34–36, 55, 57, 72, 109, 121–32, 144, 173, 200–206, 217–25, 244; response to strikes, xviii, xxvii; restructuring in 1990s, xxvii–xxviii, 8, 194, 233–37; seasonal nature of work, 54, 152, 184, 189, 221; stock libraries, 38, 96; studio building in Studio City, xvi, xxv, 61, 64, 123, 142, 174, 175, 202, 234; Taft

Broadcasting sale, xvi, xxvi, 62, 66, 98; voice actors, 45–54
Hanson, Howard, 67
Happy Harmonies, xxiii. *See also* Harman and Ising
Harlem Globetrotters, The (1970–72 series), 142, 202
Harman, Hugh, xiii, 26
Harman and Ising, xiii, xxiii, 4, 5, 18, 26
Harman-Ising animation studio, xiii, xxiii, 17–19, 22, 25–26; production units at MGM, xiii, 15, 18, 25–26
Hathcock, Jerry, 67
Hazelton, Gene, 134
Heavy Metal, 181
Heavy Traffic, 179, 224
Heidi's Song, xix, xxvii, 204–5, 217–24
Henson Creature Shop, 238
Herculoids, The, xvi, 137–38, 207
Heyyy, It's the King!, 171
Hillbilly Bears, The, 135
Home Box Office (HBO), 220
Honeymooners, The, 62–63, 78, 195, 204, 240
Honeystein, Karl, 105–6
Hope, Bob, 78
House of Mystery, The, 138
Howson, Peter, 149
How the Grinch Stole Christmas (1966 television special), 144, 212
Huber, Jack, 61
Hucker, Walt, 149–50
Huckleberry Hound, 10, 43, 48, 55, 70, 71, 73, 75, 79, 80, 82, 83, 84, 85, 87, 109, 113–14, 122, 134, 200, 218, 233–34, 239, 241
Huckleberry Hound Show, The, x, xv, xxv, 7, 13, 56, 70–74, 75, 77, 82, 84–87, 113, 114, 117, 188, 218, 225, 243
Humanitas Prize, xxvii
Hurtz, Bill, 129

Ideal Toys, 13
I Love a Mystery, 138
I Love Lucy, xxiv, 29, 78, 95
Impossibles, The, 145

ink and paint, xi–xii, xxiii, xxvii, 35, 58, 60–61, 63, 67, 71–72, 81–82, 86, 113, 148, 150, 158, 181, 182, 205
Invitation to the Dance, xxiv, 36
Irving Trust Company. *See* Barbera, Joe: banking job
Irwin, Lew, 169, 175
Ising, Rudy, 15–19, 22, 23n4, 25–26
Ito, Willie, 60

Jabberjaw, 201
Jack and the Beanstalk (1967 television special), xxvi, 134
Jack Armstrong, the All-American Boy, xv, 64, 88–89, 96
Jack Benny Show, The, 78
James Bond, 89, 127
James Hardie Industries, 155–57
Jana of the Jungle, 90, 173
Janjic, Zoran, 147–48, 152, 154
Jetsons, the: characters, xvi, 48, 50, 134; *The Jetsons* (1962–63 series), xv, xxv, 7–8, 28, 61–62, 134, 135, 139, 225, 231, 234, 241; *The Jetsons* (1985–87 series), 54; *Jetsons: The Movie* (1990 film), ix, xxvii, 230, 242
Johann Mouse, xxiv, 35
Jones, Chuck: at Cartoon Network, 235; as director/producer at Warner Bros., 141, 172; on limited animation ("illustrated radio" critique), x, 143, 218; television specials, 144
Jones, Ron, 226–31
Jones, Volus, 58
Jonny Quest: characters, 54, 109, 135, 158; *Jonny Quest* (1964–65 series), xv, xxvi, 50, 54, 64–65, 88–96, 225, 231; *The New Adventures of Jonny Quest* (1986–87 series), 227; *The Real Adventures of Jonny Quest* (1996–97 series), xxviii
Johnston, Sam, 100–101, 103, 105
Josie and the Pussycats (1970–72 series), xxvi, 164
Jungle Book, The (1967 film), 173
Justin, Eddie, 104–5

Kahl, Milt, 179
Kane, Gil, 176

Katzenjammer Kids, The, 11, 15. *See also* Captain and the Kids
Kausler, Mark, 20, 24
Keaton, Buster, 240
Keil, Bill, 58
Kellogg's, 13, 38, 117, 241
Kelly, Fred, 5
Kelly, Gene, xxiv, 36, 126, 132, 134, 179, 217
Kennedy, John F., 94
Kennedy, Kathleen, 242
Kennedy, Robert F., Jr., xvi, 127, 164, 202
Kerkorian, Kirk, 7
Keystone Cops, 143, 240
Kimball, Ward, 179
King, Martin Luther, Jr., xvi
King Features, 188–89
Kings Dominion (amusement park), xxvi
Kings Island (amusement park), xvi, xxvi, 108–11, 218
"King Who Couldn't Dance, The," 126, 132. *See also Anchors Aweigh*
Kirby, Jack, 176
Kirschner, David, xix, xxvii, 194
Kohler, Karl, 67
Kramer, Stanley, 88
Krantz, Steve, 221–22
Krazy Kat, 11, 205
Kricfalusi, John, 235

Lady and the Tramp (1955 film), 203
Lah, Mike: as animator, 25–27, 38; MGM animation unit, 59; Shield Productions collaboration with Bill Hanna (*see* Hanna, Bill: Shield Productions collaboration)
Lahr, Bert, 46, 145
Lantz, Walter, 48
Lassie (1954–71 series), 90
"Last of the Curlews" (*ABC Afterschool Special*), xxvii
Laurel and Hardy, 142, 204, 240
layout, xvii, xxiv, 16–17, 21, 26, 29, 34, 41–42, 57, 60–62, 64–67, 71, 81, 92, 95, 127–29, 133–34, 154, 161–63, 167, 171–72, 190
Legend of Robin Hood, The (1971 film), 147

Léger, Fernand, 129
Leo Burnett Company, 38
Lewis, Jerry, 53
limited animation. *See* animation, limited; "planned animation"
line production, xix, 207–9
live-action, 34–35, 72, 92, 95, 110, 122, 136, 137, 145, 172, 201, 217–18, 222, 231, 238–42
live-action and animation combination, xxiv, xxvi, 4, 7, 116, 122, 126, 134, 205, 217
Loesch, Margaret, xix, 184–93, 211–14
Looney Tunes, xxviii, 109, 125, 196
Loopy de Loop, xvi, 74
Lord of the Rings (1978 film), 224
Lost in Space (1965–68 series), 137
Lovy, Alex, 61, 81, 130
Lozzi, Art, 60
Lucas, George, 92
Lundy, Dick, 128, 132
Lusk, Don, 31–32
Lyon-Lamb video system, 176

Magilla Gorilla, xv, 156, 231
Maltese, Mike, xvii, 31, 137, 141–45
Maltin, Leonard, x, xxiin4, 218
Marco Polo Junior, 147, 151
Marmaduke, 139
Marshall, Lew, 63
Marvel Comics, 167
Marvel Productions studio, 62, 214
Marx Brothers, 65, 136, 206, 240
Mary Poppins (1964 film), xvi, 118
Mary Tyler Moore Show, The, 141
McNamara, Don, 38
Mechem, Charlie, Jr., 99, 103, 105
merchandise, xvi, xix, 13, 98, 101, 104, 107, 157, 187–88, 200, 219–20
Merrie Melodies. *See* Looney Tunes
Messick, Don, xiv, 39, 47–48, 50–54, 187
Metamorphoses (1978 film), 68
MGM: Academy Award wins, 20, 33, 76; animation production studio, ix–x, 19, 25–27, 34–36, 59, 76, 217; animation production units (*see* Avery, Tex; Hanna and Barbera; Harman, Hugh; Ising, Rudy; Jones, Chuck; Lah, Mike); Hollywood film studio, xxiii–xxiv, 41; producer Fred Quimby supervision, x, xxiv, 5, 15–20, 25–27, 29–31, 33, 235; Ted Turner purchase, 7, 234; upper management, xii, xxv, 5, 7, 11–12, 38, 41, 51, 117, 144, 203
Michaeli, John, 124
Mickey Mouse, 118, 125, 205
Mickey Mouse Club, The, 203
Midnight Snack, The, xxiv, 16–17
Mighty Mightor, 137–38
Mighty Mouse, 11
Mighty Mouse: The New Adventures, 176
Miles Laboratories, 241
Mitchell, John, 63, 104–5
Moby Dick, 142, 204
model sheet, 16, 22, 23n4, 29, 136
Monkees, The (1966–68 series), 122
Montealegre, Fernando, 60, 61, 63
Morgan, Jess, 97, 99–102
Moviola, 21, 82, 155, 208
Mr. Magoo, 56, 123
MTV, xix, xxvii, 232
Murakami-Wolf studio, 221
Murphy, Marty, 136, 171
Muse, Ken, 20, 30, 179–80, 181
Museum of Television & Radio, xxviii
music, xix, xxvi, 4, 18, 22, 29, 35, 72, 82, 93, 95, 126, 130, 150, 207, 212–13, 220–23, 225–31
Musker, John, 144
Muttley, 50, 52, 121, 122, 126, 139

National Commission on the Causes and Prevention of Violence, 126
National Educational Television, 131
NBC television, xviii–xix, 8, 40, 66, 122–23, 163, 184–93, 200–202, 211–15; *Ask NBC News*, 201
network interaction, xv–xix, xxviii, 48, 62, 66, 68, 91, 98, 100, 104, 122–23, 125–27, 131–32, 141–45, 157, 163–65, 183–93, 194–99, 200–206, 207–16

New Adventures of Huckleberry Finn, The, 8, 116–17, 134
Nichols, Margaret, 223
Nichols, Nick, 31, 62, 67, 179
Nickelodeon (cable network), 232–33
Nielsen television ratings, 121–22, 211
Nixon, Richard, 198
Nolley, Lance, xiv, 57–58, 60
Norman Rockwell Museum, xix, xxviii, 232–37
Novier, Frances, 212
Novier, John, 215

Oak Crest Market, 178–79
Officer Pooch, 18
offshore production studios: Argentina, xxvi; Australia (*see* Hanna-Barbera Australia); Brazil, 153, 154; Japan, 67, 73, 181; Mexico, xxvi, 190; Philippines (Fil-Cartoons), xxvi, 67, 157–58; Poland, xxvi; South Korea, xxvi, 67, 153, 157, 181; Spain, xxvi, 153, 154, 190; Taiwan (*see* Cuckoo's Nest; Wang Film Productions); Yugoslavia, 190
Ott, Lew, 64

Pabian, Jim, 23
Pacific Title & Art Studio, 4. *See also* Warner Bros.: Leon Schlesinger studio
Paddington Bear, 158
Parkes, Margaret, 148, 155, 158
Patterson, Ray, xiv, 28–32, 67
Paul Hamlyn Publishing, 153, 155
Peabody Award, 131
Peace on Earth, xiii, xxiv
Pearson, GeGe, 39, 40n5
pencil test (test reel), xii, 21, 25, 29, 34–35, 38, 72, 128, 143, 171–74, 176, 190. *See also* pose reel
Penelope Pitstop, xvii, 122, 129–32, 134–35
Peregoy, Walt, 129
Perez, Manny, 67
Perils of Penelope Pitstop, The, xvii, 122, 127, 131, 132, 135, 138, 142–43
Peter Pan (1953 film), 124
Peter Potamus Show, The, 65

Peyo, xxvii, 211–12, 214–16. *See also Smurfs, The*
photography, animation. *See* camera department
Phyllis, 145
Pink Panther, 154
Pinocchio (1940 film), 206
Pittman, Bob, 232
Pixie and Dixie, 47, 50, 240
"planned animation." *See* animation, limited: Hanna-Barbera production system
Popeye, 155, 179, 184–85, 188–89, 201, 205
Porky Pig, 206, 241
Porter, Eric, 147, 149, 150–51
pose reel, xii, 5, 17, 25, 27, 29–30, 34, 37, 38, 39. *See also* pencil test
Post, Mike, 226
Pound Puppies, xviii, 195–96, 230
Precious Pupp, 52
primetime animation, xiv–xv, xxv–xxvii, 7–8, 13, 74, 123, 143, 204, 206, 215
producer, animation, xiii, xiv, xvii, xix, 16, 26, 31, 35, 52, 59, 68–69, 70, 85, 93, 122, 128, 132, 143–44, 155, 157, 170–71, 196–97, 202, 207–14, 233–37
Punch and Judy (puppet shows), 51, 73
Puss Gets the Boot, ix, xii, xxiv, 5, 15–17, 18, 23n2, 23n4, 24n15, 26, 33

Quick Draw McGraw, 45, 49, 79, 84, 134, 143, 145, 241
Quick Draw McGraw Show, The, 13, 73
Quimby, Fred, x, xii, xiii, xx, xxiv, 5, 15–20, 23n2, 24n15, 26–27, 29, 30–31, 33, 37, 235. *See also* Hanna and Barbera collaboration: anonymity at MGM under Fred Quimby

racial representation/character stereotypes: Asian, 163, 201; Black, 16, 91, 163, 200, 206; Indian, xv, 21, 91; Latino, 47; Native American, 21, 91
Raft, George, 89
Raggedy Ann & Andy: A Musical Adventure, 218, 221
Raiders of the Lost Ark, 92

Reagan, Ronald, xix, 181
Record, Chet, 229
Ren & Stimpy Show, The, 235
Rescuers, The, 219
Road Runner, 202, 206
Robinson Crusoe (1719 novel), 117, 136
Rock Odyssey, 223
Rocky and Bullwinkle series, 181, 211–12
Rodriguez, Robert, 231
Rogers, Fred, 131–32
Rogers, Lawrence H., II, xvi, 97–107, 108–11
Ron Campbell Films, 180
rotoscoping, xxiv, 220
Ruby, Joe, xvii, 66, 68, 126, 135, 137–40, 171
Ruby-Spears studio, xvii, 69, 162, 171, 176, 180
Ruff and Reddy: characters, 39, 41, 50, 109; *The Ruff and Reddy Show* (1957–60 series), xxv, 7, 37–40, 42, 51, 56, 73, 104, 225
runaway production, xviii, 68, 146–60, 173, 175, 181, 190, 236. *See also* offshore production studios; subcontracting
Rushnell, Squire, xviii, 194–99, 202

Said, Fuad, 110
sales, xvi, 38, 60, 64–67, 92–94, 98–106, 117, 126, 128, 132, 155–57, 186, 195–97
Sangster, John, 150
Sanrio, 68
Saperstein, Hank, 185
Sarbry, Jay, 180
Sassa, Scott, 233, 236
Saturday morning cartoons: children's programming, xvii, xxv, 3–4, 10, 13, 39, 78, 84–87, 114, 118, 119, 131, 185, 194, 197–99, 200–203, 205–6, 211–14, 223–24; creative aspects (and/or lack of), xvii, xxv–xxvii, 53, 55, 73, 85, 92, 132, 141, 143, 176, 200–206, 208, 210, 218, 222; development, 135, 137–40, 195–98, 204; financial aspects, xvi, xvii, 123, 128, 132, 187, 224; network involvement, xviii, 186, 201, 210; production, 40, 66, 116, 156, 205–6, 207–16, 218–19; programming, ix, xxv–xxvii, 53, 121–22, 131–32,
185–86, 192, 197, 200–206, 233; ratings, x, xvii, xxvi, 98, 122, 195, 201, 211, 213–14; studio competition in industry, 122, 197, 204, 206
Saturday Night Live, 196
Schary, Dore, 41
Scheimer, Lou, 197, 198. *See also* Filmation studio
Schenck, Nicholas, 41
Schifrin, Lalo, 229–30
Schipek, Bill, 67
School of Visual Arts, 169
Scooby-Doo: characters, 52, 53, 196, 197, 200, 202, 206, 236; development, 52, 53, 66, 137–40, 196–97; merchandise, 218, 233; production, 57, 127–28, 135; *Scooby and Scrappy-Doo* (1979–80 series), 200, 218; *Scooby-Doo* (2002 film), 140, 242; *Scooby-Doo, Where Are You!* (1969–71 series), ix, xvii, xxvi, 123, 127–28, 132, 135, 137–40, 152, 164, 189; Scrappy-Doo, 196–97; voice actors, 52–53; *What's New, Scooby-Doo?* (2002–6 series), 176
scoring, music, xix, 18, 22, 220, 225–31
Scott, Art, 161
Scott, Bill, 123, 128, 130–31
Screen Actors Guild, 40n5
Screen Cartoonists Guild, 124, 170, 209, 210. *See also* Animation Guild, The
Screen Gems, xxv, 7, 8, 12, 25, 38, 56, 76, 94, 98–99, 104–5
script writing, 37, 49, 62, 66, 85, 88, 92–95, 127, 137–40, 164–65, 186, 187, 191, 202, 207, 210, 212–13, 214–15, 221, 239, 242
Sears, Ted, 5
Secret Squirrel, 65, 113
Seibert, Fred, xix–xx, xxvii, 232–37
Sgt. Bilko, 78, 118
Sheinberg, Sid, 3, 4
Sheridan College, 169
Shield Productions. *See* Hanna, Bill: Shield Productions collaboration
Sidney, George. *See* Hanna and Barbera collaboration: George Sidney relationship

INDEX 259

Silverman, Fred, xix, 66, 68, 122–23, 126, 135, 138–39, 144–45, 195, 196, 197, 211–12
Simpsons, The, xxvi, 136
Singer, Bob, 164, 167, 171
Sito, Tom, xviii, 178–83
Slafer, Eugene, 218
slapstick comedy, xxiii, 27, 73, 119, 122, 131, 201, 203
Sleeping Beauty, 58, 203
Smit, Robbert, 153, 158
Smith, Webb, 127
Smoke House (restaurant), 28, 209, 211
Smurfs, The (1981–89 series), xix, xxvii, 50, 53, 211–16, 226, 229–30, 233
Snagglepuss, 45, 46, 47, 50, 52, 145
Snow White and the Seven Dwarfs (1937 film), 32, 129, 219
Solid Serenade, 20, 23
Solomon, Ed, 171
Sommer, Paul, 62
sound editing, 71, 82
sound effects, xiv, 8, 19–20, 23, 71, 82, 130, 143, 207, 227
sound syncing, 82, 127
Southern Star Productions, 155–57
Space Angel, 88
Space Ghost and Dino Boy, xvi, xxvi, 137
Space Ghost Coast to Coast, xxviii
Space Kidettes, 137
Space Stars, 207, 212; *Space Ghost*, 212–13
Spears, Ken, xvii, 66, 68, 69, 82, 126–27, 135, 137–40, 171
Spence, Irv, 21, 28, 93, 221
Spider-Man (1967–70 series), 28
Spielberg, Steven, xx, xxviii, 13, 92, 238
sponsorship, 92–93, 113, 132, 134–35, 144, 241
Squiddly Diddly, 65
standards and practices, broadcast networks, xvii, 164, 186, 202
Star Wars (1977 film), 53, 163, 164
Steamboat Willie, 125
storyboard/storyboarding, 5, 11, 16–17, 21, 23n4, 31, 62, 65, 71, 77–81, 88, 92, 95, 127, 134, 143, 148, 153, 154, 165, 176, 186, 191–92, 205, 207–8, 209, 213, 227, 229, 236, 237
story direction, 62, 127, 131
story editing, 163, 171, 176, 212–14
story writing, 11, 13, 21, 73, 144
subcontracting, xviii, xxvi, 28, 55, 56, 146–58, 162, 175, 181, 190, 208, 215. *See also* offshore production studios
Super Friends: *The All-New Super Friends Hour* (1977–78 series), 161–64, 165, 179–80; *Challenge of the Superfriends* (1978–79 series), 163, 165, 189; characters, 163–65; *Super Friends* (1973–74 series), xvii–xviii, 67, 151, 161–65; *Super-Friends* (1980–83 series), 207, 212
Super Globetrotters, The, 200, 202
Superman, 164, 179–80, 189, 202, 206, 207
Swing Social, 16
Sword in the Stone, The, 129, 133
Sylvester the Cat, 90
syndication, broadcast, xv, xxiv, xxv, 54, 98, 104, 107, 188, 201

Taft, Hub, 97–103
Taft, Lloyd, 97
Taft Broadcasting, xvi, xix, xxvi, 8, 66, 97–107, 108–10, 147, 155, 157, 166, 192–93, 200, 218, 221, 234. *See also* Great American Broadcasting
Takamoto, Iwao, xvii, 60, 61–62, 64–65, 66–67, 126, 133–36, 175–76, 181
Taylor, Robert, 221–23
Technicolor, 36
Tee for Two, 20
Tele-Comics, 40n3
television specials, animated, xxvii, 4, 144, 146, 147, 150, 153–54, 158, 176, 215, 236
Tendlar, Dave, 172, 179
Terry, Paul, xxiii, 4
Terry and the Pirates, 89
Terrytoons, xiii, xxiii, 4, 17–19
Thomas, Frank, 124
Three Little Pigs, The (1933 short), 128, 132
Time for Beany, 46
"Tips to Remember When Submitting Gags" (Disney memo), 19

Toho studio, 185–87
Tom and Jerry: budget, 12; characters, 5, 16, 18, 23, 28–29, 33, 51, 86, 132, 240; Chuck Jones MGM series (1963–67), 144; demand from distributors, 12; design, xiii, 19, 20; development, 6, 15–24, 25–26, 86, 203; feature film appearances, xxiv, 7, 35–36, 126, 179, 217; franchise, 7, 144, 203; Golden Age animators, 170, 179, 182, 209, 217, 221; Hanna and Barbera partnership foundation, 11, 55, 70, 109, 112, 117, 125, 146, 166, 188, 201, 235, 244; MGM reissuing, xiii, 12; names, 12, 16, 26; Oscar wins, xiii, xxiv, 20, 33, 34, 86, 109, 127, 146, 201, 217, 235; style, 6, 17–23, 23n4, 26–27, 29, 131, 144, 203, 206; technique, 7, 21, 22, 28–32, 34–36, 37–38, 70, 124, 204, 206; *Tom and Jerry* (Hanna and Barbera MGM series) (1940–57), ix, x, xii–xv, xxiv, 3, 5–7, 10, 15–24, 24n15, 33, 39, 56, 75, 117, 144, 205; *Tom & Jerry Kids* (1990–94 series), 7, 10, 237; *Tom and Jerry: The Movie* (1992 film), xii–xiii, 10–11, 13; violence, xv, 10, 16, 19–20, 22, 131, 201
Top Cat, xv, xxv, 8, 77–78, 80–81, 84, 243
Tortoise and the Hare, The (1935 film), 25
To Spring, xxiii
Toth, Alex, 88, 96, 134, 162–65
Transformers, The (1984–87 series), 54
Treyz, Ollie, 100, 105
Tucker Vinson, Phyllis, 214
Tufts, Warren, 96
Turner, Ted, xix, 13, 233
Turner Broadcasting System (TBS), xxvii, 7, 199
TV Spots studio, xxiv, 38
Twentieth Century-Fox, 137–38
2001: A Space Odyssey, 110–11

union, animation labor: generational employment, xviii, 161, 170–71, 177, 179, 182; membership and rules, 93, 149, 163, 170, 175, 178, 182, 188; nonunion animation labor, xviii, 162; pay scale, 39, 60; strikes, xviii, xxvii, 124, 153–54, 181–83; work schedule, 174, 178

Universal Studios, xxvii, xxviii, 8, 13, 88, 192, 234
United Productions of America (UPA), xiii, 56, 171, 185, 186, 203

Van Beuren Studios, xxiii, 16, 17
Villa Capri (restaurant), 68
violence in television: controversy, x, xv, xvi, 84–85, 114, 118, 119, 126–27, 131–32, 164, 185, 201–2; "fun-violence," xvii, 119; prosocial cartoons, 84–87, 117–18, 164–65
Vivaldi, Antonio, 212
voice acting and actors, xiv, 28, 35, 39, 40n5, 45–49, 50–54, 71, 73, 84, 93, 136, 187, 201, 220
voice casting, 39, 53, 84, 93, 186, 187, 243
voice recording/direction, 36, 39, 47, 51–54, 62, 71, 79, 82, 93, 136, 153, 206, 207

Wacky Races, 65, 121, 122, 126, 134, 142, 240
Wait Till Your Father Gets Home, 136, 143, 152, 158
Wally Gator, 46, 48, 61, 231
Walt Disney Studios, ix, xiv, 8, 17, 19, 25, 30, 33, 55, 57–58, 60–62, 67, 110, 122, 123–25, 127, 128–29, 133, 157, 166, 168, 173–74, 179, 180, 197, 203–4, 205, 217–23
Walt Disney Television Animation, 67, 157, 176
Wang Film Productions, xviii, xxvi, 107, 153, 157–58, 173, 175, 181, 190, 208, 215. *See also* Cuckoo's Nest; Wang, James
Wang, James, 215. *See also* Cuckoo's Nest; Wang Film Productions
Ward, Jay, 37–38, 123, 128, 129, 181, 243
Warner Bros.: Hollywood film and animation studio (after Schlesinger), xiii, 11, 48, 59–60, 62, 130, 142–44, 172, 188, 189, 205, 210, 238, 240, 241; Leon Schlesinger studio, x, xiii, 11, 26, 142–44, 189, 205, 240; Warner Bros. Animation, xx, xxviii, 176
Watership Down (1972 novel), 223
Webb, Jack, 46

What a Cartoon!, xx, 236
Where's Huddles?, xxvi, 136
Wildey, Doug, xv, 64, 88–96, 134
Wile E. Coyote, 206
Williams, Esther, xxiv, 7
Wolfram, Mark, 226–28, 231
Wonder Woman, 200
Woody Woodpecker, 18
Wynn, Ed, 46

Xeroxing, 130, 150, 204

Yankee Doodle Mouse, The, xiii, xxiv, 12
Yogi Bear: at amusement parks, 156, 218; character, 7, 9, 42, 43, 45–49, 52, 65, 73, 79–81, 84, 107, 113, 115, 118, 134, 156, 157–58, 200, 218, 240–41, 243; *Hey There, It's Yogi Bear!* (1964 film), xvi, xxvi, 219; on *The Huckleberry Hound Show*, 7, 73, 82, 113; merchandise, 153, 197, 233, 241; *The Yogi Bear Show* (1961–62 series), xv, xxv, 7, 13, 82, 134; *Yogi's Space Race* (1978–79 series), 188; *Yogi's Treasure Hunt* (1985–88 series), 45, 49
Yowp (blogger), xv, 59–69

Zander, Jack, 17, 24
Zap Productions, 153

ABOUT THE EDITORS

Kevin Sandler is associate professor in the Film and Media Studies program at Arizona State University. He focuses on the US film and television industries, specializing in animation and censorship. Kevin is the author of *The Naked Truth: Why Hollywood Doesn't Make X-Rated Movies* (Rutgers, 2007), coeditor of *Titanic: Anatomy of a Blockbuster* (Rutgers, 1999), and editor of *Reading the Rabbit: Explorations in Warner Bros. Animation* (Rutgers, 1998). His forthcoming book is *Scooby-Doo, Where Are You!* (Duke University Press).

Tyler Solon Williams is assistant professor in the Department of Media Studies at the University of Virginia. His PhD dissertation is "Understanding the Early Television Cartoon" (University of Iowa, 2021). Tyler studies animation, television, cultural history, and media theory.

www.ingramcontent.com/pod-product-compliance
Lightning Source LLC
Chambersburg PA
CBHW021835220426
43663CB00005B/258